DÆMONOLOGY

An Introduction
with a
Selection of Texts

DÆMONOLOGY: AN INTRODUCTION WITH A SELECTION OF TEXTS

Cover image: *Compendium rarissimum totius Artis Magicae sistematisatae per celeberrimos Artis hujus Magistros*, circa 1775.

ISBN 978 1 907881 62 6 (HB)
ISBN 978 1 907881 63 3 (PB)
10 9 8 7 6 5 4 3 2 1

First published in Portuguese as *Thesaurus Magicus 3* by Clube dos Autores, 2015

First English edition by Hadean Press
West Yorkshire

WWW.HADEANPRESS.COM

DÆMONOLOGY

An Introduction
with a
Selection of Texts

Humberto Maggi

Contents

Foreword

This first volume in a collection devoted to the subject of the "daimon/dæmon" provides a comprehensive and detailed description of the intermediary spirits in the Western Tradition. Being a fundamental part of Magic, these spirits have important ramifications on the religions and philosophies from Late Antiquity through the present. Tracking the origins and developments of the concept of intermediary spirits under the terms "daimon/dæmon", from Homer to Augustine and beyond, revealed a very rich fountain of knowledge with direct importance to the comprehension of the worldview shared by magical practitioners from every age and culture. The "daimon/dæmon" was an essential idea for the eschatology of the pagan and Christian religions, from the cosmology of the different philosophies of the Greek-Roman culture to the practice of the magicians.

The importance and the abundance of the material researched proved too much to exhaust in one single volume. The present volume narrates the evolution of classical dæmonology until the advent of Christianity and its further uses in Renaissance magic and grimoire literature. The forthcoming books of the collection deal more deeply with specific points of the subject, being *The Greek-Roman Inheritance, The Christian Tradition, The Grimoire Literature, Torah-Talmud-Zohar* and *A Comparative Study.*

The Selection of Texts

Dæmonology is a branch of knowledge which depends almost exclusively on the reading of a vast array of texts from Archaic Greece to the most updated digressions on anthropology, and includes incursions into important precedents such as the Egyptian and Mesopotamian cultures and shamanic practices. It is a fundamental topic in the antagonism between the orthodox views of the majoritarian Christian groups and pagan religions and magical philosophies. To facilitate and enrich the reader's experience, each volume of the collection includes a selection of texts that defined or represented critical uses of the concept of the intermediary spirit during its evolution. This format allows for a more comfortable and immediate access to the pertinent original materials and opens the view to a more comprehensive understanding of the writings from the related religions, philosophies, and magical traditions mentioned.

My great thanks go to Joseph H. Peterson for the use of his digital version of *Three Books of Occult Philosophy*.

The texts of *The Discoverie of Witchcraft* in English of the sixteenth century are full of references difficult to identify. Jake Stratton-Kent, who knows very well this material, greatly helped me to understand many obscure points. However, there were cases where even our combined efforts were not enough to understand some passages.

I must also thank Gal Sofer, who very graciously helped me with Hebrew words.

DÆMONOLOGY: AN INTRODUCTION

THE DIFFICULTY IN ESTABLISHING the most ancient meanings of the word "daimon" (δαίμων) is often mentioned at the beginning of any such attempt. Here I have selected a few references made by experts which, whilst exemplifying very well this point, also give us an Ariadne's thread to follow into this complicated and obscure labyrinth. The first:

> Religious and philosophical notion at the same time, δαίμων is a polivalent term difficult to define. Characterized in a general manner, the daimon designates, in ancient Greece, one species of the divine, but, in comparison with τεός and the ἥρως, it was not circumscribed by a specific cult, neither by a mythology, neither by figurative representations. The imponderable aspect of the notion is fully reflected in the assimilation of *daimon* sometimes to destiny (μοῖρα or τύχη), sometimes to the avenging spirits (the ἀλάστορες or the Erinyes),[1] to the heroes or the souls of the dead. At the same time, this flexibility allowed the notion to be used in the attempts of rationalization and systematization of the religious representations witnessed by the works of Homer and Hesiod, attempts that will continue and become specific in the "presocratic" and platonic philosophies.[2]

[1] Τεός = teos (god); ἥρως = heros (hero, demigod); μοῖρα = moira (lot, destiny); τύχη = tike (fortune, providence, lot); ἀλάστορες = alastores (avengers); Erinyes, or Furies, chthonic deities connected to vengeance.

[2] *La Démonologie Platonicienne, Histoire de la notion de daimon de Platon aux derniers néoplatoniciens*. Andrei Timotin.

Let's begin to follow the thread with the mention made to Homer and Hesiod, to whom we owe the oldest literary works of the Western tradition.

The existence of a historical Homer remains a subject of academic debates, summarized in the expression "Homeric Question".[3] The testimonies from Herodotus and from the author of the *Life of Homer*[4] present the most extreme time indications for his biography, respectively the 9th and 12th centuries BC, but the most recent researchers consider the most likely period to be between the 9th and 8th centuries BC. The most important texts attributed to him are the *Iliad* and the *Odyssey*, considered to be the first literary works of Europe, which became the foundations of Greek culture. Plato clearly indicates the depth and extent of the influence attributed to Homer when he refers to him as the *protos didaskalos* (first teacher) of the tragedians, *hegemon paideias* (leader of the Greek culture) and, principally, *ten Hellada pepaideukon* (teacher of all Greece).[5]

It is impossible to establish one original version for these two works, which have their roots in the oral poetic traditions from the period called the Greek Dark Ages, which occurs between the mysterious fall of the Mycenaean civilization, when all the main cities of the time were destroyed and abandoned,[6] and the adoption of the Greek alphabet in the 8th century BC.[7] The division of the *Iliad* and the *Odyssey* into twenty-four books each was introduced

[3] "The Homeric Question concerns the doubts and consequent debate over the identity of Homer, the authorship of the *Iliad* and *Odyssey*, and historicity, especially of the *Iliad*. The subject has its roots in classical antiquity and the scholarship of the Hellenistic period, but has flourished among Homeric scholars of the 19th and 20th centuries." *Homeric Question*. Wikipedia.

[4] Generally referred to as the "Pseudo-Herodotus".

[5] Plato refers to Homer in these terms in his work *The Republic*.

[6] "Within a period of forty to fifty years at the end of the thirteenth and the beginning of the twelfth century almost every significant city in the eastern Mediterranean world was destroyed, many of them never to be occupied again." *The End of the Bronze Age: changes in warfare and the catastrophe ca. 1200 B.C.* Robert Drews.

[7] The "Greek Alphabet" we know comes from Phoenicia; the original Mycenaean writing was forgotten after the collapse of that civilization, and was just rediscovered in 1900 by the archeologist Sir Arthur Evans (1851-1941).

by Zenodotus,[8] the first librarian of the Library of Alexandria, who tried to organize the different manuscripts attributed to Homer. One of his sucessors, Aristarchus of Samothrace,[9] dedicated himself to the same endeavour and, possibly, is who established the standard work which was, after that, copied and copied again, although no complete manuscript dated before the 10th century survives.

The significance that the texts attributed to Homer give to the word "daimon", as it should be clear by now, are founded upon the pre-literary origins of the same, in other words, in the uses the Greeks gave to it before the poems were elaborated and, after that, put into written form. The root of the word comes from da(i), with the meanings of "share (out)" or "distribute", like in δαίομαι (daiomai), and "part" or "lot", like in δαίς (dais):[10]

> Δαίμον[11] is a derivation from the root *dai(i)* that gave δαίομαί «share, divide, distribute», δαίς «meal (where all shares are equal), feast, banquet», skr. *dáyate* «share, destroy», from whence the sense of «distributing power», of «distributor» of riches.[12]
>
> In accord with this etymology, the *daímôn* can be understood as the being that distributes lots, or as the effect of this distribution: then it is—and this is once again a significant indeterminacy—either the power that distributes lots or the lot itself that falls to

[8] "Zenodotus (Greek: Ζηνόδοτος) was a Greek grammarian, literary critic, Homeric scholar, and the first librarian of the Library of Alexandria. A native of Ephesus and a pupil of Philitas of Cos, he lived during the reigns of the first two Ptolemies, and was at the height of his reputation about 280 BC." *Zenodotus*. Wikipedia.

[9] "Aristarchus of Samothrace (Greek: Ἀρίσταρχος; c. 220—c. 143 BC) was a grammarian noted as the most influential of all scholars of Homeric poetry. He was the librarian of the library of Alexandria and seems to have succeeded his teacher Aristophanes of Byzantium in that role." *Aristarchus of Samothrace*. Wikipedia.

[10] *Dictionary of Untranslatables: A Philosophical Lexicon*. Eds. Barbara Cassin, Emily Apter, Jacques Lezra, Miguel Wood.

[11] Δαίμον = Daimon.

[12] *La Démonologie Platonicienne, Histoire de la notion de daimon de Platon aux derniers néoplatoniciens*. Andrei Timotin.

someone, whence in both cases a strong connection with the idea of fate.[13]

Two things stand out in the etymology of the word: *first*, one indeterminacy, even a certain ambiguity, which will remain in future developments, giving rise to different interpretations and uses in popular, literary, and philosophical cultures. *Secondly*, there is a significant core around which the different uses must by necessity gravitate. Andrei Timotin defends that, etymologically, the "δαίμων will then be a distributing god (of riches)", frequently connected to the gods of destiny and to the destiny of the individual.

It is the connection to something divine that is characteristic of the use of the word in Homer, where the δαίμων acquires the sense of a "non-personified divine power", indicating, generally, the influence behind one event that the characters perceive as being extraordinary, though they do not know exactly to what origin to attribute that influence. Although the narrator (Homer) in his speech names the intervenient deity, only characters of great piety, like Odysseus, can, sometimes, distinguish which divine power is acting. On the other hand, in many passages Homer uses the word δαίμων as a synonym to τεοί to indicate one identified deity, like Aphrodite, Apollo, or Zeus. This second use is also present in the Orphic texts and is frequent in the tragedies; in the lyric poetry, the δαίμων "designates currently one divine figure responsible for the fortune or misfortune of the individuals".[14]

Various aspects concerning the historicity of Hesiod also remain subject to debate, but his work, as opposed to the one attributed to Homer, is characterized for being the first European poetry where the poet himself becomes a theme: in *Works and Days,* he describes himself as a farmer, who writes this poem of more or less eight hundred lines with the objective of teaching his brother, who had litigated him with the help of corrupted judges,

---

[13] *Dictionary of Untranslatables: A Philosophical Lexicon.* Eds. Barbara Cassin, Emily Apter, Jacques Lezra, Miguel Wood.

[14] *La Démonologie Platonicienne, Histoire de la notion de daimon de Platon aux derniers néoplatoniciens.* Andrei Timotin.

on the virtue and advantages of hard work. In this writing he also mentions the migration of his father from Asia Minor, and a journey made by himself to Chalcis, where he won a musical competition and received *"an handled tripod which I dedicated to the Muses of Helicon, in the place where they first set me in the way of clear song"*.[15] In his other work, the *Theogony*, this mention of the Muses is explained in a brief narrative at the beginning of the poem, where Hesiod describes his encounter with these deities, when he received a "*rod, a shoot of sturdy olive, a marvelous thing*"; the Muses of Helicon then "*breathed into me a divine voice to celebrate things that shall be and things that were aforetime; and they bade me sing of the race of the blessed gods that are eternally, but ever to sing of themselves both first and last*".[16] If Hesiod described a real experience, a theophany which endowed him with poetic and prophetic powers, or if he was just poetically elaborating upon the discovery of his vocation, is a matter which is still debated.

The historical period atributed to Hesiod with which the majority of the historians agree falls between the 8th and the 7th centuries BC, and the tendency also is to consider him to be posterior to Homer. It is from Hesiod that we know the myth of Pandora; the historian Herodotus credited him for organizing the multiple mythologies from the different Greek cities, and he is considered to be a fundamental source on the Greek myths.

Hesiod is also important in the process of evolution of the concept of the δαίμων thanks to a passage in *Works and Days*, where he uses the word to indicate the souls of the men from the Golden Age, who after the end of their generation became the guardian spirits of the men of today.

> But after the earth covered this generation—they are called pure spirits [δαίμονες άγηοί] dwelling on the earth, and are kindly, delivering from harm, and guardians of mortal men; for they roam everywhere over the earth clothed in mist and keep watch on

[15] *Hesiod, the Homeric Hymns, and Homerica.* The Loeb Classical Library.

[16] *Hesiod, the Homeric Hymns, and Homerica.* The Loeb Classical Library.

> judgements and cruel deeds, givers of wealth; for this royal right also they received.[17]

Here in Hesiod the word begins to come near to the meaning with which it will become important in Western Magic; unlike with Homer, the emphasis is decidedly on the character of "intermediary spiritual being" and, although the connection with a deity is here indicated as being fundamental, it establishes a precedent for the use of the word δαίμων as indicative of a spirit of the dead.

It must be clear, however, that notions like "guardian spirits" and "souls of the dead" precede Greek culture and are rooted in the primitive communities of prehistoric times. What is generally interpreted and understood as being a "contact with spirits" is a phenomenon that occurs spontaneously, in statistical proportions, in every human group, and primitive societies seemed to invariably develop techniquies to profit from the experience. What this present study aims is to follow the development of the concept in order to better understand its use and meaning when it refers to spiritual beings in the magical literature, and it is important to bear in mind that this literature generally moves between the high and the popular cultures.

In *Works and Days* there is a second mention of these spirits; although Hesiod did not repeat the word δαίμων in it, it is clear that he is making again reference to the same spirits "clothed in mist":

> You, princes, mark well this punishment you also; for the deathless gods are near among men and mark all those who oppress their fellows with crooked judgements, and reck not the anger of the gods. For upon the bounteous earth Zeus has thrice ten thousand spirits, watchers of mortal men, and these keep watch on judgements and deeds of wrong as they roam, clothed in mist, all over the earth.[18]

---

[17] *Hesiod, the Homeric Hymns, and Homerica.* The Loeb Classical Library.

[18] *Hesiod, the Homeric Hymns, and Homerica.* The Loeb Classical Library.

We will establish, for our convenience, an intermediary period between the writings attributed to Homer and Hesiod and the works of Plato, a period in which for our present purposes it is better to resume the uses given to the word in the two parallel strands, in the literary and the philosophical traditions. Always in the shadows of the two giants, δαίμων in this period appears in both traditions with the following connotations:

Tutelary deity
Indeterminate divine power
Lot deity (fortune, destiny)
Avenging spirit (especially in the tragedies)
Soul of the dead
Tutelary genius[19]

These different uses are rarely unambiguous or precise, and often leave room for different hypotheses of interpretation. It is important to note that, later, Plutarch[20] attributed to Empedocles[21] the mention of the two daimones and the two fates: "*two destinies and two daimones receive and lead each of us from birth*".[22] Empedocles also disseminated a different view of the daimones, where they are seen as a group of special spiritual beings that can, when committing certain mistakes, be exiled for a time in human form. Empedocles considered himself to be one of these daimons:

---

[19] *La Démonologie Platonicienne, Histoire de la notion de daimon de Platon aux derniers néoplatoniciens.* Andrei Timotin.

[20] "Plutarch (c. AD 46–AD 120) was a Greek historian, biographer and essayist, known primarily for his *Parallel Lives* and *Moralia*. He is considered today to be a Middle Platonist." *Plutarch*. Wikipedia.

[21] "Empedocles (c. 490–c. 430 BC) was a Greek pre-Socratic philosopher and a citizen of Agrigentum, a Greek city in Sicily. Empedocles' philosophy is best known for being the originator of the cosmogenic theory of the four Classical elements. He also proposed powers called Love and Strife which would act as forces to bring about the mixture and separation of the elements." *Empedocles*. Wikipedia.

[22] *La Démonologie Platonicienne, Histoire de la notion de daimon de Platon aux derniers néoplatoniciens.* Andrei Timotin.

> There is an oracle of Necessity, an ancient decree of the gods, eternal, sealed fast with broad oaths, that when one of the divine spirits whose portion is long life sinfully stains his own limbs with bloodshed, and following Hate has sworn a false oath—these must wander for thrice ten thousand seasons far from the company of the blessed, being born throughout the period into all kinds of mortal shapes, which exchange one hard way of life for another. For the mighty Air chases them into the Sea, and the Sea spews them forth on to the dry land, and the Earth (drives them) towards the rays of the blazing Sun; and the Sun hurls them into the eddies of the Aether. One (Element) receives them from the other, and all loathe them. Of this number am I too now, a fugitive from heaven and a wanderer, because I trusted in raging Hate.[23]

The idea of Empedocles follows the opposite route to Hesiod: instead of a *post mortem* daimonification, a process of fall and expiation. The idea of a *post mortem* daimonification became popular also among the Pythagoreans; Aristotle refered to a Pythagorean belief that the founder of the sect became a "good daimon" inhabiting the Moon. Thales of Miletus said that the universe is animated and it is full with daimones; Diogenes Laertius[24] reported one fragment from the Pythagorean Memories where it is written that "*the souls who err in the air guided by Hermes, the guardian of the souls, are called* δαίμονες [daimones] or ἥρωες [heroes]".[25]

---

[23] Excerpt from the *Katharmoi* (Purifications) of Empedocles. In *Ancilla to the Pre-Socratic Philosophers*, by Kathleen Freeman.

[24] "Diogenes Laertius (fl. c. 3rd century CE) was a biographer of the Greek philosophers. Nothing is known about his life, but his surviving *Lives and Opinions of Eminent Philosophers* is a principal source for the history of Greek philosophy." *Diogenes Laertius*. Wikipedia.

[25] *La Démonologie Platonicienne, Histoire de la notion de daimon de Platon aux derniers néoplatoniciens*. Andrei Timotin.

These dubious developments in the use of the term in this period were very well expressed by Andrei Timotin:

> Despite these attempts, the philosophical notion of δαίμων never quite dispelled the ambiguity of its contents: by constantly reporting to a religious reference system, the *daimon* was assimilated, alternatively or simultaneously, to the Olympian gods, to the πρόνοία,[26] to the gods who "suffer" in the mystery cults or to Ψύχή[27] (and its divine part, the νοϋς[28]). These misconceptions were doubled by the equivalences established, from the Hellenistic period, between different religious systems of the Mediterranean world: the *daimon* (and the Latin *daemon*) could be likened to the genius and to the άγγελος.[29] These assimilations favored the conceptual contaminations and the overlays between the religious representations.[30]

[26] Πρόνοία, goddess of providence, or providence in an abstract form.

[27] Ψύχή, psique = life, mind, soul, spirit.

[28] Νοϋς = mind, reason, understanding. The higher part of the soul or of the spirit.

[29] Άγγελος, angel.

[30] *La Démonologie Platonicienne, Histoire de la notion de daimon de Platon aux derniers néoplatoniciens.* Andrei Timotin.

The Daimon of Socrates

As well as the difficulties in establishing the historicity of Homer as summarized under the "Homeric Question", attempts to identify the "real" Socrates make up the "Socratic Problem". Here, however, the problem is not to know whether Socrates really existed (as with Homer), and neither to certify the basic biographical information (as with Hesiod). Socrates lived in Athens, was born in 470 or 469 BC, and was executed in 399 at the age of seventy. A brief biography about him teaches us that:

> Socrates was born in Alopeke, and belonged to the tribe Antiochis. His father was Sophroniscus, a sculptor, or stonemason. His mother was named Phaenarete, who was a midwife. Socrates married Xanthippe, who is especially remembered for having an undesirable temperament. She bore for him three sons, Lamprocles, Sophroniscus and Menexenus. His friend Crito of Alopece criticized him for abandoning them when he refused to try to escape before his execution.[31]

The military life of Socrates is also well known; he fought at many of the battles during the Peloponnesian War. The nature of the "Socratic Problem" is different: Socrates did not write, having dedicated his life to a philosophical activity based upon the oral dialectic. Because of that, the descriptions of his thought all come from the records made by others, principally by his disciples Plato and Xenophon, which creates insoluble doubts about his ideas. Plato, particularly, used Socrates as the main figure in his philosophical dialogues, and it is especially difficult to separate the genuine thought of the master from the posterior elaborations of the disciple. Plato and Xenophon also present divergencies in the portrait they made of Socrates, motivated by their different interests. One example of these differences, important to us, is in

[31] *Socrates*. Wikipedia.

the descriptions of the "daimonic sign" (δαιμόνιον σημεῖον)[32] of the old philosopher.

> Another difference is that in Xenophon's *Apology* Socrates' "divine sign" (daimonion) is described as giving positive indications as to what should be done, while Plato's Socrates consistently and explicitly describes the sign as "turning me away from something I am about to do" but "never encouraging me to do anything".[33]

The "daimonic sign", or the "daimon of Socrates", also became the source of endless interpretations, with opinions throughout the centuries oscilating between those who considered that this daimon was only an allegory of the consciousness, or of an intuitive-mental process, and those who considered that Socrates really believed he received advice from a spiritual being. However, the double testimony of Plato and Xenophon, and also the detailed descriptions that Plato inserts in his dialogues, makes me consider that the allegorical interpretations originated in the necessity many felt of sterilizing the Philosophy, eliminating everything that could not be reconciled with what they believed to be "rationality". Without this dishonest impulse to "sanitize" Socrates,[34] the accumulation of descriptions in both sources is clear enough. First, the speech attributed to Socrates puts the "daimonic sign" as the very source of his philosophical activity:

> Then there remains, Adeimantus, only a very small group who consort with philosophy in a

[32] δαιμόνιον σημεῖον = daimonion semeion.

[33] *Apology* (Xenophon). Wikipedia.

[34] One of the most grotesque examples is found in the article of the *Encyclopædia Britannica* from 1911: "It remains for us, [...] to suppose that Socrates was subject, not indeed to delusions of mind, but to hallucinations of the sense of hearing, so that the rational suggestions of his own brain, exceptionally valuable in consequence of the accuracy and delicacy of his highly cultivated tact, seemed to him to be projected without him, and to be returned to him through the outward ear."

> way that's worthy of her. ...A very few might be drawn to philosophy from other crafts... And some might be held back by the bridle that restrains our friend Theages—for he's in every way qualified to be tempted away from philosophy, but his physical illness restrains him by keeping him out of politics. Finally, my own case is hardly worth mentioning—my daimonic sign—because it has happened to no one before me, or to only a very few. Now, the members of this small group have tasted how sweet and blessed a possession philosophy is... (Plato, Republic, Grube tr., 496 b-c).[35]

Something that Socrates atributed only to himself, or to a very small group, honestly can hardly be interpreted as an "allegory for the conscience". Of course, I am very far from being a pioneer of this conclusion:

> Mention of a daimon is not unique to the Platonic dialogues. In fact, others have claimed to have a daimon; examples are found in the *Ennead* and Porphyry's *Life of Plotinus*. Some interpret the Timaeus to be evidence that each of us has a daimonion, found in "the most sovereign part of our soul as god's gift to us, given to be our guiding spirit." Xenophon's description of the daimonion differs from Plato's in that the sign was not restricted to prohibitions. Although these alternative explanations may be helpful in another literary analysis, we will restrict our discussion to Plato's understanding of the daimonion, in light of his statement found parenthetically in the *Republic*, that "the divine sign, is hardly worth mentioning—for I suppose it has happened to few or none before [Socrates]." If this is the case, it is clear that Socrates' daimonion is

[35] *The Daemon of Socrates*. Vladimir Suchan.

> more than the common voice of conscience. James Beckman writes that the daimonion is "confined to future contingencies (as opposed to pangs of conscience after the act) and does not always have to do with judgments of moral value"; it is most often concerned with the practical consequences of Socrates' action. If Socrates' daimon is similar to the daimon that each man is able to choose in the Myth of Er, it is clear that Socrates has either made himself more able to receive daimonic alarms or his daimon is superior to others.[36]

But, we can put the question to rest just by choosing one of the many passages of Plato, where the speech of Socrates about the theme is candidly direct, and sufficiently clear:

> You have heard me give the reason for this in many places. I have a divine or spiritual sign which Meletus has ridiculed in his deposition. This began when I was a child. It is a voice, and whenever it speaks it turns me away from something I am about to do, but it never encourages me to do anything.[37]

The small divergence between the descriptions from Xenophon and Plato even increases the credibility of the matter, but the tendency is to consider Xenophon a more exempt witness, one less personally attached to the matter; the repeated description given by Plato about the "daimonic sign" always having as its aim to prevent Socrates from making a mistake, but never giving him positive indications, seems to have been a strategy in the defense of Plato against the accusations of impiety by which Socrates was condemned.

The many attempts to eradicate this daimonic element from the understanding of the Socratic philosophy derive from an

---

[36] "Socratic Knowledge and the Daimonion." Philip Kenny. *Aporia* Vol. 13 number 1–2003.

[37] *Apology* 3 1c–d. Quoted in *Socratic Knowledge and the Daimonion*, Philip Kenny.

imperfect knowledge of the cognitive functions of the human being. Although Jungian theory represents one important advance in the comprehension and valorization of these functions, which in this theory are identified with the sensation, emotion, intuition, and reason, even there it failed to identify a fundamental difference between reason and the other functions. The feeling, the emotion, and the intuition are *sources of information* for the conscience, but this information can only be understood by the use of reason, which by itself is never a source of direct information, but of conclusions about the received information. The Socratic experience reported in the Platonic dialogues is very clear on this point: the daimon does not provide the speech, and Socrates is not a "medium" who simply repeats the words from one supposed spirit; the daimon of Socrates indicates to him always one direction, which the philosopher follows through on the rational path until its ultimate logical conclusions.[38]

This consideration is at the base of my magical approach: the daimonic experience, being an experimental fact, can be induced through diverse practices collected from the magical literature and can (must) be understood as *information.* What *kind* of information it is, and what is its utility, these are the questions that reason must clarify.

[38] The text of Philip Kenny follows in detail on this point.

Plato's other daimons

In his dialogues *Politicus* and *Laws*, Plato presents one variation of the myth of the races from Hesiod, where the daimons, rather than being the souls of men, were the spirits responsible for the governance of the world during the Golden Age of Kronos. In the *Cratylus*, Socrates appears making one philosophical-linguistic analysis about the "beings that are eternal by nature", the τεοί, the δαίμονες and the ἥρωες; and, in the Myth of Er, the goddess Lachesis designates to each soul about to be reborn, one daimon whose function it is to ensure that their chosen destiny is fulfilled.

In all these descriptions, two elements stand out: (1) the intermediary character of the daimon, always hierarchically associated with a deity, and often clearly put at its service (Kronos, Lachesis); and (2) its function in the government or influence over world affairs, more specifically over the life of men. We will see these two characteristics be repeated in the description given in the dialogue *Symposium*, when Eros is defined as being a δαίμον μέγας ("great daimon").[39]

[39] δαίμον μέγας = daimon megas.

Eros as a magical daimon

A passage in Plato's *Symposium* is very important in the development of the concept of daimon from the angle that interests us—its uses in the magical literature. I reproduce the passage here in its entirety because, although it is extensive, it is fundamental:

> Eros is an intermediary between the mortal and the immortal. **Socrates:** What do you say, Diotima? **Diotima:** He is a great daimon (δαίμον μέγας), Socrates. Indeed, everything that the nature of a daimon represents (παν τό δαιμόνιον) is intermediary (μεταξύ) between the divine and the mortal. **Socrates:** What is its power?, I asked. **Diotima:** He interprets and communicates to the gods what comes from men, and to men what comes from the gods: from one side the prayers (δεήσεις) and the sacrifices (τυσίας), from the other the prescriptions and the favors that the sacrifices allow to be obtained in exchange. And as he is in the way between the gods and men, he contributes to fill the interval, to make every part to be connected to the others in the universe. From him proceeds divination (μαντική) as a whole, the art of the priests related to sacrificies (τυσίας), the initiations (τελετάς), the enchantments (έπωδάς), the entire domain of the oracles (μαντείαν) and magic (γοητείαν). The god does not come in direct contact with men; but it is through the intermediation of this daimon, that through all possible ways the gods come into connection with men and communicate with them, in a state of vigil or during sleep. One who is a specialist in these kind of things is a daimonic man (δαιμόνιος άνήρ), whilst one artesan or manual worker, who is a specialist in some other domain, is nothing more than a common man. Now these spirits or

> intermediate powers are many and diverse, and one of them is Eros.[40]

Eros as a "great daimon" is presented as an intermediary power responsible for the activities that allow human beings to cross over that space which separate us from the gods:[41]

Divination	(μαντική / mantike)
Sacrifices	(τυσίας / tisias)
Initiations	(τελετάς / teletas)
Oracles	(μαντείαν / manteian)
Magic	(γοητείαν / goeteian)

It is not surprising therefore to find between the diverse magical practices contained in the *Greek Magical Papyri*[42] an elaborate ritual to obtain the assistance of Eros:

> **Eros' as assistant. A ritual of Eros**: *consecration and preparation* (among his operations, he sends dreams or causes sleeplessness; and he releases from an evil spirit, if you use him in a proper and holy manner, for he can perform every operation). Take [wax] of Etruria and mix with it [every] kind of aromatic plant. Then make a statue of a torch-bearing Eros that is eight dactyls high and has a large base to support it. Put a bow and arrow in [his left] hand, and fashion a Psyche of the same sort as Eros. When you have completed all this, conduct a three-day consecration. You are to present to Eros fresh fruits of every kind and 7 cakes, 7 pinecones, every kind of sweetmeat, 7 lamps not colored red; also, [three]

[40] *Symposium*. (Translation into French by Brisson, quoted by Andrei Timotin; translated to English by Humberto Maggi.)

[41] It is very interesting to see how these daimonic functions attributed to Eros coincide faithfully with the attibutions of the orisha Eshu, who is also connected to the erotic-generative activity.

[42] The *Greek Magical Papyri* will be described with more detail in this text.

> daggers, votive tablets, a bow and arrow, dates, a bowl mixed with honey wine. After you make the statues and the presentation as indicated, next place your Eros on a table laden with the fruit / and holding both the 7 lamps, ablaze with clear olive oil, and all else listed so as to win the favor of wondrous Eros. On the first day, after you put him on the table and arrange things as prescribed—and I describe its form in full for you, that you may understand and lack no detail—build a pure altar; that is, take two unbaked bricks and form them into 4 horn-shaped objects, on which you lay fruit-bearing branches. Take also on the first day 7 living creatures and strangle them: one cock, a partridge, a wren, a pigeon, a turtledove, and any two nestlings you can get hold of. Do not make a burnt offering of any of these; instead, you are to take them in hand and choke them, all the while holding them up to your Eros, until each of the creatures is suffocated and their breath enters him. After that, place the strangled creatures on the altar together with aromatic plants of every variety. On the second day, strangle a male chick before your Eros and burn it as a whole offering. On the 3rd day, place another chick on the altar; while conducting this portion of the ritual, consume the chick by yourself, allowing no one else to be present. I assure you, if you perform the above actions in a holy and pure manner, you will have complete success.[43]

It was not by chance that in footnote 41 I pointed out the similarities between the Eros from the *Symposium* and the orisha Eshu; in this second example, it is possible to discern clearly the technical proximity between this magical text and the various practices of African origin, notably the offerings of food and the animal sacrifices. This proximity of methods between the

[43] PGM XII 14-95.

Mediterraneam magic of the pre-Christian period and the African traditions and, generally, with the primitive traditions preserved or known from the rest of the world, has been recognized in recent decades by leading writers such as Aaron Leitch and Jake Stratton-Kent, leading to reassessments of the methods described in several grimoires.

The sublunary daimons

Through the reconstruction of the philosophy of Xenocrates[44] it is possible to verify that, at least at some stage between the 4th and 1st centuries BC (when Plutarch described many of the ideas attributed to him), the concept of the daimon became definitively associated with the "sublunary world", a part of the cosmos that was said to occupy the space between the surface of earth and the sphere where the Moon stands. This cosmic division, which Xenocrates would have used,[45] divided the universe into the following zones:

> *Supercelestial*: where the supreme god is found.
>
> *Celestial*: the heavens, where the stars are equipared to the Olympian gods.
>
> *Sublunary Regions*: under the heavens where the stars and planets abide, the region where the daimons (ὑποσέληνοί δαίμονες[46]) live.

These daimons would participate, at the same time, in a partial manner, in the divine power (δύναμίς[47]) and in the human affections (πάθος[48]); their participation in human affections would turn some daimons evil—just as human affections can drive a human to evil—as well as would their contact with human beings.

> According to Plutarch again, Xenocrates characterized evil daemons as great and mighty natures in the

[44] "Xenocrates (c. 396/5–314/3 BC) of Chalcedon was a Greek philosopher, mathematician, and leader (scholarch) of the Platonic Academy from 339/8 to 314/3 BC. His teachings followed those of Plato, which he attempted to define more closely, often with mathematical elements." *Xenocrates*. Wikipedia.

[45] *Xenocrates' Daemons and the Irrational Soul*. Hermann S. Schibli.

[46] ὑποσέληνοί δαίμονες = iposelenoi daimones, sublunary daimons.

[47] Δύναμίς = dínamis, power, strength.

[48] Πάθος = pátos, pain, suffering; also indicates passion, affection.

> atmosphere, but surly and sullen, who delighted in days of ill omen and those festivals that entailed beatings, lamentations, fastings, blasphemies, or obscenities.[49]
>
> As Plutarch clarifies in a passage for which Xenocrates appears to be the main source, daemons, though superior to men, nonetheless do not possess the divine element unalloyed but 'it shares its lot with the nature of the soul and the sense perception of the body'; hence daemons are receptive of pleasure and pain and as many affections as attend these changes. The affections may in turn trouble even daemons, some more and some less, which also serves to explain the different degrees of virtue and vice among daemons, as among men.[50]
>
> The more daemons allow themselves to partake of human πάθη, the more disturbed and vicious they are. Evil daemons delight in sadistic and lugubrious practices among mankind because of the parasitic enjoyment they derive from such activities, in which they themselves, lacking bodies, cannot engage directly.[51]

What is noticeable is that, inside the philosophical tradition, the use of the term "daimon" got increasingly near to the popular conceptions of the various influences caused by spirits in human life; it tried to embrace all the known possibilities, but inset them into the philosophical discourse where cosmology and eschatology are part of the same subject. We must not, however, think that this was the only available term, and neither that all kinds of spiritual entities would be refered to by it; it is the notion of the "daimon"

---

[49] *Xenocrates' Daemons and the Irrational Soul*. Hermann S. Schibli.

[50] *Xenocrates' Daemons and the Irrational Soul*. Hermann S. Schibli.

[51] *Xenocrates' Daemons and the Irrational Soul*. Hermann S. Schibli.

as a being of intermediary spiritual nature who is influential in human affairs that is utilized in the magical texts. The appearance of the words κακοδαίμων[52] and εὐδαίμων[53] indicates the necessity that arose to differentiate in the discourse the nature or the inclination of these spirits.

After Plato, the daimonology following becomes an important part of the philosophical effort, and in a future volume we intend to treat the late daimonologies of Plutarch and Plotinus, amongst others.

---

[52] κακοδαίμων = kakodaimon, an evil (κακο) daimon.

[53] εὐδαίμων = eudaimon, a good (εὐ) daimon.

Agathos Daimon

It is relevant to make mention of the Agathos Daimon, as this term is recurrent in the magical literature of the Greek-Roman period:

> AGATHODAEMON, in Greek mythology, the "good spirit" of cornfields and vineyards. It was the custom of the Greeks to drink a cup of pure wine in his honour at the end of each meal (Aristophanes, *Equites*, 106). He was also regarded as the protecting spirit of the state and of individuals. He was often accompanied by Αγαθή Τύχη (good fortune), and in this aspect may be compared with the Roman Bonus Eventus (Pliny, *Nat Hist.* xxxvi. 23), and Genius. He is represented in works of art in the form of a serpent, or of a young man with a cornucopia and a bowl in one hand, and a poppy and ears of corn in the other.[54]

This designation appears in eight different magical procedures in the *Greek Magical Papyri*[55]; the glossary in Betz's edition says:

> **Agathos Daimon**: "The good genius" was originally an epithet of a god invoked at Greek banquets. In the PGM the name has become a designation for a god—one, however, who can be identified with a number of different deities.

With these last developments in the concept of the daimon, we reach the period from which we have abundant magical material; we will move then to the analyses of the understandings related to the term inside this literature.

[54] *Agathodaemon* (spirit). Encyclopædia Britannica, 1911.

[55] *The Greek Magical Papyri in Translation*. Hans Dieter Betz.

The daimon of the defixiones

Defixiones, in Greek κατάδεσμος (katadesmos), were a magical technique extremely popular in Late Antiquity, but attested since the 4th century BC, and present in all the extensions of the Roman Empire, from Athens in Greece, to the limits of the Pax Romana in Great Britain. Their use was diffused between members of every social class.

One defixio, generally, was made with one small leaf of lead with a magical formula written on it, many times accompanied by *charaktêres* and images that had the objective of gaining the assistance of spiritual entities in magical operations that targeted persons and animals. The magical effect sought after could be directly harmful, causing many kinds of ills, or could aim at gaining favors, receiving justice, or also exert a violent seduction. Although the leaves of lead were the most used material, there are examples of defixiones written in *ostraca* (broken shards of pottery), limestone, gemstones, papyrus, wax, etc. Alloys, containing lead or not, are also known.[56]

Although there is a large variety in these materials, including calligraphic differences which betray the cultural level of the makers, there are also many indications that the activity was principally exercised by professionals. Plato, for instance, mentioned the existence of professionals that prepared katadesmois for a price.[57] The existence of these professional magicians is better understood when we see, for example in the receipts found in the *Greek Magical Papyri*, that the confection of a defixio was a process much more complex than simply copying one formula over a proper material; it, in fact, included all the usual magical praxis with invocations, purifications, fumigations, prayers, instruments, rituals, etc.[58]

The last step in the preparation of one defixio could also require a very specific practical knowledge; although some of the places where the tablet should be deposited were of easy access, like a well, a sea, or river beach, others, for instance a tomb or a

---

[56] *Curse Tablets and Binding Spells from the Ancient World.* Ed. John G. Gager.

[57] *Curse Tablets and Binding Spells from the Ancient World.* Ed. John G. Gager.

[58] *Curse Tablets and Binding Spells from the Ancient World.* Ed. John G. Gager.

coffin (the main places for a defixio, in fact), implied the existence of people with proper knowledge of or connections to access and work in the cemeteries. In the modern Brazilian version of this kind of practice, what usually happens is that, for example, the Quimbandeiros establish a net of contacts with janitors and doormen who guarantee access to the space and to specific materials.

> Burial sites of those who had died young or by violent means were the preferred choices, because it was believed that their souls remained in a restless condition near the graves until their normal lifespan had been reached. In some cases, these souls were promised respite from their unhappy fate once they carried out their appointed task, as outlined in the tablet. The precise function of these "dead souls" (*nekudaimones* in Greek) is not always clear. Did they simply transmit the petition of the tablet to the gods, in their capacity as beings caught midway between the living and the dead? Or did they enact the spell themselves, under the watchful eye of the gods? Perhaps the answer is that their role changed over time and according to local beliefs. In any case, the gods were always involved in one way or the other.[59]

The names of the invoked deities tended to be from those with strong associations with the realm of the dead: Hermes (the most common), Hekate, Kore, Persephone, Hades, Gaia, and Demeter.

> On Latin tablets, the most common names are the Manes (spirits of deceased ancestors), Jupiter, Pluto (the Greek Hades), Nemesis, Mercury (the Greek Hermes), and various water nymphs. Now the 130 or so tablets from Bath, dedicated to the goddess

---

[59] *Curse Tablets and Binding Spells from the Ancient World.* Ed. John G. Gager.

> Sulis (also called Minerva) must be added at the top of the list. Finally come those highly syncretized spells, primarily from North Africa and Egypt in the third to sixth centuries C.E., where gods, daimones with secret names, personified words (for example, EULAMON), *voces mysticae* containing elements of foreign deities (IAO, ERESCHIGAL), and especially a variety of Egyptian deities come together to form the rich international blend that is so characteristic of late antique culture in all of its dimensions. Among the Egyptian contributions, the most prominent are Thoth (commonly identified with Hermes), Seth, and Osiris. In addition to contributions from Egypt, one finds significant elements from Jewish sources, from Persia, and at a later date from Christianity.[60]

As the process of syncretism of Mediterranean cultures, fostered by the Roman Empire, advanced, borrowings from other cultures, like the Egyptian (Toth, Seth, Osíris) and the Jewish (with the use of many divine and biblical names, for example) were added to the repertoire. The base of the proceedings, however, remained uniform, always more concerned with results than with theoretical elaborations. In this context, the role of the term "daimon" remained uniform in its broad generality:

> The role of images and figures as mediators of power brings us finally to the names of deities and other spiritual entities on defixiones. In discussing these names, it is essential to keep in mind three fundamental characteristics of the "spiritual universe" of ancient Mediterranean culture: first, the cosmos literally teemed, at every level and in every location, with supernatural beings; second, although ancient theoreticians sometimes tried to sort these beings into clear and distinct categories,

[60] *Curse Tablets and Binding Spells from the Ancient World*. Ed. John G. Gager.

> most people were less certain about where to draw the lines between gods, daimones, planets, stars, angels, cherubim, and the like; and third, the spirit or soul of dead persons, especially of those who had died prematurely or by violence, roamed about in a restless and vengeful mood near their buried body.[61]

I selected next an excerpt taken from one defixio where daimones which are associated with the cemetery or with the underworld are invoked; I invite the reader to later compare this text with the practices of invocation of demons and souls of the dead present in the last section of this volume (*Book XV and the Rules of Vaganostus*). This comparison is useful to understand that the manner (at the same time abusive and incoherent–making threats and promises that the magician obvisously will not fulfill) the magician must supposedly use when dealing with those spirits is not a simple result of the influence of Christianity; in fact, this disrespect from the magician has its origins in part of the Egyptian religious practices, where the gods were threatened and blackmailed. Roman Catholicism inherited this concept also, in the popular practices where the faithful "threaten" and "torture" the images of the saints.

> I bind you with the unbreakable bonds of the Fates in the underworld and powerful Necessity. For I invoke you daimones who lie here, who are continually nourished here and who reside here and also you young ones who have died prematurely. I invoke you by the unconquerable god IAÔ BARBATHIAÔ BRIMIAÔ CHERMARI. Rouse yourselves, you daimones who lie here and seek out Euphemia, to whom Dorothea gave birth, for Theon, to whom Proechia gave birth. Let her not be able to sleep for the entire night, but lead her until she comes to his feet, loving him with a frenzied love, with affection

[61] *Curse Tablets and Binding Spells from the Ancient World*. Ed. John G. Gager.

and with sexual intercourse. For I have bound her brain and hands and viscera and genitals and heart for the love of me, Theon. If you ignore me and fail to carry out quickly what I tell you, the sun will not sink below the earth, nor will Hades and Earth continue to exist. But if you bring Euphemia, to whom Dorothea gave birth, to me, Theon, to whom Proechia gave birth, I will give you Osiris NOPHRÔTH, the brother of Isis, who brings cool water and will give rest to your soul. But if you fail to do what I tell you, EÔNEBUÔTH will burn you up. I invoke you, daimones who lie here: IEÔ IIIAIA ÊIA IAÔ IAÊ IAÔ ALILAMPS. I hand over (this spell) to you in the land of the dogs. Bind Euphemia for love of me, Theon. *Daimones*, I place an oath on you in/by the stele of the gods. I place an oath on you by those (gods) in the inner sanctuary. I place an oath on you by the names of the all-seeing god: IA IA IA IÔ IÔ IÔ IE IE IE OUÔA ADÔNAI. I invoke you who are content in the temple and (are content with) the blood seized/drunk by the great god IÔTHATH (in the temple). I invoke you by the one who sits upon the four points of the winds. Do not ignore me, but act very quickly, for I have commanded you – AKRAMMACHAMARI, BOULOMENTHOREB, GENIOMOUTHIG, DEMOGENED, ENKUKLIE, ZENOBIÔTHIZ, ESKOTHORE, THOTHOUTHOTH, IAEOUOI, KORKOUNOÔK, LOULOENEL, MOROTHOEPNAM, NERXIARXIN, XONOPHOENAX, ORNEOPHAO, PUROBORUP, REROUTOER, SESENMENOURES, TAUROPOLIT, UPERPHENOUPU, PHIMEMAMEPH, CHENNEOPHEOCH, PSUCHOPOMPOIAPS, Orion the true!![62]

[62] *Curse Tablets and Binding Spells from the Ancient World.* Ed. John G. Gager.

The content of this defixio was recently translated by Celia Sanchez Natalias, from the University of Zaragoza. The superior figure, divine or daimonic, is petitioned against one "Porcellus", who is represented by the lower figure, tied or mummified.

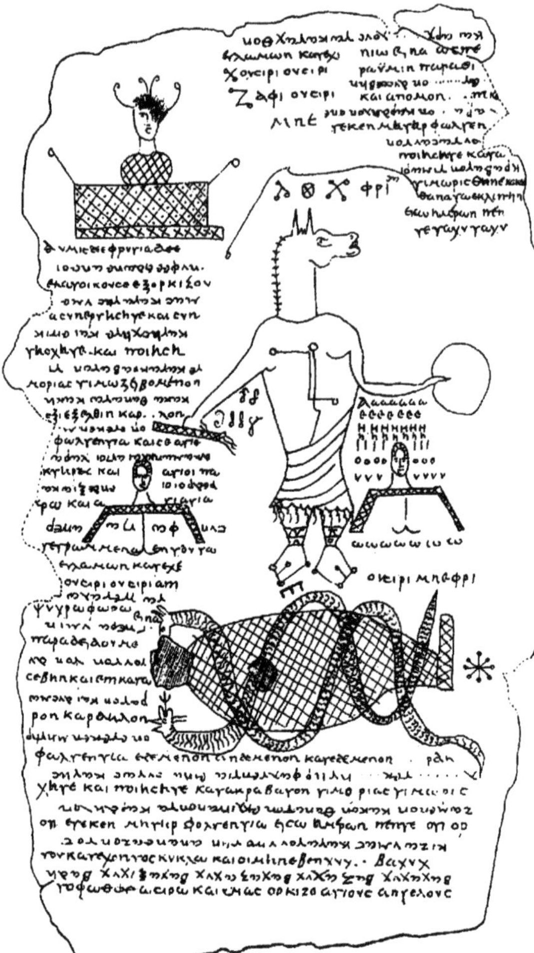

One Roman defixio, with a horse headed daimon, and the tied or mummified victim, being also attacked by two serpents.[63]

[63] *Curse Tablets and Binding Spells from the Ancient World.* Ed. John G. Gager.

The Paredos[64] of Pnouthis

The *Greek Magical Papyri*[65] is a collection of magical texts, most of which were recovered around 1827 by a diplomat and collector named Jean (or Giovanni) d'Anastasi (1765–1860). This collection contains a great "variety of magical spells and formulae, hymns and rituals"[66] covering a period which spans approximately between the 2nd century BC until the 5th century CE.

Anastasi resold the material to various European collections, including the British Museum, the Louvre, the Bibliothèque Nationale in Paris, the Staatliche Museen in Berlin and the Rijksmuseum of antiquities in Leiden.[67] The interest in the study of this material was weak at first, but it gained momentum in the 20th century. The access to the material today is primarily through the edition organized by the Old Testament and Primitive Christianity specialist Hans Dieter Betz.

According to Betz's evaluation these pieces came from the library of a scholar and collector from late Antiquity, and possibly a practitioner, who lived in Thebes. The papyri appeared on the black market almost certainly after the discovery of a *cache* during the violation of a tomb; it was common, even in the late Egyptian culture, for a magician or a priest to be buried with his books and other belongings, and stories about books found inside sepulchers were common. Another researcher, A. D. Nock, summarized the contents of this material in an introductory essay:

> This title covers a group of documents differing widely in length and not a little in character, but possessing a substantive uniformity. Some of them are brief recipes for magical processes or exorcisms, others are collections of such recipes together with

---

[64] Πάρεδρος = assistant; πάρεδροι (paredroi), plural.

[65] In Latin, *Papyri Graecae Magicae*, abbreviated PGM. "PGM", accompanied by Latin and Arabic numerals (PGM IV 1716-1870) indicates the scroll (PGM IV) and even lines of text (1716-1870).

[66] *Greek Magical Papyri in Translation*. Hans Dieter Betz.

[67] *Greek Magical Papyri*. Wikipedia.

> more ambitious invocations and methods of securing control over supernatural forces.[68]

As the late defixiones, these papyri have a rich *mélange* of diverse cultural influences, while at the same time keeping the same formal structures recognized for centuries. In fact, inside these texts we find formulas and models of the confection inclusive of defixiones. Stephen Skinner commented very well about the permanency and constancy of these techniquies when he analyzed the techniquies of Graeco-Egyptian magic:

> These papyri are the source of many magical techniques and equipment found in later European magic. The mediaeval tradition in both the Latin and Greek worlds, owe their earliest origins to the Graeco-Egyptian papyri (the PGM), not to some unknown Hebrew antecedents, not just in a general or thematic sense, but in the transmission of specific techniques, words and implements from one culture to another [...] The fact that such techniques have been utilized consistently over long periods of time often by learned people suggests that some apparent consistency of results was obtained. Otherwise if no such consistency of results had been obtained, then one might expect to find a wide and random diversity of fantasy techniques being independently invented and speculatively tried out at different times and in different cultures, but this is not the case. There is instead a systematic development of techniques with a few being dropped (such as *defixiones*) and some being added (such as the circle of protection) to the repertoire, but with the core techniques remaining the same.[69]

---

[68] *Greek Magical Papyri*. A. D. Nock.

[69] *Techniques of Graeco-Egyptian Magic*. Stephen Skinner.

Here, what interests us is a very special kind of daimon, the *daimona parhedron* that Irenaeus[70] assigned to the heretic Marcus Magus,[71] "through whom he himself seems to prophesy and through whom he rouses to prophecy those women whom he thinks worthy of participating in the grace".[72] The Clementine literature[73] also describes the source of the powers of another famous heretic and magician, Simon Magus, as deriving from an assistant spirit.[74] The idea of spirits and daimons occupying functions and being assistant to gods already existed in Hesiod, where, for instance, Aphrodite elevated Phaeton, son of Aurora, to the level of "divine daimon" (δαίμονα ίον), he becoming the guardian of her sanctuary.[75]

The best study about the figure of the paredros is the one written by Leda Jean Ciraolo,[76] which in turn served as source to

[70] "Irenaeus (early 2nd century—c. AD 202), also referred to as Saint Irenaeus, was Bishop of Lugdunum in Gaul, then a part of the Roman Empire (now Lyon, France). He was an early Church Father and apologist, and his writings were formative in the early development of Christian theology. Irenaeus' best-known book, *Adversus Haereses* or *Against Heresies* (c. 180), is a detailed attack on Gnosticism, which was then a serious threat to the Church, and especially on the system of the Gnostic Valentinus." *Irenaeus*. Wikipedia.

[71] "Marcus was the founder of the Marcosian Gnostic sect in the 2nd century AD. He was a disciple of Valentinus, with whom his system mainly agrees. His doctrines are almost exclusively known to us through a long polemic (i. 13–21) in *Adversus Haereses*, in which Irenaeus gives an account of his teaching and his school." *Marcus* (Marcosian). Wikipedia.

[72] "Magic in the Apocrypal Acts of the Apostles." Jan. N. Bremmer. In *The Metamorphosis of Magic from Late Antiquity to the Early Modern Period*. Ed. Bremmer and Veenstra.

[73] "Clementine literature (also called Clementina, Pseudo-Clementine Writings, The Preaching of Peter, Kerygmata Petrou, Clementine Romance etc.) is the name given to the religious romance which purports to contain a record made by one Clement (whom the narrative identifies as both Pope Clement I, and Domitian's cousin Titus Flavius Clemens) of discourses involving the apostle Peter, together with an account of the circumstances under which Clement came to be Peter's travelling companion, including details about his confrontation with Simon Magus." *Clementine literature*. Wikipedia.

[74] *Magic in the Apocrypal Acts of the Apostles*. Jan. N. Bremmer.

[75] *La Démonologie Platonicienne, Histoire de la notion de daimon de Platon aux derniers néoplatoniciens*. Andrei Timotin.

[76] "Supernatural Assistants in the Greek Magical Papyri." Leda Jean Ciraolo. *Ancient Magic and Ritual Power*. Ed. Meyer and Mirecki.

the texts of Eleni Pachoumi[77] and Anna Scibilia.[78] In her initial analysis, Ciraolo testifies that:

> There are ten texts within the Greek magical papyri which use the term πάρεδρος or one of its cognate forms. Πάρεδρος is an adjective meaning "sitting beside or near" from the verb παρεδρεύω, "to wait or attend upon." In classical times the adjective was used as a substantive to designate a variety of governmental and military officials. In the Greek magical papyri πάρεδρος most commonly refers to a supernatural assistant who serves the practitioner of magic.

In harmony with the origin of the term as an adjective, "the πάρεδροι are never identified simply as πάρεδροι",[79] something we already could see in the *daimona parhedron* of Irenaeus. The term appears associated with substantives like ἄγγελος,[80] δαίμων and θεός.[81]

Ciraolo divided the πάρεδροι into four general categories: *divine, celestial, spiritual, and material.* The text we already saw (PGM XII 14-95) serves as an example of a divine πάρεδρος, Eros. The paredros is also called Aion[82] in one of the texts (PGM I 164-65) that I selected for the first section of this volume (*The Magical Operation of Pnouthis*).

According to Ciraolo, "after the gods, the πάρεδροι are most frequently identified as ἄγγελοι and δαίμονες of an unspecified character". She cites as an example PGM VII 862-918 where the

[77] *Divine Epiphanies of Paredroi in the Greek Magical Papyri.* Eleni Pachoumi.

[78] "Supernatural Assistance in the Greek Magical Papyri: The Figure of the Parhedros." Anna Scibilia. *The Metamorphosis of Magic from Late Antiquity to the Early Modern Period.* Ed. Bremmer and Veenstra.

[79] *Supernatural Assistants in the Greek Magical Papyri.* Leda Jean Ciraolo.

[80] ἄγγελος (ãggelos), angel.

[81] *Supernatural Assistants in the Greek Magical Papyri.* Leda Jean Ciraolo.

[82] "Aion (Aἰών), a Hellenistic deity associated with time, the orb or circle encompassing the universe, and the zodiac." *Aion* (deity). Wikipedia.

goddess Selene is petitioned to send one of her subordinated ἄγγελος, which repeats the hierarchical pattern upon which we already commented.[83]

> These texts referring to the assistant as an ἄγγελος or a δαίμων not of a deceased person reveal some characteristics of the πάρεδροι. The term πάρεδρος is used to designate beings of diverse rank in the divine hierarchy. Some of them are powerful beings: these deserve the appellation θεός. Others are subordinate to deities: these πάρεδροι of lower rank may be termed ἄγγελοι or δαίμονες, but they are not called θεοί.[84]

Ciraolo identified the "spiritual" πάρεδροι in four texts from the papyri, and concluded that "most commonly these disembodied beings are the δαίμονες of the deceased"; in another passage, she concludes that "the πάρεδροι are frequently identified as δαίμονες, generally the δαίμονες of dead people".

Finally, Ciraolo lists in six texts the "material" πάρεδροι, which in truth must be seen as the material base of the πάρεδρος, that in which he lives or through which he manifests:

> In six of the texts the πάρεδρος is identified not only as a type of divine or spirit-being but also as a physical object. The material objects which are πάρεδροι take a variety of forms: two are skulls, one is a mummified falcon, two are statuettes of the god Eros, one of which operates in conjunction with an engraved stone, and one is an inscribed metal *lamella*.[85]

[83] PGM IV 1331-89 describes the παρέδρους of the "great god" as powerful ἀρχιδαίμονας (archidaimonas).

[84] *Supernatural Assistants in the Greek Magical Papyri*. Leda Jean Ciraolo.

[85] A plate or metal sheet.

A Few Brief Considerations

The concept of one guardian spirit, spiritual master and protector, is one of the most ancient and fundamental in all magical traditions. Different cultures interpret it according to the categories they know and, in this case, the development that leads from the πάρεδρος to the "holy guardian angel", giving continuity to the ideas about the personal δαίμων, is easily identifiable even by the observation of linguistic expressions. Terms equivalent to "holy guardian angel" and "sacred magic", that we nowadays know so well thanks to the popularization of *The Book of the Sacred Magic of Abramelin the Mage*[86] after the magical work of Aleister Crowley, appear recurrently in texts like PGM IV. 1939 ("holy angels", "guardians") or PGM I. 127 ("blessed initiate of the sacred magic"). PGM VII 862-918 mentions the goddess Selene and her ἱερόν ἄγγελος ή πάρεδρον (íeron ãggelon en páredron), "sacred angel and assistant".

Other elements, or themes, are common, between the descriptions of the operations of the Greek magical papyri, to obtain a πάρεδρος, and the text of *Abramelin*, such as the discovery or knowledge of the name of the spirit, a series of preliminary practices (purifications, obligations, abstinencies), the existence of spiritual hierarchies and, at last, the application of the powers obtained in every kind of mundane situation. The principal difference between the Angel of Abramelin and the Paredros of Pnouthis is that the text of Abramelin delegates the execution of the mundane tasks to the ἀρχιδαίμονας and δαίμονες subordinated to the Angel, whereas the Paredros, in this case, is the direct executor of the magical actions. This difference comes from the fact that the *Book of Abramelin* belongs to the "Solomonic tradition", whose primary text is the *Testament of Solomon*, a tradition where the invocation of God and his angels is considered a necessary preliminary to the invocation of demons. As we saw, however, this principle is just a variation of the pre-existent hierarchical concept.

[86] Popularized by its translation by Samuel Liddell MacGregor Mathers, *The Book of the Sacred Magic of Abramelin the Mage.*

A second line of thought, where the magical assistant is kept as the main actor, is also later present, as, for instance, in the conception of the Mephistophiles of Faustus. In a new text[87] forthcoming in *Conjure Codex* III by Hadean Press, I identified fourteen powers or abilities in common between the Mephistophiles described in the original versions of the tale (German and English) and the Paredros of Pnouthis.

Crowley's readers and followers of Thelema often ignore the late descriptions found, for instance, in *Magick Without Tears*; these descriptions bring the Angel much closer to the ancient concepts that we have appreciated; I include here a few excerpts from this work, to allow the reader to compare:

> There is only one point of theory which matters to our practice. We may readily concur that the Augoeides, the "Genius" of Socrates, and the "Holy Guardian Angel" of Abramelin the Mage, are identical. But we cannot include this "Higher Self",[88] for the Angel is an actual Individual with his own Universe, exactly as man is.[89]

> The great exception is the Holy Guardian Angel; and this as I have shewn in another letter is for exactly the same reason; He is a Person, a macrocosmic Individual. (We do not know about his birth and so on; but that is because he is, so to speak, a private God; he only appears to the world at all through some reference to him by his client; for instance, the genius or Augoeides of Socrates).[90]

---

[87] *Faustus's Good Friend: Being an Archaeology of Late Antiquity Magical Techniques obscurely found in Christian Apologetics*. Humberto Maggi.

[88] There are passages in Plato where the term *daimon* is used to indicate the superior part of the soul, or human spirit, being identified with the "nous".

[89] *Magick Without Tears*. Aleister Crowley. (Chapter XLII: This "Self" Introversion).

[90] *Magick Without Tears*. Aleister Crowley. (Chapter LXXVI: The Gods: How and Why they Overlap).

> The answer is that it depends on the Angel—for the purposes of this letter I propose to use the word "angel" to include all sorts of disembodied beings, from demons to gods—in all cases, they are objective; a subjective "angel" is different from a dream only in non-essentials.[91]
>
> I believe that the Holy Guardian Angel is a Being of this order. He is something more than a man, possibly a being who has already passed through the stage of humanity, and his peculiarly intimate relationship with his client is that of friendship, of community, of brotherhood, or Fatherhood. He is not, let me say with emphasis, a mere abstraction from yourself; and that is why I have insisted rather heavily that the term "Higher Self" implies "a damnable heresy and a dangerous delusion."[92]
>
> When I first set myself to put a name to my "mission" (...) I considered these alternatives. I thought to cut the Gordian Knot, and call it by Abramelin's title the "Holy Guardian Angel" because (I mused) that will be as intelligible to the villagers of Pu Peng as to the most learned Pundits; moreover, the implied theory was so crude that no one need be bound by it.[93]

These diverse aspects and possibilities of understanding and interpreting the different roles attributed to the magical intermediary beings can be easily discerned in the texts of this volume dating after the beginning of the Renaissance, including

[91] *Magick Without Tears*. Aleister Crowley. (Chapter XLIII: The Holy Guardian Angel is not the "Higher Self" but an Objective Individual).

[92] *Magick Without Tears*. Aleister Crowley. (Chapter XLIII: The Holy Guardian Angel is not the "Higher Self" but an Objective Individual).

[93] *Magick Without Tears*. Aleister Crowley. (Chapter XXVIII: Need to Define "God", "Self", etc.).

the acquisition of a spirit in charge of domestic labors that we see in the last section (*Book XV and the Rules of Vaganostus*), which has its correspondence in PGM Xia, where the paredros, in the form of an old woman, is invoked with that objective.

Another important aspect refers to the invocation and use of the spirits of the dead; as we will see when treating Saint Augustine, these necromantic practices were reinterpreted in Christianity as being in truth demoniac. However, many magical texts kept this distinction, and the magical secrets of the last section of this volume are very prodigal examples. It is also important to note the constancy of the necromantic method, which remained very uniform since the description given by Homer; here, I invite the attentive reader to compare the necromantic instructions given by Circe to Odysseus with the texts in the last section, and similar techniques found in other grimoires:

> When you shall have thus besought the ghosts with your prayers, offer them a ram and a black ewe, bending their heads towards Erebus; but yourself turn away from them as though you would make towards the river. On this, many dead men's ghosts will come to you, and you must tell your men to skin the two sheep that you have just killed, and offer them as a burnt sacrifice with prayers to Hades and to Proserpine. Then draw your sword and sit there, so as to prevent any other poor ghost from coming near the spilt blood before Teiresias shall have answered your questions. The seer will presently come to you, and will tell you about your voyage—what stages you are to make, and how you are to sail the sea so as to reach your home.[94]

---

[94] *The Odyssey, rendered into English prose for the use of those who cannot read the original.* Samuel Butler. Chapter X.

The Theurgy of Iamblichus

The first known ocurrence[95] of the word *theurgy*[96] comes from a mysterious text written in hexameter verses known as *The Chaldean Oracles*. These verses were adopted into the Neoplatonic tradition as being divine revelations, over which an intense and varied activity of philosophical exegesis was developed.[97] It is thanks to the writings of these philosophers that the verses come to us, since no complete copy of them survived.

These "Chaldean" verses treat in a short and enigmatic way cosmological, soteriological, and ethic themes, and contain ritualistic instructions and teachings. The ritualistic experience seems to be the source of the objective of the text. Later interpretations about the tradition attribute the elaboration of the verses to the work of a Julian the Chaldean and his son Julian the Theurgist.[98] The father would have, through religious ceremonies, endowed his son with an "archangelic soul", and the son, also through propitious ceremonies, would have received it from "the soul of Plato" and from deities like Hekate or the oracles.

Despite it being a fragmentary knowledge, it is possible to identify, in the diverse instructions and teachings, the "theurgic method" of the *Chaldean Oracles*. This method presents clear

---

[95] Another mention of the term θεουργοί (teourgoi) in the *Excerpta de musica* from the neo-Pythagorean Nicomachus of Gerasa is conjectural, and it is based upon a corrupted passage of the text. See *Theurgy in Late Antiquity: The Invention of a Ritual Tradition*, by Ilinca Tanaseanu-Doebler.

[96] In the late Latin theurgia, from Old Greek θεουργία (theourgía, "magic"), from θεός (theós, "god") + ἔργον (érgon, "work"). Being precise, The Chaldean Oracles use only the term *theurgos*.

[97] "[...] from Iamblichus to Damascius a commentary on the Oracles in oral or written guise was considered the crowning achievement of an exegetical career." "The Chaldaean Oracles: Theology and Theurgy." Polymnia Athanassiadi. *Pagan Monotheism in Late Antiquity*. Ed. Athanassiadi and Frede.

[98] "A persistent tradition, first detectable in Iamblichus, echoed by the emperor Julian and repeated by Proclus, attributes its authorship to a certain Julian the Theurgist; this claim is corroborated by the tenth-century *Suda Lexicon*, where, in two separate entries, Julian the Theurgist is described as the author of oracles in hexa-meters who lived at the time of Marcus Aurelius, and Julian the Chaldaean as his father and a philosopher." *The Chaldaean Oracles: Theology and Theurgy*. Polymnia Athanassiadi.

similarities with the ceremonies of various mystery cults of the time, and has close parallels with texts that have the same objective found in the *Greek Magical Papyri*. Steps like purification, the ascent of the soul and the reception of divine visions are perceptible. The practitioner is warned in the beginning to beware against the "hylic daimones", the spirits of Nature whose function it is to keep the soul in this world. With the adoption of these theurgic components inside Neoplatonism, the spiritual path of the philosopher is no longer merely a purification by the intellectual exercise accompanied by an ethically adequate life, and now must include the experiences of direct contact with the divine, through ritualistic practice.

> [...] theurgy aims at integrating the practitioner into the Neoplatonic hierarchy of divine beings, which includes heroes and *daimones*, gods and abstract highest hypostases such as the World Soul, the Intellect, or the One. So we will view ritual as a set of practices, of embodied actions, that are set apart and distinguished from common behavior, and are directed at bringing about a connection of the practitioner with the realm of the divine and thus at opening an avenue of communication with it.[99]

One aspect of great interest in our study comprises the descriptions of the divine visions found in the *Oracles*, because they are a link of continuity with the later descriptions we find in the grimoires about the apparition of the spirits; the reader is encouraged to compare what is mentioned in the following excerpt with diverse passages that will be found, not only in this present volume, but in many other examples of the genre. It is noteworthy that visionary images attributed earlier to the gods, later became descriptions of grimoire demons:

---

[99] *Theurgy in Late Antiquity: The Invention of a Ritual Tradition.* Ilinca Tanaseanu-Doebler.

> The gods are in themselves without form; their apparitions (φάσματα)[100] are endowed with a body for the sake of the humans who perform the ritual. The divine fire can appear in different forms, as a horse, a child in different postures, or a lion; traditional visions of a fully armed goddess—most likely Athena—are also recorded (frg. 72). The most extensive treatment of visions occurs in fragments 146-148. Frg. 146 outlines the different possible visual effects of an invocation: visions of fire in the likeness of a child leaping towards the air, formless fire whence a voice comes forth, abundant light that winds itself around the earth with a whirring sound, a horse, a child riding on a horse, fiery, covered all over with gold or naked or drawing a bow while mounted on a horse.[101]

Traditionally, Porphyry[102] is considered the first philosopher to integrate the *Oracles* in the Neoplatonic philosophy.[103] He wrote, amongst other works, a treatise titled *Philosophy from Oracles* (*De filosofia ex oraculis haurienda*) that survived only through citations in Christian texts. Despite being apparently written before his contact with the *Chaldean Oracles*, it seems to have had as a base a series of statements of divine origin confirming certain philosophical

---

[100] Φάσματα = phasmata.

[101] *Theurgy in Late Antiquity: The Invention of a Ritual Tradition*. Ilinca Tanaseanu-Doebler.

[102] "Porphyry of Tyre (c. 234—c. 305 AD) was a Neoplatonic philosopher who was born in Tyre. He edited and published the *Enneads*, the only collection of the work of his teacher Plotinus. His commentary on Euclid's *Elements* was used as a source by Pappus of Alexandria. He also wrote many works himself on a wide variety of topics. His *Isagoge*, or *Introduction*, is an introduction to logic and philosophy, and in Latin translation it was the standard textbook on logic throughout the Middle Ages. In addition, through several of his works, most notably *Philosophy from Oracles* and *Against the Christians*, which was banned by emperor Constantine the Great, he was involved in a controversy with a number of early Christians." *Porphyry* (philosopher). Wikipedia.

[103] *Theurgy in Late Antiquity: The Invention of a Ritual Tradition*. Ilinca Tanaseanu-Doebler.

truths; these statements from the gods, or oracles, were commented upon by the philosopher in the second part of the work.

> Porphyry discussesd the πολιτεία,[104] the hierarchy of the gods, the questions of true piety (εὐσέβεια[105]) and the cult of the gods (θεων θεραπεία).[106] He spoke at length about *daimones*, who are presented in a very negative way, and about the means to turn them away and purify one's body as well as one's private and cultic surroundings. An oracle about Hecate served to establish the Platonic tripartition of the soul. The problem of divination and truth is treated in several oracles, as well as questions pertaining to the summoning of the gods for oracles—the methods and the attitude of the gods towards such practices.[107]

The descriptions given in these oracles are surprisingly similar to what we know from many cults of African origins in the Americas. Here we have rituals with music, sacrifices, and the possession of the priests by the deities, answering in oracular forms. The deities' images are prepared and consecrated; the use of the χαρακτῆρες[108] in the invocations brings directly to mind the "drawn points" typical of cults like Quimbanda.

Anyone who has some deeper knowledge of these African-American cults, and of their elaborate systems of offerings and sacrifices, will appreciate the following excerpt:

> In the oracle about sacrifice, Apollo instructs the inquirer how to sacrifice to the different classes of gods—earthly, heavenly, aerial, marine and

---

[104] Πολιτεία = politeía; the existence of many gods.

[105] Εὐσέβεια = eusébeia.

[106] θεων θεραπεία = teon terapeia.

[107] *Theurgy in Late Antiquity: The Invention of a Ritual Tradition.* Ilinca Tanaseanu-Doebler.

[108] Χαρακτῆρες = karakteres; a term that the reader will see repeated many times in the magical texts selected for this volume.

netherwordly deities. The sacrifices for each class follow the established ideal patterns of Greek religion. Light-coloured victims are designed for the heavenly gods, dark victims for the chthonic entities. The description of sacrifices starts with the gods of the netherworld and proceeds until the heavenly and astral gods. The victims for the infernal deities are to be buried in a pit and then slaughtered with libations of honey and wine—reminiscent of Odysseus's sacrifice in the *Nekyia*. The gods of the air receive offerings of birds that are burned upon the altars with libations of honey, offerings of flour, barley-groats and incense. Sacrifices to marine gods are to take place on the shore, sea-water is sprinkled on the head of the victim and the body is to be thrown into the sea. Finally, the astral and heavenly gods receive the accustomed sacrifices of victims slaughtered at the altar, burnt thighs and roasted meat to be presumably eaten up by the participants while the gods feast on the smell. The prayer which was to accompany the sacrifice is not preserved. [109]

Curiously, Porphyry indicates that the gods come against their will, compelled by the intrinsic nature of the practice, "forced by a certain necessity". "Some accept their fate and form a habit of appearing, even more if they are benign, some try by all means to harm the practitioners and watch for opportunities if somebody handles the ritual all too carelessly".[110] Ilinca Tanaseanu-Dobler notes the ambiguity in these excerpts, as Porphyry sustains that all that knowledge was given by the gods themselves. Μαγεία[111], Porphyry says in one of the fragments, "was given by the gods for the solving of the workings of fate, that this [i.e. fate] may be turned aside as much as possible".

109 *Theurgy in Late Antiquity: The Invention of a Ritual Tradition*. Ilinca Tanaseanu-Doebler.

110 *Theurgy in Late Antiquity: The Invention of a Ritual Tradition*. Ilinca Tanaseanu-Doebler.

111 Μαγεία = mageía (magia).

The reader can observe, later, the same preoccupations with the coming of the spirits present in the European grimoires.

This contradiction in the oracles of Porphyry may be one of the causes of his later change of heart:

> In his treatise *On the Abstinence of Animal Food*, Porphyry attacked the practice of animal sacrifice and said such rites did not pertain to gods but to evil daimons. "For he who is studious of piety knows very well that no animated being is to be sacrificed to the Gods; but a sacrifice of this kind pertains to Daimones and to other Powers" (De Abst. II, 36, 5). In an explanation that was sure to delight Christians, Porphyry attributes the origin of these rites to the devices of bloodthirsty daimons whose life depended on ingesting the vapors of blood sacrifice (II, 42, 1). He continued: "Falsehood is allied to these malevolent beings, for they want to be considered as Gods, and the power which presides over them is ambitious to appear as the greatest God. These are they who rejoice in libations and the savour of sacrifices" (II, 42, 2; trans. T. Taylor). The philosopher should stand aloof from daimons and their misguided worshippers (II, 43, 3-4). Employing the formula of his master Plotinus, Porphyry advised the philosopher to forego all ritual activities in order to return "alone, through himself, to God alone" (II, 49, 1); while the philosopher should understand the enchantments of nature and the cults tied to its daimons, he should have nothing to do with them. "In every respect," Porphyry says, "the philosopher is the savior of himself" (II, 49, 2).[112]

It is to this later Porphyry that is attributed the philosophical questions that gave origin to the theurgic *summa* that crowned late

[112] *Theurgy and the Soul, the Neoplatonism of Iamblichus.* Gregory Shaw.

Paganism, *The Reply of the Master Abammon to the Letter of Porphyry to Anebo and the Solutions to the Difficulties Raised Therein*, that would be known later, after the Renaissance, as *De mysteriis Aegyptiorum, Chaldaeorum, Assyriorum* (*On the Mysteries of the Egyptians, Chaldeans, and Assyrians*). Despite some alleged differences in style, and in some points of doctrine, this treatise has always been attributed to Iamblichus, and his school.

Iamblichus was born in Chalcis, a region nowadays belonging to Syria; the approximate dates of his birth and death are 245-325 CE. According to traditional information, he descended from a family of priest-kings, and family pride may be the reason why he did not adopt a Greek name, as was the custom at the time. He studied with Porphyry, probably in Rome, and after that returned to Apameia, near Antioch, where he founded a philosophical school.

The *Letter of Porphyry to Anebo* shows a very different Porphyry from the one who collected and commented upon the divine oracles. Porphyry here follows more closely the negative view about the matter of the world as it was defended by his master Plotinus. This is the basis of the critical questions he asks about the rituals, while at the same time proposing an intellectualist way in opposition to the living experience of the divine proposed by theurgy. The long and detailed answer given by Iamblichus to the questions in the *Letter* constitute this treatise that "today has become notorious as an apology for the practice of magic and divination".[113]

> Porphyry, who directed a Platonic school in Rome, posed the questions and was therefore responsible for the structure of the work. Yet it was Iamblichus' answers that changed the course of Platonism; in his lengthy replies to Porphyry's questions Iamblichus solved problems that had long vexed Platonists, and he provided a philosophically viable framework for a religious way of life that Porphyry himself had longed to create.[114]

[113] *Theurgy and the Soul, the Neoplatonism of Iamblichus.* Gregory Shaw.

[114] *Theurgy and the Soul, the Neoplatonism of Iamblichus.* Gregory Shaw.

It is possible that, in his personal history, Porphyry resented not being able to experience the theophanies he described in his treatise on the oracles, at the same time becoming disgruntled by the behavior of the people officiating in the rituals he witnessed. He questions and criticizes the resource of the divine oracles in search of answers to all kinds of mundane problems (which brings to my mind a clear correlation with what we see nowadays in rituals where the orishas of African origin are consulted). It is very interesting, and even amazing, to compare the philosophical criticism of that time with the apology Umbanda writers undertook in the first half of the 20th century in Brazil, offering explanations for the material aspects of this cult when facing criticism coming from the followers of Kardec who proposed a view of spirituality also disconnected from the material world. Iamblichus endeavored in the same direction, offering reasons for the use of the material elements, and directly denied the pretension of those who thought they could threaten and constrain gods and daimons. Compare Iamblichus' criticism with the series of threats against spirits to be found in the grimoire in *Liber XV and the Rules of Vaganostus*, the last section of this volume:

> What, then, is more preposterous than these things—that a human being, inferior in dignity, should make use of threats, not to a dæmon or soul of some dead person, but to the Sun-King himself, or to the Moon, or some one of the divine ones in the sky, himself uttering falsehood in order that they may be caused to speak the truth? For the declaration that he will assail the sky, that he will reveal to view the Arcana of Isis, that he will expose to public gaze the ineffable symbol in the innermost sanctuary, that he will stop the Baris; that, like Typhon, he will scatter the limbs of Osiris, or do something of a similar character, what is it but an extravagant absurdity, threatening what he neither knows how nor is able to perform? What dejection of spirit does it not produce in those who, like children, destitute of intelligence, are

> dismayed by groundless fear and terrified by these false alarms?[115]

The excerpts I selected from the text by Iamblichus are the ones that have as their objective to clarify the doubts from Porphyry about the *discretio spirituum* of the different theurgic visions[116], in other words, how to distinguish the class of spiritual beings that manifest in a ritual. Iamblichus offers a comprehensive and very detailed description of the extensive hierarchy of intermediary beings that exist between humans and gods, not only describing their natures and functions, but also the characteristics of their *phasmatas,* of their energies, and the effects that these presences cause in the practictioner.[117]

Iamblichus dealt with "dæmons" in two sections of the *De Mysteriis,* II and IX. We selected the entire section II and excerpts of section IX here.

In section II Iamblichus proposes to identify "in what way daemons, heroes, and souls differ from each other." He uses three basic criteria discernible in the phasmata to separate them: *essence, power, and energy.*

Heroes and souls, of course, have the same origin (the hero being nothing more than a deified soul). They come from "the reasons [or effective principles] of life in divine natures," being therefore different from the dæmons that "are produced according to the generative and demiurgic powers of the Gods."

Iamblichus presents a hierarchy of seven levels for the spiritual beings, locating the dæmons in the middle. Gods, archangels and angels come first, and souls are always the lower part in the chain. But there is a confusion between heroes and archons, as in the descriptions sometimes one, sometimes the other comes after the dæmons. I am

---

[115] *Theurgia or The Egyptian Mysteries by Iamblichus.* Translated from the Greek by Alexander Wilder.

[116] *Theurgy in Late Antiquity: The Invention of a Ritual Tradition.* Ilinca Tanaseanu-Doebler.

[117] A more detailed analysis of the theurgic dæmonolgy from the *Chaldean Oracles* and from the *De mysteriis* will be offered in the forthcoming second volume of this series.

inclined to think archons are of a higher order, because when the heroes are mentoned first, it is due to a comparison made to the dæmons. When he describes the "magnitude, morphe, and figure" of the diverse phasmata, for instance, he says that "those of heroes are similar to those of dæmons; and those of souls imitate in no small degree the dæmoniacal mutation". He again compares both when he says that "the dæmoniacal and heroical self-visive spirits, have both of them beauty in definite forms, yet the former is adorned in reasons which define the essence, and the latter exhibits fortitude".

Albeit similar, prominence is always given to the dæmons, as we can see when he explains that "in the actions of the heroic phasmata, a certain magnificence presents itself to the view; but in accomplishing what they wish to effect, their energies are not so rapid as those of dæmons" and "the manifestation of heroes is still less than that of dæmons", although it "exhibits more of an elevated condition".

A further distinction is made between the dæmons: in chapter VII in section II where Iamblichus contrasts the manifestation of the "good dæmons" with that of the "avenging dæmons," and there is also mention of the "depraved dæmons" who appear "surrounded by certain noxious, blood-devouring, and fierce wild beasts".

A resumé which the reader can verify for herself in section II gives the following characteristics to the dæmonic manifestations:

> .Dreadful
> .Different forms in different times
> .Cause perturbation and disorder
> .Beauty in definite forms
> .Their operations appear to be more rapid than they are in reality
> .Present themselves to view with a turbid fire.

And, finally:

> .[The presence] of daemons renders the body heavy, afflicts with diseases, draws down the soul to nature, does not depart from bodies, and the sense allied

to bodies, and detains about this terrestrial place those who are hastening to divine fire, and does not liberate from the bonds of Fate.

The Peculiar Dæmon

In section IX Iamblichus dismisses a series of criticisms presented by Porphyry about the difficulty of discovering the personal (peculiar) dæmon after astrological calculations, proposing what he considers a more certain way to achieve this knowledge:

> What therefore hinders, but that the discovery of him may be difficult through prediction from the nativity, and yet through sacred divination, or theurgy, there may be a great abundance of scientific knowledge on this subject?

It is a bit difficult to reconcile the ideas on the dæmons from section II with the one about the peculiar dæmon. Here the dæmon again receives his traditional role of guardian of men:

> This dæmon, therefore, is established in the paradigm before the soul descends into generation; and when the soul has received him as its leader, the dæmon immediately presides over the soul, gives completion to its lives, and binds it to body when it descends. He likewise governs the common animal of the soul, directs its peculiar life, and imparts to us the principles of all our thoughts and reasonings. We also perform such things as he suggests to our intellect, and he continues to govern us till, through sacerdotal theurgy, we obtain a God for the inspective guardian and leader of the soul.

The theurgical practices described by Iamblichus are not limited to the discovery of the peculiar dæmon. As seen just above, "sacerdotal theurgy" can elevate man to the care of a higher deity.

There is a theurgic process hinted at in Iamblichus' explanations. Initially, the theurgist invokes the "one God, who is the lord of dæmons". This god seems to be "one common leader of the cosmocrators about generation" who "sends to each of us his peculiar dæmon". This God, who "from the first defined to every one his peculiar dæmon" is invoked in "a common mode by all men". If the theurgist is successful, the God "in sacred operations, unfolds to every one his proper dæmon, according to his own proper will".

The next step of the process depends on the peculiar dæmon itself:

> Hence, when the peculiar dæmon is present with each of us, he then unfolds the worship which is proper to be paid to him and his name, and likewise delivers the proper mode of invoking him.

Finally, under the implied governance of the peculiar dæmon, that now is supposed to be more direct and efficient, and through the practice of the "sacerdotal theurgy" as already mentioned, the theurgist comes under guardianship of a God.

> For then the dæmon either yields or delivers his government to a more excellent nature, or is subjected to him, as contributing to his guardianship, or in some other may is ministrant to him as to his lord.

Seventy-two Sages and The Angels Who Came Down

Unlike Porphyry, Iamblichus did not engage in disputes with the growing Christianity; however, his validation of rituals served as an important ideological support in the disputes that followed his death. His followers and admirers attributed to him the epithet "divine" and his teachings were employed by the Emperor Julian in his brief defense of paganism within the Roman Empire.

Unfortunately, by 386 CE sacrifices to the gods were already prohibited, and Christians everywhere perpetrated acts of vandalism, destroying temples, burning books, and killing people. In 370, the philosopher Hypatia was mutilated and stoned to death by Christian monks,[118] an event that for some marks the end of Clasiscal Antiquity and the beginning of the Dark Ages created by Christianity.

The violent advent of Christianity created an impoverished culture where the individual was not only forced, under the threat of torture and death, to follow the dictates of that religion, but to follow exclusively what was considered to be the *orthodox* dictates of this religion—to understand Christianity in a different way from the one voted in the turbulent concils was *also* a motive for persecution. After they eradicated Paganism, the benevolent followers of Jesus, for lack of victims, began to kill each other in outrageously stupid disputes such as, for example, the diatribes about the persons of the Holy Trinity.

Christianity waged a long ideological campaign against other religions, where the reinterpretation of the concept of "daimon" was fundamental. However, before we look at the beginnings of Christian demonology, we need to consider two previous

[118] It is opportune to remember that stoning is part of the laws of God, according to the Old Testament. People that must be stoned to death, in accordance with the divine word of the Bible, include the violated woman who did not cry for help (Dt. 22.24), a stubborn and rebellious son (Dt. 21:18-21), and the woman who loses her virginity before marriage (Dt. 22:20-21). Death by stoning is still practiced in the United Arab Emirates, Iran, Iraq, Qatar, Mauritania, Saudi Arabia, Somalia, Sudan, Yemen, North Nigeria, Brunei, and Pakistan.

cultural events: the translation of the Old Testament to the Greek Language, named the *Septuagint*, and the appearance of the figure of the "fallen angel".

SEVENTY-TWO SAGES[119]

THE *Septuagint* is the oldest translation of the Old Testament; it is written in primitive Koine Greek, one of the factors that indicates a certain authenticity in the legend about its origin, indicated in the pseudoepigraphic *Letter of Aristeas*, which attributes its elaboration to the initiative of the chief-librarian Demetrius of Phalarus and to the efforts of Ptolemy II Philadelphus. According to the letter, this king of Egypt brought 72[120] sages from Israel (six from each tribe) to the island of Pharos where, in a joint effort which lasted 72 days, they produced a text whose conformity would have been unanimously recognized by the priests and the Jewish people in Egypt.

The legend would suffer alterations to increase its legitimacy as the translation of a sacred text. Instead of being the result of an intellectual collective effort, the translation was then considered to be "divinely inspired", and the Talmud and some Christian authors began to say that the 72 Jewish sages had, separately, each one in a different cell, elaborated 72 translations that, when compared against each other, were found to be all completely identical... Even Saint Jerome[121] later rejected this part of the story.

To understand the importance that translation had, it is enough to give a quick look in the *Catholic Encyclopedia*:

---

[119] In this description of the use of the word "daimon", and its correlates, in the translation of the texts from the Old Testament, I am following almost exclusively the study "When Did Angels Become Demons?" by Dale Basil Martin. Published in the *Journal of Biblical Literature* 129, nr. 4 (2010).

[120] The name "Septuagint" comes from the seventy (and two) alleged translators. Usually it is abbreviated with the Roman algarisms "LXX". Some versions give the number of the sages as being 70.

[121] "Saint Jerome (c. 347–30 September 420) was an Illyrian Latin Christian priest, confessor, theologian and historian, who also became a Doctor of the Church. He is best known for his translation of most of the Bible into Latin (the translation that became known as the Vulgate), and his commentaries on the Gospels. His list of writings is extensive." *Jerome*. Wikipedia.

> The Jews made use of it long before the Christian Era, and in the time of Christ it was recognised as a legitimate text, and was employed in Palestine even by the rabbis. The Apostles and Evangelists utilised it also and borrowed Old Testament citations from it, especially in regard to the prophecies. The Fathers and the other ecclesiastical writers of the early Church drew upon it, either directly, as in the case of the Greek Fathers, or indirectly, like the Latin Fathers and writers and others who employed Latin, Syriac, Ethiopian, Arabic and Gothic versions. It was held in high esteem by all, some even believed it inspired. Consequently, a knowledge of the Septuagint helps to a perfect understanding of these literatures. At the present time, the Septuagint is the official text in the Greek Church, and the ancient Latin Versions used in the western church were made from it; the earliest translation adopted in the Latin Church, the Vetus Itala, was directly from the Septuagint.[122]

It was through the translation of the *Septuagint* that the word "daimon" and its correlatives came into the Jewish cultural universe and, by extension, posteriorly in the apologetic Christian elaborations. Dale Basil Martin identified the following uses given to these terms in the text:

[122] *Septuagint Version*. Catholic Encyclopedia.

	Verse	Hebrew	Greek	Text
1	Dt 32:17	שֵׁדִים shedim	δαιμόνια	They sacrificed unto **demons**, no-gods, gods that they knew not, new gods that came up of late, which your fathers dreaded not
2	Sl 105:37	שֵׁדִים shedim	δαιμονίοις	Yea, they sacrificed their sons and their daughters unto **demons**
3	Is 65:11	גַּד gad	δαιμονίῳ	But ye that forsake the LORD, that forget My holy mountain, that prepare a table for Fortune, and that offer mingled wine in full measure unto **Destiny**.
4	Is 13:21	שְׂעִירִים seirim	δαιμόνια	But wild-cats shall lie there; and their houses shall be full of ferrets; and ostriches shall dwell there, and **satyrs** shall dance there
5	Is 34.14	שָׂעִיר seir	δαιμόνια	And the wild-cats shall meet with the jackals, and the **satyr** shall cry to his fellow
6	Sl 91:6	דֶּבֶר deber	δαιμονίου	Of the pestilence that walketh in darkness, nor of the **destruction** that wasteth at noonday
7	Sl 96:5	אֱלִילִים alilim	δαιμόνια	For all the gods of the peoples are **things of nought**; but the LORD made the heavens.

I identified the exact Greek words used in the table on page 56 by resorting to the wesite ellopos.net, which includes "Elpenor's Bilingual (Greek/English) Old Testament" which has the text of the *Septuagint*; the Hebrew words, and the English text, come from the verses found on the website mechon-mamre.org in the section "Hebrew-English Bible According to the Masoretic Text and the JPS 1917 Edition".

According to Dale Basil Martin's analysis, we find two fundamental uses given to the words correlating to "daimon" in the *Septuagint*, as indicated in the table. The first, and more important, is its use in translating words and expressions that, in the original text, are directed at foreign deities, to whom cult offerings and sacrifices were offered. The plural word *shedim*,[123] for instance, is of Chaldean origin, and "the sacred writers intentionally applied the word in a dyslogistic sense to the Canaanite deities in the two passages quoted [Dt 32:17 / Sl 105:37]".[124] In the same context, to "gad" a libation would be offered, and the interpretation of "deber" as δαιμονίου follows the more archaic understanding of the Greek term:

> But also in this case, commentators point out that both *deber* and *qeteb* could be taken to be divine beings in Near Eastern contexts. The words referred both to the diseases and to the divine beings who either were or caused the diseases. The Jewish translators reveal their knowledge that Greeks would have taken daimons to be both deities that could cause disease and also the disease itself.[125]

Also δαιμόνια was used to translate "alilim" (Sl 96:5), a word of dubious meaning, but clearly pejorative, once more indicating foreign gods, and that is translated in other parts as "idol", "image"

---

123 Later, especially in the Talmud, the word *shedim* will be used to indicate a class of intermediary spiritual beings that very often act favorably towards the rabbis who could see and talk to them.

124 *Demonology*. Jewish Encyclopedia.

125 *When Did Angels Become Demons?*. Dale Basil Martin.

or as "θεός" ("god").[126] Δαιμόνια also translates to *seirim* ("hairy beings"), "to which the Israelites sacrificed in the open fields", those being "satyr-like demons, described as dancing in the wilderness. [...] To the same class belongs Azazel, the goat-like demon of the wilderness, probably the chief of the seirim".[127] Although of a status clearly inferior to the great deities, these spirits of nature apparently were credited as having power enough to deserve tributes.

Dale Basil Martin resumed well this process of translation, used by the "72 Jewish sages":

> Ancient Jews thus used δαιμόνιον to translate five or six different Hebrew words. In the original Near Eastern context, those words referred to different kinds of beings: goat-man gods; superhuman beings that either are or cause diseases; abstract qualities or goods that may also be seen as gods, such as Fortune or Fate. What they have in common, nonetheless, is that they all were thought of as gods—in fact, as the gods other people falsely worship: the gods of the nations. It is understandable why the translators took all these different words to refer to daimons. In Greek culture, "daimon" could refer simply to a god or a goddess. Even the high gods were called daimons at times, as in Homer and Hesiod but also later. Greeks could use the adjective δαιμόνιον in a less "personal" sense to refer to "the divine power" or the "divinity" of a place, person, or thing. "Destiny" and "Fate" were called "daimonic."[128]

The *Septuagint*, therefore, inaugurates one association that later would be fundamental in the development of Christian demonology, and that is still used today as the main argument in the attack, in the disrespect towards every other religion in the world: the association

---

[126] *When Did Angels Become Demons?*. Dale Basil Martin.

[127] *Demonology*. Jewish Encyclopedia.

[128] *When Did Angels Become Demons?*. Dale Basil Martin.

of the Greek word "daimon" to any and every deity belonging to another belief. This argument became so popular that, as we saw before, even the antichristian philosopher Porphyry accused the deities of the propitiatory pagan cults of being mere daimons. However, the final characterization of the daimon in Christianity depended on a second cultural process, one that developed after the 3rd century BC, which we will now approach.

The Angels Who Came Down

The oldest known mention of the concept of "fallen angel" comes from a series of texts written around the 3rd century BC that, despite the great influence they once exerted, nowadays are not part of the canon of any Jewish or Christian affiliation, with the notable exception of the Eritrean Orthodox Tewahedo Church and the Ethiopian Orthodox Tewahedo Church. These texts were gathered in a collection titled the *Book of Enoch* (also *1 Enoch*).

The *Book of Enoch* presents five different compositions that were assembled and edited to give the impression of being a continuous text; these "books" that make up the body of work are:

Book of the Watchers[129]
Book of Parables
The Astronomical Book
Book of Dream Visions
Epistle of Enoch

The idea that a group of angels disobeyed God is initially presented in the *Book of the Watchers*, after a fanciful reinterpretation of Genesis 6:2:

ב וַיִּרְאוּ בְנֵי-הָאֱלֹהִים אֶת-בְּנוֹת הָאָדָם, כִּי טֹבֹת הֵנָּה; וַיִּקְחוּ לָהֶם נָשִׁים, מִכֹּל אֲשֶׁר בָּחָרוּ.	2 that the sons of God saw the daughters of men that they were fair; and they took them wives, whomsoever they chose.[130]

[129] "Watchers" = עִיר (yir), plural עִירִין (iyrin).

[130] A Hebrew-English Bible According to the Masoretic Text and the JPS 1917

The key expression here is בְנֵי-הָאֱלֹהִים ("beni ha-elohim"), "sons of Elohim", which is repeated (in corresponding expressions) in three more passages of the Old Testament:

Job 1:6	הָאֱלֹהִים בְּנֵי	(ha-Elohim beni) the sons of Elohim
Job 38:7	אֱלֹהִים בְּנֵי	(Elohim beni) sons of divine beings
Psalm 29:1	אֵלִים בְּנֵי	(Elim beni) sons of Elim

The verse from Genesis (upon which the other passages depend), in attempts made to understand it outside the proper context, has raised questions and religious controversies that until today animate the imagination. This all stems from *a posteriori* interpretations having to come to terms with a concept of God that when the original text was written, had not yet been developed among the Jews. The expression was taken from the Ugaritic mythology and vocabulary in a period when the Jews were absorbing and copying even the names of its main gods; it is in this religion that El (another name adopted by the Jews, inclusively under the form "El Elyon", the "Highest")[131] has 70 sons, lesser gods that constantly generated children with human beings.

The author of the *Book of the Watchers* interpreted this passage as if it was referring to the "watchers", a class of celestial beings of the court of God; although the biblical text does not mention anywhere that the union of the "sons of God" with the "daughters of men" was something objectionable, the same author established a connection previously nonexistent, stating that the "wickedness of man" in the fifth verse was a consequence of the union between these watchmen and women.

> And it came to pass, when men began to multiply on the face of the earth, and daughters were born unto them, 2: That the sons of God saw the daughters of men that they were fair; and they took them wives

Edition. (http://www.mechon-mamre.org/p/pt/pt0.htm)

[131] *Deuteronomy 32:8 and the Sons of God*. Miguel S. Heiser.

> of all which they chose. 3: And the Lord said, My spirit shall not always strive with man, for that he also is flesh: yet his days shall be an hundred and twenty years. 4: There were giants in the earth in those days; and also after that, when the sons of God came in unto the daughters of men, and they bare children to them, the same became mighty men which were of old, men of renown. 5: And God saw that the wickedness of man was great in the earth, and that every imagination of the thoughts of his heart was only evil continually.[132]

The interpretation of the *beni ha-Elohim* as angels was later denied within the Jewish orthodoxy as much as within the Christian. The fundamental problem with this interpretation is the notion that angels not only have sexual desire, but would have been endowed by God with the means by which the sexual act could be carried out with human beings, including bearing children. As all of this is discordant with the Judeo-Christian notion of angels being spiritual creatures absolutely, the interpretation that prevailed in the end is that the *beni ha-Elohim* are the descendants of Seth, the third son of Adam, who, disobeying the divine will, married the female descendants of Cain.[133]

The disobedience of these angels happened for reasons far less prosaic than those later invented in Christianity:

> It happened after the sons of men had multiplied in those days, that daughters were born to them, elegant and beautiful. 2: And when the angels, the sons of heaven, beheld them, they became enamoured of them, saying to each other; Come, let us select for ourselves wives from the progeny of men, and let us beget children. 3: Then their leader Samyaza said to them; I fear that you may perhaps be indisposed

[132] Genesis 6:1-5. King James Version (KJV).

[133] This is the position adopted by Saint Augustine.

> to the performance of this enterprise; 4: And that I alone shall suffer for so grievous a crime. 5: But they answered him and said; We all swear; 6: And bind ourselves by mutual execrations, that we will not change our intention, but execute our projected undertaking. 7: Then they swore all together, and all bound themselves by mutual execrations. Their whole number was two hundred, who desdended upon Ardis, which is the top of mount Armon.[134]

If the entire idea of angels falling in love and taking wives was rejected afterwards, by both Judaism and Christianity, the fact is that the *Book of the Watchers* was successful in introducing the concept that angels could disobey God, bringing disastrous consequences to the lives of humans on earth, and suffering because of it severe punishments without any chance of remission. Despite all that, we still do not find in this text anything to equate fallen angels and daimons. The author of the *Book of the Watchers* understood that the "giants" (נפילים) from the fourth verse were the progeny of the angels with the women (an interpretation disputed later), and that, after being killed, they became the "evil spirits on earth"–which is a very interesting parallel when we think about the daimons of the Golden Age of Hesiod.

> Now the giants, who have been born of spirit and of flesh, shall be called upon Earth evil spirits, and on earth shall be their habitation. Evil spirits shall proceed from their flesh, because they were created from above; from the holy Watchers was their beginning and primary foundation. Evil spirits shall they be upon earth, and the spirits of the wicked shall they be called. The habitation of the spirits of heaven shall be in heaven; but upon earth shall be the habitation of terrestrial spirits, who are born on earth. 9: The spirits of the giants *shall be like* clouds,

[134] *The Book of Enoch the Prophet*. Richard D. Laurence.

> which shall oppress, corrupt, fall, contend, and bruise upon earth. 10: They shall cause lamentation. No food shall they eat; and they shall be thirsty; they shall be concealed, and shall not rise up against the sons of men, and against women; for they come forth during the days of slaughter and destruction.[135]

The watchers, disobedient angels who descended to earth, not only brought misfortune but generated the Nephilim, bestial beings who stood to devour everything, and to kill each other. The different sections, gathered within the *Book of Enoch*, repeat the basic narrative of the descent of the angels in search of wives, but vary in describing what happened next, and in the different assignments of blame. Chapter XIX, for instance, introduces the theme of the sacrifices "*to devils as to gods*",[136] and announces a future punishment also to "*their wives* [...] *who led astray the angels of heaven*".[137] In the *Book of Jubilees,*[138] the watchers descend to teach men, but they corrupt themselves after seeing the beauty of women; their leader Mastema "*persuades God to let one tenth of the evil spirits remain with him on earth to corrupt humanity and lead it astray.*"[139]

In one of the variations collected in the *Book of Enoch*, the angels after descending began to teach diverse arts and secrets; the catalog of names of angels with their teachings, and the following

---

[135] *The Book of Enoch the Prophet.* Richard D. Laurence.

[136] *The Book of Enoch the Prophet.* Richard D. Laurence.

[137] *The Book of Enoch the Prophet.* Richard D. Laurence.

[138] "*The Book of Jubilees*, sometimes called Lesser Genesis (*Leptogenesis*), is an ancient Jewish religious work of 50 chapters, considered canonical by the Ethiopian Orthodox Church as well as Bete Israel (Ethiopian Jews), where it is known as the *Book of Division* (Ge'ez: Mets'hafe Kufale). Jubilees is considered one of the pseudepigrapha by Protestant, Roman Catholic, and Eastern Orthodox Churches. It was well known to Early Christians, as evidenced by the writings of Epiphanius, Justin Martyr, Origen, Diodorus of Tarsus, Isidore of Alexandria, Isidore of Seville, Eutychius of Alexandria, John Malalas, George Syncellus, and George Kedrenos. The text was also utilized by the Essenes community that originally collected the Dead Sea Scrolls. It was so thoroughly suppressed in the 4th century that no complete Hebrew, Greek or Latin version is known to have survived." *Book of Jubilees*. Wikipedia.

[139] *Dictionary of Deities and Demons in the Bible.* Karel van der Toom, Bob Becking, Pieter W. van der Horst.

list of "holy angels" that did not disobey, constitute one of the oldest prototypes for the lists of spirits and functions common to European grimoires.[140] In the following tables I gathered four different translations of the text for comparison: Richard Laurence, 1848[141]; George H. Schodde, 1882[142]; R.H. Charles, 1917[143]; Andy McCracken, 2002[144].

[140] *The Book of Enoch* is possibly also one of the sources for the concept of "adversarial angels" typical of Solomonic magic.

[141] *The Book of Enoch the Prophet.* Richard Laurence.

[142] *The Book of Enoch Translated from the Ethiopic.* Rev. George H. Schodde.

[143] *The Book of Enoch.* R. H. Charles.

[144] *The Book of Enoch: A Modern English Translation of the Ethiopian Book of Enoch.* Andy McCracken.

Names and Teachings of the Fallen Angels

Richard Laurence	George H. Schodde	R.H. Charles	Andy McCracken
Azazyel taught men to make swords, knives, shields, breastplaces, the fabrication of mirrors, and the workmanship of bracelets and ornaments, the use of paint, the beautifying of the eyebrows, the use of stones of every valuable and select kind, and all sorts of dyes	Azâzêl taught mankind to make swords and knives and shields and coats of mail, and taught them to see what was behind them, and their works of art: bracelets and ornaments, and the use of rouge, and the beautifying of the eye-brows, and the dearest and choicest stones and all coloring substances and the metals of the earth.	Azâzêl taught men to make swords, and knives, and shields, and breastplates, and made known to them the metals of the earth and the art of working them, and bracelets, and ornaments, and the use of antimony, and the beautifying of the eyelids, and all kinds of costly stones, and all colouring tinctures.	Azazel taught men to make swords, and daggers, and shields, and breastplates. And he showed them the things after these, and the art of making them; bracelets, and ornaments, and the art of making up the eyes, and of beautifying the eyelids, and the most precious stones, and all kinds of coloured dyes
Amazarak taught all the sorcerers, and dividers of roots	Amêzârâk taught all the conjurers and root-cutters	Semjâzâ taught enchantments, and root-cuttings	Amezarak taught all those who cast spells and cut roots
Armers taught the solution of sorcery	Armârôs the loosening of conjurations	Armârôs the resolving of enchantments	Armaros the release of spells
Barkayal taught the observers of the stars	Baraq'âl the astrologers	Barâqîjâl (taught) astrology	Baraqiel astrologers
Akibeel taught signs	Kôkâbêl the signs	Kôkabêl the constellations	Kokabiel portents
Tamiel taught astronomy	Temêl taught astrology		Tamiel taught astrology
		Ezêqêêl the knowledge of the clouds	
		Araqiêl the signs of the earth	
		Shamsiêl the signs of the sun	
Asaradel taught the motion of the moon	Asrâdêl the course of the moon	Sariêl the course of the moon	Asradel taught the path of the moon

The Names of the Holy Angels Who Keep Watch

Richard Laurence	George H. Schodde	R.H. Charles	Andy McCracken
Uriel Presides over clamor and terror	**Uriel** who is over the world and over Tartarus	**Uriel** the angel of thunder and of trembling	**Uriel** the Holy Angel of the Spirits of Men
Raphael Presides over the spirits of men	**Raphael** who is over the spirits of men	**Rufael** the angel of the spirits of men	
Raguel Inflicts punishment on the world and the luminaries	**Raguel** who takes vengeance on the world of the luminaries	**Raguel** who takes vengeance on the earth and the luminaries	**Raguel** who takes vengeance on the world, and on the lights
Michael Presiding over human virtue, commands the nations	**Michael** he that is set over the best part of mankind and over chaos	**Michael** set over the best portion of men, over the people	**Michael** the one put in charge of the best part of humankind, in charge of the nation
Sarakiel Presides over the spirits of the children of men that transgress	**Saraqâêl** who is set over the spirits, who sin in the spirit	**Saraqâel** who is overthe spirits of the children of men who induce the spirits to sin	**Saraqael** who is in charge of the spirits of men who cause the spirits to sin
Gabriel Presides over Ikisat, over paradise, and over the Cherubim	**Gabriel** who is over Paradise and the serpents and the Cherubim	**Gabriel** who is over the serpents and over the Paradise and the Cherubim	**Gabriel** who is in charge of the Serpents, and the Garden, and the Cherubim
	Remiel whom God set over those who rise		

THE *Book of the Watchers* introduced, together with the myth of the descent of the angels, the figure of a disobedient angelic leader. The correct term for the descent of these watchers is really *disobedience*, something still distant from the revolt and confrontation that Christianity offered in the figure of the Devil. The leader of the watchers led astray, Samyaza,[145] is bound together with his companions under the Earth where they await their judgement, although the veridict was already given: eternal confinement in the lower depths of fire. He is innocent, therefore, of any further wickedness; the spirits of the dead Nephilim are the ones that torment the world.[146] In the *Book of Jubilees* these spirits have one leader, Mastema, who convinces God to leave one tenth of these spirits under his command, tempting and punishing human beings according to the will of God. The *Book of Jubilees* attributes to Mastema many biblical passages where God appears as responsible for temptations and destructions such as, for instance, the massacre of the firstborn in Egypt.

Mastema is identified with *satã*, שָׂטָן, a word that in the Old Testament appears with the definite article ("ha-satan", "*the* satan") thirteen times in *Job* and *Zechariah*, and without the article ten times in other books. In two of these passages without the article, the *Septuagint* translates satan as διάβολος[147] (Cr 21:1 e Sl 109:6); in others, where the word שָׂטָן is used to define the attitude of people, and even of angels at the service of God, as in the Book of Numbers 22:22 and 22:32, the translations generally opt for correlative terms such as "adversary".

It is in the New Testament that the figure of the adversary takes the form that Christianity still uses today, in the figure of a stupid and suicidal angel who rebels against an Omnipotent, Omnipresent, and Omniscient God and is condemned to be tortured for millions and millions of eternal years by that Just and

---

145 In the translation by Richard Laurence.

146 There are some doubts about this point, it not being clear if the spirits of the Nephilim have free range in the world, or await for some time of future reckoning.

147 From διαβάλλω (diabállo, "I slander"), from διά (diá, "across") and βάλλω (bállo, "I throw").

Merciful God. Whilst the definitive sentence is not fully applied, he endeavors to get as much company as possible to share in his future suffering, working stupidly and for free in the salvific plan of God, the creator of the stars who pretends to also torture human souls for billions and billions of centuries.

The "logic" behind the entire thing, of course, does not reveal anything beyond the elaborations of people very limited in terms of understanding, endowed with sadistic and infantile mentalities. The rereading done in the texts of the Old Testament, to which these Christians saw themselves forced to condition their reveries, can only be defined as a creative, although tedious, exercise of intellectual dishonesty; one excellent resumé of this process can be found in the Catholic Encyclopedia:

> Mention is made of the Devil in many passages of the Old and New Testaments, but there is no full account given in any one place, and the Scripture teaching on this topic can only be ascertained by combining a number of scattered notices from Genesis to Apocalypse, and reading them in the light of patristic and theological tradition.[148] The authoritative teaching of the Church on this topic is set forth in the decrees of the Fourth Lateran Council (cap. i, "Firmiter credimus"),[149] wherein, after saying that God in the beginning had created together two creatures, the spiritual and the corporeal, that is to say the angelic and the earthly, and lastly man, who was made of both spirit and body, the council continues: "*Diabolus enim et alii dæmones a Deo quidem naturâ creati sunt boni, sed ipsi per se facti sunt mali*" ("the Devil and the other demons were created by God good in their nature but they by themselves have made themselves evil").[150]

[148] That means, combining the Old and New Testament with the same apocryphal literature that the Church would later reject.

[149] In the 13th century. That means, thirteen centuries were needed to create an official version of one incongruous legend.

[150] *Devil.* Catholic Encyclopedia.

The influence of the *Book of the Watchers* can be perceived with certainty in the writings of Justin Martyr.[151] In this excerpt of his *Second Apology*, written in defense of the Christians who, at this point, suffered terrible persecutions, the narrative from the *Book of the Watchers* is repeated, but, beyond that, Justin made here a bridge that would be fundamental in the future campaign to eradicate the other religions (when the Christians would be the one perpetrating terrible persecutions)—he equated the fallen angels and their offspring ("demons")[152] to the Greek-Roman gods:

> But if this idea take possession of some one that if we acknowledge God as our helper, we should not, as we say, be oppressed and persecuted by the wicked; this, too, I will solve. God, when He had made the whole world, and subjected things earthly to man, and arranged the heavenly elements for the increase of fruits and rotation of the seasons, and appointed this divine law—for these things also He evidently made for man—committed the care of men and of all things under heaven to angels whom He appointed over them. But the angels transgressed this appointment, and were captivated by love of

[151] "Justin Martyr, also known as Saint Justin (100—165 AD), was an early Christian apologist, and is regarded as the foremost interpreter of the theory of the Logos in the 2nd century. He was martyred, alongside some of his students, and is considered a saint by the Roman Catholic Church, the Anglican Church, and the Eastern Orthodox Church. Most of his works are lost, but two apologies and a dialogue did survive. The *First Apology*, his most well known text, passionately defends the morality of the Christian life, and provides various ethical and philosophical arguments to convince the Roman emperor, Antoninus, to abandon the persecution of the fledgling sect. Further, he also makes the theologically innovative suggestion that the 'seeds of Christianity' (manifestations of the Logos acting in history) actually predated Christ's incarnation. This notion allows him to claim many historical Greek philosophers (including Socrates and Plato), in whose works he was well studied, as unknowing Christians." *Justin Martyr*. Wikipedia.

[152] From here I will use the term "demon", as the Greek "daimon" or the Latin "daemon" began to take on the meaning associated nowadays with the words "demon" and "devil". But, keep in mind that until the Renaissance, and inclusively in the work by Agrippa we will see, the Greek and Latin words were used.

women, and begat children who are those that are called demons; and besides, they afterwards subdued the human race to themselves, partly by magical writings, and partly by fears and the punishments they occasioned, and partly by teaching them to offer sacrifices, and incense, and libations, of which things they stood in need after they were enslaved by lustful passions; and among men they sowed murders, wars, adulteries, intemperate deeds, and all wickedness. Whence also the poets and mythologists, not knowing that it was the angels and those demons who had been begotten by them that did these things to men, and women, and cities, and nations, which they related, ascribed them to god himself, and to those who were accounted to be his very offspring, and to the offspring of those who were called his brothers, Neptune and Pluto, and to the children again of these their offspring. For whatever name each of the angels had given to himself and his children, by that name they called them.[153]

The association between the daimons and the offerings of the Greek-Roman cults would be repeated later by Porphyry, as we saw, but even Xenocrates had established the figure of the evil daimon (κακοδαίμων[154]) to whom he attributed the cruel and impure behaviours previously ascribed to the gods, as much as the ritualistic practice of the bloody sacrifices.[155] Plutarch also spoke of evil daimons who cause plagues and wars (ocurrences previously assigned to the gods), spirits who should be placated with sacrifices.[156]

[153] "The Second Apology of Justin for the Christians Addressed to the Roman Senate." Justin Martyr. *Early Christians Writings.*

[154] Κακοδαίμων = caco (evil) + daimon.

[155] "Démon." Stanislas Lyonnet. *Dictionaire de Spiritualite Ascetique Et Mystique Doctrine Et Histoire.* Compagnie de Jésus.

[156] "Démon." Stanislas Lyonnet.

Both developments went side by side, with Judaism transferring to the angels and evil spirits the passages in the Old Testament where God tempted and destroyed, and the pagan philosophers attributing to the daimons the mythological passages where the deities also act in questionable ways. Justin Martyr, inheriting from the Jewish side the association made in the *Septuagint* between the foreign gods and the word "daimon" and the myth of the descent of the angels from the *Book of the Watchers*, and from the Greek-Roman side the association of the daimons with the religious ceremonies, began to unite all these concepts in the creation of what will be, later, the orthodox demonological position in Christianity. In accordance with the *Book of Jubilees*, and citing texts from the New Testament, Justin attributes to the demons a leader, Satan, and invented an etymology for that name:

> [...] and by Jesus is addressed as Satan, showing that a compounded name was acquired by him from the deeds which he performed. For 'Sata' in the Jewish and Syrian tongue means apostate; and 'Nas' is the word from which he is called by interpretation the serpent, i.e., according to the interpretation of the Hebrew term, from both of which there arises the single word Satanas.[157]

In Tatian,[158] pupil of Justin, we find the demons as being, not the spirits of the children from the angels, but the angels themselves. The "first-born spirit" created by God, willing to be worshipped by men, is rejected with his followers by God and they become the demons.

---

[157] "The Second Apology of Justin for the Christians Addressed to the Roman Senate." Justin Martyr. *Ante-Nicene Fathers*, Vol I.

[158] "Tatian the Assyrian (c. 120–c. 180 AD) was an Assyrian early Christian writer and theologian of the 2nd century. Tatian's most influential work is the *Diatessaron*, a Biblical paraphrase, or 'harmony', of the four gospels that became the standard text of the four gospels in the Syriac-speaking churches until the 5th century, when it gave way to the four separate gospels in the Peshitta version. His *Oratio ad Graecos* (Address to the Greeks) condemns paganism as worthless, and praises the reasonableness and high antiquity of Christianity." *Tatian the Assyrian*. Wikipedia.

> And, when men attached themselves to one who was more subtle than the rest, having regard to his being the first-born, and declared him to be God, though he was resisting the law of God, then the power of the Logos excluded the beginner of the folly and his adherents from all fellowship with Himself. And so he who was made in the likeness of God, since the more powerful spirit is separated from him, becomes mortal; but that first-begotten one through his transgression and ignorance becomes a demon; and they who imitated him, that is his illusions, are become a host of demons, and through their freedom of choice have been given up to their own infatuation.[159]

Tatian describes a world dominated by demons, who everywhere deceive men to be adored as gods. These demons are already doomed, but before their final punishment try to control human fate, "*and the Lord of all has suffered them to besport themselves, till the world, coming to an end, be dissolved, and the Judge appear, and all those men who, while assailed by the demons, strive after the knowledge of the perfect God obtain as the result of their conflicts a more perfect testimony in the day of judgment.*".[160]

[159] *Tatian's Address to the Greeks*. Translated by J. E. Ryland.

[160] *Tatian's Address to the Greeks*. Translated by J. E. Ryland.

Augustinian Demons

In almost two centuries, between the death of Tatian and the birth of Augustine[161] of Hippo in 354 CE, the variations in the Christian doctrines concerning demons remained inside the parameters we saw. However, the social position of Christianity changed radically in that period, with the end of the persecutions in 313 CE (with the Edict of Milan which decreed tolerance for Christianity); soon after, came the establishment of Christianity as the official religion of the Roman Empire, in 380 CE.

The diversity of creeds and opinions that previously existed could no longer be accepted, and already in 325 CE the first of a long series of ecumenical councils was held in Nicaea, promulgating the *Creed of Nicaea* as the norm to be followed in all of Christianity. After 350 CE, even before the Edict of Thessalonica made Nicene Christianity the official state religion, new laws began to prescribe the death penalty for those who participated in pagan cults; temples were closed and destroyed and libraries were burnt, with Christians desecrating, looting, and vandalizing tombs and monuments.

Augustine converted to Christianity in 386 CE, becoming a strong adversary of his former faith, Maniqueism. In 395 CE he was elevated to the position of bishop in the city of Hippo Regius, located in a region that today is part of Algeria.

The text from Augustine included in this volume, *De Divinatione Daemonum* ("On the Divination of Demons") was written in the period beteween 406-408 CE. The origin of the argument, according to the text, was a conversation between the converted about the destruction of the Serapeum of Alexandria by Christians in 391 AC. The doubt brought to Augustine concerned the fact that the priests of Serapis had foreseen the fall and destruction of their temple. Rather then deny the pagan prophecy, Augustine elaborated a treatise where the nature and capacities of the demons

---

161 "Augustine of Hippo (354 – 430), also known as Saint Augustine or Saint Austin, and also sometimes as Blessed Augustine in the Eastern Orthodox Church, was an early Christian theologian and philosopher whose writings influenced the development of Western Christianity and Western philosophy. Among his most important works are *The City of God* and *Confessions*." *Augustine of Hippo*, Wikipedia.

are described, to explain the workings of the pagan cults and oracles. An example of this explanation:

> Indeed, St. Augustine in the second part of the work develops mainly three points: The demons, being of a higher nature to man, can know the future in some cases, and therefore predict it to men. Inclusively through the subtlety of their being they can know the thoughts of his interlocutors, and so deceive those who care. And, supported on the knowledge of his time, he speaks of demons as not pure spirits, but as beings that roam diffused through the air with senses so fine and subtle that they pick up, better even then telepathy, the most imperceptible of man, even to the subconscious.[162]

The writings of Saint Augustine were fundamental in the final elaboration of the doctrine that defines the fallen angels as being in fact demons, and in the rejection of the interpretation of the *beni ha-elohim* as being these angels. The myth of the fallen angels could no longer be abandoned, as passages from the Gospels and the acceptance of the *Book of Revelation* into the canon of the Church made the fall of the angels and the figure of Satan as the enemy of God points beyond argument.

> Augustine also marks the culmination of the process by which traditions about the Watchers were progressively applied to Satan and gradually dissociated from Gen 6:1–4 and the era before the Flood. Already in the second and third centuries, the figure of Satan looms even larger than the fallen angels in the Christian imagination, no doubt due to his prominent role in the increasingly elevated texts that would come to comprise the NT.[163]

---

[162] *Obras Completas de San Agustín*. Promoted by the Federación Agustiniana Española.

[163] *Fallen Angels and the History of Judaism and Christianity: The Reception of Enochic Literature*. Annette Yoshiko Reed.

Another important point of doctrine that Augustine helped to preserve, at the same time rejecting its original source in the *Book of the Watchers*, is the role of the angels as instructors of sorcery, of magic. Even more, to Augustine every magical art is possible only with help from demons. Although Iamblichus and other defenders of Theurgy had articulated a distinction between it and other practices (μαγεία, γοητεία), Augustine denounces all as "deceptive rites of demons":

> These miracles, and many others of the same nature, which it were tedious to mention, were wrought for the purpose of commending the worship of the one true God, and prohibiting the worship of a multitude of false gods. Moreover, they were wrought by simple faith and godly confidence, not by the incantations and charms composed under the influence of a criminal tampering with the unseen world, of an art which they call either magic, or by the more abominable title necromancy, or the more honorable designation Theurgy;[164] for they wish to discriminate between those whom the people call magicians, who practice necromancy, and are addicted to illicit arts and condemned, and those others who seem to them to be worthy of praise for their practice of theurgy,[165]—the truth, however, being that both classes are the slaves of the deceitful rites of the demons whom they invoke under the names of angels.[166]

---

[164] "quam uel magian uel detestabiliore nomine goetian uel honorabiliore theurgian uocant."

[165] "quos et maleficos uulgus appellat (hos enim ad goetian pertinere dicunt), alios autem laudabiles uideri uolunt, quibus theurgian deputant; cum sint utrique ritibus fallacibus daemonum obstricti sub nominibus angelorum."

[166] *St. Augustine's City of God and Christian Doctrine.* Christian Classics Ethereal Library.

Temple of Serapis, illustration from *Lyell's Principles of Geology*

The Magic of Christ

The environment of Christian victory that is perceived in the *De Divinatione Daemonum*, wherein Augustine describes a world in which Christianity triumphs over the demons and their cults, a victory very well exemplified by the destruction of the Temple of Serapis, changed significantly in the following years. The sack of Rome in 410 CE raised many doubts about the power of God in the history of salvation, and Augustine used all his argumentative capacity to justify the event:

> The sack of Rome by the Visigoths in 410 left Romans in a deep state of shock, and many Romans saw it as punishment for abandoning traditional Roman religion for Christianity. In response to these accusations, and in order to console Christians, Augustine wrote *The City of God*, arguing for the truth of Christianity over competing religions and philosophies and that Christianity is not only not responsible for the Sack of Rome, but also was responsible for the success of Rome. He attempted to console Christians, writing that, even if the earthly rule of the Empire was imperiled, it was the City of God that would ultimately triumph.[167]

"Demons" are one of the themes most treated in the *City of God*; thirty-nine chapters use the word "demons" in their titles,[168] using it to attack every form of philosophy and religion outside of Christianity, as well as every and each kind of magic. It is a remarkable exercise for the breadth of knowledge that Augustine shows, as he comments and refutes an impressive number of philosophers who had dealt with the subject of "daimons".

---

[167] *City of God*. Wikipedia.

[168] *St. Augustine's City of God and Christian Doctrine*. Christian Classics Ethereal Library.

Augustine also establishes a compromise about the presence and action of the demons in a world where, supposedly, their power had been defeated by the coming of Christ—an explanation very necessary, principally after the problems faced by the Roman Empire. Augustine proposes the present moment as being a transition between the resurrection and the second coming of Christ, during which the demons, although defeated and diminished in their powers, can still act *with God´s permission*:

> But it is to be most firmly believed that Almighty God can do whatever He pleases, whether in punishing or favoring, and that the demons can accomplish nothing by their natural power (for their created being is itself angelic, although made malign by their own fault), except what He may permit, whose judgments are often hidden, but never unrighteous.[169]

Subsequent magical texts, as prepared under the censorship of Christianity, make a casuistic use of this argument: if the demons are already in the world tempting and attacking people *with God's permission*, the conjuror needs only to direct this operation in a convenient direction. To guarantee his salvation, he resorts to the hierarchical principle of pre-Christian magic, invoking God and the angels as the source of authority and protection before asking for demonic services. This principle is already clearly defined in the *Testament of Solomon*.

---

[169] St. *Augustine´s City of God and Christian Doctrine*. Christian Classics Ethereal Library.

The Magical Renaissance

The power of Rome over the Mediterranean territories, which included parts of Europe up to Great Britain, lasted ten centuries. After the official Christianization in 380 CE, the Empire fell less than a hundred years later; the deposition of Romulus Augustulus on the 4th of September in 467 CE is, conventionally, considered to be the end of the Western Roman Empire. The Eastern Roman Empire, or Byzantine, resisted until the 15th century, when Asia Minor fell under the power of Islam. Hipona (Hippo), the city of Augustine, was less fortunate; the Muslims destroyed it in 698 CE, during the conquest and conversion of North Africa.

Paradoxically, the Muslim expansion was a key factor in the recovery of magical knowledge in Europe. First, the Muslim culture proved to be far more accessible and interested in the classical heritage:

> While Muslims were busy translating and adding their own ideas to Greek philosophies, the Latin West was still suspicious of pagan ideas. St. Jerome, for example, was hostile to Aristotle, and St. Augustine had little interest in exploring philosophy, only applying logic to theology. For centuries, Greek ideas in Europe were all but non-existent. Only a few monasteries had Greek works, and even fewer of them copied these works.[170]

This situation began to change from the twelfth century onwards, with the appearance of European universities. The *Reconquista* of the European territories previously taken by the Muslims (Toledo in 1085; Sicily in 1091) favored access to and translation of Arabic books and, among these, texts directly or indirectly related to the magical arts. The most notable example is the *Picatrix*, a treatise on astrology and talismanic magic translated in Spain in the thirteenth century.

---

[170] *Latin translations of the 12th century*. Wikipedia.

> According to Eugenio Garin "In reality the Latin version of the *Picatrix* is as indispensable as the *Corpus Hermeticum* or the writings of Albumasar for understanding a conspicuous part of the production of the Renaissance, including the figurative arts." It has significantly influenced West European esotericism from Marsilio Ficino in the 15th century, to Thomas Campanella in the 17th century.[171]

In the second place, the fall of Constantinople in 1453 caused a migration of scholars, principally to Italy, which was fundamental to the beginning of the Renaissance. This migration is directly related to the reception of two important magical texts which became major sources of the later literature of the grimoires, the *Testament of Solomon* and the *Magical Treatise of Solomon* (*Hygromanteia*). It is significant that all the surviving European manuscripts of the *Testament* are dated from the 15th century; the importance of the *Treatise* can be understood in the excerpt:

> The oldest manuscripts are from the fourteenth century, and the majority from the fifteenth century, but Pablo A. Torijano's claim that it is based on material going as far back as the sixth century is either accepted or at least regarded as plausible. Ioannis Marathakis, while not denying the possibility of Torijano's theory, suggests that some time between the thirteenth or fourteenth centuries is more likely. The *Magical Treatise of Solomon* served as a bridge between the Roman-era *Testament of Solomon* and the renaissance *Key of Solomon*. Early copies of the *Magical Treatise* were appended to or incorporated elements of the *Testament of Solomon*, while one of the earliest manuscripts of the *Key of Solomon* is also classified as a late copy of the *Magical Treatise*. Some manuscripts featured demons assigned to the

---

[171] *Picatrix*. Wikipedia.

> four cardinal directions, distinct from those found in the *Lesser Key of Solomon* and related works, but very similar to those found in later works such as the *Grand Grimoire* and *Grimoirium Verum*. Portions of the *Treatise* also have some relationship to the *Heptameron* of Pietro d'Abano, the *Lesser Key of Solomon*, and the *Sworn Book of Honorius*; and select ideas may bear distant relationships to the *Book of Abramelin*, the *Greek Magical Papyri* (particularly "The Sword of Dardanus"), *Sefer Raziel HaMalakh*, *Sepher Ha-Razim*, the *Sword of Moses*, and the *Cyranides*.[172]

That magic is closely related to the Renaissance is something evident from the life and work of one of its main initiators, Marsilio Ficino.[173] Marsilio was not only responsible for the translation of a series of works fundamental to European magic, like the *Corpus Hermeticum* and Iamblichus' treatise on Theurgy, but he was himself a practitioner and defender of a kind of astrological magic with therapeutic objectives. His disciple, Pico de la Mirandola,[174] presented the study of Kabbalah to the non-Jewish intellectual elite of his time, and this mixture of Hermetism, Neoplatonism, and Kabbalah, together with the production and diffusion of grimories, generated the magical identity that until today prevails in the West. If the reader makes reference, for instance, to the teachings

---

[172] *Magical Treatise of Solomon*. Wikipedia.

[173] "Marsilio Ficino (19 October 1433–1 October 1499) was an Italian scholar and Catholic priest who was one of the most influential humanist philosophers of the early Italian Renaissance. He was also an astrologer, a reviver of Neoplatonism in touch with every major academic thinker and writer of his day and the first translator of Plato's complete extant works into Latin. His Florentine Academy, an attempt to revive Plato's Academy, had enormous influence on the direction and tenor of the Italian Renaissance and the development of European philosophy." *Marsilio Ficino*. Wikipedia.

[174] "Count Giovanni Pico della Mirandola (24 February 1463–17 November 1494) was an Italian Renaissance philosopher. He is famed for the events of 1486, when at the age of 23, he proposed to defend 900 theses on religion, philosophy, natural philosophy, and magic against all comers, for which he wrote the famous *Oration on the Dignity of Man*, which has been called the 'Manifesto of the Renaissance', and a key text of Renaissance humanism and of what has been called the 'Hermetic Reformation'." *Giovanni Pico della Mirandola*. Wikipedia.

of the Hermetic Order of the Golden Dawn at the end of the 19th century, she will find both the arrangement of the Kabbalistic Tree of Life initiation system and the concept of the Guardian Angel derived from the grimoire of Abramelin.

This process of merger has its paradigmatic moment in the work of Cornelius Agrippa,[175] *De occulta philosophia libri tres*, or *Three Books of Occult Philosophy*. In it, Agrippa brings together all these influences in an orderly and systematic exposition which would be extremely influential; all major later Renaissance magicians, notably John Dee,[176] Giordano Bruno,[177] and Campanella,[178] were readers of Agrippa.

> Agrippa argued for a synthetic vision of magic whereby the natural world combined with the celestial and the divine through Neoplatonic participation, such that ordinarily licit natural magic was in fact validated by a kind of demonic magic sourced ultimately from

---

175 "Heinrich Cornelius Agrippa von Nettesheim (14 September 1486–18 February 1535) was a German magician, occult writer, theologian, astrologer, and alchemist." *Heinrich Cornelius Agrippa*. Wikipedia.

176 "John Dee (13 July 1527–1608 or 1609) was a mathematician, astronomer, astrologer, occult philosopher, imperialist and adviser to Queen Elizabeth I. He devoted much of his life to the study of alchemy, divination and Hermetic philosophy. Dee straddled the worlds of science and magic just as they were becoming distinguishable. One of the most learned men of his age, he had been invited to lecture on the geometry of Euclid at the University of Paris while still in his early twenties. Dee was an ardent promoter of mathematics and a respected astronomer, as well as a leading expert in navigation, having trained many of those who would conduct England's voyages of discovery. His magical system, noted during a series of invocations that have passed for years, it is one of the most popular today." *John Dee*. Wikipedia.

177 "Giordano Bruno (1548-1600), was an Italian Dominican friar, philosopher, mathematician, poet, and astrologer. He supported the new view of the Universe promulgated by Copernicus, and proposed that the stars are distant suns that could have planets with live of their own. He wrote many important treatises about Magic, Hermetism and Kabbalah, proposing a new religious form where the ideal of men as the center of the universe would be realized through theurgic practices." *Giordano Bruno*. Wikipedia.

178 "Tommaso Campanella (1568-1639), baptized Giovanni Domenico Campanella, was an Italian philosopher, theologian, astrologer, magician and poet. His main work, the *City of the Sun*, describes a Hermetic utopia inspired in ideas from the *Picatrix*." *Tommaso Campanella*. Wikipedia.

> God. By this means Agrippa proposed a magic that could resolve all epistemological problems raised by skepticism in a total validation of Christian faith.[179]

The excerpts of Agrippa I selected for this volume allow us to perceive well the presence of the old ideas about the daimons, and also the diverse tentatives of accommodation between the magical arts and the Christian doctrine. Agrippa was a cautious writer, one who endeavored to keep himself in the position of a scholar making an impersonal account of magical knowledge, and one who very rarely compromised himself with the positions he describes. This caution and fear was a major feature of European magical literature until the late nineteenth century.

> The history of learned magic in the Latin West may be understood in part as a series of attempts to reconcile theologically problematic practices and ideas with Christian orthodoxy. This was a matter that concerned not only the authors of magic books but also the scribes and collectors who transmitted or preserved such texts. The nature of each reconciliation could, in principle, be quite distinctive and depended on a wide variety of factors, including the nature of the text received, any known authoritative reactions to it or the kind of magic it promoted, the context in which it was transmitted, and the copyist's interests. A desire to see magic in terms of natural philosophy would, for example, demand a fundamentally different approach from a desire to regard it as a kind of mystical technology or religious exercise.[180]

---

179 *Heinrich Cornelius Agrippa.* Wikipedia.

180 *The Transformations of Magic: Illicit Learned Magic in the Later Middle Ages.* Frank Klaassen.

The other text included in this work, the *Isagoge: An Introductory Discourse of the nature of such Spirits,*[181] attributed to Georg Pictorius of Villingen,[182] is another good example of a confused non-orthodox demonology that, while striving to remain under the shadow of the church, courts and is fascinated with magic, not daring to take it or defend it.[183] The proximity and interest of this text to magical subjects was evident to whosoever decided to publish it together with the *Fourth Book of Occult Philosophy,* spuriously attributed to Agrippa. In this text, the reader can identify the diverse influences that we have studied, from the Archaic Greek to the elaborations of Augustine.

---

[181] *Isagoge:* An Introductory Discourse on the nature of such Spirits as are exercised in the sublunary Bounds; their Original, Names, Offices, Illusions, Powers, Prophecies, Miracles; and how they may be expelled and driven away.

[182] "Georg Pictorius of Villingen (c. 1500–1569) was a physician and an author of the German Renaissance. He became active as a physician from 1540 in Ensisheim. In his book on magic, he condemns witchcraft, endorsing the witch-trials of his time: 'if the witches are not burned, the number of these furies swells up in such an immense sea that no one could live safe from their spells and charms.'" Georg Pictorius. Wikipedia.

[183] And, very often, attacking it as a preservation strategy of both the text and the author and his readers.

The Discoverie of Witchcraft

The Renaissance had its shadow, cast by the flames at the stake over the blood shed by the religious persecution known as the Witch Hunts, or the Witch Trials. It is estimated that approximately 40,000 people were executed between the 15th and the 18th centuries, but the number of executions is far from the whole story. In Spain and Portugal, for example, where the number of executions is estimated at less than 10% of the cases investigated, the simple accusation before an Inquisition was enough to destroy the life and family of a person. An accused (male or female) could spend years in prison before the case was heard, was tortured frequently, as was his family, who besides suffering the disruption caused by his absence, suffered all manner of social rejection. Even if not sentenced to death, or even when acquitted, the accused could hardly be readmitted into society.

Some voices gradually began to rise up against the arbitrariness of the proceedings against the alleged witches and wizards. Agrippa in 1519 successfully defended a woman accused of witchcraft. His student and friend Johann Weyer[184] published in 1563 the *De Praestigiis Daemonum et Incantationibus ac Venificiis* (On the Illusions of the Demons and on Spells and Poisons), in which he argued that the confessions of the powers and the magical acts perpetrated by the witches were the result of mental problems, aggravated by the form in which the inquisitorial process was conducted.

With the same aims, Reginald Scot[185] published in 1584 *The Discoverie of Witchcraft*. He argues in the work against the reality of witchcraft from a rational viewpoint and a theology that does not

---

184 "Johann Weyer or Wier (1515–24 February 1588) was a Dutch physician, occultist and demonologist, disciple and follower of Heinrich Cornelius Agrippa. He was among the first to publish against the persecution of witches. His most influential work is *De Praestigiis Daemonum et Incantationibus ac Venificiis*." *Johann Weyer*. Wikipedia.

185 "Reginald Scot (or Scott) (c. 1538–9 October 1599) was an English country gentleman and Member of Parliament, now remembered as the author of *The Discoverie of Witchcraft*, which was published in 1584. It was written against the belief in witches, to show that witchcraft did not exist. Part of its content exposes how (apparently miraculous) feats of magic were done, and the book is often deemed the first textbook on conjuring." *Reginald Scot*. Wikipedia.

accept the possibility that human beings could have the powers the witchhunters alleged to exist. He also discredited the witnesses, resorting to the idea that the accused were people lacking mental stability, or were impostors who abused the credulity of others.

In his original edition of 1584, he included one of the texts that make up this volume, the first *Discourse on the Nature and Substance of Devils and Spirits*. It is a very comprehensive text where he comments upon and criticizes various opinions on spirits. It is especially pleasurable as a read because of its Protestant bias; Scot, like many others Protestant thinkers, accuses the Catholic practices and institutions of being magical and superstitious. It is a great irony to see the Catholic arguments of centuries past be used against the very Church where they were conceived.

Irony, however, turned against Scot's work, too. Weyer included, in the second edition of 1577 of *De Praestigiis Daemonum*, a text titled *Pseudomonarchia Daemonum*, a compilation of names of demons and magical practices, with the vowed aim of exposing the "men who are not ashamed to call themselves magi, their curiosities, deceptions, vanity, tricks, impostures, deliriums, deceiving the mind, and obvious lies, but rather that they may be unwilling, when they can be seen in the bright light of day",[186] so Scot included in his own edition (besides the *Pseudomonarchia Daemonum* itself) in its Book XV[187] what he described as the "ridiculous conjurations [...] for the most part made by T. R. (for so much of his name he bewraieth) and John Cokars, invented and devised for the augmentation and maintenance of their living, for the edifieng of the poore, and for the propagating and inlarging of Gods glorie, as in the beginning of their booke of conjurations they protest". His aim was to help unmask the "conjurors" he considered to be more guilty than the poor women accused of witchcraft. The result could not be worse—as had happened to Weyer's work, Scot's book became coveted precisely because of these magical instructions.

This interest encouraged the editor of the new edition of 1665 to include a second *Discourse concerning Devils and Spirits*, as well

---

[186] From the digital edition of Joseph H. Peterson.

[187] *The Discoverie* is internally divided into "books", and the "books" into "chapters".

as an addendum of nine chapters to "Book XV". This second discourse goes against everything Scot had originally written, being an excellent description of both magical practices and of some of the prevailing theories at the time that tried to explain the spiritual reality behind the conjurations.

The reader may notice by the reading of texts selected for this volume that the concepts of intermediate spiritual beings remained consistent even across all these centuries, and that the practices to contact them and make use of their resources also remained constant.

The adjustments required by the Christian view had more impact on the psychology of the practitioner than on their philosophy and praxis. Even the use of hierarchical divine powers, and verbal abuse against the spirits—things which seem at first as a result of Christian influence—actually existed previously.

It is also good to keep in mind that the persecution of magicians was part of pre-Christian Roman law, although, of course, it was exacerbated by the Jewish influence upon the origins of Christianity, extended initially to every other other religion, and then to what was considered unorthodox Christianity.

A Note on Etymology

Until Agrippa, inclusively, the texts used Δαίμων and Διάβολος (Greek) or Dæmon and Diabolus (Latin). In my work I used "daimon" until the moment the term acquired its modern/Christian sense, allowing me then to use "demon". In the citations, and the translations, when "dæmon" was used by the original writer, I kept it according to the text.

It is useful to mention ἄγγελος (ãggelos); it was also a decision made by the translators of the *Septuagint* not to use "daimon" when referring to the messengers and representatives of God mentioned in the Old Testament:

> Significantly, there is one being or role portrayed by a particular category of character in the Hebrew Bible that is never translated as δαίμων—מלאך[188] (angel), one of whose main roles was that of intervention, serving as an intermediary between the highest god and human beings. Thus, the most natural translation of the Hebrew word מלאך, "messenger" or "angel," should have been δαίμων, yet the translators seem conscientiously to avoid it. Instead, the translators usually render מלאך as ἄγγελος, which is a literal translation into Greek of the role signified by the Hebrew. In the Hebrew Bible, mal'āk can mean any "messenger" at all. But the word gradually becomes, one might say, a technical term rather than a common noun. That is, the word refers no longer to an activity but to a certain species of heavenly being that serves God and communicates God's messages to human beings.[189]

[188] מלאך, malak.

[189] *When Did Angels Become Demons?*. Dale Basil Martin.

Dale Basil Martin, finally, summarizes these etymological and religious developments that, as we saw, were fundamental in the creation and development of Christian demonology:

> The Jewish translators in essence created two new technical terms for Greek-speaking Jews. The Greek word ἄγγελος had not been a noun for a particular class of beings in Greek; it referred simply to any messenger. By using the translation ἄγγελοι for beings who to a Greek may have looked much like their own δαίμονες, the Jews introduced a new term into Greek, and a new class of inhabitants into cosmic demography. The mal'āk of God became not just a "messenger," but an "angel." Likewise, the Jewish translators, by using the term δαιμόνιον for several different kinds of beings in the Near East and the Hebrew Bible, thereby introduced the Greek noun for a particular class of beings into Near Eastern mythologies. They took the Greek term δαίμων and created a new species of being that included what were previously different species. The Jewish translators (if we may speak simplistically in characterizing what was really a long and complex translation history) created two new technical terms for Greek-speaking Jews: the Greek word ἄγγελος for beings they had previously known by another term, and the Greek term δαίμων for beings they had previously known by several different words. But they did not confuse the two classes of beings into one. Angels became one species of cosmic workers, and daimons another.[190]

Here follows more etymological information; the main source of consultation was the Wikitionary.

[190] *When Did Angels Become Demons?*. Dale Basil Martin.

Διαβάλλω (diabállō, “I slander”)—From **διά** (διά, “across”) and **βάλλω** (bállō, “I throw”).

Διά—From δισα (disa), from Proto-Indo-European *dwis (related to δίς (dís, “twice”) and δύο (dúo, “two”).

Βάλλω—From Proto-Indo-European *$g^w elh_1$- (“to hit by throwing”). Cognates are uncertain, but compare Sanskrit उद्गूर्ण (ud-gūrṇa) and Old Irish at·baill (“dies”).

Diabolus—Latin, from the Ancient Greek Διάβολος (Diábolos).

Devil—From Middle English devil, devel, deovel, from Old English dēofol, dēoful, from earlier dīobul (“devil”), ultimately from Ancient Greek διάβολος (diábolos, “accuser, slanderer”); the Old English word was probably adopted under influence of Latin diabolus (itself from the Greek). Other Germanic languages adopted the word independently.

Δαίμων—From Proto-Indo-European *deh_2-i- (“to divide, cut”), whence also δαίομαι (daíomai, “to divide”). For similar semantic development compare Old Persian (baga, “god”), Sanskrit भग (bhága, “dispenser, patron”) (usually applied to gods) beside Avestan (baga-, “part”) and Sanskrit भजति (bhajati, “to divide, apportion”). God, goddess, divine power, deity, guardian spirit (Latin genius), and so one’s fate, destiny, fortune; departed soul; demon, evil spirit (ecclesiastical).

Dæmon—From Latin daemon (“genius, lar, guardian spirit”), from Ancient Greek δαίμων (daímōn, “dispenser, god, protective spirit”).

Demon—From Latin daemon (“lar, genius, guardian

spirit"), from Ancient Greek δαίμων (daímōn, "dispenser, god, protective spirit"). An evil spirit. A fallen angel or Satanic divinity; a false god.

שד (shed)–From Aramaic שידא (šēḏā, "demônio"), from Akkadian šēdu, "uma divindade protetora". From Aramaic שידא (šēḏā, "demon"), from Akkadian (šēdu, "a protective deity"). A demon, devil, fiend, sprite, bogey, fantom, genie, ghost, phantom, poltergeist, shade, spirit.

ἄγγελος–Uncertain. Probably a loan word, and probably related to ἄγγαρος (ángaros, "Persian mounted courier") (whence Latin angarius), which is probably from an East Asian language (see also Sanskrit अजिरा (ajirā, "agile, swift"). Klein suggests Semitic; but it could also be from pre-Greek. Messenger. One that announces. Angel, heavenly spirit.

Angel–From Middle English angel, aungel, ængel, engel, from Anglo-Norman angele, angle and Old English ængel, engel ("angel, messenger"), possibly via an early Proto-Germanic angiluz but ultimately from Latin angelus, from Ancient Greek ἄγγελος (ángelos, "messenger"). A divine and supernatural messenger from a deity, or other divine entity. (Abrahamic tradition) The lowest order of angels, below virtues. Attendant spirit; genius; demon.

Genius–From Latin genius ("the guardian spirit of a person, spirit, inclination, wit, genius, literally 'inborn nature'"), from gignere ("to beget, produce"), Old Latin genere, the root gen; see genus.

מלאך–(mal'ákh) m (plural indefinite form מַלְאָכִים, singular construct form מַלְאַךְ, plural construct form מַלְאֲכֵי); angel; (rare) messenger.

The following table is used to correlate the terms:

	English		
Greek Latin	Demon	Devil	Angel
Δαίμων (Daimon) Dæmon *(Latin)*	From Proto-Indo-European deh$_2$-i- ("to divide, cut"), whence also δαίομαι (daíomai, "to divide").		
Διάβολος (Diabolôs) Diabolus (*Latin*)		(diabállō, "I slander"), From διά (διά , "across") and βάλλω (bállō, "I throw").	
ἄγγελος (Ãggelos) Angelus (*Latin*)			Uncertain. Probably a loan word, and probably related to ἄγγαρος (ángaros, "Persian mounted courier").
	דש Shed		ךאלמ Malak
	Hebrew		

The Selection of Texts

The texts I chose to present an overview of the magical and religious understanding of spiritual beings of intermediate nature are as follows:

The *Magical Operation of Pnouthis* is comprised of two fragments from the *Greek Magical Papyri* wherein the figure of the magical assistant is well defined; they were taken from Betz edition, with some minor adaptations to prevent the lacunas in the text interfering with the elegance of the reading.

On Angels and Daemonae & the Peculiar Dæmon, from Iamblichus' work, comes from the Thomas Taylor translation from 1822.

On the Divination of Demons, by Saint Augustine, I translated from the Spanish in the *Obras Completas de San Agustín*, from the Federación Agustiniana Española.

On the Order of the Evil Spiritis, and the Triple Good Dæmon, chapters from Agrippa's *Third Book of Occult Philosophy*, came from the eletronic version made by Joseph H. Peterson and are used with his permission. The excellent edition by Donald Tyson was much consulted.

In the same way, although I had used for the Isagoge one facsimile copy from the 1655 edition of the *Fourth Book of Occult Philosophy*, and kept (as far as I could) the use of the italics, the original form of punctuation, and the use of capital letters, the edition by Donald Tyson of this second work was also very useful.

The texts from the *Discoverie of Witchcraft* come from a facsimile of the 1886 edition.

The Magical Operation of Pnouthis

Rites of the Assistant Daimon

PGM I. 1-42

A daimon comes as an assistant who will reveal everything to you clearly and will be your companion and will eat and sleep with you.

Take together, therefore, two of your own fingernails and all the hairs from your head, and take a Circaean falcon and deify in the milk of a black cow after you have mixed Attic honey with the milk. And once you have deified it, wrap it with an undyed piece of cloth and place beside it your fingernails along with your hairs; and take a piece of choice papyrus, and inscribe in myrrh the following, and set it in the same manner along with the hairs and fingernails, and plaster it with uncut frankincense and old wine.

So, the writing on the strip is:

A EE ÊÊÊ IIII OOOOO YYYYYY ÕÕÕÕÕÕÕ

But write this, making two figures:

A
E E
Ê Ê Ê
I I I I
O O O O O
Y Y Y Y Y Y
Õ Õ Õ Õ Õ Õ Õ

Õ Õ Õ Õ Õ Õ Õ
Y Y Y Y Y Y
O O O O O
I I I I
Ê Ê Ê
E E
A

And take the milk with the honey and drink it before the rising of the sun, and there will be something divine in your heart. And take the falcon and set it up as a statue in a shrine made of juniper wood. And after you have crowned the shrine itself, make an offering of non-animal foods and have on hand some old wine. And before you recline, speak directly to the bird itself after you have made sacrifice to it, as you usually do, and say the prescribed spell:

A EE ÊÊÊ IIII OOOOO YYYYYY ÕÕÕÕÕÕÕ

Come to me, Good Husbandman, Good Daimon:

HARPON KNOUPHI BRINTANTEN SIPHRI
BRISKYLMA AROUAZAR BAMESEN
KRIPHI NIPOUMICHMOUMAÔPH

Come to me, O holy Orion, you who lie in the north, who cause the currents of the Nile to roll down and mingle with the sea, transforming them with life as it does man's seed in sexual intercourse, you who have established the world on an indestructible foundation, who are young in the morning and old in the evening, who journey through the subterranean sphere and rise, breathing fire, you who have parted the seas in the first month, who ejaculate seeds into the sacred fig tree of Heliopolis continually. This is your authoritative name:

ARBATH ABAÔTH BAKCHABRE.

But when you arE dismissed, go without shoes and walk backwards and set yourself to the enjoyment of the food and dinner and the prescribed food offering, coming face to face as companion to the god. This rite requires complete purity. Conceal, conceal the procedure and for 7 days refrain from having intercourse with a woman.

The spell of Pnouthis, the sacred scribe, for acquiring an Assistant Daimon

PGM I. 42-195

Pnouthios to Keryx, a god-fearing man, greetings.

As one who knows, I have prescribed for you this spell for acquiring an assistant to prevent your failing as you carry out this rite. After detaching all the prescriptions bequeathed to us in countless books, one out of all I have shown you this spell for acquiring an assistant as one that is serviceable to you, for you to take this holy assistant and only. O friend of aerial spirits that move having persuaded me with god-given spells but now I have dispatched this book so that you may learn thoroughly. For the spell of Pnouthis has the power to persuade the gods and all the goddesses. And I shall write you from it about acquiring an assistant.

The traditional rite for acquiring an assistant

After the preliminary purification, abstain from animal food and from all uncleanliness and, on whatever night you want to, go up onto a lofty roof after you have clothed yourself in a pure garment and say the first spell of encounter as the sun's orb is disappearing. With a wholly black Isis band on your eyes, and in your right hand grasp a falcon's head and when the sun rises, hail it as you shake its head and recite this sacred spell as you burn uncut frankincense and pour rose oil, making the sacrifice in an earthen censer on ashes from the plant heliotrope.

And as you recite the spell there will be this sign for you: a falcon will fly down and stand in front of you, and after flapping its wings in mid-air and dropping an oblong stone, it will immediately take flight and ascend to heaven. You should pick up this stone; carve it at once and engrave it later. Once it has been engraved, bore a hole in it, pass a thread through and wear it around your neck. But in the evening, go up to your housetop again and, facing the light of the goddess, address to her this hymnic spell as you again sacrifice myrrh troglitis in the same fashion. Light a fire and hold a branch of myrtle, shaking it, and salute the goddess

At once there will be a sign for you like this: A blazing star will descend and come to a stop in the middle of the housetop, and when the star has dissolved before your eyes, you will behold the angel whom you have summoned and who has been sent to you, and you will quickly learn the decisions of the gods. But do not be afraid: approach the god and, taking his right hand, kiss him and say these words to the angel, for he will quickly respond to you about whatever you want. But you adjure him with this oath that he meet you and remain inseparable and that he not keep silent or disobey in any way. But when he has with certainty accepted this oath of yours, take the god by the hand and leap down, and after bringing him into the narrow room where you reside, sit him down. After first preparing the house in a fitting manner and providing all types of foods and Mendesian wine, set these before the god, with an uncorrupted boy serving and maintaining silence until the angel departs. And you address preliminary words to the god: "I shall have you as a friendly assistant, a beneficent god who serves me whenever I say, 'Quickly, by your power now appear on earth to me, yea verily, god'!"

And while reclining, you yourself quickly speak about what you propose. Test this oath of the god on what you wish. But when 3 hours have passed, the god will immediately leap up. Order the boy to run to the door. And say, "Go, lord, blessed god, where you live eternally, as you will," and the god vanishes.

This is the sacred rite for acquiring an assistant

It is acknowledged that he is a god; he is an aerial spirit which you have seen. If you give him a command, straightway he performs the task: he sends dreams, he brings women, men without the use of magical material, he kills, he destroys, he stirs up winds from the earth, he carries gold, silver, bronze, and he gives them to you whenever the need arises. And he frees from bonds a person chained in prison, he opens doors, he causes invisibility so that no one can see you at all, he is a bringer of fire, he brings water, wine, bread and whatever you wish in the way of foods: olive oil, vinegar – with the single exception of fish – and he will bring plenty of vegetables, whatever kind you wish, but as for pork, you must not ever tell him to bring this at all! And when you want to give a dinner, tell him so. Conjure up in your mind any suitable room and order him to prepare it for a banquet quickly and without delay. At once he will bestow chambers with golden ceilings, and you will see their walls covered with marble – and you consider these things partly real and partly just illusionary – and costly wine, as is meet to cap a dinner splendidly. He will quickly bring daimons, and for you he will adorn these servants with sashes. These things he does quickly. And as soon as you order him to perform a service, he will do so, and you will see him excelling in other things: He stops ships and again releases them, he stops very many evil daimons, he checks wild beasts and will quickly break the teeth of fierce reptiles, he puts dogs to sleep and renders them voiceless. He changes into whatever form of beast you want: one that flies, swims, a quadruped, a reptile. He will carry you into the air, and again hurl you into the billows of the sea's current and into the waves of the sea; he will quickly freeze rivers and seas and in such a way that you can run over them firmly, as you want. And especially will he stop, if ever you wish it, the sea-running foam, and whenever you wish to bring down stars and whenever you wish to make warm things cold and cold things warm, he will light lamps and extinguish them again. And he will shake walls and cause them to blaze with fire; he will serve you suitably for whatever you have in mind, O blessed initiate of the sacred magic, and will accomplish it for you, this most powerful assistant, who is also the only lord of the air. And the gods will agree to everything, for without him nothing happens. Share this great mystery with no one [else], but conceal it, by Helios, since you have been deemed worthy by the lord god.

This is the spell spoken seven times seven to Helios as an adjuration of the assistant

ORI PI . . . AMOUNTE AINTHYPH PICHAROUR RAIAL
KARPHIOUTH YMOU ROTHIRBAN OCHANAU
MOUNAICHANAPTA ZO ZON TAZOTAZO PTAZO MAUIAS
SOUORI SOUO OOUS SARAPTOUMI SARACHTHI A. . .
RICHAMCHO BIRATHAU OPHAU PHAUO DAUA AUANTO
ZOUZO ARROUZO ZOTOUAR THOMNAORI AYOI PTAUCHAREBI
AOUOSOBIAU PTABAIN AAAAAAA AEEIOYOYOOIEEA
CHACHACH CHACHACH CHARCHARACHACH AMOUN O EI
IAEOBAPHRENEMOUNOTHILARIKRIPHIAEYEAIPHIRKIRALITHON
OMENERPHABOEAI CHATHACH PHNESCHER PHICHRO PHNYRO
PHOCHOCHOCH IARBATHA GRAMME PHIBAOCHNEMEO.

This is the spell spoken seven times seven to Helios.

And engraved on the stone is:

Helioros a lion-faced figure, holding in the left hand a celestial globe and a whip, and around him in a circle is a serpent biting is tail. And on the exergue of the stone is this name (conceal it):

ACHA ACHACHA CHACH CHARCHARA CHACH

And after passing an Anubian string through it, wear it around your neck.

Spell to Selene

INOUTHO PTOUAUMI ANCHARICH CHARAPTOUMI ANOCHA ABITHROU ACHARABAUBAU BARATHIAN ATEB DOUANANOU APTYR PANOR PAURACH SOUMI PHORBA PHORIPHORBARABAU BOETH AZA PHOR RIM MIRPHAR ZAURA PTAUZOU CHOTHARPARACHTHIZOU ZAITH ATIAU IABAU KANTANTOUMI BATHARA CHTHIBI ANOCH

Image of a gem engraved with the figure of Helioros[191]

Having said this, you will see some star gradually free itself from heaven and become a god. But you approach, take him by the hand, kiss him and say the same spell:

---

[191] "Helioros", article written by Gyorgy Nemeth, in *Sylloge Epigraphica Barcinonensis.*

OPTAUMI NAPHTHAUBI MAIOUTHMOU
METROBAL RACHEPTOUMI AMMOCHARI
AUTHEI A... TAMARA CHIOBITAM TRIBOMIS
ARACHO ISARI RACHI IAKOUBI
TAURABEROMI ANTABI TAUBI.

When you have spoken this, a reply will be given. But you say to him: "What is your divine name? Reveal it to me ungrudgingly, so that I may call upon it." It consists of 15 letters:

SOUESOLYR PHTHE MOTH

And this is spoken next: "Hither to me, King, I call you God of Gods, mighty, boundless, undefiled, indescribable, firmly established Aion. Be inseparable from me from this day forth through all the time of my life."

Then question him by the same oaths. If he tells you his name, take him by the hand, descend and have him recline as I have said above, setting before him part of the foods and drinks which you partake of. And when you release him, sacrifice to him after his departure what is prescribed and pour a wine offering, and in this way you will be a friend of the mighty angel. When you go abroad, he will go abroad with you; when you are destitute, he will give you money. He will tell you what things will happen both when and at what time of the night or day. And if I anyone asks you "What do I have in mind!" or "What has happened to me?" or even "What is going to happen?" question the angel, and he will tell you in silence. But you speak to the one who questions you as if from yourself.

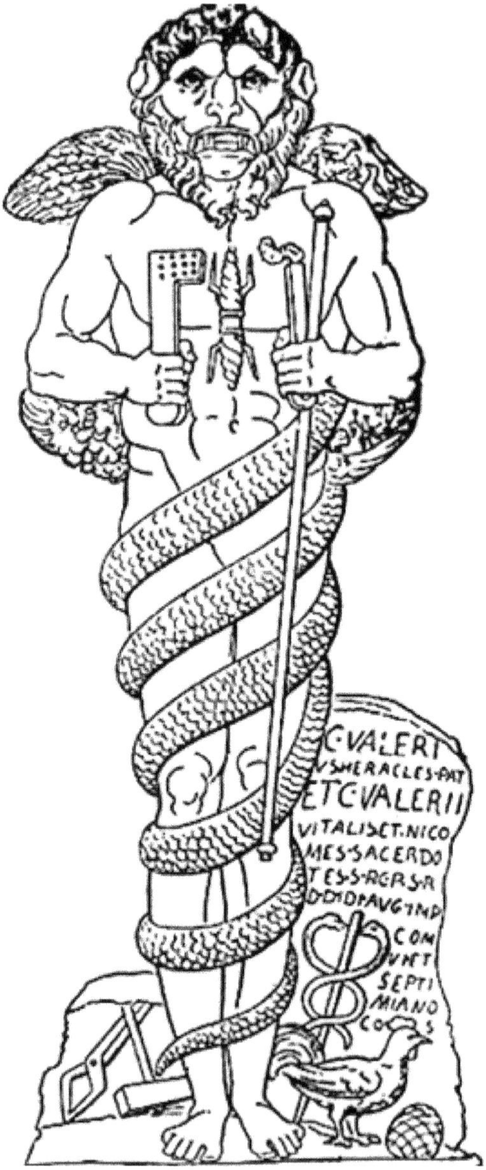

The God Aion [192]

[192] *The Mysteries of Mithras.* Franz Cumont. 1911.

When you are dead, he will wrap up your body as befits a god, but he will take your spirit and carry it into the air with him. For no aerial spirit which is joined with a mighty assistant will go into Hades, for to him all things are subject. Whenever you wish to do something, speak his name alone into the air and say: "Come!" and you will see him actually standing near you. And say to him, "Perform this task," and he does it at once, and after doing it he will say to you, "What else do you want? For I am eager for heaven." If you do not have immediate orders, say to him, "Go, lord," and he will depart. In this fashion, then, the god will be seen by you alone, nor will anyone ever hear the sound of his speaking, just you yourself alone. And he will tell you about the illness of a man, whether he will live or die, even on what day and at what hour of night. And he will also give you both wild herbs and the power to cure, and you will be worshipped as a god since you have a god as a friend. These things the mighty assistant will perform competently. Therefore share these things with no one except your legitimate son alone when he asks you for the magic powers imparted by us. Farewell.

The address to the sun requires nothing except the formula IAEOBAPHRENEMOUN and the formula IARBATHA.

On Angels and Demons & the Peculiar Demon

On Angels and Dæmonae

Chapter I[193]

IT IS ALSO NECESSARY to demonstrate to you, in what dæmons, heroes, and souls differ from each other, and whether this difference is according to essence, or according to power, or according to energy. I say, therefore, that dæmons are produced according to the generative and demiurgic powers of the Gods, in the most remote termination of progression, and ultimate distribution into parts. But heroes are produced according to the reasons [or effective principles] of life in divine natures; and from these, the first and perfect measures of souls receive their termination and distribution into parts.

Since, however, the nature of dæmons and heroes is thus generated from different causes, it is also necessary that the essence of the one should be different from that of the other. Hence, the essence of dæmons is effective, and perfective of mundane natures, and gives completion to the superintendence of generated individuals. But the essence of heroes is vital and rational, and is the leader of souls. And, with respect to the powers of each, those of dæmons must be defined to be prolific, inspective of nature, and of the bond by which souls are united to bodies. But it is requisite to attribute to heroes vivific powers, which are the leaders of men, and are liberated from generation.

Chapter II

IT FOLLOWS, therefore, that in the next place we should define the energies of them. And those of dæmons, indeed, must be surveyed as occupied about the world, and more widely extended in their effects; but those of heroes as less extended, and as converted to the order of souls. Hence, these being thus

---

[193] The main part of this selection corresponds to Section II (11 chapters) of Thomas Taylor's translation of Iamblichus' *On the Mysteries*. In the sequence, I included three chapters from Section IX (Chapters VI, VII, and IX), which treat the Peculiar (Personal) Dæmon. These three chapters follow the numeration (being now Chapters XII, XIII, and XIV) of the present section.

distinguished, soul succeeds, which proceeds as far as to the end of the divine orders; and, being allotted from these two genera certain portions of powers, is redundant with partible additions, and other prerogatives derived from itself.[194] It also produces at different times different forms and reasons and manners, which originate from different sources; and, according to each part of the world, employs various lives and ideas; becoming connascent with, and likewise receding from, whatever natures it pleases ; being assimilated to all things, and at the same time, through difference, being separated from them; drawing forth reasons allied to real beings and generated natures; and connecting itself with the Gods, according to other harmonies of essences and powers, than those by which dæmons and heroes are united to the divinities. It likewise possesses the eternity of a similar life and energy in a less degree than dæmons and heroes; yet, through the beneficent will of the Gods, and the illumination imparted by them, it frequently proceeds higher, and is elevated to a greater, i. e. to the angelic order; when it no longer remains in the boundaries of soul, but the whole of it is perfected into an angelic soul and an undefiled life. Hence, also, soul appears to comprehend in itself all-various essences and reasons, and forms or species of every kind. If, however, it be requisite to speak the truth, soul is always defined according to one certain thing, but adapting itself to precedaneous causes, it is at different times conjoined to different causes.

So great, therefore, being the difference between the energies of dæmons, heroes, and souls throughout, it is no longer proper to doubt, what it is which separates them from each other; but they are to be distinguished by the peculiar nature of each. And so far as they are able to form one conjunction, so far the communion of them must be surveyed. For thus it will be possible truly to comprehend and define separately the conception which ought to be formed of them.

Chapter III

LET US, however, now proceed to the appearances of the Gods and their perpetual attendants, and show what the difference is in their appearance. For you inquire, "*by what indication the*

[194] The idea being that the dæmons are non-human spirits, and the heroes are superior human souls. Later, the "hero" was substituted by the "saint".

presence of a God, or an angel, or an archangel, or a dæmon, or a certain archon [i. e. ruler], or a soul, may be known." In one word, therefore, I conclude that their appearances accord with their essences, powers, and energies. For such as they are, such also do they appear to those that invoke them, and they exhibit energies and ideas consentaneous to themselves, and proper indications of themselves. But that we may descend to particulars, the phasmata, or luminous appearances, of the Gods are uniform; those of dæmons are various; those of angels are more simple than those of dæmons, but are subordinate to those of the Gods; those of archangels approximate in a greater degree to divine causes; but those of archons, if these powers appear to you to be the cosmocrators,[195] who govern the sublunary element, will be more various, but adorned in order; but if they are the powers that preside over matter, they will indeed be more various, and more imperfect, than those of the archons [properly so called] ; and those of souls will appear to be all-various. And the phasmata, indeed, of the Gods will be seen shining with salutary light ; those of archangels will be terrible, and at the same time mild; those of angels will be more mild; those of dæmons will be dreadful; those of heroes (which you have omitted in your inquiry, but to which we shall give an answer for the sake of truth) are milder than those of dæmons; but those of archons, if their dominion pertains to the world, produce astonishment, but if they are material, they are noxious and painful to the spectators; and those of souls are similar to the heroic phasmata, except that they are inferior to them.

Again, therefore, the phasmata of the Gods are entirely immutable, according to magnitude, morphe,[196] and figure, and according to all things pertaining to them; those of archangels approximate to those of the Gods, but fall short of the sameness of them; those of angels are subordinate to these, but are immutable; and those of dæmons are at different times seen in a different form, and appear at one time great, but at another small, yet are still recognized to be the phasmata of dæmons. Moreover, those of such archons as are leaders are immutable; but those of such as are material are multiformly changed; those of heroes are similar to those of dæmons; and those of souls imitate in no small degree the dæmoniacal mutation. Farther still, order and quiet pertain

[195] According to Taylor, the cosmocrators, or governors of the world, are the planets.

[196] Morphe pertains to the colour, figure, and magnitude of superficies [sic]. (Note from the original text.)

to the Gods; but with archangels, there is an efficacy of order and quiet. With angels, the adorned and the tranquil are present, but not unattended with motion. Perturbation and disorder follow the demoniacal phasmata; but spectacles attend the archons, conformable to each of the particulars which we have already mentioned; the material archons, indeed, being borne along tumultuously; but those of a leading characteristic, presenting themselves to the view, firmly established in themselves. The phasmata of heroes are subject to motion and mutation; but those of souls resemble, indeed, the heroic, but at the same time are less than these. In addition also to these peculiarities, divine beauty, indeed, shines with an immense splendour as it were, fixes the spectators in astonishment, imparts a divine joy, presents itself to the view with ineffable symmetry, and is exempt from all other species of pulchritude.

But the blessed spectacles of archangels have indeed themselves the greatest beauty, yet are not so ineffable and admirable as those of the Gods. Those of angels divide, in a partible manner, the beauty which they receive from archangels. But the dæmoniacal and heroical self-visive spirits, have both of them beauty in definite forms, yet the former is adorned in reasons which define the essence, and the latter exhibits fortitude. The phasmata of archons may be divided in a twofold respect. For some of them exhibit a beauty which is spontaneous, and of a ruling characteristic; but others, an elegance of form which is fictitious and renovated. And the phasmata of souls are, indeed, adorned in definite reasons, but these reasons are more divided than those in heroes, are partibly circumscribed, and are vanquished by one form. If, however, it be requisite to define all of them in common, I say that each participates of beauty according to its arrangement, the peculiar nature which it possesses, and its allotment.

Chapter IV

PROCEEDING, therefore, to other peculiarities of them, we say, that with the Gods, indeed, there is acuteness and rapidity in the energies, which shine forth with greater celerity than those of intellect itself, though in themselves they are immoveable and stable. With archangels, the celerities are, in a certain respect, mingled with efficacious energies. Those of angels partake of a certain motion, and do not, similarly with archangels, possess a power which is effective by speaking. The operations of dæmons appear to be more rapid than they are in reality. In the motions of the heroic phasmata, a certain magificence presents itself to the view; but in accomplishing what they wish to effect, their energies are not so rapid as those of dæmons. In the phasmata of archons, the first energies appear to be most excellent and authoritative; but the second have a more abundant representation, yet in actions fall short of the end. And the phasmata of souls are seen to be more moveable, yet are more imbecile, than those of heroes.

In addition to these things also, the magnitude of the epiphanies [or manifestations] in the Gods, indeed, is so great as sometimes to conceal all heaven, the sun and the moon; and the earth itself, as the Gods descend, is no longer able to stand still. When archangels appear, certain parts of the world are moved, and a divided forerunning light precedes them. But they exhibit a magnitude of light commensurate to the magnitude of their domination. The angelic light is less than the archangelic, and more divided, but in dæmons it is still more divided, and the magnitude of the manifestation is not always equal in them. The manifestation of heroes is still less than that of dæmons, but exhibits more of an elevated condition. Again, the manifestation of such archons as preside over mundane forms, presents itself to the view as above measure great; but such of them as are distributed about matter, exhibit in their manifestations an abundance of pride and arrogance. Those of souls are not all of them seen to be equal, but appear to be less than those of heroes. And, in short, the magnitude of the manifestation is appropriately present in each of these, according to the magnitude of their powers, and the amplitude of the empire through which they extend themselves, and in which they exercise their authority.

After these things, therefore, we shall define the reasons of the self-apparent statues [or images]. Hence, in the forms of the Gods which are seen by the eyes, the most clear spectacles of truth itself are perceived, which are also accurately splendid, and shine forth with an evolved light. The images of archangels present themselves to the view true and perfect; but those of angels preserve, indeed, the same form, but fail in plenitude of indication. The images of dæmons are obscure; and those of heroes are seen to be still inferior to these. With respect, also, to archons, the images of such as are mundane, are clear; but of such as are material, obscure. Both, however, are seen to be of an authoritative nature. And the images of souls appear to be of a shadowy form.

In a similar manner, likewise, we must determine concerning the light of these powers. For the images of the Gods, indeed, are replete with a fulgid light. Those of archangels are full of supernatural light. Those of angels are luminous; but dæmons present themselves to the view with a turbid fire. The light of heroes is mingled with many things. And, with respect to archons, the light of those that have the government of the world is more pure; but of those that preside over matter, exhibits itself mingled from things of a dissimilar and contrary nature. And the light of souls manifests itself to be partibly filled with many of the mixtures which exist in generation.

Conformably, also, to what has been said, the fire of the Gods, indeed, shines forth with an indivisible and ineffable light, and fills all the profundities of the world, in an empyrean, but not in a mundane, manner. But the fire of archangels is impartible indeed, but is seen to possess about itself an abundant multitude, either preceding or following after itself. The fire of angels is divided, except that it exhibits itself in the most perfect ideas. That of dæmons is still more shortly circumscribed by a distribution into parts, is effable, and does not astonish the sight of those that have seen more excellent natures. The fire of heroes has, after a certain manner, the same things as that of dæmons, but at the same time falls short of the most accurate similitude to it. Moreover, with respect to archons, the fire of those that are of a more elevated order, is more pellucid; but of those that are material, is more dark. And the fire of souls is seen to be much divided and multiform, and is comingled from many of the natures that are in the world. Again, the fire of the Gods appears to be entirely stable. That of archangels is tranquil; but that of angels is stably moved. The fire of dæmons is unstable; but that of heroes is, for the most part, rapidly moved. The fire of those archons that are of the first rank is tranquil; but of those that are of the last order is tumultuous. And the fire of souls is transmuted in a multitude of motions.

Chapter V

MOREOVER, that which purifies souls is perfect in the Gods; but in archangels it is anagogic. Angels alone dissolve the bond of generation. Dæmons draw souls down into nature; but heroes lead them to a providential attention to sensible works. Archons either deliver to them the government of mundane concerns, or the inspection of material natures. And souls, when they become apparent, tend in a certain respect to generation.

Farther still, consider this, also, that you should attribute everything which is pure and stable in the visible image to the more excellent genera. Hence, you should ascribe to the Gods that which in the image is transcendently splendid, and which is firmly established in itself. That which is splendid, but is established as in another thing, you should give to archangels; but that which remains in another to angels. To all these, therefore, you should oppose, that which is rashly borne along, is unestablished, and filled with foreign natures, the whole of which is adapted to inferior orders.

These, also, may now be divided according to the difference of commixture. For mundane vapours are mingled with dæmons, and are unstably borne along, contrary to the motion of the world. Genesiurgic compositions of pneumatic substances are mingled with heroes, about which substances, also, they are moved. The archons of the world remain invariably the same, exhibiting the mundane nature which they possess. But the archons of matter are full of material substances. And souls are filled with an abundance of stains and foreign spirits, together with which, when they become visible, each of these genera presents itself to the view.

The following, also, will be no small indications to you [of the difference of these powers]. With the Gods matter is immediately consumed. With archangels it is consumed in a short time. With angels there is a solution of, and elevation from, matter. By dæmons matter is elegantly adorned. With heroes there is a coadaptation to it, in appropriate measures, and a skilful providential attention to it. And with respect to archons, those that are the governors of the world are present with matter in a transcendent manner, and in this way unfold themselves into light. But those that are material, exhibit themselves as entirely replete with matter. With respect to souls, also, those that are pure, present themselves to the view out of matter, but those of a contrary description are seen surrounded with it.

Chapter VI

MOREOVER, the gifts arising from the manifestations are not all of them equal, nor have the same fruits. But the presence of the Gods, indeed, imparts to us health of body, virtue of soul, purity of intellect, and in one word elevates every thing in us to its proper principle. And that, indeed, in us which is cold and destructive it annihilates; that which is hot it increases, and renders more powerful and predominant; and causes all things to accord with soul and intellect. It also emits a light, accompanied with intelligible harmony, and exhibits that which is not body as body to the eyes of the soul, through those of the body. The presence of archangels imparts likewise the same things, except that it does not impart them always, nor in all things, nor does it bestow goods which are sufficient, perfect, and incapable of being taken away; nor is their appearance accompanied with a light equal to that of the Gods. The presence of angels imparts divisibly still more partible goods, and the energy through which it becomes visible falls very short of comprehending in itself a perfect light. That of dæmons renders the body, indeed, heavy, afflicts with diseases, draws down the soul to nature, does not depart from bodies, and the sense allied to bodies, and detains about this terrestrial place those who are hastening to divine fire, and does not liberate from the bonds of Fate. The presence of heroes is in other respects similar to that of dæmons, but is attended with this peculiarity, that it excites to certain generous and great undertakings. The appearance which is visible by itself, of the mundane archons, imparts mundane goods, and every thing pertaining to human life; but that of the material archons extends material benefits, and such works as are terrestrial. Moreover, the vision of souls that are undefiled, and established in the order of angels, is anagogic, and the saviour of the soul, is accompanied with sacred hope, and imparts those goods which sacred hope vindicates to itself. But the vision of other souls draws down to generation, corrupts the fruits of [sacred] hope, and fills the spectators with passions which fix them to body.

Chapter VII

MOREOVER, in the manifestations there is an indication of the order which the powers that are seen possess. For the Gods are surrounded by either Gods or angels; but archangels have angels either preceding or coarranged with them, or following them behind, or are accompanied by a certain other multitude of angels, who attend on them as guards. Angels exhibit, together with themselves, the peculiar works of the order to which they belong. Good dæmons permit us to survey, in conjunction with themselves, their own works, and the benefits which they impart; but avenging dæmons exhibit the species of punishments [which they inflict]; and such other dæmons as are depraved are surrounded by certain noxious, blood-devouring, and fierce wild beasts.[197] Archons [of the first rank] exhibit, together with themselves, certain portions of the world; but other archons attract to themselves the inordination and confusion of matter. With respect to soul, if it ranks as a whole, and does not belong to any particular species, it presents to the view a formless fire, extended through the whole world, which is indicative of the total, one, indivisible, and formless soul of the universe; but a purified soul exhibits a fiery form, and a pure and unmingled fire. Then, also, the most inward light of it is seen, and an undefiled and stable form, and it most willingly and joyfully follows its elevating leader, and unfolds, by its works, its own appropriate order. But the soul which verges downward draws along with it the signs of bonds and punishments, is heavy with material spirits, is detained by the anomalous tumults of matter, and exhibits before itself, genesiurgic presiding dæmons. And, in short, all these genera exhibit their proper orders; *viz.* the aerial genera exhibit aerial fire; the terrestrial a terrestrial and blacker fire; and the celestial a more splendid fire. But in these three boundaries all the genera are distributed according to a triple order of beginning, middle, and end. And the Gods, indeed, exhibit the supreme and most pure causes of this triple order. But the genera of angels depend on those of archangels. The genera of dæmons appear to be subservient to those of angels; and in a similar manner to these, the genera of heroes are ministrant. They are not, however, subservient to angels in the same way as dæmons. Again, the genera of archons, whether they preside over the world or over matter, exhibit the order which is adapted to them. But all the genera of souls present themselves to the view as the last of more excellent natures. Hence, also, they exhibit places in conjunction with themselves; souls of the first rank primary, but those of the second rank secondary places, and the rest conformably to their arrangement, in each of these three genera.

---

[197] These are terrestrial daemons, to whom the Chaldean Oracles allude, which say, "The wild beasts of the earth shall inhabit thy vessel," i. e. as Psellus explains it, the composite temperature of the soul. (Note from the original text.)

Chapter VIII

MOREOVER, with respect to the tenuity and subtilty of light, the Gods extend a light so subtle that corporeal eyes cannot sustain it, but are affected in the same manner as fishes, when they are drawn upward from turbid and thick water into attenuated and diaphanous air. For men who survey divine fire are not able to breathe, through the subtilty of it, but become languid as soon as they perceive it, and are deprived of the use of their connascent spirit. Archangels, also, emit a light which is intolerable to respiration, yet their splendour is not equally pure with that of the Gods, nor similarly overpowering. The presence of angels renders the temperature of the air tolerable, so that theurgists are capable of being united to it. But when dæmons are present, the whole air is not at all affected; nor does the air, which surrounds them, become more attenuated; nor does a light precede them, in which, being previously received and preoccupied by the air, they unfold the form of themselves; nor are they surrounded by a certain splendour, which diffuses its light everywhere. When heroes appear, certain parts of the earth are moved, and sounds are heard around them; but, in short, the air does not become more attenuated, nor incommensurate to theurgists, so as to render them unable to receive it. But when archons are present, an assemblage of many luminous appearances runs round them, difficult to be borne, whether these appearances are mundane or terrestrial. They have not, however, a supermundane tenuity, nor even that of the supreme elements. And to the psychical appearances the air is more allied, and, being suspended from them, receives in itself their circumscription.

Chapter IX

IN the last place, the dispositions of the soul of those that invoke the Gods to appear receive, when they become visible, a liberation from the passions, a transcendent perfection, and an energy entirely more excellent, and participate of divine love and an immense joy. But when archangels appear, these dispositions receive a pure condition of being, intellectual contemplation, and an immutable power. When angels appear, they participate of intellectual wisdom and truth, pure virtue, stable knowledge, and a commensurate order. But when dæmons are seen, they receive the appetite of generation and a desire of nature, together with a wish to accomplish the works of Fate, and a power effective of things of this kind. If heroes are seen, they derive from the vision other such like manners and many impulses, which contribute to the communion of souls. But when these dispositions come into contact with archons, mundane or material, motions are excited in conjunction with the soul. And, together with the vision of souls, the spectators derive genesiurgic tendencies and conoascent providential inspections, for the sake of paying attention to bodies, and such other peculiarities as are allied to these.

In addition to these things, also, the manifestation of the Gods imparts truth and power, rectitude of works, and gifts of the greatest goods; but the manifestation of other powers is appropriately accompanied by such things as are commensurate to their several orders. Thus the manifestation of archangels imparts truth, not simply about all things, but definitely of certain things; and this not always, but sometimes; nor indefinitely to all, or every where, but with limitation, in a certain place, or to a certain individual. In like manner it does not impart a power effective of all things, nor always without distinction, nor every where; but a power which is effective sometimes, and in a certain place. But the manifestation of angels, in a still greater degree than that of archangels, divides, in imparting good, the circumscriptions which are always defined by them in more contracted boundaries. Again, the manifestation of dæmons does not impart the goods of the soul, but either those of the body, or goods pertaining to the body. And they impart these when the order of the world permits them. After the same manner, likewise, the manifestation of heroes imparts second and third goods, and regards as its scope the whole terrestrial and mundane polity of souls. With respect to archons, the manifestation of some of these imparts mundane benefits, and all the goods of life; but that of others of an inferior rank imparts not a few of the prerogatives of material natures. And souls, when they appear, procure for those that behold them things which contribute to the benefit of human life. Thus, therefore, we have appropriately defined the gifts of these powers, conformably to the proper order of each; and the particulars in the manifestations about which you inquired, have received a fit reply. And thus much for these questions.

Chapter X

WHAT you introduce, however, for the purpose of obtaining a knowledge of these things, whether it be your own opinion, or whether you have heard it from others, is neither true nor rightly asserted. For you say, "*that to speak boastingly, and to exhibit an adumbrative phantasm, are common to Gods and dæmons, and to all the more excellent genera of beings.*" But the thing is not as you apprehend it to be. For a God, an angel, and a good daemon, instruct men in what their proper essence consists; and never use an addition in their language which transcends their power, or their appropriate good. For truth is coexistent with the Gods, in the same manner as light with the sun. And, at the same time, we say, that divinity is not in want of any beauty or virtue which it is possible to add to him through language. Moreover, angels and dæmons always receive truth from the Gods, so that they never assert any thing contrary to this, each of them being essentially perfect, nor can they add any thing to it for the sake of commendation.

When, therefore, does the deception mentioned by you "*of speakingly boastingly*" take place. For when a certain error happens in the theurgic art, and not such autoptic, or selfvisible, images are seen as ought to occur, but others, instead of these, then inferior powers assume the form of the more venerable orders, and pretend to be those whose forms they assume; and hence arrogant words are uttered by them, and such as exceed the authority which they possess. For, as it appears to me, if any fraud germinates from the first principle, much falsehood is derived from the perversion, which it is necessary the priest should learn from the whole order in the phasmata, and by the proper observation of which they are able to confute and reject the fictitious pretext of these inferior powers, as by no means pertaining to true and good spirits. Nor is it proper to introduce errors in the true judgment of things; for neither in other sciences or arts do we judge of their works from the aberrations which may happen to take place in them. You should not, therefore, here characterize things which are scarcely performed with rectitude through ten thousand labours, from the errors which may, through ignorance, befall them; but rather assert something else of them. For if the works which take place from the appearance of these powers are such as you say, *viz.* if they are arrogant and false, yet the operations about fire of true spirits are genuine and true. For, as in all other things, such as are principal primarily begin from themselves, and impart to themselves that which they give to others; as, for instance, in essence, in life, and in motion; thus also the natures which supply all beings with truth, primarily proclaim the truth of themselves, and precedaneously unfold the essence of themselves to the spectators. Hence, likewise, they exhibit to theurgists a fire which is of itself visible. For it is not the province of heat to refrigerate, nor of light to darken or conceal any thing; nor with any other nature which essentially performs a certain thing, is a power present of at the same time effecting the contrary. But things which do not possess a [true] nature, and which are contrary to things that exist essentially; these are able to receive contraries, and are adapted to fall into evil.

We must say the same thing, therefore, concerning phantasms. For if these are not true, but other things are so which have a real existence, thus also in the appearances of spirits, they seem to be such as things which are true beings; at the same time they participate of falsehood and deception, in the same manner as the forms which present themselves to the view in mirrors; and thus vainly attract the mind about things which never take place in any of the more excellent genera. These phantasms, likewise, will consist in deceptive perversions. For that which is an imitation of [real] being, and is an obscure assimilation, and becomes the cause of deception, pertains to no one of the true and clearly existing genera. But the Gods, indeed, and those powers that follow the Gods, reveal true images of themselves, but by no means extend phantasms of themselves, such as exist in water, or in mirrors. For on what account should they exhibit these? Shall we say, as bringing with them an indication of their own essence and power? This, however, is by no means the case. For these phantasms become the cause of deception to those that believe in them, and withdraw the spectators from the true knowledge of the Gods. Shall we say, then, that it is because they afford a certain utility to those that behold them? But what advantage can be derived from falsehood? If, therefore, this is not the case, may it not be natural to divinity to extend a phantasm from itself? But how can that which is firmly established in itself, and which is the cause of essence and truth, produce in a foreign seat a certain deceitful imitation of itself? By no means, therefore, does divinity either transform himself into phantasms, nor extend these from himself to other things, but emits, by illumination, true representations of himself, in the true manners of souls. Conformably to this, also, the attendants of the Gods are emulous of the self-visible truth of the Gods. But that which you now say, "*that it is common to Gods and dæmons, and the rest of the more excellent genera, to produce fictitious images, and to speak boastingly of themselves*," confounds all the genera of superior beings in each other, and leaves no difference whatever between them. For thus all things will be common to them, and nothing singularly excellent will be given to transcendent natures. It will, therefore, be more just to ask, in opposition to you, in what will the genus of the Gods be superior to that of dæmons? These genera, however, have nothing in common, nor is the communion between them phantastic, nor is it fit from such natures as are last, and from the errors which take place in them, to estimate first essences, and the true impressions of forms which are in them. For by thus thinking concerning these essences, we shall think justly, and in a way pleasing to the Gods.

Chapter XI

IN what follows, in which you think that ignorance and deception about these things are impiety and impurity, and in which you exhort us to the true developement of these particulars, is not, indeed, attended with any ambiguity, but is acknowledged by all men. For who will not grant that the science which apprehends real being, is most adapted to a divine cause, but that ignorance which is hurried along to nonbeing, since it is most remote from a divine cause, falls off from truly existing forms ? Since, however, what is said by you is not sufficient, I will add what is wanting; and because what you assert is rather philosophical and logical, than conformable to the efficacious art of priests, on this account I think it is necessary to say something more theurgical about these particulars.

For, let "*ignorance and deception be error and impiety*," yet it does not follow that, on this account, things which are offered to the Gods, and divine works, are false. For a conception of the mind does not conjoin theurgists with the Gods; since, if this were the case, what would hinder those who philosophize theoretically, from having a theurgic union with the Gods? Now, however, in reality, this is not the case. For the perfect efficacy of ineffable works, which are divinely performed in a way surpassing all intelligence, and the power of inexplicable symbols, which are known only to the Gods, impart theurgic union. Hence, we do not perform these things through intellectual perception; since, if this were the case, the intellectual energy of them would be imparted by us; neither of which is true. For when we do not energize intellectually, the *synthemata*[198] themselves perform by themselves their proper work, and the ineffable power of the Gods itself knows, by itself, its own images. It does not, however, know them, as if excited by our intelligence; for neither is it natural that things which comprehend should be excited by those that are comprehended, nor perfect by imperfect natures, nor wholes by parts. Hence, neither are divine causes precedaneously called into energy by our intellections; but it is requisite to consider these, and all the best dispositions of the soul, and also the purity pertaining to us, as certain concauses; the things which properly excite the divine will being divine synthemata themselves. And thus, things pertaining to the Gods, are moved by themselves, and do not receive from any inferior nature a certain principle in themselves of their own proper energy.

I have, however, been thus prolix, in order that you may not think all the authority of the energy in theurgic operations is in our power, and that you may not suppose the true work of them consists in our conceptions, or the falsehood of them in our deception. For though we may know the peculiarities which are consequent to each genus, yet we may not obtain the truth which is in their works. Nevertheless, efficacious union [with divine natures] is not effected without knowledge; yet knowledge does not possess a sameness with this union. So that neither is divine purity obtained through right knowledge, as neither is purity of body procured through health; but divine purity is more undefiled than knowledge, and is more transcendently united. Hence neither this, nor any thing of the like kind which is in us, and is human, cooperates any thing to the end of divine actions.

Chapter XII[199]

IF, however, it be requisite to unfold to you the truth concerning the peculiar dæmon, we must say that he is not distributed to us from one part of the heavens, or from some one of the visible elements; but that from the whole world, the all various life contained in it, and the all various body through which the soul descends into generation, a certain peculiar portion is

[198] The inexplicable theurgic signs or symbols. (Note from the original text.)

[199] Here begins the three chapters from Section IX; this chapter in the original version is number VI from Section IX.

distributed to each of the parts in us, according to a peculiar prefecture. This dæmon, therefore, is established in the paradigm before the soul descends into generation; and when the soul has received him as its leader, the dæmon immediately presides over the soul, gives completion to its lives, and binds it to body when it descends. He likewise governs the common animal of the soul, directs its peculiar life, and imparts to us the principles of all our thoughts and reasonings. We also perform such things as he suggests to our intellect, and he continues to govern us till, through sacerdotal theurgy, we obtain a God for the inspective guardian and leader of the soul. For then the dæmon either yields or delivers his government to a more excellent nature, or is subjected to him, as contributing to his guardianship, or in some other may is ministrant to him as to his lord.

Chapter XIII[200]

FROM these things, therefore, it is easy to answer your next question. For the peculiar daemon does not rule over one of the parts in us, but, in short, over all the parts at once, and extends to every principle within us, in the same manner as he was distributed to us from the total orders in the universe. For that which it appears to you proper to add as an indication "*that dæmons preside over the parts of our body, so that one is the guardian of health, another of the form of the body, and another of the corporeal habits, and that there is one dæmon who presides in common over all these;*" this you should consider as an argument that there is one dæmon who is the guardian and governor of every thing that is in us. You must not, therefore, distribute one dæmon to the body, but another to the soul, and another to intellect: for it is absurd that the animal should be one, but the daemon that presides over it multiform. For every where the natures that govern are more simple than the natures that are governed. And it will be still more absurd if the many dæmons that rule over the parts are not connascent, but separated from each other. But you also make contrariety among them. For you speak as if "*some of them were good, but others bad.*" Evil dæmons, however, have no where a ruling allotment, nor are they oppositely divided to such as are good with equal authority and power.

[200] This chapter in the original version is number VII in Section IX.

Chapter XIV[201]

AFTER this, therefore, you also mention another disquisition concerning the peculiar dæmon, which represents "*some as worshiping two, but others three, dæmons of this kind.*" The whole of this, however, is erroneous. For it is a false mode of proceeding to divide the causes that preside over us, and not refer them to one; since this wanders from the union which has dominion over all things. The opinion, likewise, which distributes this dæmon into body, and the government of body, draws down his domination to a certain most minute part. So that what necessity is there for those who embrace this opinion to direct their attention to sacred operations, the first principle of them being futile? There is, therefore, of each of us one peculiar presiding dæmon; but it is not proper to think that this dæmon is common to all men; nor again, that he is common, but is peculiarly present with each individual. For division, according to species and difference of matter, do not receive the communion and sameness of things essentially incorporeal. "*Why then* [you say] *is the peculiar dæmon invoked by a common mode by all men?*" Because the invocation of him is effected through one God, who is the lord of dæmons; who from the first defined to every one his peculiar dæmon; and who, in sacred operations, unfolds to every one his proper daemon, according to his own proper will. For always in the theurgic order secondary are invoked through primary natures. Among dæmons, therefore, one common leader of the cosmocrators about generation sends to each of us his peculiar dæmon. Hence, when the peculiar dæmon is present with each of us, he then unfolds the worship which is proper to be paid to him and his name, and likewise delivers the proper mode of invoking him.

[201] This chapter in the original version is number IX in Section IX.

St. Augustine:

The divination of demons

First Part

The conversation of Saint Augustine with his Christian friends

Chapter I

Occasion of the Book

I.1. *Demons can know and predict.* One day, in the Octaves of Easter, there were with me in the morning, many brothers lay Christians; and as we took seat in the usual place, there was the conversation about the Christian religion, as a replica to the presumption and science of the pagans that, in a sense, is great and wonderful. Recalling that meeting, and completing it, I thought about writing without expressly naming the ones that contradicted, though they were Christians, as even more than that what they sought was how to respond properly to the pagans.

Placing the question and answer: As we discussed the divination of demons, and it was said that someone, I do not know who, had predicted the destruction of the temple of Serapis, which took place in Alexandria, I answered them that there was nothing strange in that demons could learn to predict that the destruction of the temple was imminent and say it, as with many other things, in that it is allowed to them to understand and predict.

Reply and counter-reply

2. *God also allows evil.*

They: And they replied that this kind of divination is not bad nor offends God; rather, on the contrary, the omnipotent and just God would not allow it if it were a bad and unjust thing.

Augustine: I answered them that they should not seem just because the most omnipotent and righteous God allows them, because he also allows many other things that are very clearly unjust, as are murder, adultery, theft, looting, and other similar crimes that, though they certainly offend a just God, because they are unjust, nevertheless, the same omnipotent God allows them for an array of justice, not always with impunity, but to condemn those who do what offends the just.

New reply and counter-reply

3. *God can allow what offends even in what refers to the cult.*

They: And as they contradicted me, that in no way should it be doubted that God is omnipotent and just; but that these human sins that are committed against human society, God does not care when they are committed; and that therefore crimes are committed that could certainly not occur if the Almighty had not allowed them. But, those that refer to the very cult of religion, in no way must it be supposed that they are disregarded by Him and, therefore, they would not happen if they did not please Him and, by consequence, it is not convenient to think that they are bad.

Augustine: To what I answered, too, that in reality they displease Him now, when the temples and their idols are destroyed, and when he is punishing those sacrifices that the pagans offered. For, in the same way that you say that they could not have been committed if they had displeased God, it can be said that they could not have been prohibited, destroyed and punished if they did not displease God. And therefore, if they were rightly done because it was shown that they appealed to the just God, since He allowed them to do so, by the same reasoning it can be said that now they do it wickedly, because it is shown that it is He who commands or allows them to be destroyed.

Chapter II

Why does God allow the sacrifices of the pagans

II.4. *The sacrifices of pagans are not good because God allows them.*

Against the previous statements, it was said that certanly those acts are illegal, but they are not bad. They are illegal because they are made against the laws that prohibit them, but they are not bad, because if they were bad, they would never have pleased God. Now, well, if they have never pleased God, in the same way they would never have been committed, not being allowed, by whom all can and that do not despise such acts, when they are so great that, if they are committed, go against the same religion by which God is honored.

Augustine's answer

Here I intervened: If they are not evil, because it is proved that they please God, as the Almighty allows them to be committed, how will it be good to allow them to be banned and destroyed? And if it's not good to be destroyed what pleases God, the Almighty would not allow it to take place, because this also goes against the religion in which God is honored, if what pleases God is destroyed by men. And if the Almighty allows this to be done unjustly, it is unnecessary to consider it as good because the Almighty has allowed it to take place.

New reply

5. *God allows, as Omnipotent, what he as being infinitely just disapproves.*

They: They replied to me that it is necessary to grant that currently these cults are not made; furthermore, not made at all, because now they displease the Almighty; but they pleased him when they were made. We ignore for what reason they displease him now; while it is true then they could not have been done if they had not pleased the Almighty, neither now would have disappeared if they had not displeased the Almighty.

New counter-reply

Augustine: Why, then, I replied immediately, are today made hidden similar practices that, or are kept forever hidden, or that, if discovered, are punished, if none of that the Almighty allows to be done, if it is not because it pleases him that it is just, when it is not possible that one unjust thing pleases the just?

They: To this they replied that currently, in general, such practices are not done. In effect, they insisted, these sacred cults that are written about in the Pontifical Books[202] are not

[202] "The *libri pontificales* (pontifical books) are core texts in Roman religion, which

done, which no doubt were done legally, and showed that they pleased God, since the Almighty and just allowed them to be done. In exchange, if currently some of the forbidden sacrifices are done, clandestine and illegally, it can not be compared with those pontifical sacrifices, although they are considered as such also the nocturnal rites, given that all these rites are banned and condemned as illegal by the same Pontifical Books.

Augustine: My answer was: Why, then, does God allow to be done, for example, such rites, if He does not despise any sins that are made against the religion? And, above all, even the ones that much estimate the Pontifical Books are forced to concede that He also cares for such sins, as they accept that, for being banned in these books, they are forbidden certainly by divine command? And, if they are forbidden by divine command, it is because these rites are displeasing to God who, by forbidding them, certainly not only shows that they displease him, but it also manifests that He cares and has them not disregarded? It follows that God condemns some things because they are unjust, while allowing them whilst He is omnipotent.

Conclusion

6. *Summary and statement.* After these explanations, we put ourselves in agreement that one should not judge just and good a thing because the Almighty allows it, although it displeases Him; and it should be stated that also that these evil deeds that are done against the religion in which God is worshipped, and that displease God as He is just, they are also allowed by Him while being omnipotent, for His just purposes.

Enunciation of a new question. But, let's treat another subject: From where come the divinations, from the demons, or from any of these the pagans call gods?

---

survive as fragmentary transcripts and commentaries. They may have been partly annalistic, part priestly; different Roman authors refer to them as *libri* and *commentarii* (commentaries), described by Livy as incomplete 'owing to the long time elapsed and the rare use of writing' and by Quintillian as unintelligibly archaic and obscure. The earliest were credited to Numa, second king of Rome, who was thought to have codified the core texts and principles of Rome's religious and civil law (*ius divinum* and *ius civile*)." *Glossary of ancient Roman religion*. Wikipedia.

It seems clear that one should examine this issue in order to consider if these wonders are good, not just because the Almighty allows them to be done, but because they are so extraordinary that they look like they can not be assigned unless to the power of God.

Answer from Augustine. Then, I promised to answer this question later, because at that moment, it was very necessary that I returned to the city. And, when it was offered to me some time to write, I was not careless about it, to rewrite all this, and to add what follows.

Second Part

Teachings of Saint Augustine

Chapter III

Explanation about the Diabolical Divination

III.7. *The nature of the demons.* The nature of demons is such that the sensitivity of ethereal bodies are easily seen as higher when compared to the sensitivity of earthly bodies. In addition, the speed due to the higher mobility of the same etheric body, has an advantage unmatched not only in relation to the race of any man or beast, but even to the flight of birds. Endowed with this dual faculty arising from having an ethereal body, that means the sensitive sharpness and the speed of movements, they can predict or announce many events known to them in advance, which is impressive to men due to the clumsiness of our earthly sensitivity. The demons, due to the large life span they have, acquired an experience of things much greater than what men can acquire in the brevity of our existence. Due to these properties, that the nature of the etheric body received, the demons not only predict many future things, but also do many extraordinary things. And, as men do not have power to predict and do such things, some believe that the demons are worthy of being served, and that divine honors be tributed to them, especially, if the demons stimulate their vice of curiosity, for the sake of a false and mundane happiness, and because of a temporal superiority. While those who remain pure of these desires without allowing the demons to deceive or seduce them, rather search for the good, that is always ummutable, in which participation they will be happy; they consider, in the first place, that the demons should not be considered as being superiors, after the sensory acuteness of the etheric body, in other words, because it is made of a more subtle element, because they also do not believe that, amongst the terrene bodies, we should put first the animals that presage many things with a greater subtlety; for instance, the sagacious dog, because it finds out with its subtle sense of smell the hidden beast, offering to a man a kind of warning to hunt it, certainly does not do it because of a more intelligent and developed soul, but by the sensorial subtlety of its body; or, if you prefer, the vulture, because it flies from an insuspected distance over the abandoned corpse; neither the eagle, because, they say, flying high perceives from the heights a small fish under water and, finding it, strikes against the water, taking it with its claws; neither, other species of animals that roam, feeding amongst herbs prejudicial to health without touching any that could harm them; whilst men only through experience learn how to avoid them, and fear many innoffensive things, just because we do not know them.

There is no need to put the demons above the good men. Hence, one can conjecture that the sensitivity of ethereal bodies may be more acute, without thereby any prudent person would have to believe that we must consider as superior the demons, when compared to good men. And as much I could say about the speed of the bodies; because men are also overcome on this faculty, not only by the birds but also by many quadrupeds, such that in its comparison men are considered as if they were made of lead. Therefore, as little is believed that there is to be preferred these species, which men command, hunt, and tame to adapt them for our convenience and ease, and that not by physical force, but by reason.

Chapter IV

The demons must be despised

IV. Regarding this third faculty, that because of their very large experience of things, they came to learn how to guess and predict many things, those who concern to discern carefully these divinations of the truth, which expands from the one true light, disparage them just as the good young people do not believe that the bad old men have advantage over them because they have experienced many things, and for that reason appear to be more knowing; and neither think the same about doctors, sailors, farmers, the ones between them known as being of evil will and bad life, that will not be preferred because they predict many things, some about infirmities, others about tempests and the third about the variety of trees and fruits, in a way that appear to the lay on these subjects that they predict.

8. On the other hand, the demons not only predict some future things, but also do some wonders due to the superiority of their bodies. Why wise men also would not depreciate so when often wicked and corrupt men exercise their bodies in such a way and

with so many devices can do such wonderful things, that those who do not know the secrets and did not see it gives no credence to what they hear? How many stunts the funambulists and other circus performers came to practice? How many wonders did the craftsmen and especially the mechanics? They are, therefore, better than good men, and adorned with a holy pity?

I remembered these examples to be examined without obstinacy and without vain passion of contradicting, think that if from a matter lower that the matter of his own body, from the earth, and water, and stones, just as from woods and from all metals, some men are able to perform such wonderful things, that those who give them value, contemplating them with stupor, sometimes call them divine in comparison with themselves, even when some of them are more complete in their own arts, and even some of the admirers are better men because of their customs. How largest and most prodigious effects can carry out demons by the faculties of their very subtle bodies, to say, ethereal; although, nevertheless, by the perversity of their will and, above all, for the loftiness of their pride and the malice of their jealousy, they are filthy and evil spirits?

It would be too long to demonstrate here how much better is this etheric body by which their bodies are superior for its flexibility, and by which they can set in motion many visible things, to change and alter them. And I think that all this occurs easily even to those who consider it without much thought.

Chapter V

For what reason demons divine the future

V.9. This being so, and because the issue turns on the diabolical divination, you need to know, first, that they often predict what they themselves will do. In fact, sometimes they are empowered to punish with illnesses or to vitiate the air, making it unhealthy; also to suggest to the degraded ones and to the lovers of earthly voluptuousness misdeeds that, when they suggest them, they are confident that they will consent. They make it in a wonderful and invisible way, penetrating through the subtlety of their bodies in the bodies of men who feel them, and interfering through imaginary visions in the thought of both those who watch as of those who sleep. Sometimes, they predict, not what they do but what they portend will happen by the natural signs that human senses can not perceive. And because the doctor predicts what can not predict the profane in his art, there's no reason to consider him a diviner. So, what is strange if, as the doctor through the temperature already altered or modified of the human body, predicts that health will be good or bad, so the demon, by the state and the laws of the atmospheres which are known to him but escape us, can predict the storms ahead? Also, they know well and with ease the human dispositions, not only manifested by word of mouth, but also the ones designed with the thought, because they are externalized by some intimate signs of the soul through the body. Consequently, they also predict many things that will happen, of course wonderful for those who fail to meet such secrets. Indeed, just as the most vivid emotions of the soul are reflected in the face, so that even men know from the outside something of what goes on inside, equally, it should not seem incredible if even the lighter thoughts reflect through the body some signs that the blunted sensitivity of men may not realize, but the sharpness of demons can.

Chapter VI

The diabolical divination is very far from the sublimity of divine prophecy

VI.10. *The demons deceive and are deceived.* With this faculty so prodigious demons predict many things, although they are far from the sublimity of God's prophecy, which works through his holy angels and prophets. Indeed, when they predict something about the designs of God, they listen to predict it; and when predict what they hear in this way, they do not deceive nor are deceived because the angelic and prophetic oracles are infallible and truthful. Now, some people take offense that demons predict some similar oracles, as if it is unworthy that not only the good but also the bad do not be silent about things that have been said to the intent that they would be known by men. However, even among men, we see that the principles of a good life are celebrated even by the unrighteous and the wicked, which does no harm, rather helps to a greater knowledge and prestige of truth, when speak what know of it even those that contradict it with their perverse conduct.

On the other hand, the demons are misled and deceive their other predictions, most of the time. They deceive themselves, certainly, because in predicting their own purposes, from above something is ordered offhand that upsets all their plans. So, as when men submitted to other authorities dispose of something they believe that their superiors will not prohibit, and then promise that they will do it; but those who have a higher power, by a superior decision, suddenly prohibit everything that was already prepared and ready. They are also misled when divining some things by natural causes, such as doctors, sailors, farmers do; although they know with greater sharpness and wit by their more subtle and exercised sensitivity; because all that the angels who piously serve the sovereign God can also change impromptu and suddenly, by a design unknown to the demons. Like with a sick patient, to whom the doctor predicted or promised by the true symptoms that health would come, and then something happens and he dies; or when some sailor, predicting the weather, had predicted that for a long time would roar the storm that Christ the Lord commanded to calm down when sailing with his disciples, and there was a great calm; or, if you like, when a farmer, with good knowledge of nature and the soil and the number of vines, promised for this year that it is going to produce a great harvest and, nevertheless, this year it is dried by an inclemency of heaven or it is plucked out by the order of someone powerful. For, in a similar way, a lot that is under the foresight and prediction of the demons, because they predict by the lower and common causes what will happen, is changed and transformed by most important and most secret causes. Moreover, the demons deceive with earnest striving and malicious desire to cheat to rejoice with human errors. And when they are mistaken or lying, to not lose in front of their adorers the credit of their authority, they make it so that all the blame falls on their interpreters, and on the diviners of their signals.

11. *How do the demons deceive?* And what is strange then, if being imminent the destruction of temples and idols, that God's prophets had foretold for so long, the demon Serapis revealed it to one of his worshippers, when he was withdrawing or escaping, to commend to them his intended divinity?

Chapter VII

The diabolical astuteness

VII. Let such demons be chased away and, although chained by higher orders, let them be uprooted and removed from their places, so that on those same things in which they dominated and by which they were venerated, be fulfilled God's will, he who predicted for so long what would happen to the peoples, and who ordered that it should be done so through their faithful. Why, then, would the devil not be free to predict it when he had guessed what was coming? When this prediction was attested by the prophets who had written such things, and it was granted to the wise men to understand how much surveillance would be necessary to avoid the diabolical cunning, and move away from its worship. Because, having been silent for so long in their temples about all this that would happen, and that was predicted by the prophets, they could not ignore it when the time got close, and they decided to predict it in some way so that they were not taken as ignorant and defeated. In short, and to omit other evidence: it was predicted and written so long before what was said by the prophet Sophonias: *the Lord will prevail against them, and will exterminate all the gods of the peoples of the earth; and they will worship him, every one from his place, all the islands of the Gentiles.* Or, they did not believe that this would come to them, who were venerated in the temples of the pagans, and therefore did not want to celebrate the oracles through their diviners and fanatics. So one of their poets presents Juno, who did not believe at all in what Jupiter had said about the death of Turno. And this Juno is celebrated by them as the power of air, of who thus speaks Virgil:

See, or am I mistaken, that a rigorous death threatens an innocent? Am I, rather, the plaything of a vain warning? And you, who have the power, change for the better your rigors.

I say, then, that the demons, or else, the aerial powers, doubted that would happen to them what the oracles of the prophets were saying, and because of this they did not want to disclose their prediction, and from this one can judge how they are. Or, knowing for sure what was going to happen, because of this they fell silent in their temples, so that the intelligent men would not then abandon and despise them, because they would give credit about the destruction of temples and idols that would happen, and to those prophets who forbade worship of them. But now, since there arrived that time in which are fulfilled the predictions of the prophets of the one God, who declared that these gods are false, and who commands very severely that no one gives them worship, why not also predict which is already evident so that it could appear with greater clarity: what they had previously not believed in any way, or they were afraid to announce to his worshippers; and finally that, having nothing else to do, they wanted to prove themselves apt diviners, when it was already discovered that they had for long been usurping the deity?

CHAPTER VIII

The demoniac divinations

VII.12. *Demons can guess some real things by the oracles of the prophets, but nothing can guess against the true God.* That is why the followers of the idols that remain say, that things known beforehand are also contained in some of their books, although it should be rather believed that they have been drawn up after the events have already been met, which if they were true, they should have made known a long ago time to their people, as with our prophecies, much older and famous, that are read in public not only in our churches, but also in the synagogues of the Jews, which has the strength of a much more solid testimony against all enemies.

Nevertheless, we should not be influenced by similar predictions, that only rarely and furtively, are revealed by them, if any of the demons was forced to express to his worshipers what he had learned from the predictions of the prophets, or oracles of the angels. And why would they not do that, being a prediction like that not an attack, but a witness to the truth? The only thing, in fact, that they could complain about, and that never came forward, not in the past and nor later, because what they tried to prove was just invented, it is that their gods had dared to divine or say something through their soothsayers against the God of Israel. About this God, their wisest writers who could read and know all those predictions, inquired better who God was, without being able to deny God. For this God, whom none of them dared to deny that he was the true God—and if any came to deny, would not only exposed to just condemnations, but would also be convincted with certain arguments; is this God who as I said, none of them dared to deny that it is the true God, that has predicted with a public complaint, and has commanded with a manifest power, and has complied with all truth, that these so-called gods are false, and had to be abandoned completely, and their temples with their idols and their altars were to be destroyed by their diviners, that is, by their prophets. In conclusion, who will be so naive to not elect to worship him, this God who is not forbid to be adored even by the same gods that were adored before? And, no doubt, once someone has started to worship him, will never return to these false gods that the true God that is already adored prohibits to be worshiped.

Chapter IX

The worship of the one God

IX.13. *The prophets prophesied that the worship of false gods would disappear to make way for the true God's worship.* I remembered, just before, and now I repeat, that the true God's prophets had prophesied that people would adore him after destroying the false gods worshiped before. Sophonias: *The Lord will prevail against them, and will exterminate all the gods of the peoples of the earth; and they will worship Him, each from his post, all the islands of the pagans.* Not only the islands, but all the peoples, as equally all nations, since elsewhere he does not name the islands, but the entire orb of the earth, saying: *All the ends of the earth will remember and turn to the Lord, and in his presence all the families of the peoples will prostrate.* It is sufficiently clear also through many other testimonies, and in this same psalm where I got this passage, that these predictions were to be met by means of Christ. Indeed, it is Himself, announcing his future passion through the prophet a little earlier, who says: *They pierced my hands and my feet, and counted all my bones. They observed me and targeted me triumphantly, my clothes were divided, and they threw the lots over my robe.* And, a little later, he puts the verse I cited: *All the ends of the earth will remember and turn to the Lord, etc.*

Also in this testimony I cited above, where it is said: *The Lord will prevail against them, and will exterminate all the gods of the peoples of the earth,* in this word *Prevail* it is suficiently shown that it was prophesized that the pagans would first fight against the Church, and would persecute as much as they could the Christian name to, if it would be possible, erase it completely from the earth; and, that they would be defeated by the patience of the martyrs and the greatness of the miracles, and also by the subsequent faith of the peoples, because of that it is written: *The Lord will prevail against them.* Because it would not say: *Prevail against them,* if they did not resist fighting. For that reason it was also prophesized in a psalm, this way: *Why did the nations mutiny, and the peoples plan their vain projects? They sided with the kings of the earth, and the princes took counsel together against the Lord and against his Christ.* And, a little later, says: *the Lord told me: Thou art my Son, I begot thee this day. Ask of me, and I will give thee for an inheritance the nations, and in thy possession will be the ends of the earth.* See the relation to what was also said in another psalm, which I interspersed above: *All the ends of the earth will remember and turn to the Lord.*

By these and other practical documents it is shown that was prophesied what we see is fulfilled in Christ: that would be that the God of Israel, who we recognize as the only true God, would be worshiped not by one people who were called Israel, but but by all peoples; and that He would destroy all the false pagan gods, both in their temples as in the hearts of their worshippers.

Chapter X

It is useless the pagan ostentation
about their doctrine and their science

X.14. Let them now, whoever of them dare, make the defense of their old vanities against the true worship of the true God, so that they perish loudly! It is certain that this also was prophesized about them in the psalm, with the words of the prophet: *Thou are sitting in the courtroom thou who judges the equity. Thou reproved the peoples, and the wicked perished; forever thou blotted out his name, and for ever and ever. Enemies ended in the ruin of your sword, and thou destroyed their cities. The memory of them perished loudly, but the Lord reigns forever.* It is necessary, therefore, that all this be fulfilled. And we should not be disturbed because some pagans who remained dare, however, to make ostentation of their bragging doctrines, and deride the Christians as being perfect ignorants, when we see the prophecies fulfilled in them. Surely this apparent ignorance and, as it were, madness of Christians, is what is revealed to the humble, to the saints, those who study with love, as the sublime and only true wisdom; this, I repeat, madness of Christians reduced the pagans to a tiny minority,[203] because, as the Apostle said: *God made foolish the wisdom of this world.* He adds, later, a magnificent reflection, for the one who understands, and follows well: *See that the world did not know God in the wisdom of God through wisdom; it pleased God to save the believers through the foolishness of preaching. Because Jews certainly demand signs and Greeks seek wisdom, but we predicate Christ crucified, to Jews a scandal, and to the pagans madness; in fact, for the ones called to Christ, both Jews and Greeks, it is the power of God and the wisdom of God. Because the foolish of God is wiser than men, and the weak of God stronger than men.*

Let them deride therefore as they can, of our apparent ignorance and folly, and boast of their doctrine and wisdom! I know that these jesters of ours are less this year than they were in the past. Indeed, since the nations roared, and the peoples plotted vain projects against the Lord and against his Christ, since they shed the blood of saints, and devastated the Church, to this day, and successively, they diminish day by day. We, in turn, are made strong against the outrages and proud trifles by the predictions of our God, we that see and have the joy at this point in that they are being fulfilled. Certainly, that tell us so the Prophet: *Listen to me those who know righteousness, my people, in whose hearts is my law: fear not the reproach of men, nor allow yourselves to be abated by their slander, and do give care that they despise you. For as the dress, so they will be consumed by time, and as wool will be eaten by moths; but my righteousness endures forever.*

However, read these mine reflections, if we deign to do so. And when their replies come to my attention, I'll give them the answer with the Lord's help.[204]

---

203 In fact, it was the persecutions, murders, destruction and vandalism authorized by the government.

204 However, before long, all who lived there rejected Christ, and began to follow Muhammad.

About the Orders of Evil Spirits, and the Triple Good Dæmon

Chapter I.[205]

Of Intelligences and spirits, and of the threefold kind of them, and of their diverse names, and of Infernall and subterraneall spirits.

Now consequently we must discourse of Intelligences, spirits and Angels. An Intelligence is an intelligible substance, free from all gross and putrifying mass of a body, immortall, insensible, assisting all, having Influence over all; and the nature of all intelligences, spirits and Angels is the same. But I call Angels here, not those whom we usually call Devils, but spirits so called from the propriety of the word, as it were, knowing, understanding and wise. But of these according to the tradition of the Magicians, there are three kinds, the first of which they call supercelestiall, and minds altogether separated from a body, and as it were intellectuall spheres, worshipping the one only God, as it were their most firm and stable unity or center; wherefore they even call them gods, by reason of a certain participion of the divinity; for they are always full of God, and overwhelmed with the Divine Nectar. These are only about God, and rule not the bodies of the world, neither are they fitted for the government of inferior things, but infuse the light received from God unto the inferior orders, and distribute every ones duty to all of them; The Celestial intelligences do next follow these in the second order, which they call worldly Angels *viz.* being appointed besides the Divine worship for the spheres of the world, and for the government of every heaven & Star, whence they are divided into so many orders, as there are heavens in the world, & as there are Stars in the Heavens, and they called those *Saturnine*, who rule the Heaven of *Saturn & Saturn* himself; others *Joviall*, who rule the heaven of *Jupiter* and *Jupiter* himself, and in like maner they name diverse Angels, as well for the name, as the vertue of the other Stars; and because the old Astrologers did maintain fifty five motions, therefore they invented so many Intelligences or Angels; they placed also in the Starry heaven, Angels, who might rule the signs, triplicities, decans, quinaries, degrees and Stars; for although the school of the Peripateticks assigne one onely

[205] The first chapter of this section corresponds to Chapter XVI of the *Third Book of Occult Philosophy*.

intelligence to each of the Orbs of the Stars: yet seeing every Star and small part of the heaven hath its proper and different power and influence, it is necessary that it also have his ruling intelligence, which may confer power and operate; therefore they have established twelve Princes of the Angels, which rule the twelve signs of the *Zodiack*, and thirty six which may rule the so many *Decans*, and seventy two, which may rule the so many *Quinaries* of heaven, and the tongues of men and the Nations, and four which may rule the triplicities and Elements, and seven governors of the whole world, according to the seven planets, and they have given to all of them names, and seals, which they call Characters, and used them in their invocations, incantations, and carvings, decribing them in the instruments of their operations, images, plates, glasses, rings, papers, wax lights and such like; and if at any time they did operate for the Sun, they did invocate by the name of the Sun, and by the names of *Solare* Angels, and so of the rest. Thirdly they established Angels as Ministers for the disposing of those things which are below, which *Origen* calleth certain invisible powers to which those things which are on earth, are committed to be disposed of. For sometimes they being visible to none do direct our journies [journeys] and all our businesses, are oft present at battels [battles], and by secret helpes do give the desired successes to their friends, for they are said, that at their pleasures they can procure prosperity, and inflict adversity. In like manner they distribute these into more orders, so as some are fiery, some watery, some aerial, some terrestrial; which four species of Angels are computed according to the four powers of the Celestiall souls, *viz.* the mind, reason, imagination, and the vivifying and moving nature; Hence the fiery follow the mind of the Celestiall souls, whence they concur to the contemplation of more sublime things, but the Aeriall follow the reason, and favor the rationall faculty, and after a certain manner separate it from the sensitive and vegetative; therefore it serveth for an active life, as the fiery for a contemplative, but the watery following the imagination, serve for a voluptuous life; The earthly following nature, favor vegetable nature; moreover they distinguish also these kind of Angels into *Saturnine* and *Joviall*, according to the names of the Stars, and the Heavens; further some are Orientall, some Occidentall, some Meridionall, some Septentrionall; Moreover there is no part of the world destitute of the proper assistance of these Angels, not because they are there alone, but because they reign there especially, for they are everywhere, although some especially operate and have their influence in this place, some elsewhere; neither truly are these things to be understood, as though they were subject to the influences of the Stars, but as they have correspondence with the Heaven above the world, from whence especially all things are directed, and to which all things ought to be conformable; whence as these Angels are appointed for diverse Stars, so also for diverse places and times, not that they are limited by time or place, neither by the bodies which they are appointed to govern, but because the order of wisdom hath so decreed, therefore they favor more, and patronize those bodies, places, times, stars; so they have called some Diurnall, some Nocturnall, other Meridionall; in like manner some are called Woodmen, some Mountaineers, some Fieldmen, some Domesticks. Hence the gods of the Woods, Country gods, Satyrs, familiars, Fairies of the fountains, Fairies of the Woods, Nymphs of the Sea, the Naiades, Neriades, Dryades, Pierides, Hamadryades, Potumides, Hinnides, Agapte, Pales, Pareades, Dodonæ, Feniliæ, Lavernæ, Pareæ, Muses, Aonides, Castalides, Heliconides, Pegasides, Meonides, Phebiades, Camenæ, the Graces, the Genii, Hobgoblins, and such like; whence they call them vulgar superiors, some the demi-gods [demigods] and goddesses; some of these are so familiar and acquainted with men, that they are even affected with humane perturbations, by whose instruction *Plato* thinketh that men do oftentimes wonderfull things, even as by the instruction of men, some beasts which are most nigh unto us, as Apes, Dogs, Elephants, do often strange things above their species; and they who have written the Chronicles of the Danes and Norwegians, do testifie, that spirits of diverse kinds in those regions are subject to man's commands; moreover some of these to be corporeall and mortall, whose bodies are begotten and dy [die], yet to be long lived is the opinion of the Egyptians and Platonists, and especially approved by *Proclus*. *Plutarch* also and *Demetrius* the Philosopher, and *Aemilianus* the Rhetoritian affirm the same; Therefore of these spirits of the third kind, as the opinion of the Platonists is; they report that there are so many Legions, as there are Stars in the Heaven, and so many spirits in every Legion, as in heaven it self Stars, but there are (as *Athanasius* delivereth) who think, that the true number of the good spirits, is according to the number of men ninety nine parts, according to the parable of the hundred sheep; others think only nine parts, according to the parable of the ten groats; others suppose the number of the Angels equal with men, because it is written, He hath appointed the bounds of the people according to the number of the Angels of God; and concerning their number many have written many things, but the latter Theologians following the master of the dentences, *Austin* [Augustine] and Gregory easily resolve themselves, saying, that the number of the good Angels transcendeth humane capacity; to the which on the contrary, innumerable unclean spirits do correspond, there being so many in the inferior world, as pure spirits in the superior, and some Divines affirm that they have received this by revelations; under these they place a kind of spirits, subterrany or obscure, which the Platonists call Angels that failed, revengers of wickedness, and ungodliness, according to the decree of the Divine justice, and they call them evill Angels and wicked spirits, because they oft annoy and hurt even of their own accords; of these also they reckon more legions, and in like manner distinguishing them according to the names of the Stars and Elements, and parts of the world, they do place over them Kings, Princes and Rulers and the names of them; of these, four most mischievous Kings do rule over the other [others], according to the four parts of the world; under these many more Princes of Legions govern, and also many of private offices. Hence the Gorgones, Statenocte, the furies. Hence *Tisiphone, Alecto, Megæra, Cerberus*: They of this kind of spirits, *Porphyry* saith, inhabite a place nigh to the earth, yea within the earth it self; there is no mischief, which they dare not commit; they have altogether a violent and hurtfull custome, therefore they very much plot and endeavor violent and sudden mischiefs; and when they make incursions, sometimes they are wont to lie hide [hid], but sometimes to offer open violence, and are very much delighted in all things done wickedly and contentiously.

CHAPTER II.

Of these according to the opinion of the Theologians

But our Theologians, together with *Dionysius*, maintain the three distinctions of Angels; every one of which they divide into three orders, they call these Hierarchies, those quires, whom *Proclus* also distinguisheth by the number nine. They place therefore in the superior Hierarchies, Seraphim, Cherubim, and Thrones, as it were supercelestiall Angels contemplating the order of the Divine providence; the first in the goodness of God; the second in the Essence of God, as the form; the third in the wisdom. In the middle Hierarchy they place the Dominations, Vertues, and Powers, as it were wordly Angels concurring to the government of the world; the first of these command that which the other execute; the second are Ministers to the Heavens and sometimes conspire to the working of miracles; the third drive away those things which seem to be able to disturbe the Divine Law; but in the inferior Hierarchy they place the Principalities, Archangels, [and Angels,] whom also *Iamblicus* reckoneth up, these as ministering spirits descend to take care of inferior things; the first of these take care of publike [public] things, princes and magistrates, provinces and kingdoms, every one those that belong to themselves; when we read in *Daniel*, But the prince of the Kingdom of *Persia* withstood me twenty one dayes; and *Jesus* the son of *Syrach* testifieth, that for every Nation a ruling Angel is appointed; which also *Moses* by his song in *Deuteronomy* seemeth to shew forth, saying, when the most High divided the Nations, he appointed them bounds according to the number of the Angels of God. The second are present at sacred duties, and direct the Divine worship about every man, and offer up the prayers and sacrifices of men before the gods. The third dispose every smaller matter, and to each thing each one is a preserver. There are also of these, who afford vertue to the least plants and stones and to all inferior things; to whom many things are common with God, many with men, and they are mediating Ministers; But *Athanasius*, besides Thrones, Cherubins, and Seraphins, who are next to God, and magnify him incessantly with hymns and continuall praises, praying for our salvation, nameth the other orders, which by a common name he calleth the *militia* of heaven. The first of these is the Doctrinall order, of which he was, who spake to *Daniel*, saying, Come, that I may teach thee what shall come to thy people in the last dayes: Then there is the tutelar order, of the which we read also in *Daniel*. Behold, *Michael* one of the Princes cometh to my help; and there, In that time shall rise up *Michael* a great Prince, who standeth for the sons of thy people; of this order was that *Raphael* also, who carryed forth and brought back *Tobiah* the younger; after this is the Procuratory Order, of which mention is made in *Job*, where we read, if the Angel shall speak for him, he will entreat the Lord, and the Lord will be pleased with him; and of the same order is expounded also that which is written in the sixteenth Chapter of *Ecclesiasticus*, about the end. The works of the Lord have been made by his appointment from the beginning, and he hath distributed their portions from the time they have been made, he hath adorned their works for ever, they have not hungred [hungered], nor been wearied, and have not desisted from their works, none of them shall oppress his neighbor even for ever. The Ministeriall order followeth, of which *Paul* to the Hebrews saith, Are they not all Ministring spirits, sent forth for them who shall be heirs of salvation? After these is the Auxiliary order, of which we read in *Esay*, The Angels of the Lord went forth and slew in the tent of the Assyrians 185 thousands. The Receptory order of souls followeth this, of which we read in *Luke*, the soul of *Lazarus* was carryed by Angels into the bosom of *Abraham*, and there we are taught, that we should make to our selves friends of the unrighteous Mammon, that we may be received into eternall Tabernacles. Moreover, there is the order of the Assistants, of which we reade in *Zachary*. These are the two sons of the Oyl [oil] of splendor, who assist the ruler of the whole earth, but the Theologians of the Hebrews do otherwise number and call these orders; for in the highest place are those which they call היות הקדש, [Haioth Hacadosh] that is, creatures of sanctity, or by the which God אהיה giveth the gift of being. In the second place succeed *Ophanim* אופנים, that is forms or wheels, by the which God יהוה distinguisheth the *Chaos*: In the third place are *Aralim* אראלים great, strong, and mighty Angels, by the which *Jehova* [L:Tetragrammaton] *Elohim* pronounced or *Jehova* [L: Tetragrammaton] joyned with *He* היהוה administreth form to the liquid matter: In the fourth place are *Hasmalim* השמלים by which *El* אל God framed the effigies of bodies. The fifth order is *Seraphim* שרפים by which God *Elohim Gibor* גיבר אלהים draweth forth the elements. The sixt [sixth] is *Malachim* מלאכים, that is of Angels, by which God *Eloha* אליה, produceth metals. The seventh *Elohim* אלהים that is the gods by the which God *Jehovah Sabaoth* יהוה צבאות produceth vegetables; The eighth *Beni Elohim* בני אלהים that is the sons of God, by which God *Elohim Sabaoth* אלהים צבאות procreateth Animals; The ninth & lowest *Cherubim* כרובים by which God *Sadai* שדי createth mankind; under these is the order Animasticus called *Issim* אישים that is nobles, strong men, or blessed, by which God *Adonai* אדני bestoweth prophecie.

Chapter III.

Of the orders of evil spirits, and of their fall, and divers natures

There are some of the School of the Theologians, who distribute the evill spirits into nine degrees, as contrary to the nine orders of the Angels; Therefore the first of these are those which are called false gods, who usurping the name of God, would be worshipped for gods, and require sacrifices and adorations, as that Devil, who saith to Christ, if thou wilt fal [fall] down and worship me, I will give thee all these things, shewing him all the kingdoms of the world; and the Prince of these is he who said, I will ascend ahove the height of the clouds, and will he like to the most High; who is therefore called *Beelzebub*, that is, an old god. In the second place follow the spirits of lies, of which sort was he who went forth, and was a lying spirit in the mouth of the Prophets of *Achab*; and the Prince of these is the Serpent *Pytho*; from whence *Apollo* is called *Pythius*, and that woman a witch in *Samuel*, and the other in the Gospel, who had *Pytho* in their belly. Therefore this kind of Devil joyneth himself to the Oracles, and deludeth men by divinations, and predictions, so that he may deceive. In the third order are the vessels of iniquity, which are also called the vessels of wrath, these are the inventors of evil things and of all wicked arts, as in *Plato*, that devill *Theutus* who taught Cards and Dice; for all wickedness, malice and deformity proceedeth from these; of which in *Genesis*, in the Benedictions of *Simeon* and *Levi*, *Jacob* saith, vessels of iniquity are in their habitations; into their counsel let not my soul come; whom the *Psalmist* calleth vessels of death, *Esay* vessels of fury, and *Jeremy* vessels of wrath, *Ezekiel* vessels of destroying and slaying, and their prince is *Belial*, which is interpreted without a yoak [yoke] or disobedient, a prevaricator and an Apostate, of whom *Paul* to the *Corinthians* saith, what agreement hath Christ with *Beliall*? Fourthly follow the revengers of evil, and their Prince is *Asmodeus*, *viz.* causing judgement; After these in the fifth place come the deluders, who Imitate miracles, and serve wicked conjurers and witches, and seduce the people by their miracles, as the serpent seduced *Eve*, and their Prince is Satan, of whom is written in the Revelations, that he seduced the whole world, doing great signs, and causing fire to descend from heaven in the sight of men, seducing the inhabitants of the earth, by reason of the signs, which are given him to do. Sixthly the Aeriall powers offer themselves; they joyn [join] themselves to thundering and lightnings, corrupting the aire, causing pestilences and other evils; in the number of which, are the four Angels, of whom the Revelation speaketh, to whom it is given to hurt the Earth and Sea, holding the four windes, from the four corners of the earth; and their prince is called *Meririm*; he is the *Meridian* Devill, a boyling [boiling] spirit, a devill raging in the South, whom *Paul* to the *Ephesians* calleth the Prince of the power of this air, and the spirit which worketh in the children of disobedience. The seventh mansion the furies possess, which are powers of evil, discords, war and devastations, whose Prince in the Revelations is called in Greek *Apollyon*, in Hebrew *Abaddon*, that is destroying and wasting. In the eighth place are the accusers, or the inquisitors, whose Prince is *Astarath* [Astaroth], that is, a searcher out: in the Greek language he is called *Diabolos*, that is an accuser, or calumniator, which in the Revelations is called the accuser, of the brethren, accusing them night & day before the face of our God. Moreover the Tempters and Ensnarers have the last place, one of which is present with every man, which we therefore call the evill *Genius*, and their Prince is *Mammon*, which is interpreted covetousness: But all unanimously maintain that evil spirits do wander up & down in this inferior world, enraged against all, whom they therefore call Devils, of whom *Austin* [Augustine] in his first book of the incarnation of the word to *Januarius*, saith: Concerning the devils and his Angels contrary to Vertues, the Ecclesiasticall preaching hath taught, that there are such things; but what they are and how they are, he hath not clear enough expounded: yet there is this opinion amongst most, that this Devill was an Angel, and being made an Apostate, persuaded very many of the Angels to decline with himself, who even unto this day are called his Angels: *Greece* not withstanding thinketh not that all these are damned, nor that they are all purposefully evil, but that from the Creation of the world, the dispensation of things is ordained by this means, that the tormenting of sinful souls is made over to them: The other *Theologians* say that not any Devill was created evill, but that they were driven and cast forth of Heaven, from the orders of good Angels for their pride, whose fall not only our and the *Hebrew Theologians*, but also the *Assyrians*, *Arabians*, *Egyptians* and *Greeks* do confirm by their tenents [tenets]; *Pherecydes* the *Syrian* describeth the fall of the Devils and that *Ophis*, that is, the Devilish serpent, was the head of that rebelling Army; *Trismegistus* sings the same fall in his *Pimander*, and *Homer* under the name of *Ararus*, in his verses;

and *Plutarch* in his speech of usury, signifieth, that *Empedocles* knew that the fall of the devils was after this manner: the devils also themselves often confess their fall: they therefore being cast forth into this valley of misery, some that are nigh to us wander up and down in this obscure air, others inhabit lakes, rivers and seas, others the earth, and terrifie [terrify] earthly things, and invade those who dig Wells and Metals, cause the gapings of the earth, strike together the foundation of mountains, and vex not only men, but also other creatures; some being content with laughter and delusion only, do contrive rather to weary men, then to hurt them, some heightning themselves to the length of a Giants body, and again shrinking themselves up to the smallness of the Pigmies, and changing themselves into divers forms, do disturb men with vain fear: others study lies and blasphemies, as we read of one in the third book of *Kings*, saying, I will go forth and be a lying spirit in the mouth of all the Prophets of *Achab*: but the worst sort of devils are those, who lay wait and overthrow passengers in their journeys, and rejoyce in wars and effusion of blood, and afflict men with most cruell stripes: we read of such in *Matthew*, for fear of whom no man durst pass that way; moreover the scripture reckoneth up nocturnall, diurnall, and meridionall devils, and describeth other spirits of wickedness by divers names, as we read in *Esay* of Satyrs, Scrich owls [screech owls], Syrenes, storks, Owls; and in the *Psalms* of Aspes, Basiliskes, Lions, Dragons; and in the *Gospel* we read of Scorpions and *Mammon* and the prince of this world and rulers of darkness, of all which *Beelzebub* is the prince, whom Scripture calleth the prince of wickedness. *Porphyrie* [Porphyry] saith, their prince is *Serapis*, who is also called *Pluto* by the Greeks, and also *Cerberus* is chief amongst them, that three-headed dog: *viz*. Because he is conversant in three elements, air, water, and earth, a most pernicious devill; whence also *Proserpina*, who can do very much in these three elements, is their Princess, which she testifies of her self in her answers, in these verses.

Of three fold nature I Lucina *fair,*
The daughter am, sent from above the air;
The golden Phoebe *am, and with heads trine,*
Whom many forms do change, and the trine sign
Which I bear with forms of earth, fire, and air,
I for black mastives [mastiffs] of the earth do care.

Origen's opinion concerning the devils, is: The spirits who act of their own free will, left the service of God with their Prince the devil; if they began to repent a little, are clothed with humane flesh; That further by this repentance, after the resurrection, by the same means by which they came into the flesh, they might at the last return to the vision of God, being then also freed from etheriall and aeriall bodies, and then all knees are to be bowed to God, of Celestiall, Terrestriall, and Infernall things, that God may be all in all: Moreover Saint *Ireneus* approveth the opinion of *Justine Martyr*, who hath said, Satan never durst speak blasphemy against God, before that the Lord came on the earth, because that he knew not as yet his condemnation; but there are many of the devils who are fallen, who hope for their salvation: Very many think by the History of *Paul* the *Hermite* written by *Jerome*, & reverenced by the Church with Canonical hours, also by the Legend of *Brandan*, they are so taught; and even by this Argument they maintain that their prayers are heard; that we read in the Gospels, that Christ heard the prayers of the devils, and granted that they should enter into the Herd of Swine; to these also agreeth the 71. *Psalm*, according to our supputation, but according to the supputation of the Hebrews the 72, where we read, the *Ethiopians* shall fall before him, and his enemies lick the dust; there it is read according to the Hebrew text, they that inhabit the desert, shall bend their knees before him, that is, the aiery spirits shall adore him, as the *Cabalists* affirm, and his enemies shall lick the dust, which they understand of *Zazell*, and his Army: of which we read in *Genesis*, Dust shalt thou eat all the dayes of thy life, and elsewhere the Prophet saith, because the dust of the earth is his bread; hence the Cabalists think, that even some devils shall be saved, which opinion also it is manifest that *Origen* was of.

Chapter IV.

Of the bodies of the Devils

Concerning the bodies of Angels, there is a great dissension betwixt the late Divines, and Philosophers; for *Thomas* affirms that all angels are incorporeall, yea evil angels, yet that they do assume bodies sometimes, which after awhile they put off again; *Dionysius* in *Divine Names* strongly affirms that Angels are incorporeall. Yet *Austin* [Augustine] upon *Genesis* delivers his opinion, that Angels are said to be Aery, and Fiery Animals:

because they have the nature of Aeriall bodies, neither can they be dissolved by death, because the element which is more active than passive is predominant in them; the same seem to affirm, that all Angels in the beginning of their creation had Aeriall bodies, being formed of the more pure, and superiour part of the air, being more fit to act, then to suffer; and that those bodies were after the confirmation preserved in good Angels, but changed in the evil in their fall, into the quality of more thick air, that they might be tormented in the fire: Moreover *Magnus Basilius* doth attribute bodies not only to Devils, but also to pure angels, as certain thin, Aeriall, pure spirits; to which *Gregory Nazianzen* doth agree. *Apuleius* was of opinion, that all angels had not bodies; for in the book of the *Demon* of *Socrates*, he saith, that there is a more propitious kind of spirits, which being alwayes free from corporeall bonds, are procured by certain prayers. But *Psellus* the *Platonist*, and *Christianus* do think that the nature of spirits is not without a body; but yet not that the body of angels, & devils are the same; for that is without matter; but the bodies of devils are in a manner materiall, as shadows, and subject to passion, that they being struck are pained, and may be burnt in the fire, into conspicuous ashes, which as is recorded, was done in *Tuscia*. And although it be a spirituall body, yet it is most sensible, and being touched, suffers; and although it be cut asunder, yet comes together again, as air and water, but yet in the mean time is much pained. Hence it is that they fear the edge of the sword, and any weapon. Hence in *Virgil* the *Sybill* saith to *Aeneas*,

Do thou go on thy way and draw thy sword.

Upon which *Servius* saith that she would have *Aeneas* have his sword consecrated. *Orpheus* also describes the kinds of *Demoniacall* bodies; there is indeed one body, which onely abides the fire, but being seen, doth not suffer, which *Orpheus* calls fiery, and Celestiall *Demons*: the other is contemperated with the mixtion of fire, and air, whence they are called Etheriall, and Aeriall; to which if any waterish thing was added, there arose a third kinde, whence they are called watery, which sometimes are seen: to which if any earthiness be added, this is not very thick; they are called *Terrene Demons*, and they are more conspicuous, and sensible. Now the bodies of sublime Demons are nourished of the most pure Etheriall element, and are not rashly to be seen of any, unless they be sent from God; being weaved of such bright threads, and so small, that they transmit all the rayes of our sight by their finess, and reverberate them with splendor, and deceive by their subtlety; of which *Calcidius* saith, Etheriall, and Aeriall *Demons*, because their bodies have not so much fire as that they are conspicuous, nor yet so much earth that the solidity of them resists the touch, and their whole composure being made up of the clearness of the skie [sky], and moisture of the air, hath joined [joined] together an indissoluble superficies. The other *Demons* are neither so appearable, nor invisible, being sometimes conspicuous are turned into divers figures, and put upon themselves bodies like shadows, of blood-less images, drawing the filthiness of a gross body, and they have too much communion with the Wood (which the Ancients did call the wicked soul) and by reason of their affinity with earth, and water, are also taken with *Terrene* pleasures, and lust; of which sort are hobgoblins, and Incubi, and Succubi, of which number it is no absurd conjecture to think that *Melusina* was: yet there is none of the Demons (as *Mareus* supposeth) is to be supposed male or female, seeing this difference of sex belongs to compounds, but the bodies of *Demons* are simple, neither can any of the *Demons* turn themselves into all shapes at their pleasure; but to the fiery, and aiery it is easie so to do, *viz*: to change themselves into what shapes their imagination conceives: now subterraneall and dark Demons, because their nature being concluded in the streights of a thick and unactive body, cannot make the diversity of shapes, as others can. But the waterie, and such as dwell upon the moist superfices of the earth, are by reason of the moistness of the element, for the most part like to women; of such kinde are the fairies of the Rivers, and *Nymphs* of the Woods: but those which inhabite dry places, being of dryer bodies, shew themselves in form of men, as Satyrs, or *Onosceli*, with Asses legs, or *Fauni*, and *Incubi*, of which he saith, he learned by experience there were many, and that some of them oftentimes did desire, and made compacts with women to lie with them: and that there were some Demons, which the French call *Dusii*, that did continually attempt this way of lust.

CHAPTER V.

Of the annoyance of evil spirits,
and the preservation we
have by good spirits

It is the common opinion of Divines, that all evil spirits are of that nature, that they hate God as well as men; therefore Divine providence hath set over us more pure spirits, with whom he hath entrusted us, as with Shepheards [shepherds], and Governours, that they should daily help us, and drive away evil spirits from us, and curb, and restrain them, that they should not hurt us as much as they would; as is read in *Tobia*, that *Raphael* did apprehend the *Demon* called *Asmodeus*, and bound him in the wilderness of the upper *Egypt*. Of these *Hesiod* saith, there are 30000 of *Jupiters* immortall spirits living on the Earth, which are the keepers of mortall men, who that they might observe justice and mercifull deeds, having clothed themselves with air, go every where on the Earth. For there is no Prince, nor potentate could be safe, nor any woman continue uncorrupted, no man in this valley of ignorance could come to the end appointed to him by God, if good spirits did not secure us; Or if evill spirits should be permitted to satisfie the wils [wills] of men; As therefore amongst the good spirits there is a proper keeper or protector deputed to every one, corroborating the spirit of the man to good; so of evil spirits there is sent forth an enemy ruling over the flesh, and desire thereof; and the good spirit fights for us as a preserver against the enemie [enemy], and flesh; Now man betwixt these contenders is the midle [middle], and left in the hand of his own Counsell, to whom he will give victory; we cannot therefore accuse Angels, if they do not bring the Nations entrusted to them, to the knowledge of the true God, to true piety, and suffer them to fall into errours and perverse worship: but it is to be imputed to themselves, who have of their own accord declined from the right path, adhering to the spirits of errours, giving victory to the Devill; for it is in the hand of man to adhere to whom he please, and overcome whom he will, by whom, if once the enemy the devill be overcome, he is made his servant, and being overcome, cannot fight any more with another, as a wasp that hath lost his sting: to which opinion *Origen* assents in his book *Periarchon*, concluding, that the Saints fighting against evil spirits, and overcoming, do lessen their armie [army], neither can he that is overcome by any, molest any more; As therefore there is given to every man a good spirit, so also there is given to every man an evil *Diabolicall* spirit, whereof each seeks an union with our spirit, and endeavours to attract it to it self, and to be mixed with it, as wine with water; the good indeed, through all good works conformable to it self, change us into Angels, by uniting us, as it is writ of *John Baptist* in *Malachie*: Behold I send mine Angel before thy face: of which transmutation, and union it is writ elsewhere; He which adheres to God is made one spirit with him. An evil spirit also by evil works, studies to make us conformable to it self, and to unite, as *Christ* saith of *Judas*, Have not I chosen twelve, & one of you is a devil? And this is that which *Hermes* saith, when a spirit hath influence upon the soul of man, he scatters the seed of his own notion, whence such a soul being sowen [sown] with seeds, and full of fury, brings forth thence wonderfull things, and whatsoever are the offices of spirits: for when a good spirit hath influence upon a holy soul, it doth exalt it to the light of wisdom; but an evil spirit being transfused into a wicked soul, doth stir it up to theft, to man-slaughter, to lusts, and whatsoever are the offices of evil spirits. Good spirits (as saith *Iamblicus*) purge the souls most perfectly; and some bestow upon us other good things; they being present do give health to the body, vertue to the soul, security to the soul, what is mortall in us they take away, cherish heat, and make it more efficacious to life, and by an Harmonie [harmony] do alwayes infuse light into an intelligible mind. But whether there be many keepers of a man, or one alone, *Theologians* differ amongst themselves; we think there are more, the Prophet saying, he hath given his Angels a charge concerning thee, that they should keep thee in all thy wayes: which as saith *Hierome*, is to be understood of any man, as well as of Christ. All men therefore are governed by the ministry of divers Angels, and are brought to any degree of vertue, deserts, and dignity, who behave themselves worthy of them; but they which carry themselves unworthy of them are deposed, and thrust down, as well by evil spirits, as good spirits, unto the lowest degree of misery, as their evil merits shall require: but they that are attributed to the sublimer Angels, are preferred before other men, for Angels having the care of them, exalt them, and subject others to them by a certain occult power; which although neither of them perceive, yet he that is subjected, feels a certain yoke of presidency, of which he cannot easily acquit himself, yea he fears and reverenceth that power, which the superiour Angels make to flow upon superiours, and with a certain terrour bring the inferiours into a fear of presidency. This did *Homer* seem to be sensible of, when he saith, that the *Muses* begot of *Jupiter*, did alwayes as inseparable companions assist the *Kings* begot of *Jupiter*, who by them were made venerable, and magnificent. So we read that M. *Antonius* being formerly joyned [joined] in singular friendship with *Octavus Augustus*, were wont alwayes to play together. But when as alwayes *Augustus* went away conquerour, that a certain *Magician* counselled M. *Antonius* thus: O *Antony*, what dost thou do with that yong [young] man? shun, and avoid him, for although thou art elder then he, and art more skillfull then he, and art better descended then he, and hast endured the Wars of more Emperours, yet thy *Genius* doth much dread the *Genius* of this yong man, and thy Fortune flatter his Fortune; unless thou shalt shun him, it seemeth wholly to decline to him. Is not the Prince like other men, how should other men fear, and reverence him, unless a Divine terrour should exalt him, and striking a fear into others, depress them, that they should reverence him as a Prince? Wherefore we must endeavour, that being purified by doing well, and following sublime things, and choosing opportune times, and seasons, we he entrusted or committed to a degree of sublimer, and more potent Angels, who taking care of us, we may deservedly be preferred before others.

Chapter VI.

Of obeying a proper Genius,
and of the searching out
the nature thereof

As every Region in the Celestialls hath a certain Star, and Celestiall image which hath influence upon it before others: so also in supercelestialls doth it obtain a certain Intelligence set over it, and guarding it, with infinite other ministring spirits of its order, all which are called by a common name, the Sons of *Elohim Sabaoth* בני אלהים שבאות, *i.e.* Sons of the God of hosts. Hence as often as the most high doth deliberate of War, or slaughter, or the desolation of any Kingdom, or subduing of any people in these inferiours, then no otherwise, when these shall come upon the earth, there proceeds a conflict of these spirits above, as it is written in *Isaiah*, The Lord of Hosts shall visit the Army of the high, in the heavens; and the Kings of the earth, in the earth; of which conflicts of spirits and presidents, we read also in *Daniel*, *viz.* of the Prince of the Kingdom of the *Persians*, of the Prince of the *Grecians*, of the Prince of the people of *Israel*; and of their conflict amongst themselves, of which also *Homer* seemed formerly to be sensible of, when he sang,

Great was the rumour in the Court above
When that the gods War mutually did move:
When *Phoebus* did to *Neptune* battle give,
Pallas with *Mars* the god of War did strive,
Diana did withstand in hostile way
Juno, and *Latona* did for to slay
Mercury attempt

Nevertheless seeing there he in every region spirits of all sorts, yet they are more powerfull there which are of the same order with the president of that region. So in the *Solary* region, the *Solary* spirits are most potent; in the *Lunary*, *Lunary*, and so of the rest. And hence it is that various events of our affairs offer themselves, & follow us in places and provinces, being more Fortunate in one place more then another, where *viz.* the *Demon* our *Genius* shall receive more power, or we shall there obtain a more powerfull *Demon* of the same order. So *Solary* men, if they shall travell into a *Solary* region, or province, shall he made there far more fortunate, because there they shall have more powerfull, and more advantagious conducters or *Genii*, by the present aid of whom they shall be brought beyond expectation, and their own power, to happy events. Hence it is that the choice of a place, region, or time doth much conduce to the happiness of life where any one shall dwell, & frequent, according to the nature & instinct of his own Genius. Sometimes also the change of the name doth conduce to the same, for whereas the properties of names being the significators of things themselves, do as it were in a glass declare the conditions of their forms; thence it comes to pass, that names being changed, the things often times are changed. Hence the sacred writ doth not without cause bring in God, whilest he was blessing *Abram*, and *Jacob*, changing their names, calling the one *Abraham*, and the other *Israel*. Now the ancient Phylosophers [philosophers] teach us to know the nature of the *Genius* of every man, by Stars, their influx, and aspects, which are potent in the Nativity of any one; but with instructions so divers, and differing amongst themselves, that it is much difficult to understand the mysteries of the heavens by their directions. For *Porphyrie* [Porphyry] seeks the *Genius* of the Star, which is the Lady of the Nativity: but *Maternus* either from thence, or from the Planets, which had then most dignities, or from that into whose house the Moon was to enter after that, which at the birth of the man it doth retain. But the *Caldeans* [Chaldeans] enquire after the *Genius*, either from the Sun above, or from the Moon. But others, and many *Hebrews* think it is to be enquired after from some corner of the heaven, or from all of them. Others seek a good *Genius* from the eleventh house, which therefore they call a good *Demon*; but an evil *Genius* from the sixth, which therefore they call an evil *Demon*. But seeing the inquisition of these is laborious, & most occult, we shall far more easily enquire into the nature of our *Genius* from our selves, observing those things which the instinct of nature doth dictate to, and the heaven inclines us to from our infancy, being distracted with no contagion, or those things which the minde, the soul being freed from vain cares, and sinister affections, and impediments being removed, doth suggest to us: These without all doubt are the perswasions [persuasions] of a *Genius* which is given to every one from their birth, leading, and perswading us to that whither the Star thereof inclines us to.

Chapter VII.

That there is a threefold keeper of man, and from whence each of them proceed

Every man hath a threefold good Demon, as a proper keeper, or preserver, the one whereof is holy, another of the nativity, and the other of profession. The holy Demon is one, according to the Doctrine of the Egyptians, assigned to the rationall soul, not from the Stars or Planets, but from a supernaturall cause, from God himself, the president of Demons, being universall, above nature: This doth direct the life of the soul, & doth alwaies put good thoughts into the minde, being alwaies active in illuminating us, although we do not alwaies take notice of it; but when we are purified, and live peaceably, then it is perceived by us, then it doth as it were speak with us, and communicates its voyce [voice] to us, being before silent, and studyeth daily to bring us to a sacred perfection. Also by the ayd [aid] of this Demon we may avoid the malignity of a Fate, which being religiously worshipped by us in honesty, and sanctity, as we know was done by *Socrates*; the *Pythagoreans* think we may be much helped by it, as by dreams, and signs, by diverting evill things, and carefully procuring good things. Wherefore the *Pythagorians* were wont with one consent to pray to *Jupiter*, that he would either preserve them from evill, or shew them by what Demon it should be done. Now the Demon of the nativity, which is called the Genius, doth here descend from the disposition of the world, and from the circuits of the Stars, which were powerfull in his nativity. Hence there be some that think, when the soul is coming down into the body, it doth out of the quire of the Demons naturally choose a preserver to it self, nor only choose this guide to it self, but hath that willing to defend it. This being the executor, and keeper of the life, doth help it to the body, and takes care of it, being Communicated to the body, and helps a man to that very office, to which the Celestials have deputed him, being born. Whosoever therefore have received a fortunate Genius, are made thereby vertuous in their works, efficacious, strong, and prosperous. Wherefore they are called by the *Phylosophers* [philosophers] fortunate, or luckily born. Now the Demon of profession is given by the Stars, to which such a profession, or sect, which any man hath professed, is subjected, which the soul, when it began to make choyce [choice] in this body, and to take upon itself dispositions, doth secretly desire. This Demon is changed, the profession being changed; then according to the dignity of the profession, we have Demons of our profession more excellent and sublime, which successively take care of man, which procures a keeper of profession, as he proceeds from vertue to vertue. When therefore a profession agrees with our nature, there is present with us a Demon of our profession like unto us, and sutable [suitable] to our *Genius*, and our life is made more peaceable, happy, and prosperous: but when we undertake a profession unlike, or contrary to our *Genius*, our life is made laborious, and troubled with disagreeing patrons. So it falls out that some profit more in any science, or art, or office, in a little time, and with little pains, when another takes much pains, and studies hard, and all in vain: and, although no science, art, or vertue be to be condemned, yet that thou maist live prosperously, carry on thy affairs happily; in the first place know thy good Genius, and thy nature, and what good the celestiall disposition promiseth thee, and God the distributor of all these, who distributes to each as he pleaseth, and follow the beginnings of these, profess these, be conversant in that vertue to which the most high distributor doth elevate, and lead thee, who made *Abraham* excell in justice and clemency, *Isaac* with fear, *Jacob* with strength, *Moses* with meekness and Miracles, *Joshua* in war, *Phinias* in zeal, *David* in religion, and victory, *Solomon* in knowledge and fame, *Peter* in faith, *John* in charity, *Jacob* in devotion, *Thomas* in prudence, *Magdalen* in contemplation, *Martha* in officiousness. Therefore in what vertue thou thinkest thou canst most easily be a proficient in, use diligence to attain to the height thereof; that thou maist excell in one, when in many thou canst not: but in the rest endeavour to be as great a proficient as thou canst: but if thou shalt have the overseers of nature, and religion agreeable, thou shalt finde a double progress of thy nature, and profession: but if they shall be disagreeing, follow the better, for thou shalt better perceive at some time a preserver of an excellent profession, then of nativity.

Chapter VIII.

Of the tongue of Angels, and of their speaking amongst themselves, and with us

We might doubt whether Angels, or Demons, since they be pure spirits, use any vocal speech, or tongue amongst themselves, or to us; but that *Paul* in some place saith, If I speak with the tongue of men, or angels: but what their speech or tongue is, is much doubted by many. For many think that if they use any Idiome, it is Hebrew, because that was the first of all, and came from heaven, and was before the confusion of languages in *Babylon*, in which the Law was given by God the Father, and the Gospell was preached by Christ the Son, and so many Oracles were given to the Prophets by the Holy Ghost: and seeing all tongues have, and do undergo various mutations, and corruptions, this alone doth alwaies continue inviolated. Moreover an evident sign of this opinion is, that though each Demon, and Intelligence do use the speech of those nations, with whom they do inhabit, yet to them that understand it, they never speak in any Idiome, but in this alone. But now how Angels speak it is hid from us, as they themselves are. Now to us that we may speak, a tongue is necessary with other instruments, as are the jaws, palate, lips, teeth, throat, lungs, the aspera arteria, and muscles of the breast, which have the beginning of motion from the soul. But if any speak at a distance to another, he must use a louder voice; but if neer [near], he whispers in his ear: and if he could be coupled to the hearer, a softer breath would suffice; for he would slide into the hearer without any noise, as an image in the eye, or glass. So souls going out of the body, so Angels, so Demons speak: and what man doth with a sensible voyce [voice], they do by impressing the conception of the speech in those to whom they speak, after a better manner then if they should express it by an audible voyce. So the *Platonists* say that *Socrates* perceived his Demon by sense indeed, but not of this body, but by the sense of the etheriall body concealed in this: after which manner *Avicen* believes the Angels were wont to be seen, and heard by the Prophets: That instrument, whatsoever the vertue be, by which one spirit makes known to another spirit what things are in his minde, is called by the Apostle *Paul* the tongue of Angels. Yet oftentimes also they send forth an audible voyce, as they that cryed at the ascension of the Lord, Ye men of *Galile* [Galilee], why stand ye there gazing into the heaven? And in the old law they spake with divers of the Fathers with a sensible voyce, but this never but when they assumed bodies. But with what senses those spirits and Demons hear our invocations, and prayers, and see our ceremonies, we are altogether ignorant.

For there is a spirituall body of Demons everywhere sensible by nature, so that it toucheth, seeth, heareth, without any medium, and nothing can be an impediment to it: Yet neither do they perceive after that manner as we do with different organs, but haply as sponges drink in water, so do they all sensible things with their body, or some other way unknown to us; neither are all animals endowed with those organs; for we know that many want ears, yet we know they perceive a sound, but after what manner we know not.

Chapter IX.

Of the names of Spirits, and their various imposition; and of the Spirits that are set over the Stars, Signs, Corners of the Heaven, and the Elements

Many and divers are the names of good spirits, and bad: but their proper, and true names, as those of the Stars, are known to God alone, who only numbers the multitude of Stars, and calls them all by their names, whereof none can be known by us but by divine revelation, and very few are expressed to us in the sacred writ. But the masters of the Hebrews think that the names of the angels were imposed upon them by *Adam*, according to that which is written, The Lord brought all things which he had made unto *Adam*, that he should name them, and as he called any thing, so the name of it was. Hence the Hebrew *Mecubals* think, together with *Magicians*, that it is in the power of man to impose names upon Spirits, but of such a man only who is dignified, and elevated to this vertue by some divine gift, or sacred authority: but because a name that may express the nature of divinity, or the whole vertue of angelical essences cannot be made by any humane voyce, therefore names for the most part are put upon them from their works, signifying some certain office, or effect, which is required by the quire of Spirits: which names then no otherwise then oblations, and sacrifices offered to the Gods, obtain efficacy and vertue to draw any spirituall substance from above or beneath, for to make any desired effect. I have seen, and known some writing on virgin parchment the name and seal of some spirit in the hour of the Moon: which when afterward he gave to be devoured by a water-frog, and had muttered over some verse, the frog being let go into the water, rains, and shours [showers] presently followed. I saw also the same man inscribing the name of another Spirit with the seal thereof in the hour of *Mars*, which was given to a Crow, who being let go, after a verse muttered over, presently there followed from that corner of the heaven, whither he flew, lightnings, shakings, and horrible thunders, with thick clouds: Neither were those names of spirits of an unknown tongue, neither did they signifie any thing else but their offices. Of this kinde are the names of those angels, *Raziel, Gabriel, Michael, Raphael, Haniel,* which is as much as the vision of God, the vertue of God, the strength of God, the medicine of God, the glory of God. In like manner in the offices of evill Demons are read their names, a player, deceiver, a dreamer, fornicator, and many such like. So we receive from many of the ancient Fathers of the Hebrews the names of angels set over the planets and signs: over *Saturn, Zaphiel* [Zaphkiel]; over *Jupiter, Zadkiel*; over *Mars, Camael*; over the *Sun, Raphael*; over *Venus, Haniel*; over *Mercury, Michael*; over the *Moon, Gabriel*. These are those seven Spirits which always stand before the face of God, to whom is entrusted the disposing of the whole celestiall, and terrene Kingdoms, which is under the Moon. For these (as say the more curious Theologians) govern all things by a certain vicissitude of hours, daies [days], and years, as the Astrologers teach concerning the planets which they set over; which therefore *Mercurius Trismegistus* calls the seven governors of the world, who by the heavens, as by instruments, distribute the influences of all the Stars and signs upon these inferiours. Now there are some that do ascribe them to the Stars, by names somewhat differing, saying, that over Saturn is set an intelligence called *Oriphiel*; over Jupiter *Zachariel*; over Mars *Zamael*; over the Sun *Michael*; over Venus *Anael*; over Mercury *Raphael*; over the Moon *Gabriel*. And every one of these governs the world 354 years, and four months; and the government begins from the Intelligence of *Saturn*; afterward in order, the Intelligences of *Venus, Jupiter, Mercury, Mars,* the *Moon,* the *Sun* raign [reign], and then the government returns to the Spirit of *Saturn*. *Abbas Tritemius* [Trithemius] writ to *Maximilian Caesara* speciall Treatise concerning these, which he that will thoroughly examine, may from thence draw great knowledge of future times. Over the twelve Signs are set these, *viz.* over *Aries Malchidael*; over *Taurus Asmodel*; over *Gemini Ambriel*; over *Cancer Muriel*; over *Leo Verchiel*; over *Virgo Hamaliel*; over *Libra Zuriel*; over *Scorpio Barchiel*; over *Sagittarius Advachiel*; over *Capricorn Hanael*; over *Aquarius Cambiel*; over *Pisces Barchiel*. Of these Spirits set over the planets, and Signs, *John* made mention in the Revelation, speaking of the former in the beginning; And of the seven Spirits which are in the presence of the Throne of God, which I finde are set over the seven planets, [the latter] in the end of the book, where he describes the platform of the heavenly City, saying that in the twelve gates thereof were twelve Angels. There are again twenty eight Angels, which rule in the twenty eight mansions of the Moon, whose names in order are these: *Geniel, Enediel, Amixiel, Azariel, Gabiel, Dirachiel, Seheliel [Scheliel?], Amnediel, Barbiel, Ardefiel, Neciel, Abdizuel, Jazeriel, Ergediel, Ataliel, Azeruel, Adriel, Egibiel, Amutiel, Kyriel, Bethnael, Geliel, Requiel, Abrinael, Aziel, Tagriel, Alheniel, Amnixiel.* There are also four Princes of the Angels, which are set over the four winds, and over the four parts of the world, whereof *Michael* is set over the Eastern wind; *Raphael* over the Western; *Gabriel* over the Northern; *Nariel*, who by some is called *Uriel*, is over the Southern. There are also assigned to the Elements these, *viz.* to the air *Cherub*; to the water *Tharsis*; to the Earth *Ariel*; to the Fire *Seruph*, or according to *Philon*, *Nathaniel*. Now every one of these Spirits is a great Prince, and hath much power and freedome in the dominion of his own planets, and signs, and in their times, years, months, daies, and hours, and in their Elements, and parts of the world, and winds. And every one of them rules over many legions; and after the same manner amongst evill spirits, there are four which as most potent Kings are set over the rest, according to the four parts of the world, whose names are these, *viz. Urieus*, King of the East; *Amaymon*, King of the South; *Paymon*, King of the West;

Egin, King of the North, which the Hebrew Doctors perhaps call more rightly thus, *Samuel, Azazel, Azael, Mahazuel*, under whom many other rule as princes of legions, and rulers; also there are innumerable Demons of private offices. Moreover the ancient *Theologians* of the Greeks reckon up six Demons, which they call Telchines, others Alastores; which bearing ill will to men, taking up water out of the river *Styx* with their hand, sprinkle it upon the earth, whence follow Calamities, plagues, and famines; and these are said to be *Acteus, Megalezius, Ormenus, Lycus, Nicon, Mimon*. But he which desires to know exactly the distinct names, offices, places, and times of Angels, and evill Demons, let him enquire into the book of *Rabbi Simon* of the Temples. And in his book of lights, and in his treatise of the greatness of stature, and in the treatise of the Temples of *Rabbi Ishmael*, and in almost all the Commentaries of his book of formation, and he shall finde it written at large concerning them.

Chapter x.[206]

Of the bonds of spirits, and of their adjurations, and castings out

The bonds by which spirits are bound, besought, or cast out, are three; Some of them are taken from the elementall world, as when we adjure a spirit by any inferiour and naturall things of affinity with or adverse to them, in as much as we would call upon or cast them out, as by flowers, and herbs, by animals, by snow, by ice, by hell, by fire, and such like, as these also are oftimes mixed with Divine praises, and blessings, and consecrations, as appears in the song of the three Children, and in the *Psalm*, Praise ye the Lord from the heavens, and in the consecration and blessing of the *Paschal taper*. This bond doth work upon the spirits by an apprehensive vertue under the account of love, or hatred, in as much as the spirits are present with or favour, or abhor anything that is naturall or against nature, as these things themselves love or hate one the other. Hence that of *Proclus*, As the Lion fears a cock, especially a white cock: so doth a spirit

[206] Chapters i. to ix. in this section correspond to chapters xvi. to xxiv in the *Third Book of Occult Philosophy*. This Chapter x. corresponds to Chapter xxxiii. in the same book.

appearing in the form of a lion vanish away at the sight of a cock. The second bond is taken from the Celestial world, *viz*: when we adjure them by the heaven, by Stars, by their motions, rayes, light, beauty, clearness, excellency, fortitude, influence, and wonders, and such like: and this bond works upon spirits by way of admonition, and example. It hath also some Command, especially upon the ministring spirits, and those who are of the lowest orders. The third bond is from the Intellectual and divine world, which is perfected by religion, that is to say, when we swear by the sacraments, by the miracles, by the divine names, by the sacred Seals and other mysteries of Religion; wherefore this bond is the highest of all and the strongest, working upon the spirits by Command and power; But this is to be observed, that as after the universal providence, there is a particular one; and after the universal soul, particular soules; so in the first place we Invocate by the superior bonds, and by the names and powers which rule the things, then by the inferior, and the things themselves; We must know further, that by these bonds not only Spirits, but also all creatures are bound, as Tempests, burnings, flouds [floods], plagues, diseases, force of armes, and every animal, by assuming them, either by the manner of Adjuration, or by the way of deprecation or benediction, as in the charming of Serpents, besides the naturall and celestiall, by rehearsing out of the mysteries and Religion, the curse of the Serpent in terrestriall Paradise, the lifting up of the Serpent in the wilderness; moreover by assuming that verse of the Psalm 91. Thou shalt walk upon the Aspe and the Basiliske, and shalt tread upon the Lion and Dragon: Superstition also very much prevaileth in these, by the translating of some Sacramental rites to that which we Intend to bind or hinder, as, of Excommunication, burial or exequies for the driving away of diseases, Serpents, Mice or Wormes, which thing we read to have bin thus done in divers places, and it is wont to be done even as yet.

Chapter XI.[207]

By what wayes the Magicians and Necromancers do think they can call forth the souls of the dead

By the things which have been already spoken, it is manifest that souls after death do as yet love their body which they left, as those souls do whose bodies want a due buriall: or have left their bodies by violent death, and as yet wander about their carkasses [carcasses] in a troubled and moist spirit, being as it were allured by something that hath an affinity with them; the means being known by that which in times past they were joyned to their body, they may easily be called forth & allured by the like vapours, liquors and savours, certain artificiall lights being also used, songs, sounds and such like, which do move the imaginative and spirituall Harmony of the soul; also sacred invocations, and such like, which belong to Religion, ought not to be neglected, by reason of the portion of the rationall soul, which is above nature: So the witch is said to have called up *Samuel*, and the *Thessalian* prophetesse in *Lucan*, to have caused a carcasse to stand upright: Hence we read in Poets, and those who relate these things, that the souls of the dead cannot be called up without blood and a carkasse [carcass]: but their shadowes to be easily allured by the fumigations of these things; eggs being also used, and milk, honey, oil, wine, water, flowre [flour], as it were yeelding a fit medicine for the souls to reassume their bodies, as you may see in *Homer*, where *Circe* at large instructeth *Ulysses*; yet they think, that these things can be done in those places only where these kinds of souls are known to be most conversant, either by reason of some affinity, as their dead body alluring them, or by reason of some affection imprinted in their life, drawing the soul itself to certain places, or by reason of some hellish nature of the place; and therefore fit for the punishing or purging of souls: places of this kind are best known by the meeting of nocturnall visions and incursions, and such like Phantasmes; Some are sufficiently known by themselves, as buriall places and places of execution, and where publike [public] slaughters have lately been made, or where the carkasses [carasses] of the slain, not as yet expiated, nor rightly buried, were some few yeers since put into the ground; for expiation and exorcisation of any place, and also the holy right of buriall being duely perfomed to the bodies, oftentimes

[207] Corresponds to chapter xlii.

prohibiteth the souls themselves to come up, and driveth them farther off the places of judgement; Hence *Necromancy* hath its name, because it worketh on the bodies of the dead, and giveth answers by the ghosts and apparitions of the dead, and subterrany spirits, alluring them into the carkasses [carcasses] of the dead, by certain hellish charms, and infernall invocations, and by deadly sacrifices, and wicked oblations; such we read in *Lucan* of *Erichthone* the witch, who called up the dead, who foretold to *Sextus Pompey* all the events of the *Pharsalian* War: There were also in *Phigalia* a city of *Arcadia*, certain magicians, priests most skilful in sacred rites, & raisers up of the souls of the dead: and the holy scriptures testifie, that a certain woman, a witch called up *Samuels* soul: even so truely the souls of the saints do love their bodies, and hear mote readily there, where the pledges of their reliques [relics] are preserved: but there are two kinds of Necromancy, the one called *Necromancy*, raising the carkasses [carcasses], which is not done without blood. The other *Sciomancy*, in which the calling up of the shadow only sufficeth: to conclude, it worketh all its experiments by the carkases [carcasses] of the slain, and their bones and members, and what is from them, because there is in these things a spirituall power friendly to them. Therefore they easily allure the flowing down of wicked spirits, being by reason of the similitude and propriety very familiar: by whom the *Necromancer* strengthened by their help can do very much in humane and terrestriall things, and kindle unlawfull lusts, cause dreams, diseases, hatred and such like passions, to which also they can confer the powers of these souls, which as yet being involved in a moist and turbid spirit, and wandering about their cast bodies, can do the same things that the wicked spirits commit; seeing therefore they experimentally find, that the wicked and impure souls violently plucked from their bodies, and of men not expiated, and wanting buriall, do stay about their carcases, and are drawn to them by affinity, the witches easily abuse them for the effecting of their witchcrafts, alluring these unhappy souls by the apposition of their body or by the taking of some part thereof, and compelling them by their devillish charmes, by entreating them by the deformed carkases dispersed through the wide fields, and the wandering shadowes of those that want burials, and by the ghosts sent back from *Acheron*, and the guests of hell, whom untimely death hath precipitated into Hell; and by the horrible desires of the damned, and proud devils revengers of wickednesses. But he which would restore the souls truely to their bodies, must first know what is the proper nature of the soul from whence it went forth, with how many and how great degrees of perfection it is replenished, with what intelligence it is strengthened, by what means diffused into the body, by what harmony it shall be compacted with it; what affinity it hath with God, with the intelligences, with the heavens, elements, and all other things whose image and resemblance it holdeth. To conclude, by what influences the body may be knit together again for the raising of the dead, requireth all these things which belong not to men but to God only, and to whom he will communicate them, as to *Elisha* who raised up the son of the *Shunamite*; so also *Alcestis* is reported to have been raised by *Hercules*, and to have lived long after; and *Apollonius Tyanens* is restored a dead maid to life. And here is to be noted that sometimes it happeneth to men, that their vivifying spirit is retracted in them, and they appear as dead and without sense, when as yet the intellectuall nature remaineth united to the body, and it hath the same form, and remaineth the same body, although the power of vivifying extendeth not it self into it actually, but remaineth retracted in the union with the intellectual nature; yet it ceaseth not to be; and although that man may truly be said to be dead, inasmuch as death is a want of a vivifying spirit, yet is it not truly separated; and that body can be wakened again and live; and thus many miracles appear in these; and of this kind many have been seen amongst the Gentiles and Jewes in former ages, in the number of which is that which *Plato* reciteth in his tenth book de *Republ.* [Republic], *viz.* that one *Phereus* of *Pamphilia* lay ten dayes amongst the slain in battle, and after that he had been taken away and laid to the fire two dayes, he revived and told many wonderfull things which he had seen in the time of his death; and concerning these things we have spoken partly in the first book, and shall yet speak further anon where we shall speak of Oracles, which come forth in a Rapture, Extasie [ecstasy], and in the Agony of dying men.

Isagoge:

An Introductory Discourse on the Nature of Spirits

ISAGOGE:

An Introductory Diſcourſe of the nature of ſuch Spirits as are exerciſed in the ſublunary Bounds; their Original, Names, Offices, Illuſions, Power, Propheſies, Miracles; and how they may be expelled and driven away.

By *Geo. Pictorius Villinganus* Dr. in Phyſick.

In a Diſcourſe between

CASTOR and POLLUX.

Castor. The *Greeks* do report, that *Castor & Pollux have both proceeded from one egge*; but this I scarcely credit, by reason of the difference of your mindes; for thou affectest the heavens, but he meditates upon the earth and slaughters.

Pollux. And from thence perhaps was derived that argument, *That liberty of lying was alwaies assigned to the Greeks.*

Castor. Principally.

Pollux. But it is not to be supposed, that the *Greeks* are vain in all things; but as many others, when they speak out of a three-footed thing; whereof also the Poet *Ovid* speaks in verse,

Nec fingunt omnia Græci.[208]

Castor. In this provorb I protest they are most true, without any exception, that is, αντρωπος αντρωπον δαιμονιον[209]; that is, One man to another is a devil.[210]

Pollux. Wherefore believest thou this to be most true, *Castor*?

Castor. Truely, that man to man is a devil and a ravening wolf, daily events do most certainly prove, if we do but note the treacheries that one man invents daily against another, the robberies, thefts, plunderings, rapes, slaughters, deceits, adulteries, and an hundred vipers of this nature; the fathers persecute the son, with a serpentine and poisonous biting; one friend seeks to devour another, neither can the guest be safe with his host.

Pollux. I confess it is truth thou speakest; but for ought I hear, thou dost mis understand the Etymologie of the word compared in this Proverb; for *Dæmon* here is not an horrible or odious name, but the name of one that doth administer help or succor unto another, and whom *Pliny* calleth a God.

Castor. Therefore dost thou affirm the word *Dæmon* in this Proverb to signifie any other then a cunning and malicious accuser?

Pollux. Thou hast not shot besides the mark: for, that there are more *Dæmons* then that sublunary one which thou understandest, every one may easily perceive, who hath not negligently read the opinions of the most excellent *Plato*.

Castor. I desire therefore, that thou wouldst not conceal such his writings; but that I may apprehend the marrow thereof.

---

208 "The Greeks do not invent everything."

209 "Antropos antropon daimonion."

210 The reader, who followed attentively the Introduction, can consider well the semantic difficulties in the use of the Greek phrase, an on the interpretation proposed by "Castor" (daimonion = devil). Pictorius, in the voice of Pollux, will in the following dialogue discuss the etymology given.

Pollux. I will embrace such thy desire, for truely I do delight to treat with thee concerning this subject; mark therefore, and give attention. *Plato* divided the orders of Devils or Spirits into three, which as they are distinct in the greatness of their dignity, so also they are different in the distance and holding of their places. And the first order he ascribeth to those Spirits whose bodies are nourished of the most pure element of Air, wrought and joyned together, in a manner, as it were of Spirits, with splendid threeds , not having so much reference to the element of fire, that they may be perspicuous to the fight; neither do they so much participate of the earth, that they may be touched or felt; and they do inhabit the Coelestial Theater, attending and waiting on their Prince, not to be declared by any humane tongue, or beyond the commands of the most wise God.

But the other degree is derived from those Spirits which *Apuleius* termeth rational animals, passive in their minde, and eternal in their time, understanding the apostate Spirits spread abroad from the bounds and borders of the Moon, unto us under the dominion of their Prince *Beelzebub*, which before the fall of Lucifer had pure clarified bodies; and now, like unto the former, do wander up and down, after their transgression, in the form of an aiery quality.

Castor. These I do not conceive are understood in the *Greek* Proverb: for these do hurt, and are the accusers and betrayers of men. But proceed.

Pollux. The third degree of Spirits is of a divine deitie, which is called by *Hermes*, A divine miracle to man, if he do not degenerate from the Kingly habit of his first form; whom therefore of this kinde *Greek* and *Plato* have called *Dæmons*, that is, God; and that man may be like unto God, and profitable and commodious one to another; and so also (the *Syrian* being witness) we have known Plato himself to have been called *Dæmon*, because he had set forth very many things of very high matters, for the good of the Commonwealth; and so likewise Aristotle, because he very largely disputed of sublunaries, and all such things as are subject to motion and sence. *Homer* calleth God and evil Spirits, Dæmons, without putting a discrimination.

Castor. Thou hast committed the ship to the waves, *Pollux*; therefore cease not to proceed, and declare something more concerning the Office and imployment of these Spirits, to whom *Plato* attributeth the second degree, and calleth them Lunaries.

Pollux. What shall I say?

Castor. In the first place, declare wherefore thou hast before termed these Spirits cunning and much knowing Accusers.

Pollux. Saint *Augustine* unfoldeth this difficulty, and saith, That *a Devil doth so far signife the cunning and much knowing quickness and vivacity of his deceitful wit, that by the congruent and agreeable seminal permixtures of elements, he doth so know the secrets and unknown vertues of men, as those things which may be effected and wrought by themselves successively and leisurely according to the course of nature, he by a speedy hasting or forcing of the work of nature, or by his own art, sooner bringeth the same to pass*. An example hereof he giveth in the wise men of *Pharaoh*, who immediately brought forth frogs and serpents at the commandment of the King, which nature more slowly and leisurely procreateth.

Castor. Thou hast excellently answered to the question, *Pollux*; but adde some thing concerning the original of those Spirits which do refute and refuse vertue; for often times doubting, I have been persuaded that such Erynnes as are from God, do not appear out of the earth.

Pollux. The Ecclesiastical Scripture everywhere maketh mention of the rising of them; but I will unfold such a doubt: and there do arise many and various opinions of writers, but more commonly *Peter Lombardus* in his book of Sentences, draweth his Allegations out of St. *Augustine* upon *Genesis*; to wit, That *the Divel was before his fall an Archangel and had a fine tender body, composed by God, cut of the serenity and purest matter of the Skie and Air; but then after his fall from an Archangel, he was made an Apostate, and his body no more fine and subtil; but his body was made that it might suffer the effect of a more gross substance from the quality of the more obscure and dark and spissious Air, which body also was stricken and astonished with the raging madness of pride, did draw away very many which were then Angels with him into his service and bondage, that they might be made Devils, who for him in this troublesome world do exercise their servile courses for him, and they do compel the inhabitants therein, or rather entice them; and to this purpose they undertake various endeavours, and do attempt various and manifold horrible studies, that are abominable unto God , and they serve in slavery and thraldom to* Beelzebub *their Prince, and are held in most strong captivity.*

Castor. What? Have we the fall of this Archangel nowhere else in holy writ, but in the writings of St. *Augustine*?

Pollux. We have also the fall of other Angels.

Castor. Where?

Pollux. In *Esaias*,[211] to whom thou shalt give the honour of an Evangelist, rather then a Prophet, because he so fully and plainly foretold of Christ and his kingdom: he maketh mention hereof in his 14 Chapter. And we have them also spoken of by the Apostle *Peter*, when he saith, *God spared not his Angels which sinned.* 2 Epist. 2.

Castor. Have the Devils a select place appointed them by God, which they inhabit?

Pollux. *Peter* the head of the Church, in the place before quoted, affirmeth *them to be cast headlong into hell, reserved in the the chains of hell, from whence* (as Cortesius saith) *they never go out, unless it be to tempt, provoke and delude men.* But St. *Augustine* the Champion of Christ, in his book of *The Agony of a Christian*, teacheth, That *these kinde of Spirits do inhabit in the sublunary region.* And in his 49 Epist. he sets forth, That *the most dark and obscure part of the Air, is predestinated unto them at as a prison, that they may the more nearly cast their nets of enticing and detaining.*

Castor. *Origen* hath taught, That *the punishments of the Devils are appointed for a time;* what saist thou to this?

Pollux. What shall I say? unless I should bewail and deplore the opinion of so great a man.

Castor. Wherefore shouldst thou do so?

Pollux. Truely if they have hardened themselves in wickedness, time cannot purge nor cleanse them; or if they never so much desire it, they can never be able to accomplish it; for there is no space of repentance, nor time to recal that which is past, given unto them.

Castor. Thou hast now declared that the Archangel that became an apostate, did draw away very many other Angels with him in his fall, that they might become Devils: could not he of his own proper inseparate malice after his fall sufficiently rule over his own Province, without the Angels that fell with him?

Pollux. He could: but being allured by that pride, which made him

---

[211] It is very interesting to compare the forthcoming comments on the use of Isaiah in the argument about angels with the texts from the *Discoverie of Witchcraft*.

so arrogantly affect the Majesty of God, he did so far strive to be like unto God, that he chose very many Ministers unto himfelf, to which in general he doth not commit all things he would have effected but diverse things to divers Ministers, as may be gathered from the *Hebrew* Astronomers. Those which we call *Jovii*, & *Antemeridianii*, which are false Gods, that is, lyers, which desire to be esteemed and adored for Gods and they are appointed as Servants and slaves to the Devil their Prince, that they might allure the people of the earth into a common love of themselves, which *Plato* saith, *Is the fountain of all wickedness, that they may aspire to authority and greatness, covet to be gorgeously clothed, to be called Monarchs of the earth in perpetual power, and Gods upon earth.* It is said, That it was one of these that spoke to our Saviour, shewing him all the Kingdoms of the earth, saying, *All these things will I give thee, if thou wilt fall down and worship me.*

Castor. Certainly these *Meridianii*, I have almost declared to appear a madness in *Libicus*, *Sappho*, and *Dioclesian* the Emperour, who accounted, the utmost degree of blessedness was, to be reputed for Gods.

Pollux. Truely, this is a certain natural foolishness of the minde, and of humane nature: he began, having taken certain birds to teach them by little and little to pronounce humane words, & say μεγας Θεος Ψαφον, that is, *Sapho is a great God.* Which birds when they could pronounce the words perfectly, he sent them abroad for this end and purpose, that flying everywhere abroad, they might repeat those words; and the people which were ignorant of his deceitful invention, were drawn to believe, that those words were spoken by divine instinct, and thereupon adore and worship him for a God. The other would compel his Subjects hereunto, that prostrating themselves down, and lifting up their hands, they should worship him as Almighty.

Castor. But are not they the captives of the Devil, who stir up wars, which are called *bloody men* in Scripture?[212]

Pollux. The Martialists of the North part of the world are called Executioners of vengeance, Authors of devastations, and sowers of evil, working and executing judgement with *Asmodeus*, for their King *Abaddon* or *Apollyon*, whom St. *John* in his Revelation, mentioned to be banished and expelled; for these Spirits have committed to them rapines, hatred, envy, robberies, wrath, anger, the excitements and provocations to sin, war and fury; sometimes making the Meridional Spirits their Messengers.

[212] Psalm 55:23.

And *Arioch* the Spirit of vengeance, whose work is to cause discord among brethren, to break wedlock, and dissolve conjugal love, that is impossible to be renewed; of these mention is made in the 39 Chapter of *Ecclesiasticus*. And *Esaias* the heavenly Prophet speaketh of other Spirits sent from God to the *Ægyptians* to make them erre, which were Spirits of darkness, that is, of lyes; and this kinde of Spirit they call *Bolichim*.

Castor. Is unlawful venery, and excessive gluttony, also to be imputed to the Devils?

Pollux. Yes chiefly; for *Iamblichus* doth assert, That *the Spirits of the water, of the western part of the world, and some meridional Spirits, are predestinated to this purpose; such as* Nesrach *and* Kellen*, that do so frame and contrive unlawful loves, which produce shame and dishonesty, revellings and gurmandizings, surfetings with excissive drunkenness, wanton dances, gluttony and vomiting: they wander about lakes, fish-ponds and rivers, and which are the worst, foul and most fraudulent kinde of Spirits: and by* Alcinach *an occidental Spirit, he causeth shipwracks, tempests, earthquakes, hail , rain, and frequently subverteth and overturneth ships: and if he will appear visible, he appeareth and is seen in the shape of a woman.* The *Hebrew* Astronomers before spoken of, do say, That *the Spirits of the Air do cause thunders, lightnings and thunderbolts, that so they might corrupt and infect Air, and produce pestilence and destruction.* Of such kinde of Spirits St. *John* makes mention in the 9 Chapter of the Revelation, having *Meceris* for their tutelar, which is a Spirit causing heat in the time of noon. St. *Paul* calleth him, *The Prince of the power of the Air,* and *the Spirit that ruleth the children of disobedience.*

Castor. Are there so many monsters in *Phlegeton, Pollux?*

Pollux. And many more; for the fame *Hebrew* Assertors do declare and maintain, That *there are Spirits of the fiery element, raging about like the fierce Panthers, which are conversant under the lunary regions, that whatsoever is committed to them, they forthwith execute the same. And there are Spirits of the earth, which inhabit in groves, woods and wildernesses, and are the plague and mischief of hunters, and sometimes they frequent open fields, endeavouring to seduce travellers and passengers out of their right way, or to deceive them with false and wicked illusions; or else they seek to afflict men with a hurtful melancholy, to make them furious or mad, that they may hurt them, and sometimes almost kill them. The chief of these are* Sanyaab *and* Achimael*, which are oriental Spirits, a kinde unapt for wickedness, by reason of the constancy of their dispositions. There are also subterranean Spirits, which do inhabit in dens and caverns of the earth, and in remote concavities of mountaines, that they might invade deep pits, and the bowels of the earth; these do dig up metals, and keep treasures which* *oftentimes they do transport from one place to another, lest any man should make use thereof: they stir up windes with flashing flames of fire: they smite the foundations of buildings, acting frightful daunces in the night, from which they suddenly vanish away, with making a noise and sounds of bells, thereby causing fear in the beholders; and sometimes dissembling, and faining themselves to be the Souls of the dead: notwithstanding they are ignorant in compassing their deceits upon women; of which company the* Negromancers do say, is *Gazael, Fegor and Anarazol, Meridian Spirits.*

Castor. How warily ought a man to walk, *Pollux*, amongst so many ginnes and snares?

Pollux. A man never walketh safely, unless he fortifie and strengthen himfelf with the armour of God, which is, *That his loynes be girt about with truth, and having on the brest-plate of righteousness, let him walk with his feet shod with the preparation of the Gosspel of peace, and let him take the shield of faith, and the helmet of salvation, whereby he shall dash in peices all the darts of his adversary*. But hear further: There are also besides these, other lying Spirits (although they are all lyers) yet these are more apt to lye; they are called *Pythons*, from whence *Apollo* is called *Pythius*. They have a Prince, of whom mention is made in the book of the *Kings*, where it is said, *I will be a lying Spirit in the mouth of all thy Prophets*; from whom the Spirits of iniquity do but a little differ, which also are called vessels of wrath. *Belial*, whom they have interpreted to be without any equal, and *Paul* calleth him an Apostate or transgressor, is filthily inservient for the worst inventions. *Plato* affirmeth *Theut* to have been such a one, who was the first that found out and invented Playes and Dice:[213] to whom we will joyne the Monk, who invented the use of Gunpowder, in his Engins of war. Of these *Jacob* makes mention in *Genesis*, where he blesseth his Sons: he saith, *Simeon and Levi are bloody vessels of iniquity; Oh my soul, come not thou into their counsels*. The Psalmist termeth these Spirits, *vessels of death*; *Esaias* calleth them, *vessels of fury*; *Jeremiah*, *vessels of wrath*; and *Ezekiel* calleth them, *vessels of death and destruction*. The Negromancers do call the said *Belial, Chodar, an oriental Spirit, which hath under him also the Spirits of juglers, who do imitate and endeavour to act miracles, that they may seduce false* Magicians *and wicked persons*. It is apparently manifest, that the Serpent which deceived *Eve*, was such a seducer, and *Satan* is his Prince, of whom it is spoken in the *Revelation*, that *he should deceive the whole world*. And such a one was he, that at *Tubinga*, in the sight of many people devoured a whole Chariot and some horses.

[213] Compare with the text previously seen in Agrippa's Chapter iii: *Of the orders of evil spirits, and of their fall, and divers natures.*

Castor. And what shall be the end of these false Prophets, and workers of wickedness? I can scarce believe that there is any angle or corner in the whole fabrick of the world, that is free from them.

Pollux. Scarce the smallest mite that may be seen.

Castor. Therefore dost thou truely call the world the receptacle of those false lights.

Pollux. If it were not most safely purged with the Sword of the word of God, it would forthwith be worse.

Castor. Without doubt.

Pollux. Nevertheless I have seen many that remain, whom I have not yet inscribed in this frantique Catalogue.

Castor. Who are they?

Pollux. False accusers and spies, obedient to *Astaroth*, who is called a Devil among the *Greeks*; and *John* calleth him the accuser of the brethren. Also there are tempters and deceivers that lie in wait to deceive, who are present with every man, and these we term evil Angels, which have *Mammon* for their King, & they do affect men with an insatiable avarice & thirsty desire after authority and dominion. There are others *Lucifugi*, which fly from the light, never appearing in the day, but delighting in darkness, maliciously vexing and troubling men, and sometimes by Gods permission, either by some touching, breathing or inspiration, do hurt to them; but truely they are a kind which are unapt for to do much wickedness, because they eschew & fly from any communication with men. *Pliny* the second relates, that *there was such a one at* Athens, *in a certain spacious house which* Anthenodorus *the Philosopher happened to purchase.* And *Suetonius* in his sixth book of *Cæsar*, makes mention of another to have long continued in the garden of *Lamianus*.

Castor. I desire, if it be not too irksome to thee, declare unto me what *Pliny* speaketh concerning this Spirit of *Anthenodorus*.

Pollux. The story is something long and prolixious, yet it shall not much trouble me to relate it. It is thus: *Pliny* in the seventh book of his *Epistles* writeth, *Of a certain large spacious house at Athens, which no body would inhabit by reason of the nocturnal incursions of Spirit, which were so* *formidable to the inhabitants, that sometimes in the day-time, and when they were watching, they would cast them into dreams, so alwayes, that the shapes & forms which they then saw, were ever present in their memory. Where at length a certain Philosopher named Anthenodorus happened to purchase that house, and prepared and furnished the same for himself to dwell in; and because all men had an evil suspition of that house, he forthwith commanded his servants to provide him a bed and tables, that after he had completed and finished his study he might go to bed. He therefore* (saith Pliny) *when he went in (in the evening) and applied himself to his study, suddenly heard the locks to shake open, and the chains to be moved; nevertheless he did not lift up his eyes, nor stirred from his book, but slopped his ears with his fingers, lest that furious tumult might work a vain fear upon him; but the noise still approaching neerer unto him, at length he looked up, and saw an effigies like unto a finger beckoning and calling unto him, which he little regarded, until it had touched him three times, and the noise drew neer unto the table; and then he looked up, and took a light, and beheld the Spirit, as it were an old man, worn away with withered leaness and deformity, his beard hanging down long, horrible and deformed hair, his legs and feet were as it were laden with chains and fetters: he went towards a gate which was bolted, and there left the Philosopher, and vanished away.*

Castor. What fearful things thou relatest *Pollux*, but what was the event of this sad spectacle?

Pollux. The next day he related the whole matter to the Magistrates in order, as he had seen the same, admonishing them that they should dig diligently about the threshold of the door; for there it was probable they might finde something, which might cause the house to be quiet and habitable.

Castor. What did they finde?

Pollux. Having digged up the earth, *Pliny* saith, *they found a dead carcass, bound and intangled in chains and fetters, his flesh being consumed with devouring time, which without delay they caused to be buried, according to the Christian ceremonies.* [214]

Castor. But this being performed, did the house afterwards become quiet and habitable?

Pollux. Yes, very well.

[214] Hardly, as the story happened before the rise of Christianity.

Castor. What madness therefore possesseth them who prophane and destroy Church-yards, where the sacred Organs of the holy and blessed do rest; and do give the bones of the dead for meat to the Spirit *Zazelus*,[215] of whom mention is made in the 3 of the Kings; and we read in *Pausanias*, amongst the Histories of *Delphos*, that he was called *Eurynomus*.

Pollux. Thou shalt finde, that the Governours of Cities that were of the opinion and judgement of Christians, did subvert, destroy and prophane these holy places, that herein the youth might dance their mocking interludes, after the furious sound of the drum or taber, and sing, *Io pean*; or, there the poor inferiour old women did sell base trumpery or lupines, which God would have to be purged with holy prayers, for the salvation of souls, or breaking of bread to the hungry.

Castor. But it is an impious and heathenish thing so to have touched the anointed of God.

Pollux. And worse then heathenish; for the heathens did esteem the Rites and Ceremonies of burials, as *Elpinor* is witness in *Homer*, where he yeildeth up his life; and in *Homer* he speaketh to *Ulysses*, *I intreat thee, O Ulysses, to be mindeful of me, and not depart away hence and leave me uninterred, left that, not being ritely buried, I shall be made the wrath of the Gods*. And *Archita* the Philosopher in *Flaccus*, thus speaketh to the Mariner:

What marvel, then, that when the Southern gale,
Co-mate of swift Orion, rent the sail,
I drank the Illyrian wave? But listen now:
To grant my slender boon omit not thou!
Take of the boundless sand around thee spread,
And cast it over my yet unburied head;
So may Hesperia's waves still bear thee free;
Venusium's pines divert the penalty
Of Eurus and his blast! large profit speed
Thy course, and recompense thy pious deed!
So may Jove aid thee and Tarentum's lord!
Dost thou refuse? then, sailor, heed my word:
A well-earned retribution, if it light
Not on thyself, thy children shall requite.

---

[215] According to Donald Tyson, the mention is wrong and the name does not appear in the Scriptures. *Three Books of Occult Philosophy*. Ed. Donald Tyson.

Deem not thy guilt no penal scourge incurs;
Refuse, and not a shrine thy life ensures:
Thou art in haste: I know it, thou sayest well;
Thrice cast the dust upon me, and farewell. [216]

And *Palinurus* to *Æneas* in the sixth book of *Virgils Æneids:*

And now, by winds and waves, my lifeless limbs are tossed:
Which O avert, by yon ethereal light,
Which I have lost for this eternal night!
Or, if by dearer ties you may be won,
By your dead sire, and by your living son,
Redeem from this reproach my wandering ghost.[217]

Castor. Have the *Gentiles* so greatly esteemed the ceremony of burials?

Pollux. Yes, very much; for their Religion did hold that the the Soul of a body which was uninterred, was void of any intelligible essence, and left to the power and command of a raging furious phansie, and subject to the torment and affliction of corporal qualities; so that it being an aiery body, sometimes the departed shadow would speak unto his remaining friends, and somtimes evilly vex and torment his enemies with revenge, as in the Poet, *Dido* threatneth *Æneas*, saying:

Omnibus umbra locis adero dabis improbe penas.[218]

Suetonius, as we have shown before, addeth the like concerning the dead body of C. *Caligula* the Emperour in the Garden of *Lamianus*, being not duly buried; for this body, because it was onely covered with a light turff, did very much disquiet and trouble the possessors of the Garden, with violent incursions in the night; until by his sisters, who were returned from banishment, it was taken up again and ritely and duly by them buried.

---

[216] *Horace: the Odes, Epodes, Satires, and Epistles*: Translated by the Most Eminent English Scholars and Poets, Including Ben Jonson, Milton, Dryden, Addison, Lytton, Conington, Calverley, Sir Theodore Martin, &c.

[217] Vergil (70 B.C.–19 B.C.). *Æneid*. The Harvard Classics. 1909–14. *The Sixth Book of the Æneis.*

[218] "Everywhere my shadow will be, you will pay the penalty". *Aeneid*. Book IV, verse 386.

Castor. And the house wherein the same Emperour died, could by no other way or means be freed from the fury of these shadows or Spirits, as History makes mention, but by burning thereof.

Pollux. *Aristotle* speaking of miracles, mentioneth a certain mountain in *Norway*, named *Hechelberg*, environed about with the Sea, that continually sent forth suich lamentable voices, like the yelling & howling of infernal devils, insomuch that the noise & clamour of their terrible roaring might be heard almost a mile; and the flocking together of great Ravens and Vultures neer it, did prohibit any access thereunto. And he reporteth that in *Lyppora* neer about the *Æolian* islands there was a certain Hill from whence in the night there was heard Cymbals, and sounds of tinkling instruments of brass, with certain secret & hidden screechings, laughings and roarings of Spirits. But even now, *Castor*, thou dist make mention of *Zazelus*, whom also thou didst assert to have been called *Eurynomus* by *Pausania*; I desire thee to shew me something more largely concerning this Spirit.

Castor. They do declare that he lives altogether by the flesh of the dead: so as sometimes he doth not leave the bones.

Pollux. The *Saxon* Grammarians, in the fifth book of the *Danish History*, most truely subscribe their consents and agreements to this thy Assertion; for there they set before our eyes an admirable History of one *Asuitus* and *Asmundus*, which easily proveth all thy sayings.

Castor. I beseech thee declare this unto me, *Pollux*.

Pollux. Give attention; it is thus: *Asuitus* and *Asmundus* had sworn with mutual vows each to other, that he which should live longest of them, would entomb himself alive. Now sickness did consume away *Asuitus* before *Asmundus*; whereupon *Asmundus* for his Oath of friendship sake, with his dog & his horse entombed himself alive in a vast deep den, having carried with him some meat, whereupon a longtime he fed. And at length *Ericus* the King of *Suecia* came into that place with an Army, and broke open the tombe of *Asuitus*; (supposing there had been treasure hid therein) but when the cave was opened, he drew out *Asmundus*, and brought him into the light, who was covered with a deformed sharp countenance, a deadly deformity, and gored with blood flowing from his fresh wounds.

Castor. But this story pertaineth not to our purpose.

Pollux. Truely it doth, if you diligently mark these verses, which set forth the cause of his wounds

Castor. Shew me these verses, if thou hast them.

Pollux. They are these which follow:[219]

"Why stand ye aghast, who see me colourless? Surely every live man fades among the dead. By some strange enterprise of the power of hell the spirit of Aswid was sent up from the nether world, and with cruel tooth eats the fleet-footed (horse), and has given his dog to his abominable jaws. Not sated with devouring the horse or hound, he soon turned his swift nails upon me, tearing my cheek and taking off my ear. Hence the hideous sight of my slashed countenance, the blood-spurts in the ugly wound. Yet the bringer of horrors did it not unscathed; for soon I cut off his head with my steel, and impaled his guilty carcase with a stake

Castor. I observe here, that Asmundus did cut the head of the Spirit *Zazelus* or *Eurynomus*, and struck and pierced his body with a club; what? have Spirits bodies, that may be seen and handled by men?

Pollux. *Cortesius* doth not deny, but that their natures may receive the habit and covering of vegetable bodies, and be transformed in several kindes of shapes, whereby they can the more craftily and subtilly delude and deceive the improvident wits of men. *Basilius Magnus* also testifieth the same, and witnesseth, that they have bodies appropriate to themselves, as likewise also have the pure Angels, *Psellus* a Necromancer doth also report the same; and he also teacheth That sometimes they sleep or rest, and do change their places, and shew themselves visible to the sences of men. *Socrates* asserted, That a Spirit did speak with him, which also sometimes he saw and felt; but their bodies cannot be discerned to be different in sex. But *Marcus Cherronesus*, an excellent teacher into the natures of Spirits, writeth, That they have simple bodies & that there doth belong a difference of sex to compound bodies; yet their bodies are easily drawn to motion and flexibility, and naturally apt to receive every configuration. For, saith he, *even as the clouds do shew forth the apparition and resemblance sometimes of men, and sometimes of every thing yon conceive; so likewise do the bodies of Spirits receive various shapes as they please, by reason whereof they transforme themselves into the forms sometimes of men, and sometimes of women. Nevertheless this is not free*

---

[219] As the original was in Latin, I substituted it with the version found in the "Online Medieval and Classical Library": *The Danish History*, Books I-IX, Book Five, Part II.

to them all, but onely to the fiery and aiery Spirits, For he teacheth, That the Spirits of the water have more slow and less active bodies, which by reason of the slowness and softness of that element, they do most especially resemble birds and women; of which kinde the *Naiades* and *Nereides* are, celebrated by the Poets. *Trimetius*[220] testifies, That *the Devils do desire to assume the shapes of men rather then any other form; but when they cannot finde the matter of the air convenient and befitting for that purpose.* And he saith, That *they frame such kinde of apparences to themselves, as the contrary humour or vapour will afford; and so they are seen sometimes in the form and shape of a Lion, a Wolfe, a Sow, an Ass, a Centaure, of a Man horned, having feet like a Goat*: such as it is reported were seen in the mountain of *Thrungia*, where there was heard a terrible roaring.

Castor. *Porphyrus* in *Eusebius*, in his fourth book of *Evangelical Preparations*, teacheth, *That some of these are good Spirits, and some bad*; but I have counted them to be all evil, *Pollux*.

Pollux. Then it seemeth that thou art not seduced with the assertions either of *Porphyrus*, or *Apuleius*, or *Proclus*, or of some other Plantonicks, which are mentioned in St. *Augustines* book of *The City of God*, 1, 2, and 3 Chapter, who also affirm that there are some of these Spirits good; for *Eusebius* in the said book and 6 Chapter; and St Augustine concerning the same in his book of *The City of God*, the 9 Chapter and the 8, with very great and strong Arguments do convince the Platonicks, that none of these *Dæmons* are good, but all evil; and that we do also approve of from their names, which are every where set forth in holy Scripture; for the Devil is called *Diabolus*, that is, flowing downwards: that he which swelling with pride, determined to reign in high places, fell flowing downwards to the lowest parts, like the torrent of a violent stream, as *Cassiodorus* writeth. And he is called *Sathan*, that is, an adversary; who as St. *Jerome* testifieth, by reason of the corruption of his own malice, he continually resisteth, and is an adversary against God, who is the chiefest good. He is called *Behemoth* in the 40 Chapter of Job, which signifieth an Ox; for even as an Ox desireth hay, so he with the teeth of his suggestions, coveteth to destroy the upright lives of spiritual men. And *Leviathan* in the same place, which signifies an addition, because the Devil alwaies endeavours to adde evil to evil, and punishment to punisgment. He is also called in *Revelation* 15. *Apollyon*, signifying a rooter out, for he rooteth out the vertues which God planteth

[220] Donald Tyson indicated that this reference is for Trithemius who, says he, wrote on this point in his brief treatise "Octo Quaestionum Maximiliani Cesaris". *Three Books of Occult Philosophy*. Ed. Donald Tyson.

in the Soul. He is called a *Serpent* in the 12 of the *Revelation*, by reason of his virulency. A *Lion* in the 1 Epist. *Peter* and the last Chapter, which roareth about seeking whom he may devour. He is called a cunning Workman *Isa.* 55. because by his malice the vessels that are elected and approved. He is called, Isa. 34. *Onocentaurus Erynus, Pilosus, Syren, Lamia, Ulula, Struthio.* And by David in the 90 Psal. an *Aspe, Basiliske* and *Dragon.* In the Gospel *Mammon*, the Prince of this world, and Ruler of darkness.

Castor. Why therefore have the Divines declared, That the Almighty hath given two kindes of Spirits unto men; the one good, the keeper and preserver of their lives, the other evil, resisting the good: if they are all evil?

Pollux. The holy Doctors do understand by the good Spirit a good Angel, such as we read *Raphael* was to *Tobias*, who bound the the evil Spirit *Asmodeus* in the wilderness of the furthest parts of Egypt, that he might be the more safe.

Castor. It had been more safe for every man to have been without the evil Spirits; what therefore was the will of the heavenly Father concerning them?

Pollux. That by the assistance of the good Spirits, we might couragiously wage continual war against the evil Spirits; but being clothed with the harness of righteousness, like valiant souldiers we may gird our loyns with truth, and with the sheild of faith resist and fight against all his darts.

Castor. If we condescend unto this warfare of Spirits, it seemeth good to inquire whether the Devils have power of doing hurt, granted unto them by God; or whether of themselves they can hurt as much as they please?

Pollux. If the last were true, who could compare the end of their hurting? but it is very manifest, that their authority from on high is of so great existency, that *John* the Evangelist doubteth not to name the Devils the Princes of the Earth.

Castor. In what manner therefore do they hurt?

Pollux. Although they be most mighty and powerful Spirits, yet they can do no hurt unless it be by permission; or, as *Damascenus* saith,

By dispensation. And *Chrysostome* saith, *They have a limited power; for truely without the will of God, they cannot touch a hair of any mans head*. The Devil could not have deceived the Prophets of *Ahab*, if he had not received power from God; neither could he have brought any detriment upon *Job*, either unto his body or his goods, but by the power God had given him. In the 7 *Exodus* the Magicians made Frogs and Serpents by the power of the Devil permissively; but Lice they could not bring forth, by reason of the greater power of God prohibiting them. Neither in the Gospel could the Devils hurt the Swine until Christ had given them leave.

Castor. Therefore the Devil is not so much to be feared, but the Lord our God, that either he would not suffer him to rage against us; or if at any time by his own determinate counsel he let loose his chains, that then he would defend and mercifully preserve us.

Pollux. Thou saiest well; for even as a wilde boare is not to be feared if he be bound, and held with a strong chain by a powerful strong man, and who is able by his strength to restrain the fierceness of the boare; but the man is to be feared, and requested, that he would not let loose the boare: So also *Satan* is not to be feared, being bound with the cords of the Almighty; but the Almighty rather, who holdeth him with a cord, lest at any time he should let loose his cord, for to execute his will against us.

Castor. We know that the Devils, after incarnation of the Word, were called the Lords of the earth; but I wonder, where the Word is not yet incarnate, whether they have power also over men.

Pollux. If it pleaseth God, they have very much; but take a demonstration thereof, *Castor*, from the *Caldeans*, amongst whom the Devil raged with so much power and dominion, that they made no esteem of the true God, but worshipped the elements. There needeth not a demonstration of the *Greeks*; for the fury of the Devil did so much reign amongst them that by his Arguments, they accounted *Saturn* for a very great God, devouring their own proper Children; and *Jupiter*, an adulterer and father of all filthiness, they named to be the father of Gods and men; *Bacchus*, the most wicked example of all servitude and bondage, they called a free father; Venus a strumpet, they termed a pure virgin; and they worshipped *Flora* an harlot, as a type or example of virginity. There is no man that is ignorant, that the *Egyptians* have been worse then the *Greeks*, when they made peculiar Gods to themselves, by the inanimate persuations of the Devil; for one worshipped a sheep, another a goat, another a calfe, very many did worship hoggs, crows, hawkes, vultures, eagles, crocodiles, cats, dogs, wolves, aspes, dragons; and things growing also, as onyons, garlick, and thornes; as every one that is covetous of reading, shall finde in *Damascenus*, in his History *Josaphat* and *Barlaas*, and in *Eusebius*, in the fourth Book and first Chapter of *Evangelical Preparations*; neither do I account the *Hebrews* (who glory in being the offspring of their father *Abraham*) to have been better then the former, when also by the instinct of the devil, after their coming up out of *Egypt*, with cruel hands they violently assaulted the Prophets and holy men of God, whom at length they also slew: that I may hold my peace, how diligently they have brought into their Religion the Gods, or rather Devils of the *Gentiles*.

Castor. I perceive by these thy assertions, that one Devil, and another Devil, hath been adored for Gods; for thou hast now said, That the *Greeks*, by the madness wherewith the Devil possessed them, have made unto themselves, *Saturn, Jupiter, Bacchus, Venus, and Flora*, for Gods; which *Lactantius* in his fourth book *De vera Sapientia*, also accounteth for Devils.

Pollux. Declare, I pray, thee the words of *Lactantius*.

Castor. Mark them; they are thus: *The same Devils are the gods of the Gentiles; but if any one will not believe these things of me; then let htm credit* Homer, *who joyneth the great Jupiter to the great Devils;*[221] *and the other Poets and Philosophers do call them sometimes Gods and sometimes Devils whereof there is one true and another false: for the most wicked Spirits when they are conjured, do confess themselves to be Devils; but where they are worshipped, they declare themselves to be Gods, that they may thrust men into errors, and draw them from the worship of the true God, through whom alone eternal death can be escaped.*

Pollux. It is expedient for me now to be more inquisitive in this discourse; whether there be power given to the Devils to foretell things to come? concerning which thing hitherto I have not been able to dart at the right mark; for this question seemeth sufficiently doubtful unto me.

Castor. St. *Augustine* in his book *De Natura Dæmonum,*[222] dissolveth

---

[221] With the usual Christian dishonesty, the excerpt here attributed to Lactantius plays on the fact that Homer used the word "daimon" to Zeus, in a time and context when, as we saw in the Introduction, the word had not yet acquired the meaning Christians gave to it.

[222] I agree with Donald Tyson that the work the author had in mind was probably the *De Divinatione Dæmonum*, as there is no text by Augustine with that name, and the

this *Gordoneus* knot, and saith, That *the damned Spirits, being filled full of all manner of impiety and wickedness, do sometimes challenge to themselves power of foreseeing things to come; because in the sense of their Aiery bodies, they have a far more strong and prevalent power of fore-knowing, then men of earthly bodies can have; or because of the incomparable swiftness of their aiery bodies, which wonderfully exceedeth not onely the celerity of men and wilde beasts, but also the flying of birds: by which means, they are able to declare things long before they come to be known; which we, by reason of the earthly slowness of our sense, cease not to wonder at and admire: or because of the benefit of their continual life, they obtain this wonderful experience of things; which we cannot attain to because of the shortness of our momentaneous life, which is but as it were a bubble.*

Pollux. This last assertion of S. *Augustine* seemeth unto me to be more true then the rest, because the Series of many yeers doth cause great experience.

Castor. If any one shall deny these opinions of Augustine, as erroneous, *Damascenus* setteth a greater witness of these things, without all exception, before our eyes; who in his second book of *Orthodox Faith* saith thus: *That the devils cannot foreknow things to come, for that belongs onely Unto God: but so much as they are able to know, they have from the disposition of the celestial and inferiour bodies.*

Pollux. Why therefore do the devils so willingly and of their own accord undertake Prophecies, and to answer Oracles? What benefit have they from hence?

Castor. Nothing, but that hereby they seek to get great estimation, and covet to be counted worthy of admiration, and to be adored in stead of Gods.

Pollux. We know that the devil is the father of lyes, *Castor*: from whence we are piously to believe, that those things which he foretelleth, he extracteth from his own lyes.

Castor. Furthermore, the Prophet *Esaias* saith thus: Shew the things that are to come hereafter, and tell us, that we may know that ye are gods. And the Apostle *Peter* also saith, *The prophecie came not in old time by the will of man, but holy men of God spoke as they were moved by the holy Ghost.*

---

description given matches the subjects of the known work. The *De Natura Dæmonum* was published later (1581) by one Laurentius Ananias, as we see in *Satan's Rhetoric: A Study of Renaissance Demonology*, by Armando Maggi.

Pollux. No man therefore will deny that they do sometimes foretel things to come.

Castor. No man, certainly: but for what cause that is attained to, *Chrysostome* doth most clearly teach, in these words: *It is granted, he saith, that sometimes the devil doth speak truth, that he might commend his own lying with rare verity: whereas, if he should never tell the truth, he could deceive no man, neither would his lying suffice him to tempt with.* Thus far *Chrysostome.* Notwithstanding, if he understand that he hath not grace granted unto him of himself to foretel the truth, he foretelleth things nevertheless, but so obscurely, saith S. *Augustine, that he always layeth the blame of the things by him so foretold, upon the interpreter thereof. Porphyrius*, in his book of Oracles, although he be the greatest maintainer of devils, and the most expert teacher of diabolical Arts, nevertheless he saith with the aforesaid Doctors, that *the foreknowledge of things to come, is not onely intricate to men, but also uncertain to the gods; and full of many obscurities.*

Pollux. Thou hast said, that the predictions of the devils are done in this maner, that they may gain authority to themselves amongst the credulous people, and be worshipped instead of Gods: for what end do the evil spirits work Miracles?

Castor. What is a Miracle, *Pollux*?

Pollux. A new and unwonted accident, which cometh to pass contrary to its course and custome, and draweth men into admiration thereof.

Castor. But do they work Miracles?

Pollux. They do: for whereby dost thou believe that *Æsculapius* was honoured in his Consecration for a god, but onely by the means of a Miracle, when he conveyed a Serpent from *Epidaurus* to Rome? What gave so great authority to *Juno*, but onely the working of a Miracle? when her Image of wood was asked by *Furius Camillus* whether it would be carried to *Rome*, and it answered with a humane voice, *It would.* Also, from thence *Fortune* was made a goddess, because her Statua, in the way to *Lassium*, in the hearing of many people, not once, but oftentimes spoke with a humane voice. In the 8 Chapter of the *Acts* of the Apostles, we read of Miracles done by Simon the son of Rachel; and in *Exod.* 8. of the Magicians of Pharaoh, who in the sight of many people brought forth frogs and serpents, and turned the waters into blood. *Apuleius* doth testifie the power of men to be so great in Inchantments, that the devils do not onely work Miracles by the means of men, but they are able also to subvert Nature, and with a Demoniacal Incantation, make violent streams to stay their course, To turn the windes, To make the sun stand still, To break the course of the moon, To lay impediments upon the stars, To prolong the day, and to shorten the night; as *Lucanus* excellently sheweth.

All things on earth
Change at their bidding; night usurps the day;
The heavens disobey their wonted laws;
At that dread hymn the Universe stands still[223]

And *Tibullus* of a certain Demoniacal Charm,

Her spells call forth pale spectres from their graves,
And charm bare bones from smoking pyres away:
Mid trooping ghosts with fearful shriek she raves,
Then sprinkles with new milk, and holds at bay.
She has the power to scatter tempests rude,
And snows in summer at her whisper fall. [224]

Castor. I do not any more wonder that Moses called God *Wonderful*, that he doth so connive at this sink of wickedness, and most wicked seducers, that he granteth them power to act such things so freely.

Pollux. *Firmianus* excellently sheweth why God doth so, in his last book but one of the works of God, *De opificio Dei*: for he saith, that vertue is not vertue, unless it have some like, in ruling whereof it may shew and exercise its power: for he saith, *As Victory cannot stand without Vertue, so neither can Virtue subsist without an Enemy; which virtue no sooner had the Almighty inbued man withal, but he forthwith added unto him an enemy, lest that vertue should lose its nature, being stupified with idleness. He saith, that a man cannot otherwise attain to the highest step, unless he have always an active hand; and that hand he shall establish and build up his salvation with a continual warfare and contention: for God will not that mortal men shall come to immortal blessedness with an easie Journey, but he must wrestle and strive with sayls and oars against the author and inventor of all evils and errours, who causeth and worketh execrable things and miracles.*

Castor. But sometimes it cometh to pass, that by reason of the

[223] Project Gutenberg's *Pharsalia; Dramatic Episodes of the Civil Wars*, by Lucan

[224] *The Elegies of Tibullus in English Verse.* Theodore C. Williams.

subtil snares and stratagems of the devil, which he so craftily prepareth against us, and especially against simple persons, whom he intangleth with vain Religions, so that we cannot resist him; or if we suppose our selves to be every able to withstand him, yet nevertheless we shall be very much deceived by him; as we read he oftentimes did to the good, but almost foolish Pastor, of whom *Tritemius* maketh mention.

Pollux. But what happened to this good Pastor, and whom thou termest simple?

Castor. *Tritemius* saith, *Insomuch that he was not strong in faith, therefore he made more account of the name of Saint* Blaze, *and attributed more power and custody unto it, then unto the name of* God, *the best and greatest good.*

Pollux. In what manner?

Castor. He had in his walking-staff, or Pastoral Crook, a Schedule inscribed with the name of St. *Blaze*; by the power and vertue of which staff, he did believe his swine were safely defended from the ravening of the wolves: and he did attribute so great a Deity to that Schedule, that he would leave his herd of swine to feed in the fields alone: notwithstanding, a certain time coming when the pastor was absent from his flock, and a certain man coming in the mean time, saw the devil keeping them; and he asked him what he kept here, who is the worst persecutor of the salvation of men? He answered, *I keep these swine.* The other replied, *By whose command?* The devil saith, *By the foolish confidence of the pastor: for he included a certain Schedule in his staff, unto which he ascribeth divine vertue, or to the inscripiton of the name of* St. Blaze; *and now, contrary to his own law, he beliveth that his hogs are thereby defended from the injury of wolves; inhering to me with a false superstition; where when he hath been by me called again and again, and hath not appeared, I have taken this custody upon myself in stead of* St. Blaze: *for I always freely stand instead of* God *and his Saints: so also now most freely do I keep his swine for* St. Blaze, *that J may magnifie and confirm the foolish man in his vain confidence; and thereby I may seduce him so, that he may esteem of this Schedule more then* God.

Pollux. This is a pleasant story: but I do not wonder that the devil should impose so much upon so simple a Pastor, when he doth in many things prevail over the more wise, if they do at themselves to his opportunities; which the Church contradicteth.

Pollux. But are all things wrought and brought to pass by means of the devil which men call Miracles?

Castor. No: for we must give unto Nature that which seemeth to belong unto her, who is said to be the greatest worker of Miracles; as that which we have experienced in the stone *Asbestos*, which, as *Solinus* witnesseth, being once set on fire, cannot be quenched: and the root *Baara*, described by *Josephus* in the history of *Jerusalem*, which he testifieth to be of the colour of a flame of fire, splendent and shining in the night; but so difficult to be taken, that it always flies from under the hand of him that would take it, and deceiveth his eyes so long, until it be sprinkled with the urine of a menstruous woman: and when it is retained by this means, it may not be gathered or plucked up without danger; for present death followeth him that gathereth or plucketh it up, unless he shall be fortified with a Preservative about his neck, of the same root. For which cause, they who want the same root, do scarifie it round about; and having bound the root about with a bond, they tie the same to a dog, and suddenly depart away. Whereupon, the dog, too much endeavouring to follow after him, draweth up the root; and, as if the dog were to perform the turn of his master, he forthwith dies; and afterwards the same root may be taken and handled without any danger to any man. And the same *Josephus* teacheth, that the same root is of such present force for expiations, that also those who are vexed and tormented with unclean spirits are immediately delivered, if they carry this root about them. Notwithstanding there is nothing hindereth, but that Art also may imitate Nature in the working of Miracles, as we may read in *Aristotle*, of the Greek fire that would burn in water: of which the said Author, in his singular Treatise concerning this, hath described very many compositions. And concerning the fire which is extinguished with oyl, and kindled with cold water, when it is besprinkled over therewith.

Pollux. It sometimes happeneth that the devils do clothe themselves, sometimes in more slender, and sometimes in more gross habits, that thereby they may very much affright and molest men with horrible phantasies, and terrible fights; with Ghosts appearing in divers and several shapes and aspects. What, cannot we be fortified with any thing to force and compel them to flie from us?

Castor. *Origen*, in his book against *Celsus*, saith, that there is no way more certain, then the naming of JESUS the true God. For he saith he hath oftentimes seen innumerable spirits so driven away, both from the souls and bodies of men. St. *Athanasius*, in his book *de variis Quastion*, testifieth, that the most present remedy against the insultation of evil spirits, is the beginning of the 67 *Psalm*, *Let God arise, and let his enemies be scattered*. *Cyprian*, in his book *Quod idola di non sint*, commandeth that the devils should be conjured away by the true God. Some men have declared, that Fire, which is the most holy of all elements, and the Creed, and also the instrument whereon the fire was carried, were very profitable for this purpose: from whence, in their sacrifices about the sepulchres of the dead, they diligently observed the use of lights: or else from thence that *Pythagoras* did determine, that God could be in no wise truely worshipped without lights burning. Some others do binde swords for this intent and purpose, taking the same out of the II Ode of *Homer*, where he writeth, that *Ulysses*, when he offered a sacrifice to his mother, had a sword drawn present by him, wherewith he expelled and drove away the spirits from the blood of his sacrifice. And in the sixth of *Virgil*, when the Sybil led *Æneas* into hell, she saith thus

Procul, O procul este profani,
Tuque invade viam, vaginaque, eripe ferrum [225]

Philostratus writeth, that he compelled *Apollonius*, a spirit, obvious to him and his companions, to flight, with contumelies and direful imprecations; that the vision making a noise, and with great horrour vanished away from them. Very many do much commend a Perfume of Calamint, Piony, Mint, Palma Christi, and Parley, to be used in this case. Many do keep present with them Red Coral, Mugwort, Hypericon, Rue, or Vervin, for this purpose. Some do use for this bussiness the tinkling of keys, sounding of consecrated bells, or the terrible ratling of Armour.

Pollux. I have sometimes heard from our Elders, that they made them Sigils inscribed with Pentagones; by virtue whereof, the spirits might be expelled and driven away. What sayst thou to these?

Castor. *Averrois* writing against *Algazelus*, affirmeth such things to be almost nothing worth, unless to them that have confederated with the spirits. If therefore *Averrois* saith the truth, how then can the devils kingdom stand, divided against itself?

Pollux. But we read that *Solomon*, a singular man with God, did make such Sigils.

Castor. We do read truely that *Solomon* did make them; but it was

[225] Donald Tyson offers the following translation, also referring to the use of this phrase in the opening of the sacred mysteries: “Away, O, away, ye unintiated / Cries the prophetess, withdraw wholly from the sacred grove! /And you, seize the path, and snatch your sword from its sheath.” *The Three Books of Occult Philosophy*. Ed. Donald Tyson.

at such time when he worshipped Idols, and not when he was in the state of salvation. *Tertullian* offereth a more certain Antidote then all the former, and exhorteth us, as *Job*, the most strong champion of God, to fight against all the assaults of temptations: he admonisheth us to be clothed with the silken garment of Honesty, the purple robe of Modesty and Shamefacedness, and the cloak of Patience: and he perswadeth us to meditate upon all those things which the devil doth devise and invent, to overthrow our integrity; that his falling may be proved the glory of our constancy, and that we be willing constantly to war against all machinations, which are permitted by God for this end. And the Prophet *Jeremiah* teacheth the same, in these words: *The Lord of hosts is the approver of the just.*

D. *Maximus*, in his book *de charitate*, commandeth us to binde and kill the devils. He saith we do then binde them, when by diligent observation of the Commandments of God, we do diminish and quash those affections that do boyl up in us: And we are said to kill them, when we so truely mortifie our lusts, that we cut him off from all occasions of accusing; saying with the Prophet, Depart, O *homicide, the Lord the strong warriour is with me: thou shalt fall, and shall be vanquished from me for ever. Olympiadorus*, 10. *cap.* when he interpreted the Ecclesiastical history, saith, that *all sensual appetites are to be shut out, and excluded, so that the devil may not be admitted, neither by the allurements of the eyes, nor by itching ears, nor by the petulancie and forwardness of a hurtful tongue*: for this he accounteth to be the most absolute seal against the power of the devils. Some do admonish us, in our going forth to war against the devil, to use two sorts of weapons: the one is pure Prayer, which may raise up our affections unto heaven; and true and perfect Knowledge, which may communicate and fill our understandings with wholesome doctrines, and may suggest unto us what we are to pray for, that we may pray ardently, according to St. *James*, and not doubtingly. In the Prophesie of *Isaiah*, and Epistles of St. *Paul*, we may finde the same things; *Isa*. 59. *Eph*. 6. and 1 *Thess*. 5. which may be as a remedy against vain Ghosts, that they may be expelled.

Pollux. For a remedy against Ghosts? Dost thou conceive that a Ghost is diverse and different from a spirit?

Castor. I know not truely what I may think hereof: for flowing in so spacious a sea of many opinions, I am so led in doubt, that I cannot easily attain to a certain Port of judgement: for there are some which do suppose that these Ghosts are devils, by reason of the great fear and terrour wherewith they ragingly molest men by night in their houses; and sometimes for their innate nature do to hurt. There are others that do believe these Spirits are deceitful fantasies, deceiving those that are of evil belief; who by their fallacious visions and imaginations do deceive and frighten the inhabitants in their houses: and do deny that they are Spirits indeed, because the Spirits have a body without hands and feet; wherefore they can hurt no man, nor make any tumult: being ignorant that the Angel (who also hath a body without hands and feet) did carry *Habakkuk* with his whole dinner, by the hair of his head, into *Babylon*, and afterwards brought him back again, and set him in his own place; neither considering that the Spirit of the Lord, also without a body, snatched up *Philipy* and carried him to *Azotus*: that I may forbear to speak concerning a certain incorporeal Spirit, which did so disquiet the house of my Grandfather, that by the space of almost thirty yeers he caused it to be uninhabitable, unless it were when a Lamp was burning therein; neither did that then sufficiently quiet the same: for going out of the house, they did so molest them with stones from above in the streets, that they would cast out of their hands the hearts of Pinetrees, which they used for torches. Concerning the Ghost that haunted the house of *Anthenodorus* the Philosopher, and the tumultuous spirit of *C. Caligula*, there may more be spoken: but thou hast understood the relations of them already in the foregoing discourse. From all which, we may easily convince the opinions of those, who deny that the Spirits can walk, or make any motion; but of how much truth we may hold the assertions of them, who do suppose that these tumultuous Spirits are neither devils, nor phantasms, but the souls of the dead, now hearken unto.

Pollux. Are there they who are of that opinion?

Castor. There are they who are of both opinions: for they do declare that these are the souls of them who have departed from their bodies laden and clogged in their sins; which are therefore heard to be more or less turbulent in houses, according as they have any sensible ardent spark of that sin more or less; so that except in the mean time they are expelled and driven away from thence, or expiated by Alms or Intercessions, they are compelled to a certain bound of liberty, wandering thereabouts in expectation of the last Judgement.

Pollux. Wherefore?

Castor. Because I believe that the souls of them which sleep in Christ, do live with Christ, and do not wander about the earth; and the souls of them who are oppressed and burdened with the grievous weight of their sins, since they are the members of Satan, are bound with Satan in the chains of darkness, expecting judgement in hell.

Pollux. But *Firmianus*, a Writer of no mean judgement, thinketh the contrary, in his Book which he hath written *de Divino premio.*

Castor. How is that?

Pollux. These are his words: *Let not any man conceive that the souls of the dead are judged immediately after death: for they are all detained in one common custody, until the time shall come, wherein the Almighty Judge shall make examination and inquisition of their deeds. Then they who shall be found righteous, shall receive the reward of immortality; but they whose sins and wickedness shall then be detected, shal not arise again, but shall be inclosed with the wicked in darkness, and destined to eternal punishments.*

Castor. St. *Augustine* subscribeth to *Lactantius* in his *Enchiridion*, saying, *That the time which is interposed between the death of mankinde and the last resurrection, containteh the souls in secret hidden receptacles, where every soul receiveth condigne rest or misery, for the good or evil which he did in the body while he lived.*

Pollux. Neither doth St. *Ambrose* disagree from this: In his second book of *Cain* and *Abel*, he saith, *that the soul is loosed from the body, and after the end of this life, is suspended to the ambiguous time of the last judgement.*

Castor. So also some have declared, that the soul of *Trajanus Cæsar* did wander about; but the soul of St. *George* was freed from such suffrage.

Pollux. Thou hast even now spoke, and that truely, that spacious is the sea of various opinions concerning these Spirits; for so indeed it is: but what Port thou touchest at, I desire thee it may not seem troublesome to thee to tell me: for I am not as yet satisfied of the certainty hereof by our discourse.

Castor. That which thou desirest, I conceive to be this: I hold that these tumultuous Spirits are meer images of Satan; which are not to be feared, neither is there any credit to be given to their answers: and are in no wise the souls of the dead, which either live with Christ, if they have done well; or else are bound in chains with Satan, if they have done evil.

Pollux. It remaineth that we sift out this, *Castor*: for it happeneth now sometimes, that my father appeareth to me in my sleep; perhaps that may also seem unto thee to be a Spirit.

Castor. It may seem so: but I will not in any thing contradict thee beyond Reason: of my self I will adde nothing; but at leastwise I will annihilate thy opinion with the assertions of St. *Augustine*.

Pollux. What assertions are those?

Castor. In his II book, which he intituleth *De mortuorum cura* , he offereth them as a means, saying, *Humane infirmity doth so believe of himself, that when he seeth any one that is dead, in his sleep, he supposeth that he seeth the soul of that dead person; but when he drearmeth of any one that is alive, he then is out of doubt, that neither his soul nor his body, but the similitude of the man appeared unto him: As if they could be ignorant that the souls of dead men do not appear unto them in dreams, but onely the similitudes of the persons deceased.* And he proveth both these to be done, by two examples which were at *Mediolanus*; whereof the first he sheweth to have been the image of a certain father that was dead, who appeared to his son, admonishing him that he should not pay again a debt to an unjust Creditor, which the father had paid him before: for he saith the Case was thus: The father had paid a debt to a certain Creditor, which after the death of the father, the Creditor endeavoured by force to recover the same again of his son, who was ignorant of the payment thereof: to whom the image of his father appeared when he was sleeping, and shewed him where the Writing was hid. Whereupon, the son awaking from his sleep, sought for the Paper in the place he was directed, and found it, and thereby overthrew the malice of his deceitful Creditor. The second example is, whereby the same St. *Augustine* sheweth that the living do appear to the living, in their sleep: for he saith, that *Eurologius* the Rhetorician, professing the Rhetorick of *Cicero* at *Carthage*, he found a difficult and obscure place that was not declared to him; so that waking and sleeping he vexed himself by reason of his ignorance: but in a certain night, the image of *Aurelius Augustine* appeared to him, and taught him in what maner the dark and difficult place was to be understood.

Pollux. *Augustine* doth therefore conclude, without doubt, that they are not souls.

Castor. He doth so conclude: and the greater to strengthen such his judgement, he addeth, That if the souls of the dead have any interest or counsel in the affairs of the living, he undoubtedly knew, that his own pious mother did not desert him, not for one night, but when she was living, followed him both by sea and land: neither did he at any time sustain any anguish of heart, but comforted his sorrows. And that this may not seem too hard a speech, the president of Christ teacheth, that they do not erre, who affirm that the good Angels, by the appointment of God, and Divine dispensation, do sometimes come to, and visit men, both living and sleeping, and sometimes to the place where souls endure punishment: notwithstanding, it is not unto all, but onely unto those who are so lived, that God shall judge them worthy of this mercy; or unto those upon whom, without any respect unto their deserts, God will be pleased to glorifie his unspeakable mercy; that by the prayers of the living they may obtain pardon of their sins, and deliverance from the prison of torments.

Pollux. I have sometimes read, that the same St. *Augustine* did write, that it is better for a man to doubt of secret things, then to contend about things uncertain.

Castor. That is certainly true; neither doth he declare himself to be an offence to those who do leave all these things to the unsearchable judgements of God, and labour not to finde out the secrets thereof.

Pollux. Because I have easily understood thy answers hitherto, I will not desist till thou hast fully resolved me concerning this subject. I desire therefore to know whether all Miracles which the devils perform, are done really, or imaginary phantasies.

Castor. That they perform many things really, and many things onely seemingly, we have already manifested out of the Writings of St. *Augustine*. For that great Prelate of the Christian Church, writeth, in the II Chapter of his book *de Trinitate*, That *it is a very easie thing for the wicked Spirits, through the aery substance of their bodies, to perform many things which seem wonderful (to the souls that are oppressed with earthly bodies) to be done.* He also saith, *That earthly bodies may be so qualifed with art and exercise, that in publike Theaters they may perform such wonderful things, that those who never have seen them will not believe them, but that they were done by the assistance of the devil and his ministers, to make their bodies of such an aery element, that the flesh wonders at.* Or else, which is much, he saith also, That *they do contrive with occult inspirations, forms, and fantasies of images, to delude humane sense; wherewith, waking or sleeping, they may be deceived.* Thus far *Augustine*. But, if thou wilt, I will produce also another witness without exception, *Pollux*.

Pollux. I would have thee tell me who that is.

Castor. *Abbas Tritemius*, in his third Question to St. *Maximus Emilianus*, which is spoken of before, saieth thus: *The devils, amongst unfaithful people, do see to raise up the dead to life, and to shew miracles to* *curious men, that they might as it were swallow them up with error in stead of miracles; and are altogether pertinacious and obstinate: but they cannot truely and really raise up the dead, but do variously deceive the senses of men, shewing them feigned resemblances of the dead. For it is certainly manifest, that the devils can do all things, but onely in a false similitude of holy miracles in truth.*

Pollux. Some say that the devils are obedient to wicked men, because of the similitude of their malice. How seemeth that to thee?

Castor. It seemeth to me, that they are obedient to evil men, but not to all men.

Pollux. But to whom?

Castor. To those certainly with whom they have contracted and made compacts and covenants; as those women which they call *Pythonists* are accounted, who have vowed themselves by promise unto him.

Pollux. But although they are compelled to be so serviceable unto them, yet is this service true or feigned?

Castor. It is feigned, certainly: for they are subservient unto men of their own accord, and genuine work, that they may deceive them, and allure them to themselves. Although we do not deny that their service is sometimes true, but onely towards those men, whose faith in the Lord Jesus Christ, by the merit of his holiness, hath caused them to be acceptable, and friends unto him. And that *Lactantius* also testifies, in these words, in his second book *De origine Erroris*, and 16 Chapter, That the devils do fear the just, that is, those that worship God, in whose Name they are conjured to depart out of bodies, and with whose words they are beaten as it were with scourges: and they do not onely confess that they are devils, but do declare their names: neither can they lye unto the just. And the same *Lactantius* in his fourth book *De vera Sapientia*, Chap. 27. saith, That it is necessary that they who are of the true Christian Religion, should know the course and order of the devils, and understand their subtilty, and restrain their force, and conquer and subdue them with spiritual weapons, and force them to obey him.

Pollux. I am now by thee sufficiently informed of all things which I have hitherto desired to know; wherefore I shall not any further trouble thee with my Questions, or rather Riddles, but leave thee to thy own occasions.

Castor. Neither have I counted my self idle in answering thee: but let the use thereof yeeld us each to other an equal recompence. Farewel therefore.

Pollux. And thee also.

A Discourse upon Divels and Spirits

A Discourse upon divels and spirits, and first of philosophers opinions, also the maner of their reasoning hereupon; and the same confuted.

The first Chapter.

THERE is no question nor theme (saith *Hierome Cardane*) so difficult to deale in, nor so noble an argument to dispute upon, as this of divels and spirits. For that being confessed or doubted of, the eternitie of the soule is either affirmed or denied. The heathen philosophers reson hereof amongest themselves in this sort. First, they that mainteine the perpetuitie of the soule, saie that if the soule died with the bodie; to what end should men take paines either to live well or die well, when no reward for vertue nor punishment for vice insueth after this life, the which otherwise they might spend in ease and securitie? The other sort saie that vertue and honestie is to be pursued, *Non spe præmii, sed virtutis amore*, that is, Not for hope of reward, but for love of vertue. If the soule live ever (saie the other) the least portion of life is here. And therefore we that mainteine the perpetuitie of the soule, may be of the better comfort and courage, to susteine with more constancie the losse of children, yea and the losse of life it selfe: whereas, if the soule were mortall, all our hope and felicitie were to be placed in this life, which manie Atheists (I warrant you) at this daie doo. But both the one and the other missed the cushion. For, to doo anie thing without Christ, is to wearie our selves in vaine; sith in him onelie our corruptions are purged. And therefore the follie of the Gentils, that place *Summum bonum* in the felicitie of the bodie, or in the happines or pleasures of the mind, is not onelie to be derided, but also abhorred. For, both our bodies and minds are intermedled with most miserable calamities: and therefore therin cannot consist perfect felicitie.

But in the word of God is exhibited and offered unto us that hope which is most certeine, absolute, sound & sincere, not to be answered or denied by the judgement of philosophers themselves. For they that preferre temperance before all other things as *Summum bonum*, must needs see it to be but a witnesse of their naturall calamitie, corruption and wickednes; and that it serveth for nothing, but to restraine the dissolutenes, which hath place in their minds infected with vices; which are to be bridled with such corrections: yea and the best of them all faileth in some point of modestie. Wherefore serveth our philosophers prudence, but to provide for their owne follie and miserie; whereby they might else be utterlie overthrown?' And if their nature were not intangled in errors, they should have no need of such circumspection. The justice whereof they speake, serveth but to keepe them from ravine, theft, and violence: and yet none of them all are so just, but that the verie best and uprightest of them fall into great infirmities, both dooing and suffering much wrong and injurie. And what is their fortitude, but to arme them to endure miserie, greefe, danger, and death it selfe? But what happinesse or goodnesse is to be reposed in that life, which must be waited upon with such calamities, and finallie must have the helpe of death to finish it? I saie, if it be so miserable, why doo they place *Summum bonum* therein? S. *Paule* to the *Romans* sheweth, that it cannot be that we should atteine to justice, through the morall and natural actions and duties of this life: bicause that never the Jewes nor the Gentiles could expresse so much in their lives, as the verie lawe of nature or of *Moses* required. And therefore he that worketh without Christ, doth as he that reckoneth without his host.

The second Chapter.

Mine owne opinion concerning this argument,
to the disproofe of some writers hereupon.

FOR my part doo also thinke this argument, about the nature & substance of divels and spirits, to be so difficult, as I am persuaded that no one author hath in anie certeine or perfect sort hitherto written thereof. In which respect I can neither allow the ungodly and prophane sects and doctrines of the *Sadduces* & *Peripatetiks*, who denie that there are any divels or spirits at all; nor the fond & superstitious treatises of *Plato, Proclus, Plotinus, Porphyrie*; nor yet the vaine & absurd opinions of *Psellus, Nider, Sprenger, Cumanus, Bodin, Michael, Andræas, Janus Matthæus, Laurentius Ananias, Iamblichus, &c*: who with manie others write so ridiculouslie in these matters, as if they were babes fraied with bugges; some affirming that the soules of the dead become spirits, the good to be angels, the bad to be divels; some that spirits or divels are onelie in this life; some, that they are men; some, that they are women; some, that divels are of such gender as they list themselves; some, that they had no beginning, nor shall have ending, as the *Manicheis* mainteine; some, that they are mortall & die, as *Plutarch* affirmeth of *Pan*; some, that they have no bodies at all, but receive bodies, according to their phantasies & imaginations; some, that their bodies are given unto them; some, that they make themselves. Some saie they are wind; some that they are the breath of living creatures; some, that one of them begat another; some, that they were created of the least part of the masse, whereof the earth was made; and some, that they are substances betweene God and man, and that of them some are terrestriall, some celestiall, some waterie, some airie, some fierie, some starrie, and some of each and everie part of the elements, and that they know our thoughts, and carrie our good works and praiers to God, and returne his benefits backe unto us, and that they are to be worshipped: wherein they meete and agree jumpe with the papists; as if you read the notes upon the second chapter to the *Collossians*, the Seminaries testament printed at *Rhemes*, you shall manifestlie see, though as contrarie to the word of God as blacke to white, as appeareth in the *Apocalypse*, where the angell expresselie forbad *John* to worship him.

Againe, some saie that they are meane betwixt terrestriall and celestiall bodies, communicating part of each nature; and that although they be eternall, yet that they are mooved with affections: and as there are birds in the aire, fishes in the water, and wormes in the earth; so in the fourth element, which is the fier, is the habitation of spirits and divels. And least we should thinke them idle, they saie they have charge over men, and governement in all countries and nations. Some saie that they are onelie imaginations in the mind of man. *Tertullian* saith they are birds, and flie faster than anie fowle of the aire. Some saie that divels are not, but when they are sent; and therefore are called evill angels. Some thinke that the divell sendeth his angels abrode, and he himselfe maketh his continuall abode in hell, his mansion place.

The third Chapter.

The Opinion of Psellus touching spirits, of their severall orders, and a confutation of his errors therein.

PSELLUS being of authoritie in the church of *Rome*, and not impugnable by anie catholike, being also instructed in these supernaturall or rather diabolicall matters by a monke called *Marcus*, who had beene familiarlie conversant a long time, as he said, with a certeine divell, reporteth upon the same divels owne word, which must needs understand best the state of this question, that the bodies of angels and divels consist not now of all one element, though perhaps it were otherwise before the fall of *Lucifer*; and that the bodies of spirits and divels can feele and be felt, doo hurt and be hurt: in so much as they lament when they are stricken; and being put to the fier are burnt, and yet that they themselves burne continuallie, in such sort as they leave ashes behind them in places where they have beene; as manifest triall thereof hath beene (if he saie truelie) in the borders of *Italie*. He also saith upon like credit and assurance, that divels and spirits doo avoid and shed from out of their bodies, such seed or nature, as whereby certeine vermine are ingendered; and that they are nourished with food, as we are, saving that they receive it not into their mouthes, but sucke it up into their bodies, in such sort as sponges soke up water. Also he saith they have names, shapes, and dwelling places, as indeed they have, though not in temporall and corporall sort.

Furthermore, he saith, that there are six principall kind of divels, which are not onelie corporall, but temporall and worldlie. The first sort consist of fier, wandering in the region neere to the moone, but have no power to go into the moone. The second sort consisting of aire, have their habitation more lowe and neere unto us: these (saith he) are proud and great boasters, verie wise and deceitfull, and when they come downe are seene shining with streames of fier at their taile. He saith that these are commonlie conjured up to make images laugh, and lamps burne of their owne accord; and that in *Assyria* they use much to prophesie in a bason of water. Which kind of incantation is usuall among our conjurors: but it is here commonlie performed in a pitcher or pot of water; or else in a violl of glasse filled with water, wherin they say at the first a litle sound is heard without a voice, which is a token of the divels comming. Anon the water seemeth to be troubled, and then there are heard small voices, wherewith they give their answers, speaking so softlie as no man can well heare them: bicause (saith *Cardane*) they would not be argued or rebuked of lies. But this I have else-where more largelie described and confuted. The third sort of divels *Psellus* saith are earthlie; the fourth waterie, or of the sea; the fift under the earth; the sixt sort are *Lucifugi*, that is, such as delight in darkenes, & are scant indued with sense, and so dull, as they can scarse be moved with charmes or conjurations.

The same man saith, that some divels are woorse than other, but yet that they all hate God, and are enimies to man. But the woorser moitie of divels are *Aquei*, *Subterranei*, and *Lucifugi*; that is, waterie, under the earth, and shunners of light: bicause (saith he) these hurt not the soules of men, but destroie mens bodies like mad and ravening beasts, molesting both the inward and outward parts thereof. *Aquei* are they that raise tempests, and drowne seafaring men, and doo all other mischeefes on the water. *Subterranei* and *Lucifugi* enter into the bowels of men, and torment them that they possesse with the phrensie, and the falling evill.[226] They also assault them that are miners or pioners, which use to worke in deepe and darke holes under the earth. Such divels as are earthie and aierie, he saith enter by subtiltie into the minds of men, to deceive them, provoking men to absurd and unlawfull affections.

But herein his philosophie is verie unprobable, for if the divell be earthie, he must needs be palpable; if he be palpable, he must needs kill them into whose bodies he entereth. Item, if he be of earth created, then must he also be visible and untransformable in that point: for Gods creation cannot be annihilated by the creature. So as, though it were granted, that they might adde to their substance matter and forme, &c: yet is it most certeine, that they cannot diminish or alter the substance whereof they consist, as not to be (when they list) spirituall, or to relinquish and leave earth, water, fier, aier, or this and that element whereof they are created. But howsoever they imagine of water, aier, or fier, I am sure earth must alwaies be visible and palpable; yea, and aier must alwaies be invisible, and fier must be hot, and water must be moist. And of these three latter bodies, speciallie of water and aier, no forme nor shape can be exhibited to mortall eies naturallie, or by the power of anie creature.

The fourth Chapter.

More absurd assertions of Psellus and such others, concerning the actions and passions of spirits, his definition of them, and of his experience therein.

MOREOVER, the same author saith, that spirits whisper in our minds, and yet not speaking so lowd, as our eares may heare them: but in such sort as our soules speake together when they are dissolved; making an example by lowd speaking a farre off, and a comparison of soft whispering neere hand, so as the divell entreth so neere to the mind as the eare need not heare him; and that everie part of a divell or spirit seeth, heareth, and speaketh, &c. But herein I will beleeve *Paule* better than *Psellus*, or his monke, or the moonks divell. For *Paule* saith; If the whole bodie were an eie, where were hearing? If the whole bodie were hearing, where were smelling, &c. Whereby you may see what accord is betwixt Gods word and witchmongers. [227].

[226] Epilepsy.

[227] Witchmonger. (a) Those who dealt with witches, as with wise women. (b) Those who sought them out for punishment (from the Glossary at the end of this edition of the *Discoverie*).

The papists proceed in this matter, and saie, that these spirits use great knaverie and unspeakeable bawderie in the breech and middle parts of man and woman, by tickeling, and by other lecherous devises; so that they fall jumpe in judgement and opinion, though verie erroniouslie, with the foresaid *Psellus*, of whose doctrine also this is a parcell; to wit, that these divels hurt not cattell for the hate they beare unto them, but for love of their naturall and temperate heate and moisture, being brought up in deepe, drie and cold places: marie they hate the heate of the sun and the fier, bicause that kind of heate drieth too fast. They throwe downe stones upon men, but the blowes thereof doo no harme to them whome they hit; because they are not cast with anie force: for (saith he) the divels have little and small strength, so as these stones doo nothing but fraie and terrifie men, as scarecrowes doo birds out of the corne feelds. But when these divels enter into the pores, than doo they raise woonderfull tumults in the bodie and mind of man. And if it be a subterrene divell, it dooth writh and bow the possessed, and speaketh by him, using the spirit of the patient as his instrument. But he saith, that when *Lucifugus* possesseth a man, he maketh him dumbe, and as it were dead: and these be they that are cast out (saith he) onelie by fasting and praier.

The same *Psellus*, with his mates *Bodin*[228] and the penners of M. *Mal.*[229] and others, doo find fault with the physicians that affirme such infirmities to be cureable with diet, and not by inchantments; saieng, that physicians doo onlie attend upon the bodie, & that which is perceiveable by outward sense; and that as touching this kind of divine philosophie, they have no skill at all. And to make divels and spirits seeme yet more corporall and terrene, he saith that certeine divels are belonging to certeine countries, and speake the languages of the same countries, and none other; some the *Assyrian*, some the *Chaldæan*, & some the *Persian* toong, and that they feele stripes, and feare hurt, and speciallie the dint of the sword(in which respect conjurors have swords with them in their circles, to terrifie them) and that they change shapes, even as suddenlie as men doo change colour with blushing, feare, anger, and other

[228] "Jean Bodin (1530–1596) was a French jurist and political philosopher, member of the Parlement of Paris and professor of law in Toulouse. He is best known for his theory of sovereignty; he was also an influential writer on demonology. Bodin's major work on sorcery and the witchcraft persecutions (*De la démonomanie des sorciers*) was first issued in 1580, ten editions being published by 1604. In it he elaborates the influential concept of "pact witchcraft" based on a deal with the Devil." *Jean Bodin*. Wikipedia.

[229] "The *Malleus Maleficarum* (commonly rendered into English as "Hammer of the Witches", is a treatise on the prosecution of witches, written in 1486 by Heinrich Kramer, a German Catholic clergyman. The book was first published in Speyer, Germany, in 1487. Jacob Sprenger is also often attributed as an author, but some scholars now believe that he became associated with the *Malleus Maleficarum* largely as a result of Kramer's wish to lend his book as much official authority as possible." *Malleus Maleficarum*. Wikipedia.

moods of the mind. He saith yet further, that there be brute beasts among them, and yet divels, and subject to anie kind of death; insomuch as they are so foolish, as they may be compared to flies, fleas, and wormes, who have no respect to any thing but their food, not regarding or remembring the hole from out of whence they came last. Marrie divels compounded of earth, cannot often transforme themselves, but abide in some one shape, such as they best like, and most delight in; to wit, in the shape of birds or women: and therefore the Greeks call them *Neidas*, *Nereidas*, and *Dreidas* in the feminine gender; which *Dreidæ* inhabited (as some write) the ilands beside *Scotland* called *Druidæ*, which by that meanes had their denomination and name. Other divels that dwell in drier places transforme themselves into the masculine kind. Finallie *Psellus* saith they know our thoughts, and can prophesie of things to come. His definition is, that they are perpetuall minds in a passible bodie.

To verefie these toies he saith, that he himselfe sawe in a certeine night a man brought up by *Aletus Libius* into a mountaine, and that he tooke an hearbe, and spat thrise into his mouth, and anointed his eies with a certeine ointment, so as thereby he sawe great troopes of divels, and perceived a crowe to flie into his mouth; and since that houre he could prophesie at all times, saving on good fridaie, and easter sundaie. If the end of this tale were true, it might not onelie have satisfied the Greeke church, in keeping the daie of easter, togither with the church of *Rome*; but might also have made the pope (that now is) content with our Christmas and easter daie, and not to have gathered the minuts together, and reformed it so, as to shew how falselie he and his predecessors (whome they saie could not erre) have observed it hitherto. And trulie this, and the dancing of the sunne on easter daie morning sufficientlie or rather miraculouslie proveth that computation, which the pope now beginneth to doubt of, and to call in question.[230]

The fift Chapter.

The opinion of Fascius Cardanus touching spirits, and of his familiar divell.

Fascius Cardanus had (as he himselfe and his sonne *Hierome Cardanus* report) a familiar divell, consisting of the fierie element, who, so long as he used conjuration, did give true answers to all his demands: but when he burned up his booke of conjurations, though he resorted still unto him, yet did he make false answers continuallie. He held him bound twentie & eight yeares, and

[230] Scot is mocking the alterations in the Calendar and the dates of festivities made by the Church.

loose five yeares. And during the time that he was bound, he told him that there were manic divels or spirits. He came not alwaies alone, but sometimes some of his fellowes with him. He rather agreed with *Psellus* than with *Plato*: for he said they were begotten, borne, died, and lived long; but how long, they told him not: howbeit as he might conjecture by his divels face, who was 42. yeares old, and yet appeared verie yoong, he thought they lived two or three hundred yeares; and they said that their soules and ours also died with their bodies. They had schooles and universities among them: but he conceived not that anie were so dull headded, as *Psellus* maketh them. But they are verie quicke in credit, that beleeve such fables, which indeed is the groundworke of witchcraft and conjuration. But these histories are so grosse and palpable, that I might be thought as wise in going about to confute them, as to answer the stories of Frier *Rush*, Adam Bell, or the golden Legend.

The sixt Chapter.

The opinion of Plato concerning spirits, divels and angels, what sacrifices they like best, what they feare, and of Socrates his familiar divell.

PLATO and his followers hold, that good spirits appeare in their owne likenesse; but that evill spirits appeare and shew themselves in the forme of other bodies; and that one divell reigneth over the rest, as a prince dooth in everie perfect commonwelth over men. Item, they obteine their purposes and desires, onelie by intreatie, of men and women; bicause in nature they are their inferiors, and use authoritie over men none otherwise than priests by vertue of their function, and bicause of religion, wherein (they saie) they execute the office of God. Sometimes they saie that the fierie spirits or supreme substances enter into the puritie of the mind, and so obteine their purpose; sometimes otherwise, to wit, by vertue of holie charmes, and even as a poore man obteineth for Gods sake anie thing at a princes hand as it were by importunatnesse.

The other sort of divels and defiled soules are so conversant on earth, as that they doo much hurt unto earthlie bodies, speciallie in lecherie. Gods and angels (saie they) bicause they want all material and grosse substance, desire most the pure sacrifice of the mind. The grosser and more terrestriall spirits desire the grosser sacrifices; as beasts and cattell. They in the middle or meane region delight to have frankincense, and such meane stuffe offered unto them: and therefore (saie they) it is necessarie to sacrifice unto them, all maner of things, so the same be slaine, and die not of their owne accord: for such they abhorre. Some saie that spirits feare woonderfullie vaine threats, and thereupon will depart; as if you tell them that you will cut the heavens in peeces, or reveale their secrets, or complaine of them to the gods, or saie that you will doo anie impossibilitie, or such things as they cannot understand; they are so timerous, as they will presentlie be gone: and that is thought the best waie to be rid of them. But these be most commonlie of that sort or companie, which are called *Principatus* being of all other the most easie to be conjured.

They saie *Socrates* had a familiar divell: which *Plato* relieth much upon, using none other argument to proove that there are such spirits, but bicause *Socrates* (that would not lie) said so; and partlie because that divell did ever dissuade and prohibit, not onelie in *Socrates* his owne cases, but sometimes in his freends behalfe; who (if they had beene ruled) might through his admonition have saved their lives. His disciples gathered that his divell was Saturnall, and a principall fierie divell; and that he, and all such as doo naturallie know their divels, are onlie such as are called *Dæmonii viri*, otherwise, Couseners. Item, they saie that fierie spirits urge men to contemplation, the aierie to busines, the waterie to lust; and among these there are some that are Martiall, which give fortitude; some are Joviall, giving wisedome; some Saturniall, alwaies using dissuasion and dehorting. Item, some are borne with us, and remaine with us all our life; some are meere strangers, who are nothing else but the soules of men departed this life, &c.

The seventh Chapter.

Platos nine orders of spirits and angels, Dionysius his division thereof not much differing from the same, all disprooved by learned divines.

PLATO proposeth or setteth foorth nine severall orders of spirits, besides the spirits and soules of men. The first spirit is God that commandeth all the residue; the second are those that are called *Ideæ*, which give all things to all men; the third are the soules of heavenlie bodies which are mortall; the fourth are angels; the fift archangels; the sixt are divels, who are ministers to infernall powers, as angels are to supernall; the seventh are halfe gods; the eight are principalities; the ninth are princes. From which division *Dionysius* dooth not much swarve, saving that he dealeth (as he saith) onelie with good spirits, whome he likewise divideth into nine parts or offices. The first he calleth Seraphim, the second Cherubim, the third thrones, the fourth dominations, the fift vertues, the sixt powers, the seventh principalities, the eight archangels, the ninth and inferior sort he calleth angels. Howbeit, some of these (in my thinking) are evill spirits: or else *Paule* gave us evill counsell, when he willed us to fight against principalities, and powers, and all spirituall wickednes.

But *Dionysius* in that place goeth further, impropriating to everie countrie, and almost to everie person of anie accompt, a peculiar angell; as to *Jewrie*, he assigneth *Michael*; to *Adam*, *Razael*; to *Abraham*, *Zakiel*; to *Isaach*, *Raphael*; to *Jacob*, *Peliel*; to *Moses*, *Metraton*, &c. But in these discourses he either folowed his owne imaginations and conceipts, or else the corruptions of that age. Nevertheles, I had rather confute him by M. *Calvine*, and my kinseman M. *Deering*, than by my selfe, or mine owne words. For M. *Calvine* saith, that *Dionysius* herein speaketh not as by hearesaie, but as though he had slipped downe from heaven, and told of things which he had seene. And yet (saith he) Paule was rapt into the third heaven, and reporteth no such matters. But if you read M. *Deering* upon the first chapter to the *Hebrues*, you shall see this matter notablie handled; where he saith, that whensoever archangell is mentioned in the scriptures, it signifieth our savior Christ, and no creature. And certeine it is that Christ himselfe was called an angell. The names also of angels, as *Michael, Gabriel, &c*: are given to them (saith *Calvine*) according to the capacitie of our weakenesse. But bicause the decision of this question is neither within the compasse of mans capacitie, nor yet of his knowledge, I will proceed no further to discusse the same, but to shew the absurd opinions of papists and witchmongers on the one side, and the most sober and probable collections of the contrarie minded on the other side.

The eight Chapter.

The commensement of divels fondlie gathered out of the 14. of Isaie, of Lucifer and of his fall, the Cabalists the Thalmudists and Schoolemens opinions of the creation of angels.

THE witchmoongers, which are most commonlie bastard divines, doo fondlie gather and falselie conceive the commensement of divels out of the fourteenth of *Isaie*; where they suppose Lucifer is cited, as the name of an angell; who on a time being desirous to be checkemate with God himselfe, would needs (when God was gone a litle asside) be sitting downe, or rather pirking up in Gods owne principall and cathedral chaire; and that therfore God cast him and all his confederates out of heaven: so as some fell downe from thence to the bottome of the earth; some having descended but into the midle region, and the taile of them having not yet passed through the higher region, staied even then & there, when God said, Ho. But God knoweth there is no such thing ment nor mentioned in that place.[231] For there is onlie foreshowed the deposing and deprivation of king *Nabuchadnezzar*, who exalting himselfe in pride (as it were above the starres) esteemed his glorie to surmount all others,

[231] Scot is saying that the text of Isaiah does not mention the fall of the angels.

as farre as *Lucifer* the bright morning starre shineth more gloriouslie than the other common starres, and was punished by exile, untill such time as he had humbled himselfe; and therefore metaphoricallie was called *Lucifer.*

But forsooth, bicause these great clarkes would be thought methodicall, and to have crept out of wisedomes bosome, who rather cralled out of follies breeches; they take upon them to shew us, first, whereof these angels that fell from heaven were created; to wit, of the left side of that massie moold, whereof the world was compounded, the which (saie they) was *Putredo terræ*, that is, the rottennesse of the earth. The *Cabalists*, with whome *Avicen* seemeth to agree, saie that one of these begat another: others saie, they were made all at once. The Greekes doo write that angels were created before the world. The Latinists saie they were made the fourth daie, when the starres were made. *Laurence Ananias* saith, they were made the first daie, and could not be made the fourth daie, bicause it is written; *Quando facta sunt sidera, laudaverunt me angeli*: so as (saith he) they were made under the name of the heavens.

There is also a great question among the schoolemen, whether more angels fell downe with *Lucifer*, or remained in heaven with *Michael*. Manie having a bad opinion of the angels honesties, affirme that the greater part fell with *Lucifer*: but the better opinion is (saith *Laurence Ananias*) that the most part remained. And of them that thinke so, some saie the tenth part were cast downe, some the ninth; and some gather upon S. *John*, that the third part were onelie damned; bicause it is written, that the dragon with his taile plucked downe with him the third part of the starres.

THE NINTH CHAPTER.

Of the contention betweene the Greeke and Latine church touching the fall of angels, the variance among papists themselves herein, a conflict betweene Michael and Lucifer.

THERE was also another contention betweene the Greeke church and the Latine; to wit, of what orders of angels they were that did fall with *Lucifer*. Our schoolemen saie they were of all the nine orders of angels in *Lucifers* conspiracie. But bicause the superior order was of the more noble constitution and excellent estate, and the inferior of a lesse worthie nature, the more part of the inferior orders fell as guiltie and offenders with *Lucifer*. Some saie the divell himselfe was of the inferior order of angels, and some that he was of the highest order: bicause it is written, *In cherubim extentus & protegens possui te in monte santo Dei*. And these saie further, that he was called the dragon, because of his excellent knowledge. Finallie, these great doctors conclude, that the divell himselfe was of the order of seraphim, which is the highest, because it is written, *Quomodo enim mane oriebaris Lucifer?*[232] They of this sect affirme, that *Cacodæmones* were they that rebelled against *Jove*; I meane they of *Plato* his sect, himselfe also holding the same opinion. Our schoolemen differ much in the cause of Lucifers fall. For some said it was for speaking these words, *Ponam sedem meam in aquilone, & similis ero altissimo;*[233] others saie, bicause he utterlie refused felicitie, and thought scorne therof; others saie, bicause he thought all his strength proceeded from him selfe, and not from God; others saie that it was, bicause he attempted to doo that by himselfe, and his owne abilitie, which he should have obteined by the gift of another; others saie, that his condemnation grew hereupon, for that he challenged the place of the Messias; others saie, bicause he detracted the time to adore the majestic of God, as other angels did; others saie, bicause he utterlie refused it. *Scotus* and his disciples saie that it was, bicause he rebelliouslie claimed equall omnipotencie with God: with whom lightlie the *Thomists* never agree. Others saie it was for all these causes together, and manie more: so as hereupon (saith *Laurentius Ananias*) grew a wonderfull conflict betweene Michael and the good angels on the one side, and *Lucifer* and his freends on the other: so as, after a long and doubtfull skirmish, *Michael* overthrew *Lucifer*, and turned him and his fellowes out of the doores.

The tenth Chapter.

Where the battell betweene Michael and Lucifer was fought, how long it continued, and of their power, how fondlie papists and infidels write of them, and how reverentlie Christians ought to thinke of them.

NOW where this battell was fought, and how long it continued, there is as great contention among the schoolemen, as was betwixt *Michael* and *Lucifer*. The *Thomists* saie this battell was fought in the empereiall heaven, where the abode is of blessed spirits, and the place of pleasure and felicitie. *Augustine* and manie others saie, that the battell was fought in the highest region of the aier; others saie, in the firmament; others in paradise. The *Thomists* also saie it continued but one instant or pricke of time; for they tarried but two instants in all, even from their creation to their expulsion. The *Scotists* saie, that betweene their production and their fall, there were just foure instants. Nevertheles, the greatest number of schoolemen affirme, that they continued onelie three instants: bicause it stood with Gods justice, to give them three warnings; so

[232] Isaiah 14:12.

[233] Isaiah 14:13-14.

as at the third warning *Lucifer* fell downe like led (for so are the words) to the bottome of hell; the rest were left in the aire, to tempt man. The *Sadduces* were as grosse the other waie: for they said, that by angels was ment nothing else, but the motion that God dooth inspire in men, or the tokens of his power. He that readeth *Eusebius* shall see manie more absurd opinions and asseverations of angels: as how manie thousand yeares they serve as angels, before they come to the promotion of archangels, &c.

Monsieur Bodin, M. *Mai.* and manie other papists gather upon the seventh of *Daniel*, that there are just ten millians of angels in heaven. Manie saie that angels are not by nature, but by office. Finallie, it were infinite to shew the absurd and curious collections hereabout. I for my part thinke with *Calvine*, that angels are creatures of God; though *Moses* spake nothing of their creation, who onelie applied himselfe to the capacitie of the common people, reciting nothing but things seene. And I saie further with him, that they are heavenlie spirits, whose ministration and service God useth: and in that respect are called angels. I saie yet againe with him, that it is verie certeine, that they have no shape at all; for they are spirits, who never have anie: and finallie, I saie with him, that the scriptures, for the capacitie of our wit, dooth not in vaine paint out angels unto us with wings; bicause we should conceive, that they are readie swiftlie to succour us. And certeinlie all the sounder divines doo conceive and give out, that both the names and also the number of angels are set downe in the scripture by the Holie-ghost, in termes to make us understand the greatnesse and the manner of their messages; which (I saie) are either expounded by the number of angels, or signified by their names.

Furthermore, the schoole doctors affirme, that foure of the superior orders of angels never take anie forme or shape of bodies, neither are sent of anie arrand at anie time. As for archangels, they are sent onelie about great and secret matters; and angels are common hacknies about evere trifle; and that these can take what shape or bodie they list: marie they never take the forme of women or children. Item they saie that angels take most terrible shapes: for *Gabriel* appeared to *Marie*, when he saluted hir, *Facie rutilante, veste coruscante, ingressu mirabili, aspectu terribili, &c*: that is, with a bright countenance, shining attire, wonderfull gesture, and a dredful vissage, &c. But of apparitions I have spoken somewhat before, and will saie more hearafter. It hath beene long, and continueth yet a constant opinion, not onelie among the papists; but among others also, that everie man hath assigned him, at the time of his nativitie, a good angell and a bad. For the which there is noreason in nature, nor authoritie in scripture. For not one angell, but all the angels are said to rejoise more of one convert, than of ninetie and nine just. Neither did one onelie angell conveie *Lazarus* into *Abrahams* bosome. And therefore I conclude with *Calvine*, that he which referreth to one angell, the care that GOD hath to everie one of us, dooth himselfe great wrong: as may appeare by so manie fierie chariots shewed by *Elizæus* to his servant. But touching this mysterie of angels, let us reverentlie thinke of them, and not curiouslie search into the nature of them, considering the vilenes of our condition, in respect of the glorie of their creation. And as for the foresaid fond imaginations and fables of *Lucifer, &c*: they are such as are not onelie ridiculous, but also accomptable among those impious curiosities, and vaine questions, which *Paule* speaketh of: neither have they anie tittle or letter in the scripture for the maintenance of their grosse opinions in this behalfe.

THE ELEVENTH CHAPTER.

Whether they became divels which being angels kept not their vocation, in Jude and Peter; of the fond opinions of the Rabbins touching spirits and bugs, with a confutation thereof.

WE doo read in *Jude*, and find it confirmed in *Peter*, that the angels kept not their first estate, but left their owne habitation, and sinned, and (as *Job* saith) committed follie: and that God therefore did cast them downe into hell, reserving them in everlasting chaines under darkenes, unto the judgement of the great daie. But manie divines saie, that they find not anie where, that God made divels of them, or that they became the princes of the world, or else of the aire; but rather prisoners. Howbeit, divers doctors affirme, that this *Lucifer*, notwithstanding his fall, hath greater power than any of the angels in heaven: marrie they say that there be certeine other divels of the inferiour sort of angels, which were then thrust out for smaller faults, and therefore are tormented with little paines, besides eternal damnation: and these (saie they) can doo little hurt. They affirme also, that they onelie use certeine jugling knacks, delighting thereby to make men laugh, as they travell by the high waies: but other (saie they) are much more churlish. For proofe heereof they alledge the eighth of *Matthew*, where he would none otherwise be satisfied but by exchange, from the annoieng of one man, to the destruction of a whole heard of swine. The *Rabbines*, and namelie *Rabbi Abraham*, writing upon the second of Genesis, doo say, that God made the fairies, bugs, *Incubus*, Robin good fellow, and other familiar or domesticall spirits & divels on the fridaie: and being prevented with the evening of the sabboth, finished them not, but left them unperfect; and therefore, that ever since they use to flie the holinesse of the sabboth, seeking darke holes in mountaines and woods, wherein they hide themselves till the end of the sabboth, and then come abroad to trouble and molest men.

But as these opinions are ridiculous and fondlie collected; so if we have onelie respect to the bare word, or rather to the letter, where spirits or divels are spoken of in the scriptures, we shall run into as dangerous absurdities as these are. For some are so carnallie minded, that a Spirit is no sooner spoken of, but immediatlie they thinke of a blacke man with cloven feet, a paire of homes, a taile, clawes, and eies as broad as a bason, &c. But surelie the divell were not so wise in his generation, as I take him to be, if he would terrifie men with such uglie shapes, though he could doo it at his pleasure. For by that meanes men should have good occasion & oportunitie to flie from him, & to run to God for succour; as the maner is of all them that are terrified, though perchance they thought not upon God of long time before. But in truth we never have so much cause to be afraid of the divell, as when he flatteringlie insinuateth himselfe into our harts, to satisfie, please, and serve our humors, entising us to prosecute our owne appetits and pleasures, without anie of these externall terrors.

I would weete of these men, where they doo find in the scriptures, that some divels be spirituall, and some corporall; or how these earthie or waterie divels enter into the mind of man. *Augustine* saith, and diverse others affirme, that sathan or the divell while we feed, allureth us with gluttonie: he thrusteth lust into our generation; and sloth into our exercise; into our conversation, envie; into our traffike, avarice; into our correction, wrath; into our government, pride: he putteth into our harts evill cogitations; into our mouthes, lies, &c. When we wake, he mooveth us to evill works; when we sleepe, to evill and filthie dreames; he provoketh the merrie to loosenesse, and the sad to despaire.

THE TWELFE CHAPTER.

That the divels assaults are spirituall and not temporall, and how grosselie some understand those parts of the scripture.

UPON that, which hitherto hath beene said, you see that the assaults of sathan are spirituall, and not temporall: in which respect *Paule* wisheth us not to provide a corselet of Steele to defend us from his clawes; but biddeth us put on the whole armour of God, that we may be able to stand against the invasions of the divell. For we wrestle not against flesh and bloud; but against principalities, powers, and spirituall wickednesse. And therefore he adviseth us to be sober and watch: for the divell goeth about like a roring lion, seeking whome he may devoure. He meaneth not with carnall teeth: for it followeth thus, Whome resist ye stedfastlie in faith. And againe he saith, That which is spirituall onelie discerneth spirituall things: for no carnall man can discerne the things of the spirit. Why then should we thinke that a divell, which is a spirit, can be knowne, or made tame and familiar unto a natural man; or contrarie to nature, can be by a witch made corporall, being by God ordeined to a spirituall proportion.

The cause of this grosse conceipt is, that we hearken more diligentlie to old wives, and rather give credit to their fables, than to the word of God; imagining by the tales they tell us, that the divell is such a bulbegger,[234] as I have before described. For whatsoever is proposed in scripture to us by parable, or spoken figurativelie or significativelie, or framed to our grosse capacities, &c: is by them so considered and expounded, as though the bare letter, or rather their grosse imaginations thereupon were to be preferred before the true sense and meaning of the word. For I dare saie, that when these blockheads read *Jothans* parable in the ninth of Judges to the men of *Sichem*; to wit, that the trees went out to annoint a king over them, saieng to the olive tree, Reigne thou over us: who answered and said, Should I leave my fatnesse, &c? They imagine that the woodden trees walked, & spake with a mans voice: or else, that some spirit entred into the trees, and answered as is imagined they did in the idols and oracles of *Apollo*, and such like; who indeed have eies, and see not; eares and heare not; mouthes, and speake not, &c.

The XIII. Chapter.

The equivocation of this word spirit,
how diverslie it is taken in
the scriptures, where (by the waie)
is taught that the scripture
is not alwaies literallie to be interpreted,
nor yet allegoricallie to be understood.

SUCH as search with the spirit of wisedome and understanding, shall find, that spirits, as well good as bad, are in the scriptures diverslie taken: yea they shall well perceive, that the divell is no horned beast. For,[235] sometimes in the scriptures, spirits and divels are taken for infirmities of the bodie; [236] sometimes for the vices of the mind; sometimes also for the gifts of either of them. Sometimes[237] a man is called a divell, as *Judas* in the sixt of *John*, and *Peter* in the xvi. of *Matthew.* Sometimes[238] a spirit is put for the Gospell; sometimes for the mind or soule of man; sometimes[239] for the will of man, his mind and counsell; sometimes[240] for

[234] From the Glossary in this edition of the Discoverie: "Terrifying goblins. I see no difficulty in the derivation from Bul, a bull, or bull's face, it being terrifying enough, especially when, enraged or mad, it is directly opposed to you; and a bulbegger is an over-bold beggar, etc."

[235] Exodus 31.1

[236] Acts 8.19

[237] John 6, Matthew 16

[238] Cor 1.3, Gal. 3, Cor. 1.2, Cor 2.7

[239] Luke 9, Cor 1.5, Phillip 1, Thes 1.5

[240] John 1.4

teachers and prophets; sometimes[241] for zeale towards God; sometimes [242] for joie in the Holie-ghost, &c.

And to interpret unto us the nature and signification of spirits, we find these words written in the scripture; to wit, The spirit of the Lord shall rest upon him; The spirit of counsell and strength; The spirit of wisedome and understanding; The spirit of knowledge and the feare of the Lord. Againe, I will powre out my spirit upon the house of *David, &c*: The spirit of grace and compassion. Againe, Ye have not received the spirit of bondage, but the spirit of adoption. And therefore *Paule* saith. To one is given, by the spirit, the word of wisedome; to another, the word of knowledge by the same spirit; to another, the gift of healing; to another, the gift of faith by the same spirit; to another, the gift of prophesie; to another, the operation of great works; to another, the discerning of spirits; to another, the diversitie of toongs; to another, the interpretation of toongs: and all these things worketh one and the selfesame spirit. Thus farre the words of *Paule*. And finallie, *Esaie* saith, that the Lord mingled among them the spirit of error. And in another place, The Lord hath covered you with a spirit of slumber.

As for the spirits of divination spoken of in the scripture, they are such as was in the woman of *Endor*, the *Philippian* woman,[243] the wench of *Westwell*,[244] and the holie maid of *Kent*,[245] who were indued with spirits or gifts of divination, whereby they could make shift to gaine monie, and abuse the people by slights and craftie inventions. But these are possessed of borrowed spirits, as it is written in booke of Wisedome; and spirits of meere cousenage and deceipt, as I have sufficientlie prooved elsewhere. I denie not therefore that there are spirits and divels, of such substance as it hath pleased GOD to create them. But in what place soever it be found or read in the scriptures, a spirit or divell is to be understood spirituallie, and is neither a corporall nor a visible thing. Where it is written, that God sent an evill spirit betweene *Abimelech*, and the men of *Sichem*, we are to understand,

---

241 Tim 1.4

242 Ephesians 5, Isaiah 11.2

243 A slave in the Greek city of Philippi who predicted the future, through one spirit that possessed her, with great profit for her owners, until she was exorcized by Paul. Acts 16:16-19.

244 "Mildred Norrington de Westwell, in Kent. Her story was told in a pamphlet, according to which she was possessed by Satan in 13 of October of 1574, and, with the voice changed by the spirit, she kept many conversations with notable people from the region." *England's First Demonologist*. Philip C. Almond.

245 "Sister Elizabeth Barton (1506–1534), known as 'The Nun of Kent', 'The Holy Maid of London', 'The Holy Maid of Kent' and later 'The Mad Maid of Kent', was an English Catholic nun. She was executed as a result of her prophecies against the marriage of King Henry VIII of England to Anne Boleyn." *Elizabeth Barton*. Wikipedia.

that he sent the spirit of hatred, and not a bulbegger. Also where it is said; If the spirit of gelosie come upon him: it is as much to saie as; If he be mooved with a gelous mind: and not that a corporall divell assaulteth him. It is said in the Gospell; There was a woman, which had a spirit of infirmitie 18. yeeres, who was bowed togither, &c: whome Christ, by laieng his hand upon hir, delivered of hir disease. Wherby it is to be scene, that although it be said, that sathan had bound hir, &c: yet that it was a sicknes or disease of bodie that troubled hir; for Christs owne words expound it. Neither is there any word of witchcraft mentioned, which some saie was the cause thereof.

There were seven divels cast out of Marie Magdalen. Which is not so grosselie understood by the learned, as that there were in hir just seven corporall divels, such as I described before elsewhere; but that by the number of seven divels, a great multitude, and an uncerteine number of vices is signified: which figure is usuall in divers places of the scripture. And this interpretation is more agreeable with Gods word, than the papisticall paraphrase, which is; that Christ, under the name of the seven divels, recounteth the seven deadlie sinnes onelie. Others allow neither of these expositions; bicause they suppose that the efficacie of Christs miracle should this waie be confounded: as though it were not as difficult a matter, with a touch to make a good Christian of a vicious person; as with a word to cure the ague, or any other disease of a sicke bodie. I thinke not but any of both these cures may be wrought by meanes, in processe of time, without miracle; the one by the preacher, the other by the physician. But I saie that Christs worke in both was apparentlie miraculous: for with power and authoritie, even with a touch of his finger, and a word of his mouth, he made the blind to see, the halt to go, the lepers cleane, the deafe to heare, the dead to rise againe, and the poore to receive the Gospell, out of whom (I saie) he cast divels, and miraculouslie conformed them to become good Christians, which before were dissolute livers; to whome he said, Go your waies and sinne no more.

The xiiii. Chapter.

That it pleased God to manifest the power of his sonne and not of witches by miracles.

JESUS CHRIST, to manifest his divine power, rebuked the winds, and they ceased; and the waves of water, and it was calme: which if neither our divines nor physicians can doo, much lesse our conjurors, and least of all our old witches can bring anie such thing to passe. But it pleased God to manifest the power of Christ Jesus by such miraculous & extraordinarie meanes, providing and as it were preparing diseases, that none otherwise could be cured, that his sonnes glorie, and his peoples faith might the more plainelie appeere; as namelie, leprosie, lunacie, and blindnesse: as it is apparent in the Gospell, where it is said, that the man was not stricken with blindnesse for his owne sinnes, nor for any offense of his ancestors; but that he was made blind, to the intent the works of God should be shewed upon him by the hands of Jesus Christ.[246] But witches with their charmes can cure (as witchmongers affirme) all these diseases mentioned in the scripture, and manie other more; as the gowt, the toothach, &c : which we find not that ever Christ cured.

As touching those that are said in the Gospell to be possessed of spirits, it seemeth in manie places that it is indifferent, or all one, to saie; He is possessed with a divell; or, He is lunatike or phrentike: which disease in these daies is said to proceed of melancholie. But if everie one that now is lunatike, be possessed with a reall divell; then might it be thought, that divels are to be thrust out of men by medicines. But who saith in these times with the woman of *Canaan*; My daughter is vexed with a divell, except it be presupposed, that she meant hir daughter was troubled with some disease? Indeed we saie, and saie truelie, to the wicked, The divell is in him: but we meane not thereby, that a reall divell is gotten into his guts. And if it were so, I marvell in what shape this reall divell, that possesseth them, remaineth. Entreth he into the bodie in one shape, and into the mind in another? If they grant him to be spirituall and invisible, I agree with them.

Some are of opinion, that the said woman of *Chanaan* ment indeed that hir daughter was troubled with some disease; bicause it is written in sted of that the divell was cast out, that hir daughter was made whole, even the selfesame houre. According to that which is said in the 12. of *Matthew*; There was brought unto Christ one possessed of a divell, which was both blind and dumbe, and he healed him: so as, he that was blind and dumbe both spake and sawe. But it was the man, and not the divell, that was healed, and made to speake and see. Whereby (I saie) it is gathered, that such as were diseased, as well as they that were lunatike, were said sometimes to be possessed of divels.

The xv. Chapter.

Of the possessed with divels.

HERE I cannot omit to shew, how fondlie diverse writers; and namelie, *James Sprenger*,[247] and *Henrie Institor*[248] doo gather and note the cause, why the divell

[246] And this is the god of the Christians.

[247] "Jacob Sprenger (1436/1438–1495) was a German priest. He was born in Rheinfelden, Further Austria. Scholars now believe that he became associated with the *Malleus Maleficarum* largely as a result of Kramer's wish to lend his book as much official authority as possible." *Jacob Sprenger*. Wikipedia.

[248] "Heinrich Kramer (1430–1505), was a German churchman and inquisitor, tha

maketh choise to possesse men at certeine times of the moone; which is (saie they) in two respects: first, that they may defame so good a creature as the moone; secondly, bicause the braine is the moistest part of the bodie. The divell therefore considereth the aptnesse and conveniencie thereof (the moone having dominion over all moist things) so as they take advantage therby, the better to bring their purposes to passe. And further they saie, that divels being conjured and called up, appeere and come sooner in some certeine constellations, than in other some: thereby to induce men to thinke, that there is some godhead in the starres. But when Satile was releeved with the sound of the harpe, they saie that the departure of the divell was by meanes of the signe of the crosse imprinted in *Davids* veines. Whereby we maie see how absurd the imaginations and devises of men are, when they speake according to their owne fansies, without warrant of the word of God. But me thinks it is verie absurd that *Josephus* affirmeth; to wit, that the divell should be thrust out of anie man by vertue of a root. And as vaine it is, that Ælianus writeth of the magicall herbe *Cynospastus*, otherwise called *Agla[o]photis*; which is all one with *Salomons* root named *Baaros*, as having force to drive out anie divell from a man possessed.

The xvi. Chapter

That we being not throughlie informed of the nature of divels and spirits, must satisfe our selves with that which is delivered us in the scriptures touching the same, how this word divell is to be understood both in the singular and plurall number, of the spirit of God and the spirit of the divell, of tame spirits, of Ahab.

THE nature therfore and substance of divels and spirits, bicause in the scripture it is not so set down, as we may certeinlie know the same: we ought to content and frame our selves faithfullie to beleeve the words and sense there delivered unto us by the high spirit, which is the Holie-ghost, who is Lord of all spirits; alwaies considering, that evermore spirits are spoken of in scripture, as of things spirituall; though for the helpe of our capacities they are there sometimes more grosselie and corporallie expressed, either in parables or by metaphors, than indeed they are. As for example (and to omit the historic of *Job*, which elsewhere I handle) it is written; The Lord said, Who shall entise *Ahab*, that he maie fall at *Ramoth Gilead, &c*? Then came foorth a spirit, and stood before the Lord, and said; I will entise him. And the Lord said, Wherewith? And he said; I will go and be a lieng spirit in the mouth of all his prophets. Then he said; Go foorth, thou shalt prevaile, &c.

---

author of the *Malleus Maleficarum*." *Heinrich Kramer*. Wikipedia.

This storie is here set foorth in this wise, to beare with our capacities, and speciallie with the capacitie of that age, that could not otherwise conceive of spirituall things, than by such corporall demonstrations. And yet here is to be noted, that one spirit, and not manie or diverse, did possesse all the false prophets at once. Even as in another place, manie thousand divels are said to possesse one man: and yet it is also said even in the selfe same place, that the same man was possessed onelie with one divell. For it is there said that Christ met a man, which had a divell, and he commanded the fowle spirit to come foorth of the man, &c. But *Calvine* saith; Where sathan or the divell is named in the singular number, thereby is meant that power of wickednesse, that standeth against the kingdome of justice. And where manie divels are named in the scriptures, we are thereby taught, that we must fight with an infinite multitude of enimies; least despising the fewnesse of them, we should be more slacke to enter into battell, and so fall into securitie and idlenes.

On the other side, it is as plainelie set downe in the scripture, that some are possessed with the spirit of God, as that the other are endued and bound with the spirit of the divell. Yea sometimes we read, that one good spirit was put into a great number of persons; and againe, that diverse spirits rested in and upon one man: and yet no reall or corporall spirit meant. As for example; The Lord tooke of the spirit that was upon Moses, and put it upon the seventie elders, and when the spirit rested upon them, they prophesied. Why should not this be as substantiall and corporall a spirit, as that, wherewith the maid in the Acts of the apostles was possessed? Also *Elisha* intreated *Elia*, that when he departed, his spirit might double upon him. We read also that the spirit of the Lord came upon *Othniel*, upon *Gedeon, Jeptha, Samson, Balaam, Saule, David, Ezechiel, Zacharie, Amasay*: yea it is written, that *Caleb* had another spirit than all the Israelits beside: & in another place it is said, that *Daniel* had a more excellent spirit than anie other. So as, though the spirits, as well good as bad, are said to be given by number and proportion; yet the qualitie and not the quantitie of them is always thereby ment and presupposed. Howbeit I must confesse, that Christ had the spirit of God without measure, as it is written in the evangelist *John*. But where it is said that spirits can be made tame, and at commandement, I saie to those grosse conceivers of scripture with *Salomon*, who (as they falslie affirme was of all others the greatest conjuror) saith thus in expresse words; No man is lord over a spirit, to reteine a spirit at his pleasure.

The xvii. Chapter.

Whether spirits and soules can assume bodies, and of their creation and substance, wherein writers doo extreamelie contend and varie.

SOME hold opinion, that spirits and soules can assume & take unto them bodies at their pleasure, of what shape or substance they list: of which mind all papists, and some protestants are, being more grosse than another sort, which hold, that such bodies are made to their hands. Howbeit, these doo varie in the elements, wherewith these spirituall bodies are composed. For (as I have said) some affirme that they consist of fier, some thinke of aier, and some of the starres and other celestiall powers. But if they be celestiall, then (as *Peter Martyr* saith) must they follow the circular motion: and if they be elementarie, then must they follow the motions of those elements, of which their bodies consist. Of aier they cannot be: for aier is *Corpus homogenium*; so as everie part of aier is aier, whereof there can be no distinct members made. For an organicall bodie must have bones, sinewes, veines, flesh, &c: which cannot be made of aier. Neither (as *Peter Martyr* affirmeth) can an aierie bodie receive or have either shape or figure. But some ascend up into the clouds, where they find (as they saie) diverse shapes and formes even in the aier. Unto which objection *P. Martyr* answereth, saieng, and that trulie, that clouds are not altogether aier, but have a mixture of other elements mingled with them.

The xviii. Chapter.

Certeine popish reasons concerning spirits made of aier, of daie divels and night divels, and why the divell loveth no salt in his meate.

MANIE affirme (upon a fable cited by M. *Mali.*) that spirits are of aier, bicause they have beene cut (as he saith) in sunder, and closed presentlie againe; and also bicause they vanish awaie so suddenlie. But of such apparitions I have alreadie spoken, and am shortlie to saie more, which are rather scene in the imagination of the weake and diseased, than in veritie and truth. Which sights and apparitions, as they have beene common among the unfaithfull; so now, since the preaching of the gospell they are most rare. And as among faintharted people; namelie, women, children, and sicke folkes, they usuallie swarmed; so among strong bodies and good stomachs they never used to appeare; as elsewhere I have prooved: which argueth that they were onelie phantasticall and imaginarie. Now saie they that imagine divels and spirits to be made of aier, that it must needs be that they consist of that element; bicause otherwise when they vanish suddenlie awaie, they should leave some earthie substance behind them. If they were of water, then should they moisten the place where they stand, and must needs be shed on the floore. If they consisted of fier, then would they burne anie thing that touched them: and yet (saie they) *Abraham* and *Lot* washed their feete, and were neither scalded nor burnt.

I find it not in the Bible, but in *Bodin*, that there are daie divels, and night divels. The same fellow saith, that *Deber* is the name of that divell, which hurteth by night; and *Cheleb* is he that hurteth by daie: howbeit, he confesseth that Sathan can hurt both by daie and by night; although it be certeine (as he saith) that he can doo more harme by night than by daie; producing for example, how in a night he slew the first borne of *Ægypt*. And yet it appeareth plainelie in the text, that the Lord himselfe did it. Whereby it seemeth, that Bodin putteth no difference betweene God and the divell. For further confirmation of this his foolish assertion, that divels are more valiant by night than by daie, he alledgeth the 104. *Psalme*, wherein is written, Thou makest darknesse, and it is night, wherein all the beasts of the forrest creepe foorth, the lions rore, &c: when the sunne riseth, they retire, &c. So as now he maketh all beasts to be divels, or divels to be beasts. Oh barbarous blindnes! This *Bodin* also saith, that the divell loveth no salt in his meate, for that it is a signe of eternitie, and used by Gods commandement in all sacrifices; abusing the scriptures, which he is not ashamed to quote in that behalfe. But now I will declare how the scripture teacheth our dull capacities to conceive what maner of thing the divell is, by the verie names appropriated unto him in the same.

The xix. Chapter.

That such divels as are mentioned in the scriptures,
have in their names their nature and qualities expressed,
with instancies thereof.

SUCH divels as are mentioned in the scriptures by name, have in their names their nature and qualities expressed, being for the most part the idols of certeine nations idolatrouslie erected, in steed, or rather in spight of God. For *Beelzebub*, which signifieth the lord of the flies, bicause he taketh everie simple thing in his web, was an idol or oracle erected at *Ekron*, to whom *Ahaziah* sent to know whether he should recover his disease: as though there had beene no God in Israell. This divell *Beelzebub* was among the *Jewes* reputed the principall divell. The *Græcians* called him *Pluto*, the *Latines Sumanus*, *quasi summun deorum manium*, the cheefe ghost or spirit of the dead whom they supposed to walke by night: although they absurdlie beleeved also that the soule died with the bodie. So as they did put a difference betweene the ghost of a man and the soule of a man: and so doo our papists; howbeit, none otherwise, but that the soule is a ghost, when it walketh on the earth, after the dissolution of the bodie, or appeareth to anie man, either out of heaven, hell, or purgatorie, and not otherwise. *Nisroch* signifieth a delicate tentation, and was worshipped by *Senacherib* in *Assyria*. *Tarcat* is in English, fettered, and was the divell or idoll of the *Hevites*. *Beelphegor*, otherwise called *Priapus*, the gaping or naked god was worshipped among the *Moabits*. *Adramelech*, that is, the cloke or power of the king, was an idoll at *Sepharvais*, which was a citie of the *Assyrians*. *Chamos*, that is feeling, or departing, was worshipped among the *Moabits*. *Dagon*, that is, corne or greefe, was the idoll of the *Philistines*. *Astarte*, that is, a fold or flocke, is the name of a shee idoll at *Sydonia*, whom *Salomon* worshipped: some thinke it was *Venus*. *Melchom*, that is, a king, was an idoll or divell, which the sonnes of *Ammon* worshipped.

Sometimes also we find in the scriptures, that divels and spirits take their names of wicked men, or of the houses or stats of abhominable persons: as *Astaroth*, which (as *Josephus* saith) was the idol of the *Philistines*, whome the *Jewes* tooke from them at *Salomons* commandement, and was also worshipped of *Salomon*. Which though it signifie riches, flocks, &c: yet it was once a citie belonging to Og the king of *Basan*, where they saie the giants dwelt. In these respects *Astaroth* is one of the speciall divels named in *Salomoms* conjuration, and greatlie emploied by the conjurors. I have sufficientlie prooved in these quotations, that these idols are *Dii gentium*, the gods of the Gentiles: and then the prophet *David* may satisfie you, that they are divels, who saith *Dii gentium dæmonia sunt*, The gods of the Gentiles are divels.[249] What a divell was the rood of grace[250] to be thought, but such a one as before is mentioned and described, who tooke his name of his courteous and gratious behaviour towards his worshippers, or rather those that offered unto him. The idolatrous knaverie wherof being now bewraied, it is among the godlie reputed a divell rather than a god: and so are diverse others of the same stampe.

---

[249] Scot is reffering to the quote from Psalm 96 from the Vulgate. See in the Introduction about the use of the word "daimon" and its correlatives in the *Septuagint*.

[250] The "rood of grace" was a crucifix made with mobile parts, used as a kind of puppet in the Abbey of Boxley in Kent. The fraud was denounced in 1538. Scot is comparing it to the false idols denounced in the Old Testament which were also considered to be demons.

The XX. Chapter.

Diverse names of the divell, whereby his nature and disposition is manifested.

IT hath also pleased GOD to informe our weake capacities, as it were by similitudes and examples, or rather by comparisons, to understand what manner of thing the divell is, by the verie names appropriated and attributed unto him in the scripture: wherein sometimes he is called by one name, sometimes by another, by metaphors according to his conditions. *Elephas* is called in *Job*, *Behemoth*, which is, *Bruta*; whereby the greatnes and brutishnes of the divell is figured. *Leviathan* is not much different from *Elephas*; whereby the divels great subtiltie and power is shewed unto us. *Mammon* is the covetous desire of monie, wherewith the divell overcommeth the reprobate. *Dæmon* signifieth one that is cunning or craftie. *Cacodæmon* is perverslie knowing. All those which in ancient times were worshipped as gods, were so called. *Diabolus* is *Calumniator*, an accuser, or a slanderer. Sathan is *Adversarius*, an adversarie, that troubleth and molesteth. *Abaddon* a destroier. *Legio*, bicause they are manie. Prince of the aire. Prince of the world. A king of the sonnes of pride. A roring lion. An homicide or manslear, a lier, and the father of lies. The author of sinne. A spirit. Yea somtimes he is called the spirit of the Lord, as the executioner and minister of his displeasure, &c. Sometimes, the spirit of fornication, &c. And manie other like epithets or additions are given him for his name. He is also called the angell of the Lord. The cruell angell. The angell of sathan. The angell of hell. The great dragon, for his pride and force. The red dragon for his blouddines. A serpent. An owle, a kite, a satyre, a crowe, a pellicane, a hedghog, a griph, a storke, &c.

The xxi. Chapter.

That the idols or gods of the Gentiles are divels, their diverse names, and in what affaires their labours and authorities are emploied, wherein also the blind superstition of the heathen people is discovered.

AND for so much as the idols of the gentiles are called divels, and are among the unlearned confounded and intermedled with the divels that are named in the scriptures; I thought it convenient here to give you a note of them, to whome the Gentiles gave names, according to the offices unto them assigned. *Penates* are the domesticall gods, or rather divels that were said to make men live quietlie within doores. But some thinke these rather to be such, as the Gentiles thought to be set over kingdomes: and that *Lares* are such as trouble private houses, and are set to oversee crosse waies and cities. *Larvæ* are said to be spirits that walke onelie by night. *Genii* are the two angels, which they supposed were appointed to wait upon each man. *Manes* are the spirits which oppose themselves against men in the waie. *Dæmones* were feigned gods by poets, as *Jupiter, Juno,* &c. *Virunculi terrei* are such as was Robin good fellowe, that would supplie the office of servants, speciallie of maids; as to make a fier in the morning, sweepe the house, grind mustard and malt, drawe water, &c: these also rumble in houses, drawe latches, go up and downe staiers, &c. *Dii geniales* are the gods that everie man did sacrifice unto at the daie of their birth. *Tetrici* be they that make folke afraid, and have such ouglie shape, which manie of our divines call *Subterranei*. *Cobali* are they that followe men, and delight to make them laugh, with tumbling, juggling, and such like toies. *Virunculi* are dwarfes about three handfulles long, and doo no hurt; but seeme to dig in mineralles, and to be verie busie, and yet doo nothing. *Guteli* or *Trulli* are spirits (they saie) in the likenes of women, shewing great kindnesse to all men: & hereof it is that we call light women, truls. *Dæmones montani* are such as worke in the mineralles, and further the worke of the labourers woonderfullie, who are nothing afraid of them. *Hudgin* is a verie familiar divell, which will doo no bodie hurt, except he receive injurie: but he cannot abide that, nor yet be mocked: he talketh with men freendlie, sometimes visiblie, and sometimes invisiblie. There go as manie tales upon this *Hudgin*, in some parts of *Germanie*, as there did in England of Robin good fellowe. But this *Hudgin* was so called, bicause he alwaies ware a cap or a hood; and therefore I thinke it was Robin hood. Frier *Rush* was for all the world such another fellow as this *Hudgin*, and brought up even in the same schoole; to wit, in a kitchen: in so much as the selfe-same tale is written of the one as of the other, concerning the skullian, which is said to have beene slaine, &c: for the reading whereof I referre you to Frier *Rush* his storie, or else to John Wierus *De præstigiis dæmonum*.

There were also *Familiares dæmones*, which we call familiars: such as *Socrates* and *Cæsar* were said to have; and such as *Feats* sold to doctor *Burcot*. *Quintus Sertorius* had *Diana* hir selfe for his familiar; and *Numa Pompilius* had *Aegeria*: but neither the one nor the other of all these could be preserved by their familiars from being destroied with untimelie death. *Simon Samareus* boasted, that he had gotten by conjuration, the soule of a little child that was slaine, to be his familiar, and that he told him all things that were to come, &c. I marvell what privilege soules have, which are departed from the bodie, to know things to come more than the soules within mans bodie. There were spirits, which they called *Albæ mulieres*, and *Albæ Silyllæ*, which were verie familiar, and did much harme (they saie) to women with child, and to sucking children. *Deumus* as a divell is worshipped among the *Indians* in *Calecute*, who (as they thinke) hath power given him of God to judge the earth, &c: his image is horriblie pictured in a most ouglie shape. *Thevet* saith, that a divell in America, called

Agnan, beareth swaie in that countrie. In *Ginnie* one *Grigrie* is accounted the great divell, and keepeth the woods: these have preests called *Charoibes*, which prophesie, after they have lien by the space of one houre prostrate upon a wench of twelve yeares old, and all that while (saie they) he calleth upon a divell called *Hovioulsira*, and then commeth foorth and uttereth his prophesie. For the true successe whereof the people praie all the while that he lieth groveling like a lecherous knave. There are a thousand other names, which they saie are attributed unto divels; and such as they take to themselves are more ridiculous than the names that are given by others, which have more leasure to devise them. In litle bookes conteining the cousening possessed, at *Maidstone*, where such a woonder was wrought, as also in other places, you may see a number of counterfeit divels names, and other trish trash.

The xxii. Chapter.

Of the Romanes cheefe gods called Dii selecti, and of other heathen gods, their names and offices.

THERE were among the Romans twentie idolatrous gods, which were called *Dii selecti sive electi*, chosen gods; whereof twelve were male, and eight female, whose names doo thus follwe: *Janus, Saturnus, Jupiter, Genius, Mercurius, Apollo, Mars, Vulcanus, Neptunus, Sol, Orcus* and *Vibar*, which were all hee gods: *Tellus, Ceres, Juno, Minerva, Luna, Diana, Venus*, and *Vesta*, were all she gods. No man might appropriate anie of these unto himselfe, but they were left common and indifferent to all men dwelling in one realme, province, or notable citie. These heathen gentiles had also their gods, which served for sundrie purposes; as to raise thunder, they had *Statores, Tonantes, Feretrii*, and *Jupiter Elicius*. They had *Cantius*, to whome they praied for wise children, who was more apt for this purpose than *Minerva* that issued out of *Jupiters* owne braine. *Lucina* was to send them that were with child safe deliverie, and in that respect was called the mother of childwives. *Opis* was called the mother of the babe new borne, whose image women with child hanged upon their girdles before their bellies, and bare it so by the space of nine moneths; and the midwife alwaies touched the child therewith, before she or anie other laied hand thereon.

If the child were well borne, they sacrificed therunto, although the mother miscaried: but if the child were in any part unperfect, or dead, &c: they used to beate the image into powder, or to burne or drowne it. *Vagianus* was he that kept their children from crieng, and therefore they did alwaies hang his picture about babes necks: for they thought much crieng in youth portended ill fortune in age. *Cuninus*, otherwise *Cunius*, was he that preserved (as they thought) their children from misfortune in the cradell. *Ruminus* was to keepe their dugs from corruption. *Volumnus* and his wife *Volumna* were gods, the one for yoong men, the other for maids that desired marriage: for such as praied devoutlie unto them, should soone be married. *Agrestis* was the god of the fields, and to him they praied for fertilitie. *Bellus* was the god of warre & warriers, and so also was *Victoria*, to whome the greatest temple in *Rome* was built. *Honorius* was he that had charge about inkeepers, that they should well intreat pilgrimes. *Berecynthia* was the mother of all the gods. *Aesculanus* was to discover their mines of gold and silver, and to him they praied for good successe in that behalfe, *Aesculapius* was to cure the sicke, whose father was *Apollo*, and served to keepe weeds out of the corne. *Segacia* was to make seeds to growe. *Flora* preserved the vines from frosts and blasts. *Sylvanus* was to preserve them that walked in gardens. *Bacchus* was for droonkards, *Pavor* for cowherds; *Meretrix* for whores, to whose honour there was a temple built in Rome, in the middest of fortie and foure streets, which were all inhabited with common harlots. Finallie *Colatina*, alias *Clotina*, was goddesse of the stoole, the jakes, and the privie, to whome as to everie of the rest, there was a peculiar temple edified: besides that notable temple called *Pantheon*, wherein all the gods were placed togither; so as everie man and woman, according to their follies and devotions, might go thither and worship what gods they list.

The xxiii. Chapter.

Of diverse gods in diverse countries.

THE *Aegyptians* were yet more foolish in this behalfe than the *Romans* (I meane the heathenish *Romans* that then were, and not the popish *Romans* that now are, for no nation approcheth neere to these in anie kind of idolatrie.) The *Aegyptians* worshipped *Anubis* in the likenesse of a dog, because he loved dogs and hunting. Yea they worshipped all living creatures, as namelie of beasts, a bullocke, a dog, & a cat; of flieng fowles, *Ibis* (which is a bird with a long bill, naturallie devouring up venemous things and noisome serpents) and a sparrowhawke; of fishes they had two gods; to wit, *Lepidotus piscis*, and *Oxyrinchus*. The *Saitans* and *Thebans* had to their god a sheepe. In the citie *Lycopolis* they worshipped a woolfe; in *Herinopolis*, the *Cynocephalus*; the *Leopolitans*, a lion in *Lætopolis*, a fish in *Nilus* called *Latus*. In the citie *Cynopolis* they worshipped *Anubis*. At *Babylon*, besides *Memphis*, they made an onion their god; the *Thebans* an eagle; the *Mændeseans*, a goate; the *Persians*, a fier called *Orimasda*; the *Arabians*, *Bacchus*, *Venus*, and *Diasaren*; the *Boeotians*, *Amphiaraus*; the *Aphricans*, *Mopsus*; the *Scithians*, *Minerva*; the *Naucratits*, *Serapis*, which is a serpent; *Astartes* (being as *Cicero* writeth the fourth *Venus*, who was she, as others affirme, whom *Salomom* worshipped at his concubines request) was the goddesse of the *Assyrians*. At *Noricum*, being a part of *Bavaria*, they worship *Tibilenus*; the *Moores* worship *Juba*; the *Macedonians*, *Gabirus*; the

Poenians, *Uranius*; at *Samos Juno* was their god; at *Paphos*, *Venus*; at *Lemnos*, *Vulcane*; at *Naxos*, *Liberus*; at *Lampsacke*, *Priapus* with the great genitals, who was set up at *Hellespont* to be adored. In the ile *Diomedea*, *Diomedes*; at *Delphos*, *Apollo*; at *Ephesus*, *Diana* was worshipped. And bicause they would plaie small game rather than sit out, they had *Acharus Cyrenaicus*, to keepe them from flies and flieblowes; *Hercules Canopius*, to keepe them from fleas; *Apollo Parnopeius*, to keepe their cheeses from being mouseaten. The *Greeks* were the first, that I can learne to have assigned to the gods their principall kingdomes and offices: as *Jupiter* to rule in heaven, *Pluto* in hell, *Neptune* in the sea, &c. To these they joined, as assistants, divers commissioners; as to *Jupiter, Saturne, Mars, Venus, Mercurie, and Minerva*: to *Neptune, Nereus, &c. Tutilina* was onelie a mediatrix to *Jupiter*, not to destroie corne with thunder or tempests, before whom they usuallie lighted candels in the temple, to appease the same, according to the popish custome in these daies. But I may not repeate them all by name, for the gods of the gentiles were by good record, as *Varro* and others report, to the number of 30. thousand, and upward. Whereby the reasonable reader may judge their superstitious blindnesse.

The xxiiii. Chapter.

Of popish provinciall gods, a comparison betweene them and heathen gods, of physicall gods, and of what occupation everie popish god is.

NOW if I thought I could make an end in anie reasonable time, I would begin with our antichristian gods, otherwise called popish idols, which are as ranke divels as *Dii gentium* spoken of in the psalmes: or as *Dii montium* set foorth & rehearsed in the first booke of the kings; or as *Dii terrarum* or *Dii populorum* mentioned in the second of the Chronicles 32. & in the first of the Chronicles 16. or as *Dii terra* in Judges 3. Or as *Dii filiorum Seir* in the second of the Chronicles 25. or as *Dii alieni*, which are so often mentioned in the scriptures.

Surelie, there were in the popish church more of these in number, more in common, more private, more publike, more for lewd purposes, and more for no purpose, than among all the heathen, either heretofore, or at this present time: for I dare undertake, that for everie heathen idoll I might produce twentie out of the popish church. For there were proper idols of everie nation: as S. *George* on horssebacke for *England* (excepting whome there is said to be no more horssemen in heaven save onelie saint *Martine*) S. *Andrew* for *Burgundie* and *Scotland*, S. *Michael* for France, S. *James* for *Spaine*, S. *Patrike* for *Ireland*, S. *Davie* for *Wales*, S. *Peter* for *Rome*, and some part of *Italie*. Had not everie citie in all the popes dominions his severall patrone? As *Paule* for *London*, *Denis* for *Paris*, *Ambrose* for *Millen*, *Loven* for *Gaunt*, *Romball* for *Mackline*, S. *Marks* lion for *Venice*, the three magician kings for *Cullen*, and so of other. Yea, had they not for everie small towne, and everie village and parish, (the names wherof I am not at leisure to repeat) a severall idoll? As S. *Sepulchre*, for one; S. *Bride*, for another; S. All halowes, All saints, and our Ladie for all at once: which I thought meeter to rehearse, than a bedroll of such a number as are in that predicament. Had they not hee idols and shee idols, some for men, some for women, some for beasts, and some for fowles, &c. Doo you not thinke that S. *Martine* might be opposed to *Bacchus*? If S. *Martine* be too weake we have S. *Urbane*, S. *Clement*, and manie other to assist him. Was *Venus* and *Meretrix* an advocate for whoores among the Gentiles? Behold, there were in the Romish church to encounter with them, S. *Aphra*, S. *Aphrodite*, and S. *Maudline*. But insomuch as long Meg was as verie a whoore as the best of them, she had wrong that she was not also canonized, and put in as good credit as they: for she was a gentlewoman borne; whereunto the pope hath great respect in canonizing of his saints. For (as I have said) he canonizeth the rich for saints, and burneth the poore for witches. But I doubt not, Magdalen, and manie other godlie women are verie saints in heaven, and should have beene so, though the pope had never canonized them: but he dooth them wrong, to make them the patronesses of harlots and strong strumpets.

Was there such a traitor among all the heathen idols, as S. *Thomas Becket*? Or such a whoore as S. *Bridget*? I warrant you S. *Hugh* was good a huntesman as *Anubis*. Was *Vulcane* the protector of the heathen smithes? Yea forsooth, and S. *Euloge* was patrone for ours. Our painters had *Luke*, our weavers had *Steven*, our millers had *Arnold*, our tailors had *Goodman*, our sowters had *Crispine*, our potters had S. *Core* with a divell on his shoulder and a pot in his hand. Was there a better horseleech among the gods of the Gentiles than S. *Loy*? Or a better sowgelder than S. *Anthonie*? Or a better toothdrawer than S. *Apolline*? I beleeve that *Apollo Parnopeius* was no better a ratcatcher than S. *Gertrude*, who hath the popes patent and commendation therefore. The *Thebans* had not a better shepherd than S. *Wendeline*, nor a better gissard to keepe their geese than *Callus*. But for physicke and surgerie, our idols exceeded them all. For S. *John*, and S. *Valentine* excelled at the falling evill, S. *Roch* was good at the plague, S. *Petronill* at the ague. As for S. *Margaret*, she passed *Lucina* for a midwife, and yet was but a maid: in which respect S. *Marpurge* is joined with hir in commission.

For mad men, and such as are possessed with divels, S. *Romane* was excellent, & frier *Ruffine* was also pretilie skilfull in that art. For botches and biles, *Cosmus* and *Damian*; S. *Clare* for the eies, S. *Apolline* for teeth, S. *Job* for the pox. And for sore brests S. *Agatha* was as good as *Ruminus*. Whosoever served *Servatius* well, should be sure to loose nothing: if *Servatius* failed in his office, S. *Vinden* could supplie the matter with his cunning; for he could cause all things that were lost to be restored againe. But here laie a strawe for a while, and I will shew you the names of some, which exceed these verie far, and might have beene canonized for archsaints; all the other saints or idols being in comparison of them but bunglers, and benchwhistlers. And with your leave, when all other saints had given over the matter, and the saints utterlie forsaken of their servitors, they repaired to these that I shall name unto you, with the good consent of the pope, who is the fautor, or rather the patrone of all the saints, divels, and idols living or dead, and of all the gods save one. And whereas none other saint could cure above one disease, in so much as it was idolatrie, folle I should have said, to go to *Job* for anie other maladie than the pox; nothing commeth amisse to these. For they are good at anie thing, and never a-whit nice of their cunning: yea greater matters are said to be in one of their powers, than is in all the other saints. And these are they S. mother *Bungie,*[251] S. mother *Paine*, S. *Feats,*[252] S. mother *Still,*[253] S. mother *Button,*[254] S. *Kytrell,*[255] S. *Ursula Kempe,*[256] S. mother *Newman,*[257] S. doctor *Heron,*[258] S. *Rosimund*[259] a good old father, & diverse more that deserve to be registred in the popes kalendar, or rather the divels rubrike.

---

[251] Mother Bungie from Rochester in Kent; a witch denounced as a fraud by Reginald Scot, executed around 1584. *England's First Demonologist.* Philip C. Almond.

[252] One Thomas Hilles (aka Feats), Sorcerer, Magician, Conjuror, is mentioned in the list *Witches in Early Moderns England.* Uszkalo, Kirsten C. The Witches in Early Modern England Project. 2011. <http://witching.org>

[253] Very likely, she is Mother Elizabeth Stiles, one of the four "witches of Windsor", executed in 1579. *England's First Demonologist.* Philip C. Almond.

[254] Possibly Mother Dutton, one associate of Elizabeth Stile.

[255] "S. Kytrell" and "Paine" were the only mentions I could not identify; as the whole paragraph is a mockery offering people accused of witchcraft to be canonized by the Church, "Kytrell"and "Paine" probably are not exceptions.

[256] "Ursula Kemp or Ursley Kempe alias Grey (ca. 1525–1582) was an English wise woman and midwife judged and hanged for witchcraft in 1582." *Ursula Kemp.* Wikipedia.

[257] "Alice Newman, a friend of Ursula Kemp, one of the six women acused and hanged." *Ursula Kemp.* Wikipedia.

[258] "A professor of Physic and Surgery, presumably from Rochester in the county of Kent, who allegedly taught Mother Bungy about human anatomy and surgery." Uszkalo, Kirsten C. The Witches in Early Modern England Project. 2011. <http://witching.org>

[259] "Father Rosimond is a magician and wiseman from Windsor in the county of Berkshire, alias Osborne. He can allegedly transform himself into various animal shapes, and has a reputation for both curing the bewitched and causing bewitchments himself. Elizabeth Stile, in her confession, alleges that his daughter is also a witch." A *Rehearsal both Strange and True.* London: 1579. Uszkalo, Kirsten C. The Witches in Early Modern England Project. 2011. <http://witching.org>

The xxv. Chapter.

A comparison betweene the heathen and papists, touching their excuses for idolatrie.

AND bicause I know, that the papists will saie, that their idols are saints, and no such divels as the gods of the Gentiles were: you may tell them, that not onelie their saints, but the verie images of them were called *Divi.* Which though it signifie gods, and so by consequence idols or feends: yet put but an (ll) thereunto, and it is *Divill* in English.[260] But they will saie also that I doo them wrong to gibe at them; bicause they were holie men and holie women. I grant some of them were so, and further from allowance of the popish idolatrie emploied upon them, than greeved with the derision used against that abuse. Yea even as silver and gold are made idols unto them that love them too well, and seeke too much for them: so are these holie men and women made idols by them that worship them, and attribute unto them such honor, as to God onelie apperteineth.

The heathen gods were for the most part good men, and profitable members to the commonwealth wherein they lived, and deserved fame, &c: in which respect they made gods of them when they were dead; as they made divels of such emperors and philosophers as they hated, or as had deserved ill among them. And is it not even so, and woorsse, in the commonwealth and church of poperie? Dooth not the pope excommunicate, cursse, and condemne for heretikes, and drive to the bottomlesse pit of hell, proclaming to be verie divels, all those that either write, speake or thinke contrarie to his idolatrous doctrine? *Cicero*, when he derided the heathen gods, and inveied against them that yeelded such servile honor unto them, knew the persons, unto whom such abuse was committed, had well deserved as civill citizens; and that good fame was due unto them, and not divine estimation. Yea the infidels that honored those gods, as hoping to receive benefits for their devotion emploied that waie, knew and conceived that the statues and images, before whome with such reverence they powred foorth their praiers, were stockes and stones, and onelie pictures of those persons whome they resembled: yea they also knew, that the parties themselves were creatures, and could not doo so much as the papists and witchmongers thinke the Roode of grace,[261] or mother *Bungie* could doo. And yet the papists can see the abuse of the Gentils, and may not heare of their owne idolatrie more grosse and damnable than the others.

---

[260] Scot uses a fake philology here as an argument. He is not the first Christian writer to do this, as we have seen before. Interestingly, this feature is now used against the Church.

[261] "'Rood of Grace', a crucifix with mobile parts, used as a puppet in the Abbey of Boxley in Kent. The fraud was denounced in 1538." *Rood of Grace.* Wikipedia.

The XXVI. Chapter.

The conceipt of the heathen and the papists all one in idolatrie, of the councell of Trent, a notable storie of a hangman arraigned after he was dead and buried, &c.

BUT papists perchance will denie, that they attribute so much to these idols as I report; or that they thinke it so meritorious to praie to the images of saints as is supposed, affirming that they worship God, and the saints themselves, under the formes of images. Which was also the conceipt of the heathen, and their excuse in this behalfe; whose eiesight and insight herein reached as farre as the papisticall distinctions published by popes and their councels. Neither doo anie of them admit so grosse idolatrie, as the councell of *Trent* hath doone, who alloweth that worship to the Rood that is due to Jesus Christ himselfe, and so likewise of other images of saints. I thought it not impertinent therfore in this place to insert an example taken out of the Rosarie of our Ladie, in which booke doo remaine (besides this) ninetie and eight examples to this effect: which are of such authoritie in the church of *Rome*, that all scripture must give place unto them. And these are either read there as their speciall homilies, or preached by their cheefe doctors. And this is the sermon for this daie verbatim translated out of the said Rosarie, a booke much esteemed and reverenced among papists.

A certeine hangman passing by the image of our Ladie, saluted hir, commending himselfe to hir protection. Afterwards, while he praied before hir, he was called awaie to hang an offendor: but his enimies intercepted him, and slew him by the waie. And lo a certeine holie preest, which nightlie walked about everie church in the citie, rose up that night, and was going to his ladie, I should saie to our ladie church. And in the churchyard he saw a great manie dead men, and some of them he knew, of whome he asked what the matter was, &c. Who answered, that the hangman was slaine, and the divell challenged his soule, the which our ladie said was hirs: and the judge was even at hand comming thither to heare the cause, & therefore (said they) we are now come togither. The preest thought he would be at the hearing hereof, and hid himselfe behind a tree; and anon he saw the judiciall seat readie prepared and furnished, where the judge, to wit Jesus Christ, sate, who tooke up his mother unto him. Soone after the divels brought in the hangman pinnioned, and prooved by good evidence, that his soule belonged to them. On the other side, our ladie pleaded for the hangman, prooving that he, at the houre of death, commended his soule to hir. The judge hearing the matter so well debated on either side, but willing to obeie (for these are his words) his mothers desire, and loath to doo the divels anie wrong, gave sentence, that the hangmans soule should returne to his bodie, untill he had made sufficient satisfaction; ordeining that the pope should set foorth a publike forme of praier for the hangmans soule. It was demanded, who should doo the arrand to the popes holines? Marie quoth our ladie, that shall yonder preest that lurketh behind the tree. The preest being called foorth, and injoined to make relation hereof, and to desire the pope to take the paines to doo according to this decree, asked by what token he should be directed. Then was delivered unto him a rose of such beautie, as when the pope saw it, he knew his message was true. And so, if they doo not well, I praie God we may.

The XXVII. Chapter

A confutation of the fable of the hangman, of manie other feined and ridiculous tales and apparitions, with a reproof e thereof.

BY the tale above mentioned you see what it is to worship the image of our ladie. For though we kneele to God himselfe, and make never so humble petitions unto him, without faith and repentance, it shall doo us no pleasure at all. Yet this hangman had great freendship shewed him for one point of courtesie used to our ladie, having not one dramme of faith, repentance, nor yet of honestie in him. Neverthelesse, so credulous is the nature of man, as to beleeve this and such like fables: yea, to discredit such stuffe, is thought among the papists flat heresie. And though we that are protestants will not beleeve these toies, being so apparentlie popish: yet we credit and report other appearances, and assuming of bodies by soules and spirits; though they be as prophane, absurd, and impious as the other. We are sure the holie maide of *Kents* vision was a verie cousenage: but we can credit, imprint, and publish for a true possession or historie, the knaverie used by a cousening varlot at *Maidstone*; and manie other such as that was. We thinke soules and spirits may come out of heaven or hell, and assume bodies, beleeving manie absurd tales told by the schoolemen and Romish doctors to that effect: but we discredit all the stories that they, and as grave men as they are, tell us upon their knowledge and credit, of soules condemned to purgatorie, wandering for succour and release by trentals and masses said by a popish preest, &c: and yet they in probabilitie are equall, and in number farre exceed the other.

We thinke that to be a lie, which is written, or rather fathered upon *Luther*; to wit, that he knew the divell, and was verie conversant with him, and had eaten manie bushels of salt and made jollie good cheere with him; and that he was confuted in a disputation with a reall divell about the abolishing of private masse. Neither doo we beleeve this report, that the divell in the likenes of a tall man, was present at a sermon openlie made by *Carolostadius*;[262] and from this sermon went to his house, and told his sonne that he would fetch him awaie after a daie or twaine: as the papists saie he did in deed, although they lie in everie point thereof most maliciouslie. But we can beleeve *Platina*[263] and others, when they tell us of the appearances of pope *Benedict* the eight, and also the ninth; how the one rode upon a blacke horsse in the wildernesse, requiring a bishop (as I remember) whome he met, that he would distribute certeine monie for him, which he had purloined of that which was given in almes to the poore, &c: and how the other was scene a hundred yeares after the divell had killed him in a wood, of an heremite, in a beares skinne, and an asses head on his shoulders, &c: himselfe saieng that he appeared in such sort as he lived. And diverse such stuffe rehearseth *Platina*.

Now bicause S. *Ambrose* writeth, that S. *Anne* appeared to *Constance* the daughter of *Constantine*, and to hir parents watching at hir sepulchre: and bicause *Eusebius* and *Nicephorus* saie, that the *Pontamian* virgine, *Origins* disciple, appeared to S. *Basil*, and put a crowne upon his head, in token of the glorie of his martyrdome, which should shortlie followe: and bicause *Hierome* writeth of *Paules* appearance; and *Theodoret*, of S. *John* the *Baptist*; and *Athanasius*, oh *Ammons, &c*: manie doo beleeve the same stories and miraculous appearances to be true. But few protestants will give credit unto such shamefull fables, or anie like them, when they find them written in the Legendarie, Festivall, Rosaries of our Ladie, or anie other such popish authors. Whereby I gather, that if the protestant beleeve some few lies, the papists beleeve a great number. This I write, to shew the imperfection of man, how attentive our eares are to hearken to tales. And though herein consist no great point of faith or infidelitie; yet let us that professe the gospell take warning of papists, not to be carried awaie with everie vaine blast of doctrine: but let us cast awaie these prophane and old wives fables. And although this matter have passed so long with generall credit and authoritie: yet manie grave authors have condemned long since all those vaine visions and apparitions, except such as have beene shewed by God, his sonne, and his angels. *Athanasius* saith, that soules once loosed from their bodies, have no more societie with mortall men. *Augustine* saith, that if soules could walke and visit their freends, &c: or admonish them in sleepe, or otherwise, his mother that followed him by land and by sea would shew hir

[262] "Andreas Rudolph Bodenstein von Karlstadt (1486 -1541), better known as Andreas Karlstadt or Andreas Carlstadt or Karolostadt, was a German Christian theologian during the Protestant Reformation." *Andreas Karlstadt.* Wikipedia.

[263] "Bartolomeo Sacchi (1421-1481), known as Platina, was an Italian Renaissance humanist writer and gastronomist. Persecuted, arrested and tortured by the Pope Paul II, he wrote an inovative and influential history about the popes and became the Vatican librarian in 1475, under the new Pope Sixtus IV." *Bartolomeo Platina.* Wikipedia.

selfe to him, and reveale hir knowledge, or give him warning, &c. But most true it is that is written in the gospell; We have Moses and the prophets, who are to be hearkened unto, and not the dead.

The xxviii. Chapter

A confutation of Johannes Laurentius,[264] *and of manie others, mainteining these fained and ridiculous tales and apparitions,*
And what driveth them awaie: of Moses and Helias appearance in mount Thabor.

FURTHERMORE, to prosecute this matter in more words; if I saie that these apparitions of soules are but knaveries and cousenages; they object that Moses and Helias appeared in mount Thabor, and talked with Christ, in the presence of the principall apostles: yea, and that God appeared in the bush, &c. As though spirits and soules could doo whatsoever it pleaseth the Lord to doo, or appoint to be doone for his owne glorie, or for the manifestation of his sonne miraculouslie. And therefore I thought good to give you a taste of the witchmongers absurd opinions in this behalfe.

And first you shall understand, that they hold, that all the soules in heaven may come downe and appeare to us when they list, and assume anie bodie saving their owne: otherwise (saie they) such soules should not be perfectlie happie. They saie that you may know the good soules from the bad verie easilie. For a damned soule hath a verie heavie and sowre looke; but a saints soule hath a cheerefull and a merrie countenance: these also are white and shining, the other cole blacke. And these damned soules also maie come up out of hell at their pleasure; although *Abraham* made *Dives*[265] beleeve the contrarie. They affirme that damned soules walke oftenest: next unto them the soules of purgatorie; and most seldome the soules of saints. Also they saie that in the old lawe soules did appeare seldome; and after doomes daie they shall never be scene more: in the time of grace they shall be most frequent. The walking of these soules (saith *Michael Andr.*) is a most excellent argument for the proofe of purgatorie: for (saith he) those soules have testified that which the popes have affirmed in that behalfe; to wit, that there is not onelie such a place of punishment, but that they are released from thence by masses, and

[264] "Giovanni Lorenzo d'Anania or Gian Lorenzo d'Anania (Latin: Johannes Laurentius Anania, 1545–1609), Italian geographer and theologian." *Giovanni Lorenzo D'Anania*. Wikipedia.

[265] "Dives", Latin word meaning "rich man". The reference is to a parable of Jesus (Lc. 16:19-31).

such other satisfactorie works; whereby the goodnes of the masse is also ratified and confirmed.

These heavenlie or purgatorie soules (sale they) appeare most commonlie to them that are borne upon ember daies,[266] bicause we are in best state at that time to praie for the one, and to keepe companie with the other. Also they saie, that soules appeare oftenest by night; bicause men may then be at best leasure, and most quiet. Also they never appeare to the whole multitude, seldome to a few, and most commonlie to one alone: for so one may tell a lie without controlment. Also they are oftenest seene by them that are readie to die: as *Trasilla* sawe pope *Fælix*; *Ursine*, *Peter* and *Paule*; *Galla Romana*, S. *Peter*; and as *Musa* the maid sawe our Ladie: which are the most certeine appearances, credited and allowed in the church of *Rome*: also they may be seene of some, and of some other in that presence not seene at all; as *Ursine* sawe *Peter* and *Paule*, and yet manie at that instant being present could not see anie such sight, but thought it a lie: as I doo. *Michael Andræas* confesseth, that papists see more visions than protestants: he saith also, that a good soule can take none other shape than of a man; marie a damned soule may and dooth take the shape of a blacke moore, or of a beast, or of a serpent, or speciallie of an heretike. The christian signes that drive awaie these evill soules, are the crosse, the name of Jesus, and the relikes of saints: in the number whereof are holiwater, holie bread, *Agnus Dei, &c.* For *Andrew* saith, that notwithstanding *Julianus*[267] was an Apostata, and a betraier of christian religion: yet at an extremitie, with the onelie signe of the crosse, he drave awaie from him manie such evill spirits; whereby also (he saith) the greatest diseases and sicknesses are cured, and the sorest dangers avoided.

---

[266] "In the liturgical calendar of the Western Christian churches, Ember days are four separate sets of three days within the same week – specifically, the Wednesday, Friday, and Saturday – roughly equidistant in the circuit of the year, that were formerly set aside for fasting and prayer. These days set apart for special prayer and fasting were considered especially suitable for the ordination of clergy. The Ember Days are known in Latin as the quattuor anni tempora (the "four seasons of the year"), or formerly as the jejunia quattuor temporum ("fasts of the four seasons")." *Ember Days*. Wikipedia.

[267] "Flavius Claudius Iulianus Augustus (331-363), was Roman Emperor from 361 to 363, as well as a notable philosopher and author in Greek He was the last non-Christian ruler of the Roman Empire, and it was his desire to bring the Empire back to its ancient Roman values in order to, as he saw it, save it from dissolution. He purged the top-heavy state bureaucracy and attempted to revive traditional Roman religious practices at the cost of Christianity. His anti-Christian sentiment and promotion of Neoplatonic paganism caused him to be remembered as Julian the Apostate." *Julian (emperor)*. Wikipedia.

The xxix. Chapter.

A confutation of assuming of bodies, and of the serpent that seduced Eve.

THEY that contend so earnestlie for the divels assuming of bodies and visible shapes, doo thinke they have a great advantage by the words uttered in the third of Genesis, where they saie, the divell entered into a serpent or snake; and that by the cursse it appeareth, that the whole displeasure of God lighted upon the poore snake onlie. How those words are to be considered may appeare, in that it is of purpose so spoken, as our weake capacities may thereby best conceive the substance, tenor, and true meaning of the word, which is there set downe in the manner of a tragedie, in such humane and sensible forme, as woonderfullie informeth our understanding; though it seeme contrarie to the spirituall course of spirits and divels, and also to the nature and divinitie of God himselfe; who is infinite, and whome no man ever sawe with corporall eies, and lived. And doubtles, if the serpent there had not beene taken absolutelie, nor metaphoricallie for the divell, the Holie-ghost would have informed us thereof in some part of that storie. But to affirme it sometimes to be a divell, and sometimes a snake; whereas there is no such distinction to be found or scene in the text, is an invention and a fetch (me thinks) beyond the compasse of all divinitie. Certeinlie the serpent was he that seduced Eve: now whether it were the divell, or a snake; let anie wise man (or rather let the word of God) judge. Doubtles the scripture in manie places expoundeth it to be the divell. And I have (I am sure) one wiseman on my side for the interpretation hereof, namelie *Salomon*; who saith, Through envie of the divell came death into the world: referring that to the divell, which Moses in the letter did to the serpent.[268] But a better expositor hereof needeth not, than the text it selfe, even in the same place, where it is written; I will put enmitie betweene thee and the woman, and betweene thy seed and hir seed: he shall breake thy head, and thou shalt bruse his heele. What christian knoweth not, that in these words the mysterie of our redemption is comprised and promised? Wherein is not meant (as manie suppose) that the common seed of woman shall tread upon a snakes head, and so breake it in peeces, &c: but that speciall seed, which is Christ, should be borne of a woman, to the utter overthrow of sathan, and to the redemption of mankind, whose heele or flesh in his members the divell should bruse and assault, with continuall attempts, and carnall provocations, &c.

[268] Poor wretches, to this day, delude themselves that it was this Moses who wrote Genesis.

The xxx. Chapter.

The objection concerning the divels assuming of the serpents bodie answered.

THIS word Serpent in holie scripture is taken for the divell: The serpent was more subtill than all the beasts of the feeld. It likewise signifieth such as be evill speakers, such as have slandering toongs, also heretiks, &c: They have sharpned their toongs like serpents. It dooth likewise betoken the death and sacrifice of Christ: As *Moses* lifted up the serpent in the wildernesse, so must the sonne of man be lifted up upon the crosse. Moreover, it is taken for wicked men: O yee serpents and generation of vipers. Thereby also is signified as well a wise as a subtile man: and in that sense did Christ himselfe use it; saieng, Be ye wise as serpents, &c. So that by this breefe collection you see, that the word serpent, as it is equivocall, so likewise it is sometimes taken in the good and sometimes in the evill part. But where it is said, that the serpent was father of lies, author of death, and the worker of deceipt: me thinks it is a ridiculous opinion to hold, that thereby a snake is meant; which must be, if the letter be preferred before the allegoric. Trulie *Calvines* opinion is to be liked and reverenced, and his example to be embraced and followed, in that he offereth to subscribe to them that hold, that the Holie-ghost in that place did of purpose use obscure figures, that the cleare light thereof might be deferred, till Christs comming. He saith also with like commendation (speaking hereof, and writing upon this place) that *Moses* doth accommodate and fitten for the understanding of the common people, in a rude and grosse stile, those things which he there delivereth; forbearing once to rehearse the name of sathan. And further he saith, that this order may not be thought of *Moses* his owne devise; but to be taught him by the spirit of God: for such was (saith he) in those daies the childish age of the church, which was unable to receive higher or profounder doctrine. Finallie, he saith even hereupon, that the Lord hath supplied, with the secret light of his spirit, whatsoever wanted in plainenes and clearenes of externall words.

If it be said, according to experience, that certeine other beasts are farre more subtill than the serpent: they answer, that it is not absurd to confesse, that the same gift was taken awaie from him, by God, bicause he brought destruction to mankind. Which is more (me thinkes) than need be granted in that behalfe. For Christ saith not; Be yee wise as serpents were before their transgression: but, Be wise as serpents are. I would learne what impietie, absurditie, or offense it is to hold, that *Moses*, under the person of the poisoning serpent or snake, describeth the divell that poisoned *Eve* with his deceiptfull words, and venomous assault. Whence commeth it else, that the divell is called so often, The viper, The serpent, &c: and that his children are called the generation of vipers; but upon this first description of the divell made by *Moses*? For I thinke none so grosse, as to suppose, that the wicked are the children of snakes, according to the letter: no more than we are to thinke and gather, that God keepeth a booke of life, written with penne and inke upon paper; as citizens record their free men.[269]

The xxxi. Chapter.

Of the cursse rehearsed Gen. 3. and that place rightlie expounded, John Calvines opinion of the divell.

THE cursse rehearsed by God in that place, whereby witchmongers labour so busilie to proove that the divell entered into the bodie of a snake, and by consequence can take the bodie of anie other creature at his pleasure, &c: reacheth (I thinke) further into the divels matters, than we can comprehend, or is needfull for us to know, that understand not the waies of the divels creeping, and is farre unlikelie to extend to plague the generation of snakes: as though they had beene made with legs before that time, and through this cursse were deprived of that benefit. And yet, if the divell should have entred into the snake, in maner and forme as they suppose; I cannot see in what degree of sinne the poore snake should be so guiltie, as that God, who is the most righteous judge, might be offended with him. But although I abhorre that lewd interpretation of the familie of love,[270] and such other heretikes, as would reduce the whole Bible into allegories: yet (me thinkes) the creeping there is rather metaphoricallie or significativelie spoken, than literallie; even by that figure, which is there prosecuted to the end. Wherein the divell is resembled to an odious creature, who as he creepeth upon us to annoie our bodies; so doth the divell there creepe into the conscience of *Eve*, to abuse and deceive hir: whose seed nevertheles shall tread downe and dissolve his power and malice. And through him, all good christians (as *Calvine* saith) obteine power to doo the like. For we may not imagine such a materiall tragedie, as there is described, for the ease of our feeble and weake capacities.

---

[269] The reference is to the village registers indicating the men considered "free", that means, not being servants in the property of some noble.

[270] "The Familists or Family of Love (English term) was a mystic religious sect known as the Familia Caritatis (Hus der Lieften; Huis der Liefde; Haus der Liebe), founded in the sixteenth century by Henry Nicholis, also known as Niclaes. The outward trappings of Nicholis's system were Anabaptist. His followers were said to assert that all things were ruled by nature and not directly by God, of denying the dogma of the Trinity, and repudiating infant baptism. They held that no man should be put to death for his opinions, and apparently, like the later Quakers, they objected to the carrying of arms and to anything like an oath; and they were quite impartial in their repudiation of all other churches and sects." *Familist*. Wikipedia.

For whensoever we find in the scriptures, that the divell is called, god, the prince of the world, a strong armed man, to whome is given the power of the aier, a roring lion, a serpent, &c: the Holie-ghost mooved us thereby, to beware of the most subtill, strong and mightie enimie, and to make preparation, and arme our selves with faith against so terrible an adversarie. And this is the opinion and counsell of *Calvine*, that we seeing our owne weakenes, & his force manifested in such termes, may beware of the divell, and may flie to God for spirituall aid and comfort. And as for his corporall assaults, or his attempts upon our bodies, his nightwalkings, his visible appearings, his dansing with witches, &c: we are neither warned in the scriptures of them, nor willed by God or his prophets to flie them; neither is there anie mention made of them in the scriptures. And therefore thinke I those witchmongers and absurd writers to be as grosse on the one side, as the *Sadduces* are impious and fond on the other; which saie, that spirits and divels are onlie motions and affections, and that angels are but tokens of Gods power. I for my part confesse with *Augustine*, that these matters are above my reach and capacitie: and yet so farre as Gods word teacheth me, I will not sticke to saie, that they are living creatures, ordeined to serve the Lord in their vocation. And although they abode not in their first estate, yet that they are the Lords ministers, and executioners of his wrath, to trie and tempt in this world, and to punish the reprobate in hell fier in the world to come.

The xxxii. Chapter.

Mine owne opinion and resolution of the nature of spirits, and of the divell, with his properties.

BUT to use few words in a long matter, and plaine termes in a doubtfull case, this is mine opinion concerning this present argument. First, that divels are spirits, and no bodies. For (as *Peter Martyr* saith) spirits and bodies are by antithesis opposed one to another: so as a bodie is no spirit, nor a spirit a bodie. And that the divell, whether he be manie or one (for by the waie you shall understand, that he is so spoken of in the scriptures, as though there were but one, and sometimes as though one were manie legions, the sense whereof I have alreadie declared according to *Calvinus* opinion), he is a creature made by God, and that for vengeance, as it is written in *Eccl.* 39. *verse.* 28: and of himself, though emploied by God to necessarie and good puposes. For in places, where it is written, that all the creatures of God are good; and againe, when God, in the creation of the world, sawe all that he had made was good: the divell is not comprehended within those words of commendation. For it is written that he was a murtherer from the beginning, and abode not in the truth, because there is no truth in him; but when he speaketh a lie, he speaketh of his owne, as being a lier, and the father of lies, and (as *John* saith) a sinner from the beginning. Neither was his creation (so farre as I can find) in that weeke that God made man, and those other creatures mentioned in *Genesis* the first; and yet God created him purposelie to destroie. I take his substance to be such as no man can by learning define, nor by wisedome search out. M. *Deering* saith, that *Paule* himselfe, reckoning up principalities, powers, &c: addeth, Everie name that is named in this world, or in the world to come. A cleere sentence (saith he) of *Paules* modestie, in confessing a holie ignorance of the state of angels: which name is also given to divels in other places of the scripture. His essence also and his forme is so proper and peculiar (in mine opinion) unto himselfe, as he himselfe cannot alter it, but must needs be content therewith, as with that which God hath ordeined for him, and assigned unto him, as peculiarlie as he hath given to us our substance without power to alter the same at our pleasures. For we find not that a spirit can make a bodie, more than a bodie can make a spirit: the spirit of God excepted, which is omnipotent. Nevertheles, I learne that their nature is prone to all mischeefe: for as the verie signification of an enimie and an accuser is wrapped up in *Sathan* and *Diabolus;* so dooth Christ himselfe declare him to be in the thirteenth of Matthew. And therefore he brooketh well his name: for he lieth dailie in wait, not onelie to corrupt, but also to destroie mankind; being (I saie) the verie tormentor appointed by God to afiflict the wicked in this world with wicked temptations, and in the world to come with hell fier. But I may not here forget how M. *Mal.* and the residue of that crew doo expound this word *Diabolus*: for *Dia* (saie they) is *Duo*, and *Bolus* is *Morsellus*; whereby they gather that the divell eateth both bodie and soule at two morselles. Whereas in truth the wicked may be said to eate up and swalloue downe the divell, rather than the divell to eate up them; though it may well be said by a figure, that the divell like a roring lion seeketh whome he may devoure: which is ment of the soule and spirituall devouring, as verie novices in religion may judge.

The xxxiii. Chapter.

Against fond witchmongers, and their opinions concerning corporall divels.

Now, how *Brian Darcies*[271] he spirits and shee spirits, Tittie and Tiffin, Suckin and Pidgin, Liard and Robin, &c: his white spirits and blacke spirits, graie spirits and red spirits, divell tode and divell lambe, divels cat and divels dam, agree herewithall, or can stand consonant with the word of GOD, or true

[271] The Justice in the case of the witches of Saint Osyth, where Ursula Kemp was tried. *England's First Demonologist*. Philip C. Almond.

philosophic, let heaven and earth judge. In the meane time, let anie man with good consideration peruse that booke published by W. W.[272] and it shall suffice to satisfie him in all that may be required touching the vanities of the witches examinations, confessions, and executions: where, though the tale be told onlie of the accusers part, without anie other answer of theirs than their adversarie setteth downe; mine assertion will be sufficientlie prooved true. And bicause it seemeth to be performed with some kind of authoritie, I will saie no more for the confutation thereof, but referre you to the booke it selfe; whereto if nothing be added that may make to their reproch, I dare warrant nothing is left out that may serve to their condemnation. See whether the witnesses be not single of what credit, sex and age they are; namelie lewd, miserable, and envious poore people; most of them which speake to anie purpose being old women, & children of the age of 4. 5. 6. 7. 8. or 9. yeares.

And note how and what the witches confesse, and see of what weight and importance the causes are; whether their confessions be not woonne through hope of favour, and extorted by flatterie or threats, without proofe. But in so much as there were not past seventeene or eighteene condemned at once at S. *Osees*[273] in the countie of *Essex*, being a whole parish (though of no great quantitie) I will saie the lesse: trusting that by this time there remaine not manie in that parish. If anie be yet behind, I doubt not, but *Brian Darcie* will find them out; who, if he lacke aid, *Richard Gallis*[274] of *Windsor* were meete to be associated with him; which *Gallis* hath set foorth another booke to that effect, of certeine witches of *Windsore* executed at *Abington*. But with what impudencie and dishonestie he hath finished it, with what lies and forgeries he hath furnished it, what follie and frensie he hath uttered in it; I am ashamed to report: and therefore being but a two pennie booke, I had rather desire you to buie it, and so to peruse it, than to fill my booke with such beastlie stuffe.[275]

[272] W. W. is the anonimouys writer of the pamphlet about the witches of Osyth: *A true and just Recorde of the Information, Examination and Confession of all the Witches, taken at S. Oses in the countie of Essex*, published in 1582. *England's First Demonologist.* Philip C. Almond.

[273] Saint Osyth.

[274] The writer of *A brief treatise containing the most strange and horrible cruelty of Elizabeth Stile alias Rockingham and her confederates, executed at Abingdon. England's First Demonologist.* Philip C. Almond.

[275] This first Discourse ends with a very lengthy discussion about the nature of the Holy Spirit, and with a refutation of the *Pneumatomachi*, also known as Macedonians or Semi-Arians in Constantinople and the Tropici in Alexandria, who were an anti-Nicene Creed sect which flourished in the countries adjacent to the Hellespont during the latter half of the fourth, and the beginning of the fifth century. They denied the Godhead of the Holy Ghost, hence the Greek name Pneumatomachi or 'Combators against the Spirit'. As it is outside the scope of this volume, I left it out.

[This second Book of "A Discourse concerning Devils and Spirits", like the Chapters in Appendix I, were added to the third edition, 1665, by someone unknown.][276]

BOOK II

Chap. I

Of Spirits in General; What they are and how to be considered: Also how farr the Power of Magitians and Witches is able to operate in Diabolical Magick.

1. Because the Author in his foregoing Treatise, upon the *Nature of Spirits and Devils*, hath only touched the subject thereof superficially, omitting the more material part; and with a brief and cursory Tractat, hath concluded to speak the least of this subject which indeed requires most amply to be illustrated; therefore I thought fit to adjoyn this subsequent discourse; as succedaneous to the fore-going, and conducing to the compleating of the whole work.

2. The Nature of Spirits is variously to be considered, according to the source to which each *Caterva*[277] doth belong: for as some are altogether of a divine and celestial nature; not subject to the abominable Inchantments and Conjurations of vitious mankind; so others are the grand Instigators, stirring up mans heart to attempt the enquiry after the darkest, and most mysterious part of Magick, or Witchcraft: neither is this their suggestion without its secret end: that is, that by the private insinuation, and as it were incorporating themselves into the affection, or desire of the Witch, or Magician; they may totally convert him into their own nature: reducing him at last by constant practice, to such obdurateness and hardness of heart, that he becometh one with them, and delighted with their association, being altogether dead to any motions in himself that may be called good.

[276] This note is at the beginning of the second Discourse or Book II; the reference to Appendix I concerns the text presented as Book XV—this being in fact a grimoire inserted between the two Discourses, which should be understood as a complement to Book XV of the original edition. This grimoire, together with the original Book XV, comprise the last section of this volume.

[277] *Caterva* is a word of Latin origin, meaning a group, crowd, etc.

3. And if we may credit example, which is the surest proof; the very imaginations, and affection of a Magician, doth create an evil Essence or Devil; which was not before in being: for, as the Astral Spirits are believed by many to Germinate and procreate one another so likewise are the infernal Spirits capable of multiplication in their power and essence, according to their Orders, Ranks and Thrones; by means of the strong imagination in a Witch, or malevolous person, earnestly desiring their assistance.

4. Not that the Spirits or Devils so begotten do any whit add or contribute to the number in general; for as they are capable of increasing into distinct and separated substances, so are they likewise again contracted, and as it were annihilated; when the force of that Imagination is gone, which was the cause of their production: The nature of a spirit, whither heavenly or hellish, being to dilate, or contract themselves into as narrow compass, as they please; so that in a moment they can be as big in circumference as an hundred worlds, and on a sodain reduce themselves to the compass of an atome.

5. Neither are they so much limited as Tradition would have them; for they are not at all shut up in any separated place: but can remove millions of miles in the twinkling of an eye, yet are they still where they were at first: for, out of their own element, or quality, they can never come: go whither they will, they are in darkness: and the cause is within them, not without them: as one whose mind is troubled here in England, can remove his Carcase from the place where it was before; but should he go to the utmost bounds of the Earth, he cannot leave his perplexed and tormented minde behind him.

6. As for the shapes and various likenesses of Devils, It is generally believed, that according to their various capacities in wickedness, so their shapes are answerable after a Magical manner: resembling spiritually some horrid and ugly monsters, as their conspiracies against the power of God, were high and monstrous, when they fell from Heaven: for the condition of some of them is nothing but continual horrour and despair; others triumph in firie might and pomp, attempting to pluck God from out of his Throne; but the quality of Heaven is shut from them, that they can never find it, which doth greatly add to their torment and misery.

7. But that they are materially vexed and scorched in flames of fire, is inferiour to any to give credit to, who is throughly verst in their nature and existence: for their substance is spiritual; yea their power is greater, then to be detained or tormented with any thing without them: doubtless their misery is sufficiently great, but not through outward flames; for their Bodies are able to pierce through Wood and Iron, Stone, and all Terrestrial things: Neither is all the fire, or fewel of this World able to torment them; for in a moment they

can pierce it through and through. But the infinite source of their misery is in themselves, and is continually before them, so that they can never enjoy any rest, being absent from the presence of God: which torment is greater to them, then all the tortures of this world combined together.

8. The wicked souls that are departed this life, are also capable of appearing again, and answering the Conjurations of Witches, and Magicians, for a time: according to *Nagar the Indian,*[278] and the *Pythagoreans*. And it cannot be easily conceived, that their torment is much different from the rest of the Devils: for the Scripture saith: *every one is rewarded according to their works*. And, *that which a man sows, that he shall reap*. Now as the damned Spirits, when they lived on earth, did heap up vanity, and load their souls with iniquity, as a treasure to carry with them into that Kingdom, which sin doth naturally lead into: so when they are there, the same abominations which here they committed, do they ruminate and feed upon; and the greater they have been, the greater is the torment, that ariseth before them every moment.

9. And although these Infernal Spirits, are open Enemies to the very means which God hath appointed for mans salvation; yet such is the degenerate and corrupted mind of mankind, that there is in the same an itching after them for converse and familiarity, to procure their assistance, in any thing that their vain imagination suggesteth them with: to effect which, they inform themselves in every Tradition of Conjuration and Exorcism; as also in the names, natures and powers of Devils in general, and are ever restless, till their souls be totally devoted to that accursed and detestable nature, which is at enmity with God and goodness.

10. Now to proceed in the description of these Infernal Spirits and separated *Dæmons*, or *Astral Beings*, as also of those in the Angelical Kingdom; they that pertain to the Kingdom of Heaven, are either Angels which are divided into their degrees and orders; or else the righteous souls departed, who are entred into rest: And it cannot be, but that the life of Angels and Souls departed, is the same in Heaven, as also the food that nourisheth them, and the fruits that spring before them: Nor is it possible for any, how expert soever in Magical Arts, to compel either of them, of what degree soever they

[278] The poet and dramaturgist John Dryden (1631-1700) adapted these mentions of "Nagar the Indian" in his tragedy in verses *Tyrannick Love*. In the study *The Works of John Dryden* (edited by Novak and Guffey), it is noted that: "These names [Nakar/Damilkar] are adapted from 'Anti-Scot's' *[referring to the unknown author who added these passages to the Discoverie]* account of the relation between 'Nagar the Indian' and his good demon or genius Damilkar *[described next, in Chapter II]*. Since resort to Indian manuscripts was a common device in hermetic and occult writings, there is not necessarily a genunie source for the account."

be, to present themselves, or appear before them: Although many have written large Discourses and Forms of Convocation, to compel the Angels unto communication with them by Magical Rites and Ceremonies.

11. It may indeed be believed, that seeing there are infinite numbers of Angels, they are also imployed for the glory of God, and protection of mankind, (but not subject to Conjurations:) And that they accompany many righteous men Invisibly, and protect Cities and Countries from Plagues, War, and infestings of wicked Spirits, against which Principalities and Powers of Darkness, it is their place to contend and war, to the confusion of the Kingdom of Darkness.

12. But such Spirits as belong to this outward World, and are of the Elemental quality, subject to a beginning and ending, and to degrees of continuance; These may be solicited by Conjurations, and can also inform Magicians in all the secrets of Nature; yet so darkly, (because they want the outward organ); that it is hardly possible for any that hath fellowship with them, to learn any manual operation perfectly and distinctly from them.

13. Many have insisted upon the Natures of these Astral Spirits: some alledging, *That they are part of the faln Angels, and consequently subject to the torments of Hell at the last Judgment*: Others, *That they are the departed souls of men and women, confined to these outward Elements until the Consummation*: Lastly, others, As *Del rio*, *Nagar* the *Indian* Magician, and the *Platonists* affirm, *That their nature is middle between Heaven and Hell; and that they reign in a third Kingdom from both, having no other judgment or doom to expect for ever.*

14. But to speak more nearly unto their natures, they are of the source of the Stars, and have their degrees of continuance, where of some live hundreds, some thousands of years: Their food is the *Gas* of the Water, and the *Blas* of the Air: And in their Aspects, or countenances, they differ as to vigour and cheerfulness: They occupy various places of this world; as Woods, Mountains, Waters, Air, fiery Flames, Clouds, Starrs, Mines, and hid Treasures: as also antient Buildings, and places of the slain. Some again are familiar in Houses, and do frequently converse with, and appear unto mortals.

15. They are capable of hunger, grief, passion, and vexation: they have not any thing in them that should bring them unto God: being meerly composed of the most spiritual part of the Elements: And when they are worn out, they return into their proper essence or primary quality again; as Ice when it is resolved into Water: They meet in mighty Troops, and wage warr one with another: They do also procreate one another; and have power sometimes to make great commotions in the Air, and in the Clowds, and also to cloath themselves with

visible bodies, out of the four Elements, appearing in Companies upon Hills and Mountains, and do often deceive and delude the observers of Apparitions, who take such for portents of great alterations, which are nothing but the sports and pastime of these frolick Spirits: as Armies in the Air, Troops marching on the Land, noises and slaughter, Tempest and Lightning, &c.

16. These Astral Spirits are variously to be considered; some are beings Separate and absolute, that are not constitute to any work or service: Others are subservient to the Angels that have dominion over the Influences of the Stars: Others are the Astral Spirits of men departed, which (if the party deceased was disturbed and troubled at his decease,) do for many years, continue in the source of this world; amongst these airy Spirits, to the great disquietness of the soul of the person, to whom they belong : Besides the causes are various that such Spirits rest not; I. When by Witchcraft they are inchanted, and bound to wander so many years; as thrice or fourtimes seven, before they can be resolved into nothing. 2. When the person hath been murthered; so that the Spirit can never be at rest, till the crime be discovered. 3. When desires and lusts, after Wife, or Children, House, Lands, or Money, is very strong at their departure; it is a certain truth, that this same spirit belonging to the Starrs will be hanckering after these things, and drawn back by the strong desires and fixation of the Imagination, which is left behind it: Nor can it ever be at rest, till the thing be accomplished, for which it is disturbed. 4. When Treasure hath been hid, or any secret thing hath been committed by the party; there is a magical cause of something attracting the starry spirit back again, to the manifestation of that thing. Upon all which, the following Chapters do insist more largely and particularly.

Chap. II.

Of the Good and Evil Dæmons *or* Genii:
Whither they are; what they are, and how they are manifested; also of their names, powers, faculties, offices; how they are to be considered.

1. According to the disposition of the mind, or soul, there is a good or evil *Dæmon* that accompanies the party visibly, or invisibly; and these are of such rancks and orders, and names, as the capacity of the persons soul is, to whom they belong: Their Office is said to be, fore-warning the person of eminent danger, sometimes by inward instinct, sometimes by dreams in the night, and sometimes by appearing outwardly. The *Dæmon* or *Genius* changeth its nature and power, as the person changeth his: and if from good, the party degenerate

to iniquity; then by degrees the good Angel leaves him, and an evil *Dæmon* doth naturally succeed: for each thing draws after that which is like it self.

2. Magicians mention three several wayes of enjoying the society of the Bonus Genius; first by intellectual association, when secret and mental instigations do arise in their hearts, to do this or that, and to forbear the other: as in the Manuscript of *Nagar* the *Indian*, his own testimony of himself is to this effect: *My blessed Guardian* **Damilkar**, *hath now so sweetly communicated himself unto me; That by all the manifestations, whereby a holy* Dæmon *can attend and converse with mankind, he appeareth unto me: first in the intellectual way, he is ever present, and every moment prompts me, what to act, what to forbear from acting: Ah had he not rushed up through the powers of my soul, and suddenly warned me in my Travel to* Quiansi *in* China, *through the airy Region, to turn nimbly to the right hand, at an instant, a mighty Troop of Devils, whose Leader was* **Grachnock**, *coming through that tract of air, had crusht me into a thousand peices:* This is the first degree of its appearing.

3. Then he proceedeth in the language of *Sina*, describing the second way of its manifestation: *And when the deepest sleep hath overpoured me, I am never without him; sometimes my* **Damilkar** *stands before me like a glorious Virgin, administring to me a Cup of the drink of the Gods, which my Intellectual man exhausteth: sometimes he brings celestial Companies, and danceth round about me; and when after the weariness of the Senses, through contemplation I fell into gentle sleep on the holy Mountain of Convocation, which is called* Adan, *he shewed me the motion of the Heavens, the nature of all things, and the power of every evil* Dæmon.

4. Thirdly, he continueth to describe the External appearance of the *Genius*, to this effect: **Damilkar** *appears before me at my desire; for my desires are as his desires: When I slept a long space in my private dwelling, he appeared outwardly, and watering me with the dew of the fourth Heaven, I awakned, when he had thrise said* **Nankin Nagar**; *so the time being come, we mounted through the Air, unto the holy Mountain of Convocation.*

5. In this Example the three degrees of the Apparition of the *Bonus Genius*, or *Good Dæmon* are excellently deciphered, which is also the same in the appearance of the *bad Genius*: and according to the deepest Magicians, there be *seven good Angels*, who do most frequently become particular Guardians, of all others, each to their respective capacities; and also *seven evil Dæmons*, that are most frequent in association with depraved persons, as Guardians to them.

6. These are the seven good *Angels*, or *Dæmons*.

Jubanladace[279] a mighty Prince in the Dominion of Thrones, he cometh unto such as follow national affairs, and are carryed forth unto war and conquest; he beareth alwayes a flaming Sword, and is girded about, having a helmet upon his head, and appearing still before the party in the Air: he must be sollicited and invocated with Chastity, Vows, Fumes, and Prayers: and this is his Character to be worn as a Lamin.

Yah-Li-Yah one of the Powers, accompanying such as are Virgins, and devoted to Religion, and a Hermits life: he teacheth all the names and powers of Angels, and gives holy Charms against the assaults of *Evil Dæmons*: he must be addrest unto by Prayer, resignation, and fasting, with a celestial Song out of the Canto's of *Nagar*: this is his Character.

Nal-gah appearing to those that are devoted to the knowledge of Magick; teaching them how to exercise Infernal Witchcraft without danger, and in despight to the Devils: he must be sought by hours, minutes, constellations, privacy and blood, *&c.* He hath a bow bent in his hand, and a Crown of Gold upon his head: this is his Character.

---

[279] Jubanladace appears in the writings of John Dee (p. 18, Cotton Appendix XLVI 1); Joseph Smith (1805–1844), the founder of Mormonism, invoked Jubanladace in his search for treasure.

Maynon one of the Powers who hath the ability of subservient administration; that is, at one time to be present with many; he resembleth a Ew with Lamb, typifying his nature in that appearance.

Gaonim an Angel, causing his Pupil to go invisible, and transporting him at his pleasure in a moment, to the outmost parts of the earth.

Halanu the Instructer in Manual operations, by whom *Bezaliah*, and *Aholibah*[280] were divinely inspired for the structure of the Tabernacle.

Rama-umi who is the Instructer in Cabalistical Magick, and reveals the secrets of numbers, the names of Angels, and the virtue of *Boim.*[281]

7. These are the seven bad *Angels* or *Dæmons.*

As the power and capacity of the good, proceeds from the strength of God, in the quality of heaven; so is the force of the *evil Genii*, in the hellish quality correspondent: for it is to be noted, that these *evil Angels* did before their fall, enjoy the same places and degrees that now the *good* or *holy Angels* do: so that as their power is to instruct men in Government, Abstinence, Philosophy, Magick, and Mechanick Arts, for a good intent, and for the glory of God: The power of the *evil* ones, is the very same to inform and instigate unto the same attainments, as farr as they may be instrumental for the Devil, or the Kingdom of Darkness therein.

8. Their names are 1. **Panalcarp**, like a Crocodile with two heads. 2. **Baratron** appearing like a Conjurer in a Priestly habit. 3. **Sondennah** like a Hunts-man. 4. **Greizmodal** accompanying his Pupil like a Spaniel-Dog. 5. **Ballisargon** the grand Inticer to theeving and robbery, till he hath brought his followers to destruction. 6. **Morborgran** who can put on various likenesses, especially appearing as a Serving-man. 7. **Barman** who most commonly possesseth the soul of those that are joyned unto him.

9. These are the names of the good and evil *Dæmons*; according to the antient writing, on the Magical Art: who do also to many particular Cities and Countries, ascribe certain good and evil Angels; the one whereof protects and defends, the other inflicts Pestilence and Famin upon them: Like unto which is the story recorded by *Sigbertus* in *Chronicis*: *That in the 11th year of the reign of* Constans, *a good Angel and a bad were seen by the whole City of* Constantinople,

---

[280] See footnote 452.

[281] I could not identify this reference; in this context, it must refer to some term in Hebrew.

nightly to fly about the City; and as often as by the command of the good Angel, the other smote any house with a dart in his hand, such was the number that dyed in that house, according to the stroaks given.

10. And indeed it is to be feared, that whosoever have ever pretended, or do at present alledge, that they enjoy familiarity with a familiar Spirit; I say its greatly to be suspected, that all such familiars belong to the Kingdom of Darkness; for such are too too officious, and ready to attend the depraved desires of mortal men; whereas if communication with Angels, or good and holy Guardians be at all attainable, yet such is the difficulty of the attainment, that the examples thereof, if true, are exceeding rare: But in general, the writings of Magicians and Naturallists do plentifully abound with examples of this nature; whether good or evil, is yet to be determined. I have been told of a certain Country-man, in these dayes, who was continually pestered with the company of a woman, discerned by none but by himself: If he was upon Horse-back, she would be behind him: if at dinner, she sate at his elbow; if lying on his bed, there she was also present; And if at any time he had taken a journey, or gone about some unprofitable business, at such a time she accompanyed him not; and seldom escaped he some mischief when she was absent: But at last, for all her dutiful pretences, as she accompanyed him, riding through a deep and swift running River, she tumbled him into the deepest part, and lay upon him till she had strangled or drowned him.

11. Amongst the *Jews* this kind of Idolatry was frequent, to consult with and associate themselves unto familiar Spirits, whom they compelled to do them domestick service, dressing their Camels, lifting their burthens, and doing their messages: for the attaining their service they had many blasphemous Forms, and superstitious Ceremonies and Sacrifices; making the holy Names of God subservient to their accursed practices: one whose name was **Baal-hemammin**, was adjudged by the Law of *Moses* to be burnt for the like practices; being condemned in the time of one *Judah* a high Priest in the Captivity for killing an Infant, and with its blood performing Sacrifice to **Baalzebub**, with various ceremonies intermixed; by which means his God had bequeathed unto him a certain Lacky from the Infernal Troop to attend and serve him for his whole life time: this is to be found in *Zoars* Coment upon *Berosus*, and *Belus*, who affirms, *That at his tryal he endeavoured to prove, that the same was the good Angel or Genius given unto him by the mercy of God.*

12. Both the *Hebrew Cabalists* and *Heathen Magicians*, as also those addicted to Magick in Christianity, have all of them laid down certain forms of attaining the company of a good, or evil Angel, by number and astrological Observations, fitted to the rules of Conjuration and Invocations: And many of the superstitious *Rabbi*'s have affirmed, *That they were able by such practices, to*

cause the ghost of Adam, Eve, *or any of the holy Patriarchs to appear unto them*: which was surely the delusion of Satan to harden their hearts. But in the Addition to the 15th Book of the *Discovery* this Subject is more practically handled; where many forms of obtaining the Society of the *Bonus*, or *Malus Genius*, are plainly decyphered: so far as with safety and convenience they could be described.[282]

Chap. III.

Of the Astral Spirits of men departed:
What they are: And why they appear again:
And what Witchcraft may be wrought by them.

1. As the Astral Spirits separate, which belong not to any deceased person, do for many years survive, or continue; so if party deceased hath departed in discontent, and melancholy, it is often known that they return again, and causing terrour to families and houses, do wait for opportunity to disburthen themselves, that at length they may come into their desired rest.

2. The opinion of many is, *That the Devill in their likenesse is all that appears:*[283] But the more Learned have sufficiently demonstrated, through Example, and Experience; *That the apparition is really proper to the person deceased.* Nor can it easily be denyd, That to every man, and woman, while they live the natural Life, there belongs a *Syderial*, or *starry Spirit*; which takes its original wholly from the Elemental property: And according to the weaker, or stronger capacity of the party, it hath the longer, or shorter continuance, after the bodyes decease.

3. Such persons as are secretly murthered, and such as secretly murthur themselves, do most frequently appear again, and wander near the place where their Carcase is, till the radical moisture be totally consumed: according to the opinion of *Paracelsus*, after the consumption whereof, they can reappear no longer, but are resolved into their first being, or *Astrum*, after a certain term of months, or years, according to the vigour, or force of that first attraction which was the only cause of their returning.

---

[282] He is referring to the grimoire that, in that edition of the Discoverie, appears between the First and Second Discourses and should be understood as an adition to Book XV from the first edition of the *Discoverie*. This additional material in this present volume corresponds to the beginning of the section named "Book XV and the Rules of Vaganostus", with material selected from Book XV original coming next.

[283] In the "opinion of many", it is the Devil who presents himself as the ghosts of the deceased.

4. The manner and seasons of their appearing are various: Sometimes before the person, unto whom they do belong, depart this life, they[284] do by external presentations forewarn him, near the time, that the day of death approacheth. As it is reported of *Codrus Laoenus*, to whom an empty, meager Ghost appeared at midnight, signifying unto him, *how sad and lachrymable a Tragedy was shortly to attend him*; and also adding, *that he would visit him in the Execution thereof*: which proved not contrary to the words of the apparition; for at the very instant, when his Treacherous Wife had stabed him at the heart, on a suddain he beheld the same, with preparations for his interment, whilst he yet survived, after the fatall wound was given.

5. Sometimes the starry spirit of a person appears to his beloved Companion, many hundred of miles asunder, who was ignorant of the death of the party: And it hath often been heard, that when none of the kindred or family of the said party deceased, have ever been disturbed by it, or in the least been sensible of its appearing; yet to some of its most intimate acquaintance, it discovers it self, and importunes them to perform some ceremony, or other, that it may be returned into rest; or else discovers some treasure, which was hid by the party whilest alive, or else some murther which it had commited: But the most frequent cause of their returning, is when the party hath himself been privately murthered.

6. For such is the poysonous malice, and bloudy spirit of the murtherers, that it sufficeth them not to have privately bereaved them of their Lives; but also by certain earnest Wishes, Curses, and Conjurations, they do afterwards adjure them, that for such a term of years, they shall never have power to appear again: Which wishes, being earnestly given forth, from the hellish root in the murtherer, do exceedingly torment the murthered parties spirit, taking deep impression thereon; so that it is alwayes in continual sorrow, and anguish, till the term of years be expired, and till the murther be made manifest to the world: after which discovery, it returns to perfect rest; This is well known to those that are exercised in Witchcraft, and cruell Murthers, though not common to those that murther but once.

7. There be many Ancient families, in Europe, to whom the Ghost of their first Progenitor, or Ancestor appears immediately before the departure of some Heir, or chief in the same family: which assertion is confirmed by *Cardan*, in an Example of "an Antient family, in the Dukedome of *Parma*, called the *Tortells*, to whom there belongs an ancient Castle, with a spatious Hall; near the

[284] The appearances of the astral, sidereal or stellar spirit; the idea that the author seems to want to develop is that there is an astral body belonging to each person, but it takes some degree of independence when it dies, or is close to dying.

Chimney of the said Hall an old decrepit Woman, for these hundreds of years, is wonted to appear, when any of the Family is about to dye: And it is reported amongst them that the same is the Ghost of one belonging to the same name, and family, who for her Riches, was murthered by some of her Nephews, and thrown into a pit."

8. Many such apparitions do for many years continue to be seen in one particular place; ever watching for opportunity, to discover some murther, or Treasure hid: And the cause of the difficulty of the said discovery, consists in the nature of their substance; for could they make use of the organ of the Tongue, they might quickly discover it: or if they had the outward benefit of Hands, they might produce the said Treasure, or Carcase murthered, but this they are seldome able to accomplish; being destitute of the outward Organs, and mediation of Hands to hold withall, or Tongue to vent their grievances: And that this is true, the manner of their appearance doth confirm it : For all that they are able to effect, If they have been murthered, is commonly to appear near the very place, where their body lies, and to seem as if they sunk down, or vanished in the same; or else to appear in the posture of a murthered person, with mangled, and bloudy wounds, and hair dissheveled: But it is rarely known, that any such apparitions have plainly spoken, or uttered by words, the time of their murther, with the cause, the persons name, or place; unless the murther, by circumstances hath been more then ordinary, horrid, and execrable: then the remembrance of the same doth sometimes enable the apparition to frame a voice, by the assistance of the Air, and discover the fact.

9. But to speake in general concerning apparitions, why they are so seldome seen; and why such spirits as appear, can not without mans assistance accomplish their design; It may easily be apprehended, that all Spirits, or spiritual Substances, and Devills, have their life, breath, and motion in another source, or Element then this external world; And as any creature, whom the Element of Water hath nourished, and bred, can live but short while upon the Land; So its with them, when they come out of their proper habitations: which is the cause of the rarity of apparition; it being as difficult for any spirit to manifest it self in this outward principle, of the four Elements, as for a man to continue with his head under water: yea it is rather pain, then pleasure for any spirit, whether good, or bad, to come into this outward world.

10. Great is the villany of Necromancers, and wicked Magicians, in dealing with the spirits of men departed; whom they invocate, with certain forms, and conjurations, digging up their Carkasses again, or by the help of Sacrifices, and Oblations to the infernal Gods; compelling the Ghost to present it self before them: how this was performed in antient times, by Hags, and Witches, is notably described in the Æthi*opian* History of *Heliodorus*, in the practice of an antient

woman, who coming into the Camp, in the dead of night; where amongst many slaughtered bodies, the body of her Son was also slain; whose carkase she laid before her, digging a hole, and making a fire on each side, with the body in the midst; Then taking an earthen pot from a three footed stool, she poured honey out of it, into the pit; then out of another pot, she poured milk; and likewise out of the third:[285] Lastly, she cast a Lump of hardned dough[286], in the form of a man into the pit: the Image was Crowned with Lawrell: then she threw in some of the Shrub called *Bdellium*: This done, with a sword she ran frantickly up and down, cutting herself; and with a Lawrell branch sprinkled of her blood into the fire: at length whispering at her Sons ear, she caused him to arise, and questioning him of the fortune of his Brother, what was become of him, he answered dubiously speaking prosperity to two persons that secretly beheld her, and telling her, That suddain death for her impiety attended her, which came to passe ere she left the place; after all these predictions, the Carcase ceased to answer any more: and tumbled groveling on the ground again.

11. And although by most men, as also by the Author in his foregoing Discovery,[287] it is constantly believed, that the Witch of *Endor* raised not *Samuel*, nor the Ghost of *Samuel*, as not beleeving that there is an *Astral Spirit* or Ghost belonging unto every Man; yet it is very probable, that by her conjurations she caused his *Sydereal Spirit* to appear: which is possible to be effected: and hath been often done: as *Weaver*[288] in his *Funeral Monuments* records of *Edward Kelly*, who in the Park of *Walton Ledale* in the County *Lancaster*, with one *Paul Waring*; Invocated a Devil, and afterwards digged up the Corps of a poor man, that had been buried that very day, in a place near the same, called *Law Church-yard*: whom he compelled by Incantations, and Conjurations to speak, and utter prophetical words, concerning the master of one of his Assistants.

12. According to the state and condition wherein a person dyes, so is it with their *Astral Spirit*: for if they died in perfect peace, and had come through the valley of true Repentance; being dead to this Life before it left them; then their *starry Spirit* doth enter into rest, in its proper source, or quality at the instant of their Decease: nor is it possible for all the Conjurations in Hell, to cause them to return, or appear again.

---

[285] Although the contents of the third pot is not mentioned, the custom was milk, honey and wine, as seen elsewhere in this volume.

[286] Made with flour and water, used to make bread.

[287] The anonymous author, who added the second Discourse, here refers to Reginald Scot, author of *The Discoverie of Witchcraft*.

[288] "John Weever (1576–1632) was an English antiquarian and poet. His work *Ancient Funerall Monuments* (1631), is about epitaphs and religious monuments." *John Weever*. Wikipedia.

Original image from "*The Astrologer of the Nineteenth Century*" by Ebenezer Sibley. Although the two figures have been identified as Edward Kelley and John Dee, in fact the image is a recreation of the story from the book of Weever. There are no records of John Dee performing Necromancy.

13. But some might object, *That Samuel was an Holy Prophet, and attaind unto a perfect Life*; which is thus to be answered, that before Christ came into the world, none of the most Holy Prophets of God, did ever attain to that degree of blessednesse, that the Christians after Christ possessed: for in the time of the Law, a covering, or vail was spread over the faces of all people: and something there was that letted, or hindred their souls from any plain and perfect vision, and fruition of God; otherwise then through types, and shaddows, which partition wall, the end of Christs Incarnation was to break down.

14. In the writings of *Plato*, there be many strange Relations of the apparitions of Souls, of their torments, and purgations, of the cause of their returning, what their nature is, what their substance and property is, and what their food, and nourishment is: but he mistakes the *Soul* for the *Astral Spirit*: for the Soul in its returning and apparition is farr different; if a Holy Soul appear, it is to persons like it self, and that in sleep, warning them of dangers, and discovering heavenly secrets unto them: And if a Damned Soul appear, it is likewise to such as are of a nature like it self: whom it instigates, asleep, teaching them notorious Villanies in Dreams; and provoking them to every wicked cogitation.

15. The sect of *Pythagoras* have strange and antick opinions, concerning Souls, and Ghosts, or starry Spirits: whom they alledge to be frequently converted into *Gods*, or *Dæmons*, or *Demi-Gods*, and *Heroes*: (as the Platonicks do). And that there is a continual traduction, and transmigration of Souls, from one to another, till they attain to be deify'd at last; and then that they do frequently appear, to those that be like themselves; instructing, and forewarning them: It was also the belief of many wise, and antient Philosophers, that the *Oracles* were from such *Dæmons*, as had been the Ghosts, or Souls of wise and excellent men: as *Apollo's Oracle*, and the *Oracle* of *Pallas*, or *Minerva*: which opinions have much of reason and probability.

16. It is also the opinion of some, that the particular Spirits of famous men do after the death of the body, take up some particular habitations, near such places Cities, Towns, or Countries, as they most do affect, as Tutelaries, and Guardians unto them; Which is reported by *Vopiscus*, of *Apollonius Thyaneus*; That when his City *Thyana* was taken by *Aurelianus* the Emperour: and when he was in his Tent, pondering furiously how to destroy the same; the Ghost of *Apollonius* appeared unto him saying, Aurelianus, *if thou desirest to be a Conquerour, suppose not to slay these my Citizens:* Aurelianus, *if thou wilt be a Ruler, shed no innocent blood:* Aurelianus, *be meek, and gentle, if thou wouldst be a Conquerour.*

17. I have heard many wonderful Relations from Lunaticks or such as are almost natural fools, who have asserted, *That being for many daies together conversant amongst Faeries in Woods, Mountains, and Caverns of the Earth, they have feasted with them, and been magnificently Entertaind with variety of dainties, where they have seen several of their Neighbours or Familiar acquaintance in the habit they were wont to weare, notwithstanding they were known to have been dead some years before.*

18. And many Learned Authors have also insisted upon this particular, alledging, *That when such as the Faeryes have brought into their Society do feast and junket with them, though they have a real and perfect knowledge of their neighbours and acquaintance amongst the rest, yet their Language they are not able to understand, neither do these Acquaintance of theirs acknowledge or take notice of them at all, but do either sit (both they and all the rest) in a profound and tedious silence, or else discourse in a most stupendious kinde of Gibberish, not intelligible to strangers.*

19. But more particularly to illustrate this conjecture, I could name the person who hath lately appeared thrice since his Decease, at least some Ghostly being or other, that calls it self by the name of such a person who was dead above an hundred years agoe, and in his life time accounted as a Prophet or Praedicter by the assistance of Sublunary Spirits. And now at his appearance did also give out strange Praedictions concerning Famine, and Plenty, Warrs, and Bloodshed, and the end of this world.

20. By the affirmation of the person that had Communication with him, the last of his Appearances was on this following manner; *I had been*, said he, *to sell a Horse at the next Market Town, but not attaining my price, as I returned home by the way I met this man aforesaid who began to be familiar with me, asking what news, and how affairs moved throughout the Country*; I answered as I thought fit; withall I told him of my Horse whom he began to cheapen, and proceeded with me so far, that the price was agreed upon; so he turned back with me and told me, *that if I would go along with him, I should receive my Money*; on our way we went, I upon my Horse and he on another milk white beast; after much discourse I askt him where he dwelt, and what his name was; he told me, *That his dwelling was about a mile off, at a place called Farran*; of which place I had never heard though I knew all the Country round about; he also told me, *That he himself was that person of the Family of* Learmonts *so much spoken off for a Prophet*; At which I began to be somewhat fearful, perceiving us in a road which I had never been in before, which increased my fear and admiration more. Well on we went till he brought me under ground I know not how into the presence of a beautiful woman that payd me the moneys without a word speaking; he conducted me out again through a large and long entry, where I saw above 600 men in Armour layd prostrate on the ground as if asleep: at last I found my self in the open field by the help of Moon-light in that very place where first I

met him, and made shift to get home by three in the morning, but the money I received was just double of what I esteemed it, and what the woman payd me, of which at this instant I have several pieces to show consisting of nine pences, thirteen pence halfpennies, *&c.*

21. The variety of Examples throughout the writings of Learned men may serve as stronge inducements to confirm this particular of *Astral Spirits*, or *Ghosts* that belong unto Mortal men, returning after death untill the cause of their returning be taken away. In Ancient times before the name of Christianity, there was nothing more frequent than millions of Apparitions in fields where battails had been fought, seeming to fight as they had done at first, which the Ancient Heathens believed to proceed from the want of Burying. And from this arose the Poetical Romance of the *wandring of Ghosts besides the River Styx for an hundred years*. And the custome of Solemn Interment amongst them.

22. But with more probability. The Custome of the Funeral Piles used by the *Romans*, and the Urns to reduce their Corpses into Ashes, was instituted at first to prevent the torment of the Deceased, least his Ghost should wander, or return, which doubtlesse from a natural cause may have the same effect, that the reducing of the carcase into Ashes suddainly after its decease may prevent the return of the Astral Spirit; for if it be true what is affirmed by *Paracelsus*, that *the starry Spirit can continue no longer then the radical moisture in the body*; it will naturally follow that its appearance is at an end when the body is burnt, seeing that the moisture is totally exterminate and consumed thereby. And in some sense the Ceremony may be said to be Laudable and Judicious, having so beneficial a consequence.

23. As there is some semblance of a natural cause in the custome of the Antient urns, so likewise may the Interment of slaughtered bodies by the like cause prevent the like Appearances; for many are the examples that I have read of such as appeared to their surviving kindred and acquaintance, after they had been slaughtered in the Warrs, beseeching them to perform unto their bodies the Sacred Funeral Rites that their Ghosts might return into Rest, for which many have consulted with the Oracles to be informed whether the deceased deserved Burial, because they held it unlawful to bury Murtherers, Incestuous and Sacriligious, persons, which Nature her self doth also seem to hold if this following Relation be not false: which was, That some Learned men returning from *Persia* where they had been to see the King *Cosroes*, by the way interred a dead Carcase which they found unburied: And in the following night the Ghost of an Ancient Matron, as if it had been the Spirit of the World or Madam Nature her self, appeard unto them, saying, *Why Interr ye that nefarious Carcase? let the Dogs devoure it; The Earth who is the Mother of us all admitts not of that man that depraves his Mother*: So returning they found the Carcase yet unburied.

24. To confirm the verity of *Astral Spirits* proper, and their returning, I shall conclude this Chapter with the Example of famous *Aristeus* the Poet who in the Isle *Marmora* dyed suddainly, at which instant a certain Philosopher of *Athens* arriving there, affirmed, *That he had lately been in Company and discourse with him.* In the mean time going to Bury him they found him yet alive, but never after that had he any constant residence amongst Mortals. Seven years after that he was seen at *Proconnesus* his native Town, and remaind a while composing several Poems and Verses called *Arimaspei*, and then vanished. In *Metapontis* he was seen 300 years after that, charging that *Apollo*'s Altar should be erected by the name of *Aristeus Proconnesius*. The like stories are reported of *Apollonius*, and *Pythagoras*, whom their followers would have to be *Ubiquitaryes*, affirming, *That at one instant of time they were seen in several places thousands of miles in distance.* And though in *Iamblichus* who hath wrote the Life of *Pythagoras*, in *Philostratus* that wrote the Life of *Apollonius Tyanus*, there be many fabulous things reported as to the *Astral Spirits* separation, and return unto the body; Yet I have sufficiently here endeavoured to separate the true from the more Poetical part in this particular Subject of the *starry Spirits* belonging to every individual man and woman, and their returning after the body falls away.

Chap. IV.

Of Astral Spirits or separate Dæmons in all their distinctions, flames, and natures, and places of Habitation, and what may be wrought by their Assistance.

1. Having in the foregoing Chapter sufficiently illustrated the nature of the Astral Spirits proper, that belong to every individual; The subject of this present Chapter shall be of Astral Spirits separate; which are not constitute to any peculiar work or service, but do only, according to their nature and temper, haunt such places in the sublunary world as are most correspondent to their natures, and existence.

2.According to the Judgment of Magicians, the Seven Planets have seven Starry Spirits peculiar to themselves, whose natures are answerable to that peculiar Planet under which they are constitute. And they are said to be substitute under the seven Cæslestial Angels that govern the influences of the superiour Spheres, being equal in their name and continuance with that planet whose Spirit they are, that is, till the Consummation of all things visible.

3. And in that houre, month, day or year, wherein their Planet hath the most dominion, then is their efficacy most prevalent, and their operation the most powerful upon inferiour bodies, whether to the destruction or prosperity

of that animal vegitative or mineral subject to their Influences, according to the dignification of the Planet at that instant Dominion; for if ill affected, their nature is to blast with Mildew, Lightning, and Thunder any Vegetative proper to their Planet; To deprive any Animal of sight or the motion of the nerves under their Dominion; And lastly, bring Plagues, Pestilence, and Famine, Storms, and Tempests, or on the Contrary to bring sweet and excellent Influences upon Animals, or Vegetatives under their Planetary Regiment, if well and honourably dignified.

4. Innumerable are the Spirits that inhabit the Aiery Region, Spirits of the germinating amongst themselvs as Magicians affirm, and begetting one another after a Mystical manner. It is their property to be instant in storms and boistrous weather, which is said to be joy and delight unto them; And in such a season they may with most facility be calld upon, and make their appearance, which they do accordingly to their age, and youthfulness, seeming young or old at their appearance answerable to their years. Besides they march in mighty Troops through the Aiery Region, waging warr amongst themselves, and destroying one anothers beings or Existences, after which they are reduced to the primary source or nature of the Starrs. This is likewise to be observed that according to the Language, Vigour, Life, and Habit of that Region wherein they live, such is their Habit, Language, and Ability, one *Caterva* or Company being ignorant of their Neighbours, or Enemies Language, so that they have need of the Assistance of such Spirits as dwell *in onmibus Elementis*, to be their Interpreters.

5. And doubtless from hence arise the various deceptions that men are incident unto in their judgments of Apparitions, perswading themselves that they are portents and foretokens of Warr and Famine, when such numerous Spirits are beheld Fighting or Marching either in the Air, Earth, or Water: whereas it is nothing else but the bare effect of the Natures and Tempers of such Aerial beings to fight and randevouse immediately after sun-set, or else later in the Summer evenings, which is their principal time of such Conventions. And though it must be confest that such Spirits may be, and are the Devils Instruments as appertaining to the Kingdom whereof he is Ruler; Yet considered in themselves, their Nature is wholly harmless, as to ought that may be called *innate Evill*, having nothing in them that is eternal as the Soul of Man: and consequently nothing in them that is able to make them capable of enjoying Heaven, or induring the torments of Hell.

6. And it is believed by some, that according to the motion of the spheres, there are certain companies of Aerial Spirits good and bad that follow them in their motions round the earth, the good distilling influences that are good, and the bad, such influences as are destructive to every thing that is under

their Dominion. It is also believed that by the assistance of Devils, and damned Spirits, such Aerial Spirits are given for Familiars to some Magicians and Witches with whom they are said to have actual copulation, and the enjoyment of every dainty meat through their assistance, being able thereby to go invisible, to fly through the air, and steal Treasures and Jewels from the Coffers of Princes, as also carouse in Wine-sellers, and Pantries of those that are most amply provided with the choisest Daynties.

7. Subordinate unto these of the Air are the Terrestrial Spirits, which are of several degrees according to the places which they occupy, as Woods, Mountains, Caves, Fens, Mines, Ruins, Desolate places, and Antient Buildings, calld by the Antient Heathens after various names, as *Nymphs, Satyrs, Lamii, Dryades, Sylvanes, Cobali, &c.* And more particularly the *Faeries*, who do principally inhabit the Mountains, and Caverns of the Earth, whose nature is to make strange Apparitions on the Earth in Meddows, or on Mountains being like Men, and Women, Souldiers, Kings, and Ladyes Children, and Horse-men cloathed in green, to which purpose they do in the night steal hempen stalks from the fields where they grow, to Convert them into Horses as the Story goes. Besides, it is credibly affirmed and beleeved by many, That such as are real Changlings, or Lunaticks, have been brought by such Spirits and Hobgoblins, the true Child being taken away by them in the place whereof such are left, being commonly half out of their wits, and given to many Antick practices, and extravagant fancies, which passions do indeed proceed from the powerful influence of the Planet in their nativity, and not from such foolish conjectures.

8. Such jocund and facetious Spirits are sayd to sport themselvs in the night by tumbling and fooling with Servants and Shepherds in Country houses, pinching them black and blew, and leaving Bread, Butter, and Cheese sometimes with them, which if they refuse to eat, some mischief shall undoubtedly befall them by the means of these Faeries. And many such have been taken away by the sayd Spirits, for a fortnight, or a month together, being carryed with them in Chariots through the Air, over Hills, and Dales, Rocks and Precipices, till at last they have been found lying in some Meddow or Mountain bereaved of their sences, and commonly of one of their Members to boot.

9. Certainly the *Lares* and *Penates*, or houshold Gods of the antient Heathens were no other than such like Spirits who for several years would keep their residence in one house till upon some displeasure offered, or offences done by any of the sayd Family, they departed and were never afterwards heard of. There are plenty of such examples to be found in *Olaus Magnus*, and *Hector Boethus* in his History of *Scotland*, relating wonderful passages of *Robin-goodfellows*, and such as have been familiar amongst mankind.

10. **Luridan** a familiar of this kinde did for many years inhabit the island *Pomonia*, the largest of the *Orcades* in *Scotland*, suplying the place of Man-servant and Maid-servant with wonderful diligence to these Families whom he did haunt, sweeping their rooms, and washing their dishes and making their fires before any were up in the morning. This Luridan affirmed, That he was the *genius Astral*, of that Island that his place or residence in the dayes of *Solomon* and *David* was at Jerusalem; That then he was called by the *Jewes* **Belelah**, and after that he remaind Long in the Dominion of *Wales*, instructing their Bards in *Brittish* Poesy and Prophesies being called **Urthin**, **Wadd**, **Elgin**: And now said he, I have removed hither, and alas my continuance is but short, for in 70 years I must resigne my place to **Balkin** Lord of the *Northern* mountains.

11. Many wonderful and incredible things did he also relate of this **Balkin**, whom he called the Lord of the *Northern* Mountains, affirming that he was shaped like a Satyr and fed upon the Air, having Wife and Children to the number of 12 thousand which were the brood of the *Northern* Faeries inhabiting *Southerland* and *Catenes* with the adjacent Islands; And that these were the Companies of Spirits that hold continual wars with the Fiery Spirits in the Mountain *Heckla* that vomits fire in *Islandia*. That their speech was antient Irish, and their dwelling the Caverns of the Rocks, and Mountains, which relation is recorded in the Antiquities of *Pomonia*[289].

12. I have read another wonderful relation in a book *de Annulis Antiquorum*, Concerning a young man from whom the power of *Venus* was taken away so that he could not Company with his new marryed Wife. The Story is briefly thus; Being busy at play or exercise with some of his Companions on his marriage day, he put his wedding Ring on the finger of the Statue of *Venus* that stood besides the place least it should be lost; when he had done, returning to take his Ring, the finger was bended inward, so that he could by no means pluck off the Ring to his great amazement, at which instant he forsooke the place, and in the night the Image of *Venus* appeared unto him, saying, Thou hast espoused me, and shalt not meddle with any other: in the morning returning, the Ring was gone, and the finger made straight again, which troubled him mightily, so that he consulted with a Magician, who wrote a Letter to some Principal Spirit in that Dominion to which *Venus* belonged, bidding the party stand watching at such a place at such an houre till he saw many troops of Spirits pass by him, and describing one in a Chariot, of stern and terrible Countenance, to whom he bad him deliver the

---

[289] "The Orkney Islands is an archipelago off the north coast of Great Britain, 16 kilometres (10 mi) north of the coast of Caithness. Orkney comprises approximately 70 islands, of which 20 are inhabited. The largest island, Mainland, often referred to as "the Mainland", is sometimes called 'Pomona' (or 'Pomonia'), a name originated from a translation mistake that is rarely used by its inhabitants." *Orkney*. Wikipedia.

Letter; All which he performed, and after the person in the Chariot had read the contents thereof, he broke out into this expression, great God, how long shall we be subject to the insolencies of this accursed Rascal, naming the Magitian: But withal calling to a most beauteous Woman from amongst the Company, he charged her to deliver back the Ring which at length she did with much aversness, and after that he injoyd his Marriage rites without impediment.

13. Besides the innumerable Troops of Terrestrial Spirits called *Faeryes* there are also *Nymphs* of the Woods, Mountains, Groves, and Fountains, as **Aegle, Arethusa, Io, Menippa, Irene**, &c. who are sayd to be altogether of the fæminine kinde, sporting and dancing, and feasting amongst the trees in Woods, and bathing in clean and limpid Fountains; such have been seen by many, and are often alluded to, by the *Roman* and *Greek* Poets. There is also a relation of a *German* Prince, who being exceeding thirsty and weary with hunting and hawking, lost his Company in the Woods, on a suddain beheld an opening at a little hillock amongst the trees, and a most beautiful Maiden offering a Golden Horn full of Liquor, which he received and drunk, and after rid quite away with the sayd Horn, not regarding the Virgins tears, who lamented after him; tis sayd that having spilt some of the sayd Liquor, it fetcht the hair from off his Horses skin, and the horn is yet to be seen in *Germany*, which I have been told by one that hath seen and handled it, affirming, *That the Gold for purity cannot be parallel'd.*

14. Another sort are the **Incubi**. and **Succubi**, of whom it is reported, that the Hunns have the original, being begotten betwixt these Incubi, and certain Magical women whom *Philimer* the King of the *Goths* banished into the deserts, whence arose that savage and untamed Nation, whose speech seemed rather the mute attempts of brute Beasts, than any articulate sound and well distinguished words. To these *Incubi* are attributed the diseases of the blood called the Night-hag, which certainly have a natural cause, although at the instant of time when the party is oppressed, it is probable that certain malevolent Spirits may mix themselvs therein and terrifie the soul and minde of the afflicted party.

15. And amongst such Spirits as are resident amongst mortals, there is a very froward kinde, who take delight to pull down what man hath builded, who have been seen at the building of strong and mighty Castles to come in the night and tumble all to the ground that the workmen had reared the day before; of this sort were **Horon, Stilkon, Glaura**, and **Ribbolla**, four pestiferous, and turbulent Animals that for many years infested the first founders of the Emperours *Seraglio*[290]: Till one of the holy Musselmans did by certain Charms,

[290] "Seraglio or serail is the sequestered living quarters used by wives and concubines in an Ottoman household. The term harem refers to the women themselves, but has

and Exorcisms constrain and bind them, to tell their names, and the cause of their disturbing, which they declared, and were by him confined to destroy the mines of Copper in *Hungaria*.

16. There is also a Relation extant in the life of *Paul* the Hermit of a Satyr appearing to him in the Woods, and discoursing with him that it was a mortal Creature as he, and served the same God, dehorting the people to worship them for demi-Gods, as they had been accustomed to; Like unto this is the Story of the Death of the great God *Pan*; That a Mariner sailing by the Island of *Cicilia*, was called by his name from the shore, and by a certain voice was bid to tell the Inhabitants of the next Island, that the great God *Pan* was dead, which he obeyed, and though in the next Island there were no Inhabitants, yet when he approached he proclaimed, towards the shoar that *Pan* was deceased, immediately after which Proclamation he could sensibly hear most doleful and lachrymable Cryes, and noyses, as of those that lamented his departure.

17. **Janth** is sayd by Magitians, to be a water Spirit, who is ever present when any are drownd in the water, being delighted much in the destruction of mankinde, that it may enjoy the Company of their Astral Spirits after their decease; for according to the four Complexions or Constitutions of the body of Man, The Astral Spirit associates it self with separated substances; The Phlegmatick, to the watry Spirits: The Sanguine, to those of the Aire ; The Cholerick, to the Fire; and the Melancholy, to the Terrestrial Spirits. But this is only to be supposed of such persons as dyed in discontent, and restlesness.

18. Of another sort are such *Aquatick Animals* as in former times Watry Spirits have conversed, and procreated with mankinde bearing divers Children; And at length snatching all away into the watry Element again, whereof there are variety of Examples in *Cardanus* and *Bodin*. Of this sort was the Familiar of *Paulus* a Mendicant Frier, called by him **Florimella**, and entertaind as his Bed-fellow for forty years, though unknown and unseen to any but himself, till upon some unhandsome carriage of the Fryer, his Companion accompanymg him over the *Danube*, leapt into the River and was never after seen.

19. Innumerable are the reports and accidents incident unto such as frequent the seas, as fisher-men and sailers who discourse of noises, flashes, shadows, ecchoes, and other visible appearances nightly seen, and heard, upon the surface of the water. And as the disposition of the Heavens is according to the constellations, and climates, so are these spectres appropriate to particular parts, and coasts, from the North to the Southern Pole. But more especially, abounding in the North, about *Norweigh Isleland*, *Green Land*, and *Nova Zembla*.

---

also come to be used to refer to these sequestered living quarters." *Seraglio*. Wikipedia.

20. Neither are the Storyes of the Greek, and Latine Poets all together to be sleighted in this particular; for many verities are interwoven with their fictions, they speak of vocal Forrests, as *Dodona*, of *Talkative* Rivers, as *Scamander*, of sensitive Fountains as *Arethusa*, *Menippa*, and Æagle; Which more credible Historians have partly confirmed in the Relation of *Dodona*, asserting that the trees do seem to speak by reason of the various Apparitions, and Phantasms, that attend the Forrest. And also in the Story of the River *Scamander*, which is sayd at this day to afford plenty of spectres, and prophetical Spirits, that have nightly conversation with the *Turkish* Sailers coming by that way with Gallyes into the *Mediterranean*.

21. The like is reported of a Castle in *Norweigh* standing over a Lake wherein a Satyr appeareth sounding a Trumpet before the death of any Souldier, or Governour belonging to the same, tis sayd to be the Ghost of some murdered Captain that hath become so Fatal, and Ominous to his Successors. But with more probability may be called a Spectre proper to the place according to the Constellation.

22. And it hath been the conjecture of eminent speculators that from the Loins of such arise the numerous brood of *Elves*, *Faeryes*, *Lycanthropi*; And *Pigmyes*, sometimes visible, sometimes invisible in Green-Land and the adjacent rocks where they have no concomitants, but bears and scurvy-grass to mix, and make merry withal, except they pass from thence to the *Northern* parts of America, where they shall find their off-spring adored for Gods, and Goddesses, by the ignorant Inhabitants about new *Albion*, and as far *South* as *Mexico*, as is amply related in the discourses of *Drake, Cortes* and *Purchas* concerning the conquest and discovery of these Territoryes.

23. By Apparitions upon the water many have been tempted to leap into the Sea in pursuit thereof till they were drowned, of which spectres there is a sort called by *Psellus*, *Ordales*, who do appear like Ducks or other Water fouls, till they by fluttering upon the water, do entice their followers to pursue them so farr that many perish in the attempt, which doth greatly delight these faithless Spirits who (as we have said before) do long to accompany their Astral Spirits after their decease. An Example of this kinde I my self knew, besides the numerous relations I have had from the mouths of others, which confirm the opinions of the antient Magicians concerning these water Spirits, that of all the rest they are the most deceitful, and dangerous, like the flattering Seas, and swift gliding Torrents, that when they have wonn any thing, to admire, and sound them, do carry them violently into the abysse of their own Element.

24. But we will leave the waters and insist a little on the nature of *Igneous* or *Fiery Spirits* that inhabit the Mountains in *Hecla*, Ætna, *Propo Champ*, and

Poconzi; Where the Courts, and Castles of these puissant Champions are kept. The opinion of some is, *That they are not Astral, but Infernal Spirits, and Damned Souls, that for a term of years are confined to these burning Mountains for their Iniquities*: Which opinion although it be granted, yet we may assert, That for the most part the apparitions, sounds, noices, clangors, and clamors, that are heard about the Mountains in *Hecla* in *Island* and other places, are the effects of separated Starry beings, who are neither capable of good nor evill, but are of a middle vegetative nature, and at the dissolution of the *Media Natura* shall be again reduced into their primary Æther.

25. And from natural Causes, it may be easily demonstrated, That there is great Correspondence betwixt such substances, and the Element of fire, by reason of the Internal Flagrat and Central Life proceeding from the Quintessence or one only Element which upholds them, in Motion, Life, and Nourishment. As every natural, and supernatural being is upheld, and maintained out of the self-same root from whence it had its original, or rise; So the Angels feed upon the *Celestial Manna*, The Devils of the fruits of Hell, which is natural to their appetite, as trash for swine; the Astral beings, of the source of the stars, the Beasts, Birds, or Reptiles of the fruits of the Earth, and the gas of the Air, the fishes of the blass of the Water; But more particularly, every thing is nourished by its Mother, as Infants at the Breast, either by exhausting or fomentation.

26. Such Spirits are very officious in the burnings of Towns, or Cole-pits, delighting much to dance and exult amidst the flames, and become Incendiaries worse then the material Cause of the Combustion, often tempting men in drunkeness, to burn their own Houses, and causing Servants carelesly to sleep, that such unlucky accidents may happen. As the Story of *Kzarwilwui* a Town in Poland doth confirm, which was reduced to ashes by three of these pestilentious Animals, called **Saggos**, **Broundal**, and **Baldwin**, who after many open Threatnings for six months together, that they would destroy the City, and Citizens, did on a dark and stormy night, set all on fire on a suddain in twenty or thirty several places, which irrecoverably destroyed the Inhabitants.

27. As for the nourishment of fiery Spirits, it is radical heat, and the influence of the Aery Region; their sport and pastime consisteth for the most part in tumbling, and fooling one with another when the flames are most impetuous, and violent in the Mountains: And it is likewise credited by some that their office is to cruciate and punish some Evil Livers, retaining, and tormenting their Souls, or Astral Spirits for many years after the Bodies decease, which is too empty a notion to be hearkened unto by any that are well informed of their natures.

28. Neither is it to be wondered at that they are so much delighted with the fiery quality in regard of their affinity and appropriation with infernal spirits, whose state and being is altogether damnable and deplorable; for although they have not the ability of attaining either the Heavenly or Infernal quality, by reason that they are utterly voyd of the innermost Center, and may be rather called bruits, then rational Animals, yet because they belong to the outermost principle, such is their innate Affinity, and Unity with the dark World, or infernal Kingdome that they do often become the Devils Agents to propagate his works upon the face of the Earth.

29. By the Instigations of infernal Spirits they are often sent to terrifie men with nocturnal visions, in the likeness of monstrous Beasts or Ghosts of their deceased Friends. They are moreover often abetted to tempt and provoke melancholy people to execute themselves; besides innumerable wayes they have of executing the pleasures of iniquous Spirits through malicious Instigations, and secret Stratagems projected by them to the destruction of mortal men, especially when the work to be effected by the Devil is too hard for his subtle and spiritual nature to bring to pass, because the same belongs to the Astral source or outward principle to which these dubious Spirits do properly belong; then are they frequently sollicited to mediate in such treacherous actions, as the hellish Spirits have conspired against the Lives of mortal men.

30. More particularly, These Spirits that belong to the fiery Element, are most officious in this kinde of service, being naturally such as the Antecedent matter hath sufficiently demonstrated; but according to the ranks and Categoryes to which they belong, some of them are more inveterate, and malicious in their undertakings then the rest. But every kinde of Astral Spirit is obsequious to the Kingdome of darkness, that the devilish Spirits can effect little or nothing without their assistance in this external principle of the Starrs and Elements upon the bodies or possessions of Mankind; because their bodies are too crude and rough for the conveyance of their influence, either in Dreams, Raptures, Philtes, Charms, or Constellations, as the following Chapter of the nature of Infernal beings shall make plain, wherein the nature and capacity of every damned Spirit is deciphered according to the truth of the antient Philosophy.

31. Leave we now the Spirits of the fire, to illustrate the natures of subterranean Beings, whose Orders, Species, and Degrees, are various; for they consist in these distinctions, *viz.* Spirits of men deceased, Souls of men deceased, separated Spirits Astral, separate Spirits semi-Infernal[291], Spirits

[291] The reader may note that the unknown author used repeatedly the term "separated"

appropriate to the Constellations where any of the seven metals, *viz. Saturn, Jupiter, Mars, Sol, Lima, Venus, Mercury*, are found in the bowels of the Earth; and as farr as the natures of Minerals are distinct one from the other, so much distant are these Subterranean Spirits in Nature and Faculty in respect of their places, shapes, names, and qualities.

32. But they are not all confined unto the metallick Kingdome; for there are also Spirits of the Mountains, Vallies, Caves, Deeps, Hiata's, or Chasma's of the Earth, hidden Treasures, Tombs, Vaults, and Sepultures of the Dead. To the last belong the Astral Spirits of deceased Mortals, that delight to hover over the antient Carcases to which they belonged, seeking still to be dissolved, and diligently enquiring the Cause of their retention; such are resident in silent Caves, and solitary Vaults, where the deceased lie till the Humidum Radicale be exciccate, and totally dryd up, after which their tricks are no more manifest, but are utterly extinguished, and annihilated.

33. To the next, belong such Spirits as are Protectors of hidden Treasures, from a natural Cause, from whence they do exceedingly envy mans benefit, and accomodation in the discovery thereof, ever haunting such places where money is concealed, and retaining malevolent and poysonous Influences, to blast the Lives and Limbs of those that dare to attempt the discovery thereof: Peters of Devonshire with his confederates, who by Conjuration attempted to dig for such defended Treasures, was crumbled into Atomes, as it were, being reduced to Ashes with his Companions in the twinkling of an eye.

34. And upon this particular, we have plenty of Examples of the destruction of such as by Magical experiments have discovered hidden Treasures; which instances do rather seem to prove, That such as haunt these places do more nearly belong to the Infernal, then to the Astral Hierarchy, in regard that they are so infesting and inveterate to Mortal men, that the Grand Intention of the Prince of darkness may be accomplished in their designs.

35. But of all the rest such as haunt Mines and mettle men, are the most pernicious, and frequent from the same Cause with the former. The nature of such is very violent; they do often slay whole Companies of Labourers, they do sometimes send inundations that destroy both the Mines, and Miners, they bring noxious and malignant vapours to stifle the laborious workmen; briefly,

to identify a kind of spirit of non-human origin. Even Jake Stratton-Kent, who knows very well this work, considers this passage a "tough one, 'separate' could indicate a soul gone on to another state than merely deceased; separate from the mere dead. Or that their region/habitation is distinct from ours, separated by some barrier or distance". (From a private conversation with Jake Stratton-Kent. Used with permission.)

their whole delight and faculty consists in tormenting, killing, and crushing men that seek such Treasures, that mankind may never partake thereof to relieve their Cares, and worldly necessities.

36. Such was *Anæbergius* a most virulent Animal that did utterly confound the undertakings of those that laboured in the richest Silver mine in *Germany*, called *Corona Rosacea*. He would often shew himself in the likeness of a he-goat with Golden horns, pushing down the workmen with great violence, sometimes like a Horse breathing flames, and pestilence at his Nostrils. At other times he represented a Monk in all his *Pontificalibus*, flouting at their Labour, and imitating their Actions with scorn and dedignation, till by his daily and continued molestation he gave them no further ability of perseverance.

37. Thus, I have hinted the various distinctions, and sub-distinctions of Astral Spirits proper or common, illustrating their natures according to the opinions of the Learned; from thence I proceed to say what the Infernal Hierarchy is, and whereof it doth consist in this fifth Chapter following.

Chap. V.

Of the Infernal Spirits, or Devils, and damned Souls treating, what their Natures, Names, and Powers are, &c.

1. Leaving the Astral Kingdome, I will now proceed to describe the natures, and distinctions of Infernal Spirits or Devils, and damned Souls, who are to be considered according to their ranks, and orders, exactly correspondent to the Quires, and Hierarchies of the Angels, or Celestial beings, wherein I will insist upon their names, shapes, places, times, orders, powers, and capacities, proceeding gradually from a general narration, to a particular Anatomy of every sort of Spirit in its proper place and order.

2. As for the Locality or Circumscription of the Kingdome of darkness, it is farr otherwise to be considered then the vulgar account it, who esteem the hellish habitation, a distinct Chasma or Gulph in a certain place, above, under, or in the Center of the Earth, where innumerable Devils, and wicked Souls inhabit, who are perpetually scorched, and tormented with material flames of fire. This is the opinion which naturally all men are addicted and prone unto. But if we will rightly consider the Kingdome of Heaven and Hell, in respect of one another, we must look upon the similitude of light and darkness in this outward world, who are not circumscribed, nor separate as to Locality from one another; for when the sun arises, the darkness of the night disappeareth, not that it removes it self to some other place or Country, but the brightness of

the light overpowereth it, and swallows it up, so that though it disappeareth, yet it is as really there as the light is.

3. This is also to be considered in the description of the Habitations of good, or evill beings, that they are really in one another, yet not comprehended of one another, neither indeed can they be, for the evil Spirits if they should remove ten thousand miles, yet are they in the same quality and source, never able to finde out or discover where the Kingdome of Heaven is to be found, though it be really through, and through with the dark Kingdome, but in another quality which makes them strangers to one another.[292]

4. A similitude hereof we have in the faculties of the humane Life, as to the indowments of the Soul considered in the just, and in the wicked; for to be good, pure, and holy, is really present as a quality in *potentia* with the depraved soul, although at that instant the Soul be cloathed with Abominations, so that the eye which should behold God or Goodness is put out. Yet if the soul would but come out of it self, and enter into another source or principle, in the center it might come to see the Kingdome of Heaven within it self, according to the Scripture, and *Moses*, *The word is nigh thee, in thy heart, and in thy Mouth.*

5. True it is that the Devils and damned Souls cannot sometimes manifest themselvs in this Astral World, because the nature of some of them is more near unto the external quality then of others, so that although properly the very innermost and outermost darkness be their proximate abode, yet they do frequently flourish, live, move, and germinate in the Aery Region, being some of them finite and determinate Creatures.

6. But according to their fiery nature, it is very difficult for them to appear in this outward world, because there is a whole principle or gulph betwixt them, to wit, they are shut up in another quality or existence, so that they can with greater difficulty finde out the being of this World, or come with their presence into the same, then we can remove into the Kingdome of Heaven, or Hell with our intellectual for if it were otherwise, and that the Divels had power to appear unto Mortals as they list, how many Towns, Cities, &c. should be destroyed, and burnt to the ground, how many Infants should be kild by their malicious power! yea few or none might then escape in Lives, or Possessions, and sound minds, whereas now all these enjoyments are free amongst mortals, which proves, that it is exceeding hard

[292] This confused and elaborate exhibition has indeed a very interesting principle and represents a concept well in advance of the time it was published. In more modern terms, it can clearly be understood as indicating that the different "homes" of spiritual beings are separated by different vibrational levels ("quality" and "source"), or different dimensions, etc.

for evill Spirits to appear in the third principle of this world, as for a man to live under water, and fishes on the Land. Yet must we grant, that when the imaginations, and earnest desires of some particular Wizards, and envious Creatures have stirred up the center of Hell within themselvs, that then the Devil hath sometimes access to this world in their desires, and continues here to vex, and torment so long as the strength of that desire remains which was the first attractive Cause.

7. For the very cause of the paucity of appearances in these dayes, is the fulness of time, and the brightness of Christianity, dispelling such mists, as the sun doth cause the clouds to vanish, not by any violence or compulsion, but from a natural cause; even so the Kingdome of Light as it grows over mans soul, in power and dominion, doth naturally close up the Center of darkness, and scatter the influences of the Devil so that his tricks lye in the dust, and his will at length becomes wholly passive as to man.

8. In the time of the Law, when the wrath and jealousie of the Father, had the dominion in the Kingdom of Nature, all Infernal Spirits had more easie access unto mankind then now they have; for before the Incarnation of Christ, the anger of God had more dominion over the soul of Man, and was more near in nature unto the same; so that the Devils could with more facility spring up in the element of Wrath, to manifest themselves in this outward principle, because the very Basis and Foundation of Hell beneath, is built and composed of the Wrath of God, which is the channel to convey the Devil into this sublunary World.

9. But when Christ began to be manifest unto the World, the multiplicity of Appearances, and possessed with Devils, began insensibly to decay and vanish. And if any should object, *That betwixt the space of his Incarnation and his Suffering, such accidents were rather more frequent than in the times before*: To this I answer, That the Devil knowing well that his time was but short; and also knowing, that till the great Sacrifice was offered up, he had leave to range and rove abroad the Kingdom of this World; therefore he imployed all his forces and endeavours to torment those miserable souls and captives to whom Christ came to Preach Deliverance.

10. But after the Partition wall was broken down, and the vail of Moses, and of the anger of God from off the soul in the death of Christ,[293] there was a sensible and visible decay of the Devils prancks amongst mortals, and that little remnant of Lunaticks and Possessed, which continued after Christ, did

[293] The reference is possibly to Ephesians 2:14, where is mentioned the fall of the "wall of hostility" or "of separation" that existed between Jews and Gentiles, broken by Jesus Christ when he was crucified.

the Apostles relieve and set at liberty, through the influence and virtue of the promise of the Son of God (to wit) *the Holy Ghost*, or the *Comforter*, which could not come until he went away: And on the day of *Pentecost*, whilst they waited in humility for the fulfilling of his promise, the very effect of Christs birth and sufferings did first manifest it self, when the Holy Ghost sprung up amongst them, to the destruction of Sin and Satan.

11. And so long as the purity of Christianity continued in the Primitive Church, there were very few that the Devil could personally or actually lay hold of in the Astral Man, for the space of two hundred years after the death of Christ, until that from Meekness and Abstinence, the Christians began to exalt themselves in Loftiness and Worldly Honours; then the Devil began to exalt his head amongst the Lip-Christians, bewitching them into every Lust; and captivating their inward and outward faculties at his pleasure. As all along in Popery is clearly seen.

12. Yet notwithstanding, the coming of Christ hath prevented the Devils force in general. Such Nations as have never embraced the Christian Faith, are still deluded and bewitched by him; because the center hath never been actually awakened in any of them, so that the Devils power prevails over them mightily, to seduce them to worship things visible, and not the true God: For where the most darkness is in Religion and Worship, or in natural understanding, there his power is most predominant; As in *Tartary*, *China*, and the *East-Indies*; also in *Lapland*, *Finland*, and the *Northern Islands*.

13. In the West-Indies or America, his access is very facil and freequent to the Inhabitants, so that by custom and continuance they were at the first discovery thereof, become so much substitute and obsequious to his power, that though they knew him to be a power of Darkness, yet they adored him lest he should destroy them and their Children. And unto such a height were they come at the Landing of *Cortes*, *Drake*, and *Vandernort*, that they could familiarly convert themselves into Wolves, Bears, and other furious Beasts; in which Metamorphosis their *Enthusiasms* and *Divinations* were suggested, and such were held in greatest esteem.

14. Till upon the Invasion of the *Spaniards*, the greater evil drove out the less, and the cruel Murthers of that Antichristian tradition, did both depopulate the Islands and most of the Continent; and also by accident, though not through any good intention, extirpate the race of such as addicted themselves to this infamous sort of Divination. In which devastation, and bloody inquisition, their Idols were discovered with their Oracles and Inchantments, far different from the *European* Conjurers, and any of their Ceremonies.

15. But that which is the most remarkable in the Infernal proceedings, is this, That there is not any Nation under the Sun, but the Devil hath introduced himself amongst them through their Ceremonies and Worship, though quite opposite to one another: For in the Kingdom of *China*, by the sacrifice of Blood and *Panaak*, he is Conjured and Exorcized through the repetitions of several Superstitious Invocations to the Sun and Moon. In *Tartary* the Magicians go quite another way to work, with Offerings to the Ocean, to the Mountains, and the Rivers, fuming Incense, and divers sorts of Feathers; by which means the Devils are compelled to appear. So that we see how this *Proteus* can dispose himself in the divers Kingdoms of this World; being called by other names in *Tartary*, *China*, the *East* and *West-Indies*, &c. then amongst the *European* Conjurers. Likewise the *Greeks* and *Romans* could Invocate Spirits by Prayers unto the Moon, and divers Sacrifices of Milk, Honey, Vervine, and Blood. And those that are addicted to Conjurations in Christianity, have attained to a more lofty and ample manner of Incantation and Conjuring with Magical Garments, Fire, Candles, Circles, Astrological Observations, Invocations, and holy Names of God, according to the *Kaballa* of the *Jews*.

16. So that every distinct Nation hath conformed its Conjuration unto the Ceremonies of that Religion which it professeth: And it is to be observed, That from a natural cause every Nation hath its Conjurations and Names of Devils, from the Constellation under which the Countrey lyeth, and from the Air or Wind to which such particular Dominations do belong; so that no effect would follow, if one Countrey should traditionally inure themselves to the Forms and Exorcisms that are used by another Nation. And therefore is it that so many attempts are offered in vain amongst professed Christians to raise Spirits, because they have little or nothing from their own Constellation, but make use of what they have borrowed from the *Greeks* and *Romans*, or the ancient Imbecillity of the Ægyptians Priests; I mean, their simple forms of Invocation.

17. But because we are rather upon the discovery of the Infernal Kingdom, as it hath no dependence upon the doings of mortal Men; therefore we will proceed to discover what the Antients have said concerning it: So the next which we fall upon after the description of their Habitations, and the manner of their Appearances, is their Names and Appellations diversly considered. First, from the Creation of the World to the coming of Christ, they retained the Hebrew names, as **Belial**, **Baal**, **Baalzebub**, **Lelah**, **Ador**, **Abaddon**, &c. according to the *seculum* under which they were Invocated ; assuming names according to the present occasion about which they were imployed.

18. Under the Constellation of China, they are Invocated by the Names **Kan**, **Sinoam**, **Nantam**, **Bal**, **Balial**, **Sheall**, the six Governours or Presidents: **Chaneangian** the chief of the Devils **Po**, **Paym**, **Nalkin**, **Nebo**,

the Devils of the four Winds: **Lean**, **Lan**, **Pan**, **Adal**, the Devils of the four Elements. And according to the nature of their language or words which do all consist of no more then one syllable, so are the Devils named. Yea, as it is conjectured by many learned Magicians, this language of the *Chinenses* is more Magical and adapted to Conjurations, then all the *Oriental Tongues*, because of the consonancy and copiousness thereof, together with the numerous and various Characters used by them.

19. In the *East-Indies*, and in *Tartary*, the Names are the same with those of *China*, though the Ceremonies differ. In *Persia, Arabia, Natolia, Ægypt, Ethiopia*, the Names are the same with the *Jewish Rabbins*. But the *Greeks* and *Romans* have different from the rest, according to their Language and Superstitions. The *Turks, Muscovites, Russians, Lapponians, and Norwegians*, make use of the *Sclavonian* tongue in all their Conjurations. The *West-Indians* have very strange and antick Names and Ceremonies of their own, nothing depending on the Traditions and Practices of the old World; for, as is related before, the Devil is sufficiently capable of introducing himself through the Religious Superstitions of any Nation whomsoever, according to the Constellations, although strangers to the Rites and Ceremonies of others.[294]

20. But though their Names be conformable to the Language and Climate of that Nation where they are raised or called; yet have they divers Names, suppose twenty or thirty to one Devil, according to the several ministrations they have had from the Creation to this day, leaving a several name behinde them at each of their appearances upon the earth; for, according to the testimony of the Devil himself, if credit may be given to Devils, they, as they are abstractively considered in their own Kingdom, have no imposed Names of distinction, but are forced to assume them when they rise up in the external principle of this World: although in some measure it must be granted, that there be some principal Kings and Dukes in the Infernal Hierarchy, that have Names established upon them which cannot be transferr'd or altered.

21. As for the Names that are recorded in this precedent *Discovery of Witchcraft* by Reginald Scot Esq; being a Catalogue of Devils in their Rancks and Hierarchies, they are supposed to be fictitious and totally imaginary, being taken out of *Bodin* or *Wyerus*, which they recorded from the mouth of Tradition, and obscure Manuscrips: And indeed were there any certainty in this List of Devils,[295] it were to be preferred as the most ample and exact delineation that

[294] From this we conclude that the Devil is much more competent than Jesus, whose "word of salvation" took 1500 years to come to the New World where it was, as ususal, implanted by massacres and destruction.

[295] He is making reference to the use that Scot made of the text *Pseudomonarchia*

is extant. But it is the rather to be suspected, because of the little coherence it hath with the former received Names of Devils eitheir in *Europe, Asia, Africa,* or *America.*

22. But if we would speak of Damned Souls and their Names or Appellations, they are farr otherwise to be considered then the Devils; for such as their imposed Names were here on earth, such is the Name they have in the Kingdom of Darkness, after a Magical manner, according to the language of nature in the first principle of Darkness; as the Saints in heaven retain their Names in a Cœlestial manner: And also, as the Astral Spirit of a Man deceased, retains its antient Name according to the Astral source in the principle of the one only Element.

23. For as the language of Nature is found in the second Principle, it is likewise manifest in the dark Worlds property, according to the first Principle of Wrath; as also the monstrous shapes of Devils and Damned Souls is correspondent to the Magical postures of their Souls whilst they were alive; of which I shall speak more largely when their Shapes are to be described. According unto which, as also according to the rest of their attributes, *viz.* their Rancks, Numbers, Times, Powers, Places, &c. their Names are fitted and conformed according to the uniformity of name and thing in the principles of the eternal and external nature.

24. And as all other Nations have their various Appellations for Devils and Damned Souls, like their natural tone or language; so we can mention one Kingdom more admirable then the rest, *viz.* the Kingdom of *Fiacim* at the *Northern Pole*, where all the Counsellors are Magicians; and the Names which they use in Invocations, are Mathematically disposed in a wonderful harmony and efficacy, to the performance of Magical operations. So much of the Places and Names of Infernal Beings; the next to be considered is their Shapes and Likenesses.

25. The Shapes of Devils are answerable to the cause of their Fall, and the Dominions to which they belong. Those that belong to the Supreme Hierarchy, when they are called by Magicians, do at first appear in the form of fierce and terrible Lyons, vomiting fire, and roaring hideously about the Circle; from thence they convert themselves into Serpents, Monkies, and other Animals, till the Magician do repeat the form of Constriction or Confinement to a Trine or Triangle, as before is mentioned in the Fifteenth Book of the *Discovery*.

Daemonum, published by Johann Weyer as an appendix to his *De praestigiis daemonum* from 1577. Scot included it in Book XV, but here we omitted it.

26. After the Conjuration is repeated, they forsake these bestial shapes, and indow the humane form at first like troops of Armed Men; till at last by frequent repetitions of other Ceremonies, they appear as naked Men of gentle countenance and behaviour. Yet is the Magician to take care that they deceive him not by insinuations; for their fraudulency is unspeakable in their appearance and dealings with Mankind; because we may be assured they appear not willingly, but are by forceable Conjurations compelled: so that they will ever minde their own ends in medling with man; that is, to deprave his minde, or subvert the Lives and Estates of others through his means and assistance.

27. The rest of the Infernal Dominions have various appearances. The two next Orders affect to represent the beautiful colours of Birds, and Beasts, as Leopards, Tygers, Pecocks, &c. But by Conjurations they may be likewise reduced to a Manlike form, wherein they will readily answer every demand within the compass of their capacity, answerable to the Order unto which they belong; Yet many of them appear in Monstrous forms, and can hardly be conjured to desert them. Though the Exorcist Charm them never so wisely, they will shew him a pair of Crocodiles jaws, or a Lyons paw, with other dreadful menaces, enough to terrifie any Novice from such Damnable Injunctions as the practice of Magick.

28. But more especially, the opinion of the antients is, That according to the division of the clean and unclean Beasts in the Law given unto *Moses*, the Shapes of Devils are disposed in the Infernal Kingdom: So that the most perverse and potent amongst the Devils represent the most ugly and mischievous amongst the Beasts, according to this following division; *viz*. such Devils as **Astaroth**, **Lucifer**, **Bardon**, **Pownok**, who incline men and instigate them to pride and presumptuousness, have the shapes of Horses, Lyons, Tygars, Wolves. Such as instigate to Lust and Covetousness have the forms of Hogs, Serpents, and other filthy reptiles or envious Beasts, as Dogs, Cats, Vultures, Snakes, &c. Such as incline to Murther, have the shapes of every Bird and Beast of prey. Such as Answer Questions humane in Philosophy, or Religion, have more tolerable shapes, almost manly, but with crooked Noses, like Mermaids, or Satyres. And of all the rest it is to be observed, that as not one single Lust or Vice hath dominion without mixture in the evil Spirits, so they are not of a distinct shape lik one single Beast, but compounded into Monsters, with Serpents-tails, four eyes, many feet and horns, &c.

29. And as in general, these are the shapes of Devils, so the particular shapes of Damned Souls are to be considered in the same manner with the rest, only with this difference, that they are more addicted to metamorphose themselves and vary their appearances. Though, for the most part, the Damned Souls retain the humane shape after a Magical manner, so that the greatest part

of that numberless number are in their antient shapes, especially when they appear in sleep to their surviving acquaintance. Their aspects are very dismal and melancholy like the Ghosts of the Astral source.

30. Now to speak of the Times and Seasons of their Appearance. The better sort of Magicians to square their times with Astrological hours, especially of *Saturn*, *Luna*, and *Venus*, in the Moons increase, and the middle of the night, or twelve a clock at noon: In which hours they do likewise compose their Garments, Caps, Candlesticks, Figures, Lamins, Pentacles, and Circles for Conjuration. As for the Times in respect of their Infernal Courses, the fittest are when they spring up in the Wrath, or when they sink in the Dispair, which is a mystery to the learned Conjurers of Europe.

31. In respect of this exterior World, they can most easily appear in solitary places, when the Sun is down; for they are naturally at enmity with the Sun, because it stands as a type of the Mediator, or Heart and Centre which they lost utterly in their fall, and now are destitute of, like a wheel without an axletree. And indeed, the want of this is the chief cause of all their torment, and of the rising of the gnawing Worm, when they consider of their irrevocable sentence, and irrecoverable loss.

32. In storms of Hail, or Snow, Wind, Tempest, and Lightning, is accounted amongst Magicians, a time for Conjuring at an easie rate. And they say, That such Ceremonies will prove very effectual, if a Conjurer begin his Exorcisms in the hour and day of *Luna*, in the middest of a furious storm of Lightning, Rain, and Thunder, in a low Vault or Celler that is close and retired. Also when the Wind blows high, without Rain, they say, the Devils are more near the Kingdom of this World, and may with great facility be sollicited or raised at such a season, because they delight in all extremities of weather, being themselves the first cause of the disorder of the properties in the Kingdom of Nature.

33. But in some Countries they can more easily appear then in others, according to the Constellations, for they delight much in the extremities of the two Poles toward *Lapland*, *Nova Zembla*, *Greenland*, *Tartary*; and in the South towards the Islands scattered about the confines of *Terra Incognita*. They are likewise easily Invocated on the shoar amongst lofty Rocks and Precipices, or Deserts and Wildernesses far from Towns or Inhabitants. And it is said, they do much respect the motion of the Seas in their appearance unto such as solicite them in places *Maritime* or *Plagiary*.

34. As for their Rancks or Orders, there is some difficulty in the true discovery thereof, by reason that we know not certainly of what Orders they

were that *Fell.* The opinion of most men is, *That of every Order many fell.* But those that better know the nature of the Heavenly Hierarchies, have sufficiently proved, *That of any Ranck or Order none can fall unless all do follow.* Therefore with more reason may it be judged, That before the Devils fell, the Hierarchy of Heaven did consist of three Rancks or Orders; to wit, the Order of **Uriel**, of **Michael**, of **Lucifer**: That of **Lucifer** is totally in Hell: The other which is under Michael, is the dominion of Heaven: The last which is Uriels, are more in the dominion of this third principle of the *Stars*, having the *Planets* in their dominion, with the influences thereof.

35. So that the foregoing Catalogue, transcribed by the Author of this *Discovery*, is utterly feigned and fictitious, because it makes these many sorts of Devils to have Dominion over several Legions in several distinctions of *Seraphims, Powers, Thrones, Dominations, Cherubims*, &c. Whereas the whole Kingdom of Hell consists but of one only Hierarchy, which is that of **Lucifer** and his *Legions*, reduced by their exorbitances into that Lacrymable posture wherein they now are and shall be for ever. Which Doctrine seriously weigh'd will prove the attempts of Conjurers and Magicians to be utterly vain, and their forms of Invocation vanity and falshood.

36. Their number may be thought upon more narrowly, if we consider that they consist of one Hierarchy and no more; yet must we confess that the limit is not to be put thereunto, because their nature is to Germinate and Multiply as they please, contracting and dilating themselves according to the force of their imaginative powers and faculties. But although this be granted, yet there is a setled number of Devils that varyeth not.[296] Though of Damned Souls the number is numberless and unfathomable; yet as to their extent of room or place, it is never the more because of their multitude, they being able to truss a thousand Legions into the carcass of a man. As for the opinions of Authors, they are various; it is believed by some, *That the Starrs are answerable to their number*; others speak of *the Sands upon the Sea-shore*: however it be, this is certain, *They are even innumerable in respect of humane Capacities.*

37. Their Natures are now to be considered as they belong to the hellish source or quality. In themselves they rest not, neither are they capable of the length or shortness of time, nor of the alternate courses of day and night. The wickedness which they committed in this life, are their continual torment, which do Magically gnaw and corrode them, rising and boyling up perpetually within them, all the refrigeration which they have, is by intercourse when the height of Wickedness begins to stirr them in blasphemies against God, and towring up above heaven and goodness, in their adulterated Imaginations,

[296] The reader may feel free to try to understand this contradiction.

which is unto them as sport and pastime with one another, and lasteth such a space as with us makes up forty minutes. Neither doth this any whit advantage them, but rather adds to their torment; for pain discontinued is the greater: neither would vexation be vexation, if it had no respite or forbearance; That the contrary might be also manifest. *Nam contraria juxta se posita majus elucescunt.* Yet is their torment exceedingly different, so that the torment of one, in respect of another, is but a Dream or Phansie; I mean, amongst the Damned Souls, and not the Devils, for the pain and sorrow of the Devils is greater then the greatest of the lost Souls, by many thousand degrees, according to the course of nature and reason; for that which falls highest, suffers most, and *optima corrupta fiunt pessima.*

38. But wonderful and manifold are the torments which all in general of the Infernal troops, do suffer according to the various lusts they reigned in whilst they lived upon the earth. The cruel Murtherers that died in the boyling source of blood and envy, their torment is the greatest, they are continually Murthering in their imaginations, and seeking, like dreaming men, to do what the want of the Organ will not suffer them; for according to the saying of the wisest upon this Subject, this is the torment and misery of all the Damned, *That they are continually wishing and woulding; and in wouldings they generate Ideas and representations, which are the species of their continual aggravations and deceiving phansies.*

39. Those that were buryed in Lust and Gluttony, Drunkenness and Lasciviousness, are also in miserable torments, yet much inferiour to the first; they are continually imagining their former pleasures in the *Magia* as in a dream, which when they wake, torments them cruelly; they are often hanging, stabbing, and mangling themselves for love, and perpetually sinking down in sorrow and despair, if they were such as died in love, or in the height of their Astral affections, leaving behind them a heap of desires and lusts, which are the only cause of all their torment. And we may well compare the passions of Melancholy persons, or such as in Deserts, Woods, and Mountains, pine away for love of Women, unto their torments; which indeed being the trouble of the mind, are absolutely the greatest and heaviest that the source or property of this World affordeth, I mean, the perturbations of the minde in general.[297]

40. Such souls in whom the boyling source of Anger and Rage, hath had a dwelling or receptacle, if they depart unmortified, do also enter into a most dreadful kind of torment, which continually ariseth as a biting Worm and

[297] We must bear in mind that the writer, being a Protestant, is against the institution of ecclesiastical celibacy, and here it seems he is criticizing the tradition of tales about the "temptations" of saints, so popular in Catholicism.

hungry fire to double and accumulate the excess of despair upon them, if they have much domineered therein whilst they lived in this World. Also these that reigned in Pride and Envy, are ever seeking to pluck God from his Throne, and towring up in their Imaginations, as men that dream, still seeking for the Kingdom of heaven, to insult and boast therein; but the quality thereof is utterly occult and estranged from them; so that they can never finde, taste, hear, nor see it, though it be through and through with their own peculiar principle.[298] This adds perpetually to their misery, and ariseth at times with horrible pangs and gnawings, like the irksome and vexatious pains and aches subject to Mans body, which cease a while and then begin to shoot and ake by intercourse, as the Gowt, Tooth-ach, Head-ach, Convulsion, Gripings, and the Stone.

41. Thus their torments are in brief described, but indeed the capacity of Man is not able to reach the description of their cruel miseries, and continual pangs which they contracted upon themselves; for every faculty is sufficiently plagued. The Sence of Hearing is disturbed with harsh and rugged sounds, which are as an antipathy to that Organ; as rough and scraping sounds externally offend the ears, and set the teeth on edge, by affecting the tender fibres of the same. Their Sight is likewise cruelly offended and affrighted with monstrous appearances and Ideas represented continually to their imaginations. And there is not any loathsome taste in the Kingdome of this World, either Animal, Vegetative, or Mineral, which they are at any time void of, being continually pestered and suffocated with filthy fumes and smoaks of hellish fruits, as of Sulphurean stinks, and abominations.

42. Neither are the other Sences of the Touch and Smell behind in participation of the like Torments, which their own iniquities do perpetually excite and create unto them; besides, they are ever vexing one another; and if any be in the same misery with whom they had acquaintance here on earth, the very Magical knowledge, and perceivance, or remembrance thereof, doth beyond utterance or conception, most miserably afflict and macerate their Souls and all their Sences.

43. For the nature of their habitation is such, that their torment is exceedingly aggravated thereby, because the extremity of the four Elements is there converted into a whole Principle of wrath and vexation. The excess of cold and heat, drought and moisture, are continually raging amongst them by

298 A notion exposed earlier in this text; the idea here seems to be the concept that God is everywhere, even in hell and in the condemned beings, and that these, however, no matter how much they want it, cannot see it. The "own peculiar principle", according to an earlier passage, is the divine Wrath.

intercourse. Neither is there any light or lustre to be seen within their Courts, but that which comes from their fiery Eyes, as a deadly glance or glimmering, being sudden fiery flashes and sparkling, as the enkindling of Gunpowder, or *Aurum fulminans*[299] for a similitude.

44. And as every kinde of Being feeds upon somewhat of its own nature, property, and element, whither it be Plant, Animal, or Metalline kinde; so the Devils are neither destitute of meat, drink, nor cloathing, according to their own Kingdom and quality, having fruits springing and growing before them of hellish, sour and poysonous natures, which are real and palpable unto them, and not imaginary or typical, though to us magical and invisible; neither is this to be wondered at, if we consider the nature of Man's Soul, *In Media Natura*; for if it feed not upon the internal and substantial Word, which is the very Bread of Life it self, it must of necessity ruminate on something else, *viz.* the fruits of Iniquity, which it takes in and drinketh up as the Oxe drinks water, so that to the soul the sin becomes palpable, glutting, and satiating; yea, so substantial unto the Soul, as Dirt or Ink upon fair white Linnen is to our external Eyes; neither can the Soul be freed from these spots till the water above the Firmament wash them away.

45. Also in respect of the Astral source they are not destitute of food, when they bring themselves into the same; for the gas of the air and bias of the water is their nourishment, while they stay here, as is before alledged: These influences of the air and water they take into their *Limbus*, and convert into their own poisonous natures; as of sweet and wholsome herbs the filthy Toads and other venemous Beasts do make their poyson, converting them into a nature like themselves. And on the contrary, the poysonous herbs are converted into good and wholesome nourishment by other cleanly Beasts.

46. And as the Infernal Troops are considered in respect of the four Elements, they have a distinct and peculiar tone or language, which they exercise and speak one amongst one another, as mortals do. But they have utterly lost the dignity of their sounds according to the eternal nature. And are likewise totally corrupted in their pronouncing, or Dialect, since they fell from their first cælestial glory; so that their speech is harsh, doleful, and terrible, like the fruits they feed upon, and the life they dwell in. Which depravation is very apparent in the Kingdom of this World in the divided Languages of every Region, according to the Constellation under which they are situated: The true and magical Language of nature being hid from all the Countreys of the earth.

---

[299] Fulminate of gold, an explosive compound of gold; called also fulminating gold, and *aurum fulminans.*

47. But when they appear in the outward Elements, they do many times express themselves in *Irish*, *Welch*, *Latine*; or *Russian*, are the Languages most affected by them to answer unto Conjurations, or Compacts. So that if any Magician, who is ignorant of these aforesaid Languages do at any time Raise or Exorcise such Spirits, he must be mindful to confine them to his mother tongue; least their gibberish prove altogether unintelligible; for as every thing appears in what it most affecteth, or is addicted to; even so the Spirits have their distinct affections, passions, and postures, both in word, habit, shape, and gesture; so that the Magician must be wary in Exorcizing with them, that he confine them to a different place, posture, shape, and language, to answer their intentions without impediment.

48. For they are very variable and unconstant in their dealings with mankind, nor will they stand to any thing that hath not bound them by the obligations of Words, Characters, and Imprecations, except the skill of the Exorcist be such, that he is able to confine them into a Magical Triad, which hath the certain force of obliging or compelling them to utter truth, and nothing false in all their Answers, or Informations. But with such miserable men and women as they have made Covenants and Indentures for body, soul, and works; with such I say, they keep no faith, nor are they lyable to their commands; but on the contrary, have them hampered and subjected to their will and power, till they have terminated their lives in their destruction.

49. Yet have not any of the most potent Princes in the Hellish Power, the least ability to destroy the least of the sons of men, without the consent of the mind and senses of the Soul; for until the will of the Soul be opened unto him, his threatnings, sleights and stratagems are without any power or force, as the nerves of a dead man. Although naturally every evil Spirit boasteth, as if all the world were at its command, and every Soul were subject to its authority and beck, with the Goods or Possessions of the external World.

50. When any evil Spirit is raised up by Conjurations, without League, or Compact; these Spirits so raised, are exceeding fraudulent and deceitful, as stubborn servants that do their Masters will by constraint, and not by any natural act of obedience unto his Commands. But with such as they have compacted, they are frequent and officious,[300] imploying them as Agents for the destruction of others and their substance: and being marryed unto such, they are even become one with them, being incorporated into them, so that they are nothing different from incarnate Devils, save that the spark of divine Light, which was the gift of God unto repentance, is not totally eradicated until the body fall away.

---

[300] This passage seems to contradict the one before.

51. From such as Covenant with these unconstant Spirits, do they daily obtain Fumigations, Odours, and Offerings, or Sacrifices of Blood, Fire, Wine, Ointments, Incense, Fruits, Excrements, Herbs, Gums, Minerals, and other Ingredients, by which from a Magical cause, they have more influence and authority over the bewitched party to insinuate into their affectfon, peircing even through their bones and marrow, till they have so habituated them to their service, that the same becomes their daily bread and sole delight in accomplishing every villany and abomination which the malicious and subtle instigation of Satan leads them to.

52. Thus have I Essayed to illustrate the Natures of Infernal Beings, which notwithstanding is a Subject so intricate and copious in it self, that great difficulty accompanies the Explication thereof; by reason of the variety of their natures in the source of darkness, wherein they live, move, eat, breath, and inhabit, having qualities, actions, and passions innumerable, to us men-kinde utterly unknown and incomprehensible: So that to attempt an ample demonstration of this present Subject, would require deeper speculation then the matter doth deserve, in regard that there be so many *Protei* and *Changlings* in that gloomy Kingdom, who do never stay or continue in the same nature, property, and form for an hour together; but may be compared to the swiftness of the Windes, or the likeness and form of swift running Waters, that pass away as a thought; and are no more remembered. So it is with the Spirits of Darkness, whose life is a meer anguish and inconstancy from one sorrow to another unto all Eternity.

Chap. VI.

Treating of the Nature, Force and Forms of Charms, Periapts,Amulets, Pentacles, Conjurations, Ceremonies, &c.

1. Before Appearances are made, after forms of Conjuration are repeated, the Infernal Spirits make various and wonderful shews, noises, and attempts as fore-runners to their appearance: At the first attempts of novices in Conjuration, they are accompanyed with noises, tremblings, flashes, bowlings, and most dreadful shriekes, till after further progress and experience therein they approach nearer unto this Elemental nature, till by degrees they can manifestly be apparent unto their Exorcist.

2. When *Chiancungi*, and his sister *Napala*, did first attempt to call up Spirits, they begun with the Spirit **Bokim**, in the twentieth degree: they hung a vault under ground with black both on the top and bottom, lining

it therewith; and having drawn the Circle of the Order of Thrones, with the seven Planets, and their Magical Characters in the Center, they proceeded to the Ceremonies of Conjuration after they had frequently repeated the forms of calling, and nothing as yet appeared; they were grown so desperate therein, that forsaking the Circle, and every defensive Character or Ceremony, they at last betook themselves to the most accursed and detestable branch of Magick, which consists of Compacts, or Confederacy; and having by a solemn League summoned the aforesaid Spirit **Bokim**, they obtained 155. years from the Spirit, Covenanting therewith for body, soul, and works.

3. In which damned life they continued exercising strange wonders in every Countrey. By the help of this Magician the *Tartars* did destroy above 100 sail of Ships belonging unto *China*; many losses did he bring upon that Kingdom in their Children, Fruits, Corn, Silk, and Navigation; he could frequently transport himself through the Air, and carry in one hand a thousand pound weight, to the astonishment of all that knew him. He had many publick contests with Magicians of other Countries, being tryals of skill in Magical Art, wherein he was said to excel all that ever went before him.

4. Such another was *Lewis Gaufridi* a French Priest, who had compacted with the Devil, and served him 14 years in these detestable works, sacrificing Infants unto him, worshipping him in a filthy shape, and tempting others to their Magical society or nocturnal Conventions; in which, as it is reported, they did ever feast and junket with varieties and dainties, which though they did seem delectable, were yet notwithstanding gustless and unsavoury.

5. Leaving these relations, something shall be said of *Charms* and *Spells*, as they are divided in this following manner; first, such Amulets as being engraven and molded in the fashion of Money, or Coyn, do serve to provoke any one desired unto love and familiarity, being hung about the neck in certain Planetary hours. Secondly, Spells or Charms in Parchment with Magical Characters, as Periapts to Cure diseases; to make one valiant, memorative, and constant. Thirdly, Corselets, which are an ancient *Danish* Charm of Necklaces, composed of Thunderstones ingraven with Magical Letters, to resist all noxious influences, and the danger of Lightning.

6. *Pentacles* are a fourth sort of appendix, which Conjurers, Charmers, and Magicians use, being made with five corners, according to the five Senses, and the operation thereof inscribed upon the corners; the matter whereof they are composed, is fine Linnen doubled, and done with Cere-cloth[301] between. This figure the Magician holds in his hand, lifting it up from the skirt of his Garment

[301] Fabric coated with wax used to cover the dead.

to which it is annexed, when Spirits that are raised are stubborn and rebellious, refusing to be conformable unto the Ceremonies and Rites of Magick.

7. Also by the holding forth *Pentacles*, with these words, **Glauron**, **Amor**, **Amorula**, **Beor**, **Beorka**, **Beroald**, **Anepheraton**, repeated at the instant. The evil Spirits that possess the bodies of bewitched people are cruelly tortured and amazed, being by the frequent repetition thereof forced at last to depart by the assistance of the Exorcism of the sixth Cannon for the order of Seraphims.

8. When Magicians exercise Conjuration by Moon-light in the Mountains or Valleys, they have another sort of Charm by way of Telesms, which they bury within a hundred paces of the place where the Circle is composed towards the *East*, *West*, *North*, and *South*; For such spells have the secret power to hinder any living creature for coming near them, till their Exercize be done, except the Infernal Spirit, whose presence they do so ardently desire.

9. Such Spells as are made in some *Edible matter*, with Characters upon them, are given for Agues, Head-ach, Epilepsie, Mother, &c. Especially being powerful in operation, when the party is ignorant of the Charm taken in; many such I know have taken wonderful effect. But as for *Philtres*, *Potions*, and *Love-cups*, they proceed rather from a natural cause; whether their effects be to afflict with Diseases to Poyson, or to provoke unto Love of a Party whom they disdain: Neither are such to be numbered amongst Charms; because their effect is meerly natural, from a natural cause.

10. But to insist further upon the nature of Conjuration, Magicians do much exercise their time in *Fumigations* unto those Spirits whom they are about to provoke; their fumes being distributed according to the nature of the Spirit under any of the seven Planets, which the antient Conjurers were very punctual in observing, though in these days it be much forgot, as superfluous, or rather dangerous to insert amongst the Ceremonies of Conjuration. A division of Fumigations according to the Influence of the Planets, and Orders of Spirits, we will here set down in this manner.

11. *Fumigations for Saturn* are made of Frankincense Trees, Pepperwort Roots, Storax, and Galbanum; by these the Spirits **Marbas**, **Corban**, **Stilkon**, **Edos**, And all of the first order in the astringency are appeased and provoked, when the *fumes* are put upon a *Tripod* in the hour of *Saturn* according to the Planetary division. These Fumigations make these Spirits appear like old men, with promiss beards, and meager looks; like Serpents, Cats, Wolves, Badgers, Panthers; like old Men in Armour; like Trumpeters in many ranks and divisions.

12. For Spirits under Jupiter, they take Lignum Aloes, Ashen-Keys, Benjamin, Storax, Peacocks-feathers, and *Lapis Lazuli*, mixing the same with the blood of a Stork, a Swallow, or a Hart; the brains being also added. The *fumes* are kindled in *Jupiters* hour, and in a place appropriate to his nature. And by this sacrifice the Spirits of the next order are called up, like glorious Kings with many attendants, and mighty pomp; with Heralds before them, and Ensign-bearers, Trumpeters, Guards, and all sorts of musical Instruments.

13. They make *Fumigations* unto such Spirits of the order of Powers, as are under *Mars*, in the Planetary division with Aromatick Gum, Bdellium, Euphorbium, Load-stone, Hellebore white and black, and an addition of Sulphur to make them into an Amalgama, with Man's blood, and the blood of a black Cat; which mixtures are said to be exceeding magical: so that without any other addition, they say, this *fumigation* is able of it self to make such Spirits to appear before the Exorcist; at their appearance they come with weapons brandishing, and shining Armour, being terrible in their looks; yet of power inferiour to the Spirits of *Saturn*, though they can likewise shew themselves as Lions, Wolves, Tygers, Bears, and all other cruel or ravenous Beasts.

14. They do likewise unto the Spirits under Sol, being of the order of Thrones, *Suffumigate* Saffron, Musk, Laurel, Cinnamon, Amber-griece, Cloves, Myrrhe, and Frankincense, Musk, and the Balsamick Tree mixed up together with the brain of an Eagle, and the blood of a white Cock, being made up like Pills, or little Balls, and put upon the *Tripod*; their appearances are Castles, Gardens, Mountains, Rivers, Fisher-men, Hunters, Reapers, Dogs, Sheep, Oxen, and other domestick Beasts.

15. Under *Venus* are the Spirits of the sixth order in the Powers; their appearances are very stately, like the nature of the Planet; like Courtiers, Ladies, Princes, Queens, Infants, Children, and fragrant smells. The fumigations appropriate unto them are Roses, Coral, *Lignum Aloes*, and *Sperma Ceti* made up with Sparrows, brains and blood of Pidgeons to be fumigated with a Song.

16. *Mercury* sendeth Horsemen, Fishers, Labourers, Priests, Students, Servants, *&c.* Also, Foxes, Serpents, Dogs, Hares, Hyena's, Hydra's, and other Monstrous Animals; unto him they *fumigate* Frankincense, Mastick, Cinkfoyl, incorporated with the brain of a Fox, and the blood of a Mag-Pye.

17. Spirits under *Luna* are like Ghosts and shadows, very gastly to behold; though in humane shape sometimes male, sometimes female. *Fumigations* are offered unto them of Frogs dryed, white Poppy-seed, Bulls Eyes, Camphire, and Frankincense, incorporated with Gooses blood, and the menstruous blood of Women.

18. These are the divisions of *fumigations*, neither can it be denyed, but that in many Ceremonies of this kind, there is great inherent virtue according to the Doctrines of Sympathy and Antipathy, hereby every thing is drawn by its like in the Idea, whither by words or actions, according to the saying, *In verbis, herbis & lapidibus latet virtus,*[302] so that the Ceremonies and Charms, with other circumstances used by Magicians, are doubtless prevalent to the accomplishment of that work which they undertake; to wit, *The calling up and Exorcizing of Infernal Spirits by Conjurations.*

Chap. VII.

Being the Conclusion of the Whole; wherin divers antient Spells, Charms, Incantations and Exorcisms are briefly spoken of

1. Besides what the Author hath set down, there be many other *Spells* and *Charms*, which Tradition hath left unto Posterity, being many of them effectual for the thing intended by them, as in the precedent Chapter is set down, wherein the *Orders* of *Fumigations* are described. Besides there are *Magical Characters* attributed to the Planets, whereof *Telesms, Periapts, Amulets*, and *Philters*, are composed by *buryings, writings, bindings, engravings, alligations,* &c. to effect various purposes in Astrological hours. To conquer Enemies, cure diseases, overturn Cities, stop Inundations, render bodies Invulnerable, and the like; which are all effected by medium's of this kind, with the assistance of Imagination.

2. Yet are there many natural Compositions, which have very stupendious effects of themselves, without assistance of Superstition; for the commixtion of things is of two-fold force or vertue: First, When the Celestial vertues are duly disposed in any natural body; so that in one thing are couched various Influences of superiour Powers. The second is, from Artificial mixtures and Compositions of natural things amongst themselves, in a certain proportion to agree with the Heavens under certain Constellations. This proceeds from the correspondence of natural things amongst themselves, whereby things are effected even unto admiration, as Agrippa declares, Cap. 35. *lib.* I.

---

302 A Medieval Latin proverb, which occurs in numerous versions, declares that there is power (vim or virtus) in plants, in stones, and in words. Interestingly, in a sixteenth century medical text (Kindheart's Dream), the words "in verbis et in herbis, et in lapidibus sunt virtutes" appear as part of a spell for the cure of toothache. Claire Fanger in *Things Done Wisely by a Wise Enchanter: Negotiating the Power of Words in the Thirteenth Century.*

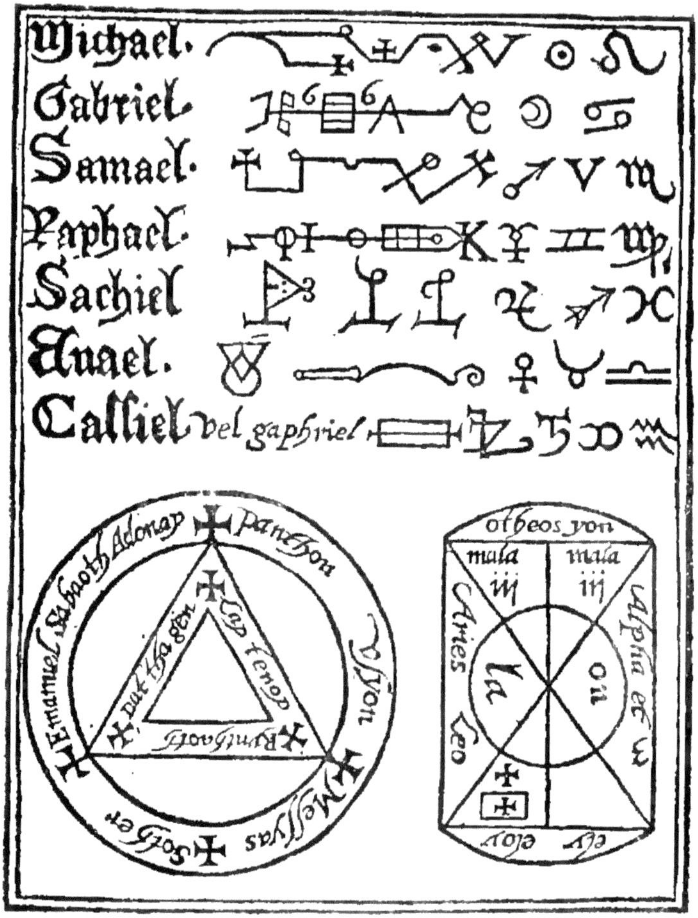

An example of magical caracteres with planetary associations; the image comes from the original Book XV from the Discoverie.[303]

[303] This image, and the one called "Seales of the Earth" (see page 316), with their brief descriptions, appear in the "seventh chapter" of the original Book XV. The description says: "The characters of the angels of the seaven daies, with their names: of figures, seales and periapts." The characters of the angels come from the *Heptameron*.

3. And as unto every Planet certain fumigations are ascribed; so unto such Spirits as are under them, certain Places are adopted for the Ceromonies of Conjuration, which Magicians chose when they set upon their works of Darkness. Unto *Saturn* are ascribed dark melancholy Places, Vaults, Tombes, Monasteries, empty Houses, Dens, Caves, Pits. Unto *Jupiter*, Theaters, Schools, Musick houses, Judgment seats. To *Mars*, Fields where Battels have been fought, Bake—houses. Glass-houses, Shambles, Places of Execution. To *Sol*, Palaces, Mountains, Meddows, Sunshine, Groves, and upper Rooms. To *Venus*, Fountains, Meadows, Gardens, and the Sea-shore. Unto *Mercury*, all publick places belonging unto Cities. To *Luna*, Wildernesses, Woods, Rocks, Forrests, Ships, High-wayes, &c.

4. In like manner are *Spells* and *Charms* adapted to the thing which they must effect, according to the matter, form and place of their composition; as for the *procuring of Love*, they bury Rings, Ribbons, Seals, Pictures, Looking-Glasses, &c. in Stews, Baths, Beds, that in such places they may contract some Venereal faculty: When they gather Herbs or other Ingredients; they chuse the hour and place, when such Planets have Dominion as are over these Herbs, which they collect, ever remembring to turn their faces to the *East*, or *South*, when *Saturnine*, *Martial* or *Jovial* Herbs are gathered, because their Principal houses are Southern signs; for *Venereal*, *Mercurial*, or *Lunary* herbs, they must look towards the *West* or *North*, because their houses are chiefly Northern signs. Yet in any *Solar* or *Lunar* operations the body of the Sun and Moon must be respected in the operation.

5. Colours are also much regarded amongst Magicians, according to the Planet, as black, leaden, brown, unto *Saturn*; saphire, vernal, green, purple, golden, unto *Jupiter*; red, burning, violet, bloody, and iron colours unto *Mars*; golden, saffron, scarlet, &c. unto the *Sun*; white, fair, green, ruddy, pleasant mixed colours unto *Venus*, *Mercury* and *Luna*. In like manner they ascribe colours unto the twelve Houses, and according to the Planets have also certain compositions for fire that produce wonderful operations; as Lamps of Serpents skins will make Serpents to appear. Oyl that hath stood under Grapes, being lighted, presenteth the Chamber full of Grapes. Centaury and the Lapwings blood makes people seem like Gyants, and in the open air will make the Stars seem to move up and down in the Elements. The fat of a Hare lighted in a Lamp, will cause Women to be exceeding merry and facetious. And Candles composed of things that are Saturnine, raise terrours and melancholy in the party that lights them, and in those that are lighted by them.

6. Such wonderful effects have natural things being fitted unto their Hours and Constellations, as also when they are used to prove such effects as the nature of the things doth produce of it self, though in a weaker degree.

To raise *Tempests* Magicians burn the Liver of a Camælion on the house top. To cause strange sights they hang the Gall of a Ox over their Beds; to bring *Apparitions* and *Spirits*, they make a strange fume of a Mans Gall, and the Eyes of a black Cat; *Which, Agrippa* saith, *he hath often made experience of.* There is also a strange Magical Candle described amongst *Chymical* Authors, which being lighted, foretells the death of the party to whom it belongs. The manner thereof is thus; *They take a good quantity of the venal blood luke-warm as it came out of the vein, which being Chymically prepared with Spirit of Wine and other Ingredients, is at last made up into a Candle, which being once kindled, never goes out till the death of the party whose blood it is composed of; for when he is sick, or in danger, it burns dim and troubled; and when he is dead, it is quite extinguished;* of which Composition a Learned man hath wrote an intire Tractate, *De Biolychnio*, or, *The Lamp of Life.*

7. But to proceed to the nature of *Characters, Sigils*, and other *Ceremonies*, we find that not only such as pretend to command over all sorts of Spirits; but also they that do make Compacts, and have sold themselves unto him, do make use of such; which instance is sufficient to prove what a wise man hath asserted, that although Evil Spirits have so blinded Mens Eyes, as to make them believe they are defended by such Ceremonies, and that these Characters are as Munitions against the Devils malignancy; Yet these very *Characters, Sigils, Lamins*, &c., are *Compacts* themselves, which the Devils did at first cunningly disguise with strange Repetitions in uncouth Language.

8. So that we have grounds to believe, that none is able absolutely without *Compact* to call up any *Spirit*. But that whosoever hath pretended to be famous in the Art of Magick or Conjuration, hath (to himself unknown) *compacted* with and *worshipped the Devil*, under strange *Repetitions* and mystical *Characters*, which to him seemed to have effects quite contrary to what they really had.

9. Neither is this to be admired, that without the Knowledge or Consent of the Magician, a *Contract* is made with *Evil Spirits*; when we consider the magical strength of *Words* and *Characters*, which of themselves can cure Diseases, pull down, infect, save, destroy, charm and inchant without the Parties assistance, either in knowledge of the Cause, or in belief of the Consequence or Effect.

10. But on the contrary, I could instance a multitude of Examples of such as have spent much time in *Conjurations* to no purpose, still attempting by Exorcisms and Defensive Prayers to conjure a Spirit, or cause Personal Appearances, with severe Imprecations and powerful Charges, and yet notwithstanding have never attain'd their purpose, nor at any time heard, or seen any Beeing, which may be called *Spectre*, or *Apparition*.

11. Which is nothing wonderful, if we minde the *sympathy* of things in Nature, how each desires its *like*, and hunteth after it as the Loadstone draws Iron; the male coveteth the female; the evil after the evil, and the good after the good; which is seen in wicked Men and their Association, in Birds and Beasts of prey; while on the contrary, the Lamb delights not in the Lyon, nor the Sheep in the society of the Wolf; neither doth the nature which is totally depraved and estranged from God, care to be forced or drawn compulsively by another contrary nature, *viz.* innocent, just, and harmless.

12. Neither doth it consist with natural reason, That *Evil Spirits* should affect the society of those that are their Enemies, who make use of the dreadful and holy Names of God in Conjurations to call them up; whereas they are rather antidotes against Apparations: as may be seen in various Examples of holy Men, who by Prayers and Exorcisms have banished *Evil Spirits* in all Ages, which is also further evident, in that the very form of *Dispossessing*; and *Exorcising* is made up of divers Prayers and Defensive Blessings against the obnoxious influences of *Infernal Spirits*.

13. Therefore though I would be far from describing an undenyable course of Conjuring Spirits, or of causing Apparitions: Yet this I must assert conclusively from what is before alledged, That if any thing would be called or wrought upon, it must be with something which is of its own nature, as a bait to catch or tempt it; for in catching Birds, Beasts, or Fishes, such esculents as are properly for these Animals, are made use of to allure them, neither can mankind command them by any threats to come into his custody.

14. How much less is mankind able to compel the Infernal Spirits, the very least of which Kingdom, is able, if let loose, to exterminate a thousand lives, and utterly over-turn poor mortals and their doings, as various by-past accidents can evince: But whosoever hath compacted with them for body, soul, and works, such they are at unity with, and unto such they appear for the advancement of their Kingdom in the destruction of others; for they are grafted into them and incorporated into their very heart and soul, which unavoidably becomes their wages when the body falls away.

15. Yet many wayes there be by *Images*, *Telesms*, and *Amulets*, which have little or no dependance upon Conjuration, or the strength thereof, being rather effectual from sympathetical Causes, as many natural conclusions prove. And *Paracelsus* speaks of a way by the Image of any Bird or Beast to destroy that Animal, though at a distance; so by hair, fat, blood, excrements, excrescences, &c. of any Animal or Vegetable, the ruin or cure of that thing may be effected

16. Which is seen in the Armary Unguent,[304] and the Sympathetical Powder.[305] In the instance of divers Histories, of such as used Waxen Images, composed in divers postures, and under certain Constellations, whereby several have been tormented and macerated even unto death; and according to the punishment or torment which the Magician intends to afflict, accordingly do they dispose the hour of the Composition, and the posture or semblance of the Image.

17. For if a malitious minded Witch intends to consume and pine away the Life or Estate of any miserable Man or Woman, she makes his Image of Wax in such an ominous aspect as may conduce to her design, making several magical Characters upon the sides of the head, describing the Character of the hour or Planetary time upon the breast of the Image; the name of the party on his forehead; the intended effect to be wrought upon him upon his back. When they cause aches, pains, and violent pangs in the sinews and the flesh, they stick thorns and pins in divers places of their arms, breasts, and legs. When they cast them into Feavers and Consumptions, they spend an hour in every day to warm and turn the Image before a doleful and lingring fire, composed of divers exotick Gums, and magical Ingredients of sweet Odours, and strange Roots of shrubs, efficient for their purpose.

18. Wonderful are the various postures and pranks which Magicians play with Images; neither will I mention the most perfect and prevalent part of the practice of Images, and the powerful operations thereof, least the evil minded should work abominations therewith upon the Persons or Possessions of their neighbours.

19. According to the nature of what they would effect they frame their Images; if by Images they would provoke two parties to love, or be enamoured on one another, they frame their Images naked, with Astrological Observations and Imbraces of those that are Venereal; to provoke unto enmity they place malignant Characters and Aspects, and the Images in a fighting posture.

20. If their intentions be for good, all their Characters are engraven upon the foreparts of the body. But if they would afflict the party with Consumption, or with death, they thrust Needles through the hearts, and engrave their Characters upon their Posteriors, or upon their shoulders, using all their Conjurations retrograde, and repeating every Charm opposite to the former.

---

[304] The *unguentum armarium*, or Weapon Salve, was a popular preparation to apply on the weapon that had caused the injury, and through sympathy it was believed to heal the wound.

[305] "Powder of sympathy was a form of sympathetic magic, current in the 17th century in Europe, whereby a remedy was applied to the weapon that had caused a wound in the hope of healing the injury it had made." *Powder of Sympathy.* Wikipedia.

21. Thousands of strange and uncouth Charms might be here described, according to the exact form wherein Tradition hath left them; But I have only insisted upon the description of the natures in General; And as by *Images* and *Telesms*, the *Europeans* have effected admirable things: so the *Tartars* have a wonderful way of producing the like effects, by *Botles*, *Sheep-skins*, *Rods*, *Basins*, *Letters*, or *Missives*, unto certain Spirits, and many otherwayes unheard of in *Europe*.

22. As for the *Tying of the Point*, which is a strong impediment in Conjugal Rites, to restrain the acts of secresie betwixt two marryed persons; This knot or ligament is become so notorious both in the practice and effect throughout *France*, *Italy*, and *Spain*, as also in all the *Eastern* Countries, that the Laws of several Nations have prohibited the performance thereof; neither is it fit to be openly described in this place.

23. Other stratagems they have by *turning the Sive* with a pair of Sizzers[306] by *voices uttered* out of *skins*, which is in common amongst the *Turks* by *Letters* wrote unto certain Spirits, which by due appointments will have their answers returned. By the *Turning* of the *Cord* with several names wrapped round the same, which with certaian repetitions will of it self be tyed into several strange knots which unty themselves again. Besides the many wayes by Lots, in extractings Scrolls, consulting with the Staff and the empty Pot, with others tedious to be enumerated.

24. The *Art of Transplantation* is also reckoned amongst Charms with the vulgar. And indeed one member thereof, *viz.* the Transferring of Diseases is really Magical, and much in practice amongst the Witches; for by certain baits given to any domestick Beasts they remove Feavers, Agues, and Consumptions from Martial men, or from one to another by burying certain Images in their neighbours ground they bring all evil fortune to the owner of the ground, yet

[306] "Coscinomancy is a form of divination utilising a sieve and shears, used in ancient Greece, medieval and early modern Europe and 17th century New England, to determine the guilty party in a criminal offense, find answers to questions, etc. The term comes into English via both New Latin and Medieval Latin coscinomantia, and is ultimately derived from the Ancient Greek koskinomantis (Greek: κοσκινομάντης) a diviner using a sieve, from koskinon (Greek: κόσκινον) a sieve. The word is mentioned by a number of Ancient Greek writers, including Philippides, Julius Pollux, Lucianus and, most famously, Theocritus. Agrippa believed that the movement of the sieve was performed by a demon, and that the conjuration *Dies, mies, jeschet, benedoefet, dowima, enitemaus* actually compelled the demon to perform the task. He further notes that the words of this conjuration were understood neither by the speaker nor anyone else (*nec sibi ipsis, nec aliis intellectua*)." *Coscinomancy*. Wikipedia.

though they add strange Words and Conjurations in the practice, the effects thereof are more from Nature then Conjuration.

25. For, by the same Cause, those that are profound, can destroy diseases, take off Warts, and other Excrescences, kill, cure, purge and poyson at a distance from the party, by their hair, fatt, blood, nails, excrements, &c. or by any root, or carnuous substance, rubbed upon their hands, breasts or leggs, by burying which, they free them from Diseases, which experiments take effect according to the *Mediums* and their Consumption under ground.

26. And as by natural reason every Magical Charm or Receipt had its first institution; In like manner have Magicians disposed the Matter and Manner together with the times of their Utensils and Instruments, according to the Principles of Nature: As the Hour wherein they compose their Garments, must either be in the hour of *Luna*, or else of *Saturn*, in the Moons increase.

27. Their Garments they compose of White Linnen, black Cloth, black Cat-skins, Wolves, Bears, or Swines skins. The Linnen because of its abstracted Quality for Magick delights not to have any Utensils that are put to common uses. The skins of the aforesaid Animals are by reason of the *Saturnine* and *Magical qualities* in the particles of these beasts: Their sowing thred is of silk, Cats guts, mans Nerves, Asses hairs. Thongs of skins from Men, Cats, Bats, Owls, Moles, and all which are enjoyn'd from the like Magical cause.

28. Their Needles are made of Hedge-hog prickles, or bones of any of the abovesaid Animals: Their *Writing-pens* are of Owls or Ravens, their Ink of Mans blood: Their *Oyntments* Mans fat, Blood, Usnea, Hoggs-grease, Oyl of Whales. Their *Characters* are ancient *Hebrew* or *Samaritan*: Their *Speech* is *Hebrew* or *Latine*. Their *Paper* must be of the Membranes of Infants, which they call *Virgin-parchment*, or of the skins of Cats, or Kids. Besides, they compose their *Fires* of sweet Wood, Oyl or Rosin; And their *Candles* of the Fatt or Marrow of Men or Children: Their *Vessels* are Earthen, their *Candlesticks* with three feet, of dead mens bones: Their *Swords* are steel, without guards, the poynts being reversed. These are their Materials, which they do particularly choose from the Magical qualities whereof they are composed.

29. Neither are the peculiar shapes without a natural cause. Their *Caps* are Oval, or like Pyramids with Lappets on each side, and furr within: Their *Gowns* reach to the ground, being furred with white Fox-skins, under which they have a Linnen Garment reaching to their Knee. Their *Girdles* are three inches broad, and have many Caballistical Names, with Crosses, Trines and Circles inscribed thereon. Their *Knives* are Dagger-fashion: and the *Circles* by which they defend themselves are commonly nine foot in breadth, but the *Eastern* Magicians give

but seven. And these are the matter and manner of their Preparations, which I thought fit here to insist upon, because of their affinity with the *Instruments* of *Charms*, for both which a natural cause is constantly pretended.

30. Thus I have briefly spoken of the Nature of every Spirit *good* or *evil*, so farr as *safety* or *convenience* would permit; adding also this last Discourse of *Charms* and *Conjurations*, in their *speculative part*, forbearing to describe the *Forms themselves*, because many of them are not only *facil*, but also of *mighty power* when they are seasonably applyed: So that to describe distinctly, by what means Magicians *kill*, *cure*, or *conquer*, were to strengthen the hands of the Envious against their Neighbours Lives and Fortunes. And therefore the Readers must rest contented with what is here related of the *Nature* of *Astral* or *Infernal Spirits*.

FINIS

Book XV

and the

Rules of Vaganostus

Chap. I.

Of Magical Circles, and the Reason of their Institution [307]

Magitians, and the more learned sort of Conjurers, make use of Circles in various manners, and to various intentions. First, when convenience serves not, as to time or place that a real Circle should be delineated, they frame an imaginary Circle, by means of Incantations and Consecrations, without either Knife, Pensil, or Compasses, circumscribing nine foot of ground round about them, which they pretend to sanctifie with words and Ceremonies, spattering their Holy Water all about so far as the said Limit extendeth; and with a form of Consecration following, do alter the property of the ground, that from common (as they say) it becomes sanctified, and made fit for Magicall uses.

How to consecrate an imaginary Circle.

Let the Exorcist, being cloathed with a black Garment, reaching to his knee, and under that a white Robe of fine Linnen that falls unto his ankles, fix himself in the midst of that place where he intends to perform his Conjurations: And throwing his old Shooes about ten yards from the place, let him put on his consecrated shooes of russet Leather with a Cross cut on the top of each shooe. Then with his Magical Wand, which must be a new hazel-stick, about two yards of length, he must stretch forth his arm to all the four Windes thrice, turning himself round at every Winde, and saying all that while with fervency:

I who am the servant of the Highest, do by the vertiie of his Holy Name Immanuel, *sanctifie unto my self the circumference of nine foot round about me,* ✠✠✠ *from the East,* **Glaurah**; *from the West,* **Garron**; *from the North,* **Cabon**; *from the South,* **Berith**; *which ground I take for my proper defence from all malignant spirits, that they may have no power over my soul or body, nor come beyond these Limitations, but answer*

[307] Here begins the material that was added to the 1665 edition of *The Discoverie* [Appendix I.]. This material comes at the end of the edition from 1886 which I used, and is presented in the following form (before the beginning of the first chapter): "The nine chapters forming the beginning of the fifteenth Book in the third edition, 1665, are numbered Ch. I, etc., and Scot's Ch. I made Ch. X, and so onward." Chapter I to V from Book XV by Scot correspond to the text of the *Pseudomonarquia Daemonun*, which Scot copied from Weyer's work. We omitted it here. Chapter VI of Scot has only some astrological tables, and I moved it to the end so it is now the current Chapter XXIII. Chapter VII contains only the "characters of the angels" which I put on page 300, and the "Seals of the Earth", now on page 316. In this way, in this section, Chapter X corresponds to the "The viii. Chapter" of the original Book XV.

truely being summoned, without daring to transgress their bounds: **Worrh.**[308] **worrah. hareot. Gambalon.** ✠✠✠

Which Ceremonies being performed, the place so sanctified is equivalent to any real Circle whatsoever. And in the composition of any Circle for Magical feats, the fittest time is the brightest Moon-light, or when storms of lightning, winde, or thunder, are raging through the air; because at such times the infernal Spirits are nearer unto the earth, and can more easily hear the Invocations of the Exorcist.

As for the places of Magical Circles, they are to be chosen melancholly, dolefull, dark and lonely; either in Woods or Deserts, or in a place where three wayes meet, or amongst ruines of Castles, Abbies, Monasteries, *&c.* or upon the Sea-shore when the Moon shines clear, or else in some large Parlour hung with black, and the floor covered with the same, with doors and windowes closely shut, and Waxen Candles lighted. But if the Conjuration be for the Ghost of one deceased, the fittest places to that purpose are places of the slain, Woods where any have killed themselves. Church-yards, Burying-Vaults, *&c.* As also for all sorts of Spirits, the places of their abode ought to be chosen, when they are called; as Pits, Caves, and hollow places, for Subterranean Spirits: The tops of Turrets, for Aerial Spirits: Ships and Rocks of the Sea, for Spirits of the Water: Woods and Mountains for Faries, Nymphs, and Satyres; following the like order with all the rest.

And as the places where, so the manner how the Circles are to be drawn, ought to be perfectly known. First, for Infernal Spirits, let a Circle nine foot over be made with black, and within the same another Circle half a foot distant, leaving half a foot of both these Circles open for the Magitian and his assistant to enter in: And betwixt these Circles round about, write all the holy Names of God, with Crosses and Triangles at every Name; making also a larger triangle at one side of the Circle without on this manner with the names of the Trinity at the seven corners, *viz.*, **Yehowah, Ruah Kedesh, Emmanuel**, written in the little circles.[309]

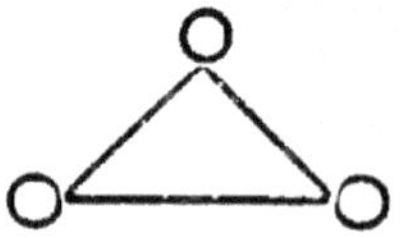

[308] A note in the original book questions if "Worrh" should not be "Worrah" (as the second word).

[309] I really could not understand the reference to the "seven corners", which makes even less sense when it is explained in relation to the (three) "little circles". Later (on page 314) he mentions the "four corners of the World"; maybe he had in mind some relationship between the three corners of the triangle and the four corners of the world?

The reason that Magitians give for Circles and their Institution, is, That so much ground being blessed and consecrated by holy Words, hath a secret force to expel all evil Spirits from the bounds thereof; and being sprinkled with holy water, which hath been blessed by the Master, the ground is purified from all uncleanness; besides the holy Names of God written all about, whose force is very powerful; so that no wicked Spirit hath the ability to break through into the Circle after the Master and Scholler are entered, and have closed up the gap, by reason of the antipathy they possesse to these Mystical Names. And the reason of the Triangle is, that if the Spirit be not easily brought to speak the truth, they may by the Exorcist be conjured to enter the same, where by vertue of the names of the Sacred Trinity, they can speak nothing but what is true and right.

But if Astral Spirits as Faries, Nymphs, and Ghosts of men, be called upon, the Circle must be made with Chalk, without any Triangles; in the place whereof the Magical Character of that Element to which they belong, must be described at the end of every Name.

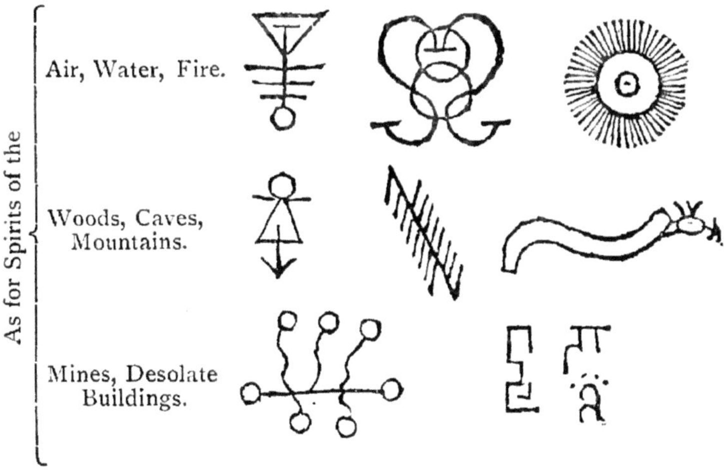

Magical Characters of the Elements[310]

[310] The table has only three elements, following a tradition similar to the *Sepher Yetzirah*; the other characters refer to places associated with diferent kinds of spirits.

CHAP. II.

How to raise up the Ghost of one that hath hanged himself.

This experiment must be put in practice while the Carcass hangs; and therefore the Exorcist must seek out for the straightest hazel wand that he can find, to the top whereof he must binde the head of an Owl, with a bundle of *St. John's Wort*, or *Milliès Perforatum*: this done, he must be informed of some miserable creature that hath strangled himself in some Wood or Desart place (which they seldom miss to do) and while the Carcass hangs, the Magitian must betake himself to the aforesaid place, at 12 a clock at night, and begin his Conjurations in this following manner.

First, stretch forth the consecrated Wand towards the four corners of the World, saying, *By the mysteries of the deep, by the flames of* **Banal**, *by the power of the East, and the silence of the night, by the holy rites of* **Hecate**, *I conjure and exorcize thee thou distressed Spirit, to present thy self here, and reveal unto me the cause of thy Calamity, why thou didst offer violence to thy own liege life, where thou art now in beeing, and where thou wilt hereafter be.*

Then gently smiting the Carcase nine times with the rod, say, *I conjure thee thou spirit of this* N. *deceased, to answer my demands that I am to propound unto thee, as thou ever hopest for the rest of the holy ones, and the ease of all thy misery; by the blood of Jesu which he shed for thy soul, I conjure and bind thee to utter unto me what I shall ask thee.*

Then cutting down the Carcass from the tree, lay his head towards the East, and in the space that this following Conjuration is repeating, set a Chafing-dish of fire at his right hand, into which powre a little Wine, some Mastick, and Gum Aromatick, and lastly a viol full of the sweetest Oyl, having also a pair of Bellows, and some unkindled Charcole to make the fire burn bright at the instant of the Carcass's rising. The Conjuration is this:

I conjure thee thou spirit of N. *that thou do immediately enter into thy antient body again, and answer to my demands, by the virtue of the holy resurrection, and by the posture of the body of the Saviour of the world, I charge thee, I conjure thee, I command thee on pain of the torments and wandring of thrice seven years, which I by the power of sacred Magick rites, have power to inflict upon thee; by thy sighs and groans, I conjure thee to utter thy voice; so help thee God and the prayers of the holy Church. Amen.*

Which Conjuration being thrice repeated while the fire is burning with Mastick and Gum Aromatick, the body will begin to rise, and at last will stand upright before the Exorcist, answering with a faint and hollow voice, the questions proposed unto it. Why it strangled it self; where its dwelling is; what its food and life is; how long it will be ere it enter into rest, and by what means the Magitian may assist it to come to rest: Also, of the treasures of this world, where they are hid: Moreover, it can answer very punctually of the places where Ghosts reside, and how to communicate with them; teaching the nature of Astral Spirits and hellish beings, so far as its capacity reacheth.

All which when the Ghost hath fully answered, the Magitian ought out of commiseration and reverence to the deceased, to use what means can possibly be used for the procuring rest unto the Spirit.

To which effect he must dig a grave, and filling the same half full of quick Lime, and a little Salt and common Sulphur, put the Carcass naked into the same; which experiment, next to the burning of the body into ashes, is of great force to quiet and end the disturbance of the Astral Spirit.

But if the Ghost with whom the Exorcist consulteth, be of one that dyed the common death, and obtain'd the ceremonies of burial, the body must be dig'd out of the ground at 12 a clock at night; and the Magician must have a companion with him, who beareth a torch in his left hand, and smiting the Corps thrice with the consecrated rod, the Exorcist must turn himself to all the four winds, saying:

By the virtue of the holy resurrection, and the torments of the damned. I conjure and exorcise thee spirit of N. *deceased, to answer my liege demands, being obedient unto these sacred ceremonies on pain of everlasting torment and distress:* Then let him say, **Berald, Beroald, Balbin gab gabor agaba**: *Arise, arise, I charge and command thee.*

After which Ceremonies, let him ask what he desireth and he shall be answered.

But as a faithful caution to the practicer of this Art, I shall conclude with this, That if the Magician, by the Constellation and Position of the Stars at his nativity, be in the predicament of those that follow Magical Arts, it will be very dangerous to try this experiment for fear of suddain death ensuing, which the Ghosts of men deceased, can easily effect upon those whose nativities lead them to Conjuration: And which suddain and violent death, the Stars do alwayes promise to such as they mark with the *Stigma* of Magicians.[311]

[311] A dubious piece of advice, as it says that people born to be Magicians should not practice the Art, as it is more dangerous to them...

Chap. III.

How to raise up the three Spirits,
Paymon, Bathin, and Barma:
And what wonderful things may
be effected through theirassistance.

The Spirit *Paymon* is of the power of the Air, the sixteenth in the ranck of Thrones, subordinate to *Corban* and *Marbas*.

Bathin is of a deeper reach in the source of the fire, the second after *Lucifers* familiar, and hath not his fellow for agility and affableness, in the whole Infernal Hierarchy.

Barma is a mighty Potentate of the order of Seraphims, whom 20 Legions of Infernal Spirits do obey; his property is to metamorphose the Magician or whom he pleaseth, and transport into foreign Countreys.

These three Spirits, though of various ranks and orders, are all of one power, ability and nature, and the form of raising them all is one. Therefore the Magician that desireth to consult with either of these Spirits, must appoint a night in the waxing of the Moon, wherein the Planet Mercury reigns, at 11 a clock at night; not joyning to himself any companion, because this particular action will admit of none; and for the space of four dayes before the appointed night, he ought every morning to shave his beard, and shift himself with clean linnen, providing beforehand the two Seals of the Earth, drawn exactly upon parchment, having also his consecrated Girdle ready of a black Cats skin with the hair on, and these names written on the inner side of the Girdle: **Ya, Ya** ✠ **Aie, Aaie** ✠ **Elibra** ✠ **Elohim** ✠ **Saday** ✠ **Yah Adonay** ✠ *tuo robore* ✠ *Cinctus sum* ✠.

"These figures are called the seales of the earth, without the which no spirit will appeere, except thou have them with thee."

Upon his Shooes must be written **Tetragrammaton**, with crosses round about, and his garment must be a Priestly Robe of black, with a Friers hood, and a Bible in his hand.

When all these things are prepared, and the Exorcist hath lived chastly, and retired until the appointed time: Let him have ready a fair Parlour or Cellar, with every chink and window closed; then lighting seven Candles, and drawing a double Circle with his own blood, which he must have ready before hand: let him divide the Circle into seven parts, and write these seven names at the seven divisions, setting at every Name a Candle lighted in a brazon Candle-stick in the space betwixt the Circles.

The names are these, **Cados** ✠ **Escherie** △ **Anick** ✠ **Sabbae** ⊠ **Sagun** ✠✠ **Aba** ✠ **Abalidoth** △

When the Candles are lighted, let the Magician being in the midst of the Circle, and supporting himself with two drawn Swords, say with a low and submissive voyce:

I do by the vertue of these seven holy Names which are the Lamps of the living God, Consecrate unto my use this inclosed Circle, and exterminate out of it all evill Spirits, and their power; that beyond the limit of their circumference they enter not on pain of torments to be doubled, **Yah**, **Agion**, **Helior**, **Heligah**, *Amen.*

When this Consecration is ended. Let him sprinkle the Circle with consecrated Water, and with a Chafing-dish of Charcole, perfume it with Frankincense and Cinamon, laying the Swords a cross the Circle, and standing over them; then whilest the fumigation burneth, let him begin to call these three Spirits in this following manner:

I Conjure and Exorcize you the three Gentle and Noble Spirits of the power of the North, by the great and dreadful name of **Peolphan** *your King, and by the silence of the night, and by the holy rites of Magick, and by the number of the Infernal Legions, I adjure and invocate you; That without delay ye present your selves here before the Northern quarter of this Circle, all of you, or any one of you, and answer my demands by the force of the words contained iti this Book.*

This must be thrice repeated, and at the third repetition, the three Spirits will either all appear, or one by lot, if the other be already somewhere else imployed; at their appearance they will send before them three fleet Hounds opening after a Hare, who will run round the Circle for the space of half a quarter of an hour; after that more hounds will come in, and after all, a little ugly Æthiop, who will take the Hare from their ravenous mouths, and together with the Hounds vanish; at last the Magician shall hear the winding of a Huntsmans horn, and a Herald on Horseback shall come galloping with three Hunters behind upon black Horses, who will compass the Circle seven times, and at the seventh time will make a stand at the Northern quarter, dismissing the Herald that came up before them, and turning their Horses towards the Magician, will stand all a brest before him, saying; **Gil pragma burthon machatan dennah**; to which the Magician must boldly answer,

Beral, Beroald, Corath, Kermiel; *By the sacred rites of Magick ye are welcome ye three famous Hunters of the North, and my command is, that by the power of these Ceremonies ye be obedient and faithful unto my summons, unto which I conjure you by the holy Names of God,* **Yah, Gian, Soter, Yah, Jehovah, Immanuel, Tetragrammaton, Yah, Adonay, Sabtay, Seraphin**; *Binding and obliging you to answer plainly, faithfully and truly, by all these holy names, and by the awful name of your mighty King* **Peolphon**.[312]

Which when the Magician hath said, the middle Hunter named **Paymon**, will answer, **Gil pragma burthon machatan dennah**, *We are the three mighty Hunters of the North, in the Kingdom of* Fiacim, *and are come hither by the sound of thy Conjurations, to which we swear by him that liveth to yield obedience, if* Judas *that betrayed him be not named.*

Then shall the Magician swear, *By him that liveth, and by all that is contained in this holy Book, I swear unto you this night, and by the mysteries of this action, I swear unto you this night, and by the bonds of darkness I swear unto you this night, That Judas the Traitor shall not be named, and that blood shall not be offered unto you, but that truce and equal terms shall be observed betwixt us.* Which being said, the Spirits will bow down their heads to the Horses crests, and then alighting down will call their Herald to withdraw their Horses; which done, The Magician may begin to bargain with all, or any one of them, as a familiar invisibly to attend him, or to answer all difficulties that he propoundeth: Then may he begin to ask them of the frame of the World, and the Kingdoms therein contained, which are unknown unto Geographers: He may also be informed of all Physical processes and operations; also how to go invisible and fly through the airy Region: They can likewise give unto him the powerful Girdle of Victory, teaching him how to compose and consecrate the same, which hath the force, being tyed about him, to make him conquer Armies, and all men whatsoever. Besides, there is not any King or Emperour throughout the world; but if he desires it, they will engage to bring him the most pretious of their Jewels and Riches in twenty four hours; discovering also unto him the way of finding hidden treasures and the richest mines.

---

[312] Previously spelled "Peolphan".

And after the Conjurer hath fulfilled his desires, he shall dismiss the aforesaid Spirits in this following form.

I charge you ye three officious Spirits to depart unto the place whence ye were called, without injury to either man or Beast, leaving the tender Corn untouched, and the seed unbruised; I dismiss you, and licence you to go back untill I call you, and to be alwayes ready at my desire, especially thou nimble Bathin, *whom I have chosen to attend me, that thou be alwayes ready when I ring a little Bell to present thy self without any Magical Ceremonies performed; and so depart ye from hence, and peace be betwixt you and us. In the Name of the Father, Son, and Holy Ghost. Amen.*

When the Magician hath repeated this last form of dismission, he will hear immediately a horn winding, after which the Herald with the jet black Horses, and the three Spirits will mount upon them, compassing the Circle seven times, with the Herald winding his horn before them, and at every Candle they will bow towards the Horses crest, till coming towards the Northern quarter, they will with great obeysance seem to march away out through the solid wall as through a City gate.

CHAP. IV.

How to Consecrate all manner of Circles, Fumigations, Fire, Magical Garments, and Utensills.

Consecrations are related either to the person or the thing conscerated. The person is the Magitian himself, whose consecration consisteth in Abstinence, Temperance, and holy Garments. The things consecrated are the Oyl, the Fire, the Water. The Fumigations consisting of oriental Gums and Spices; the magical Sword, Pensils, Pens and Compasses, the measuring Rule and waxen Tapers, the Pentacles, Periapts, Lamins, and Sigils, Vests, Caps, and Priestly Garments; these are the materials to be consecrated.

The sacred Pentacles are as signs and charms for the binding of Evil Dæmons, consisting of Characters and Names of the Superior order of the good Spirits opposite unto those evil ones whom the Magitian is about to Invocate: And of sacred Pictures, Images, and Mathematical Figures adapted to the names and natures of separated Substances whither good or evil. Now the form of Consecrating such Magical Pentacles is to name the vertue of the holy Names and Figures, their Antiquity and Institution with the intention of the Consecration purifying the Pentacle by consecrated fire, and waving the same over the flames thereof.

When the Exorcist would consecrate Places or Utensils, Fire or Water for magical uses, he must repeat the Consecration or Dedication of *Solomon* the King at the building of the Temple, the Vision of *Moses* at the Bush, and the Spirit of the Lord on the tops of the Mulberry-trees, repeating also the sacrifice of it self being kindled; the Fire upon *Sodom*, and the Water of Eternal Life: Wherein the Magitian must still remember to speak of the seven golden Candle-sticks, and *Ezekiels* Wheels,[313] closing the Consecration with the deep and mysterious Names of God and holy Dæmons.

When particular Instruments are to be sanctified, the Magitian must sprinkle the same with consecrated Water, and fumigate them with fumigations, anoint them with consecrated Oyl: And lastly, Seal them with holy Characters; after all which is performed, an Oration or Prayer must follow, relating the particulars of the Consecration with Petitions to that Power in whose Name and Authority the Ceremony is performed.

And in like manner shalt thou consecrate and sanctifie every Utensil whatsoever, by Sprinklings, Fumigations, Unctions, Seals, and Benedictions, commemorating and reiterating the sanctifyings in the holy Scripture, of the Tables of the Law delivered to Moses; of the two Testaments in the New Covenant, of the holy Prophets in their Mothers wombs, and of *Aholiah*, and *Aholibah*,[314] whom the Spirit of God inspired to frame all sorts of curious workmanship for the Tabernacle. This is the sum of Consecration.

---

[313] What is possibly being suggested here is the Reading of the Bible's verses where these events are mentioned.

[314] There is an "Oholiab" or "Aholiab", son of Ahisamakh that, in the Old Testament, worked under Bezalel in the preparation of the Tabernacle and the instruments lodged in it, including the Ark of the Covenant. He is described in Exodus 38:23 as a master of carpentry, weaving, and embroidery. The similarity of the names possibly induced the writer to the mistake, because Oholah (אהלה) and Oholibah (אהליבה) (or: Aholah and Aholibah) are derogatory names given by the Prophet Ezekiel to Samaria in the Kingdom of Israel and Jerusalem in the Kingdom of Judah, respectively. (Ezek. 23). The correct mention, according to custom, is to Aholiab and Bezalel as being divinely inspired artisans.

Chap. V.

Treating more practically of the Consecration of Circles, Fires, Garments, and Fumigations.

In the Construction of Magical Circles, the hour, day, or night, and season of the year, and the Constellation are to be considered; as also what sort of Spirits are to be called; and to what Region, Air, or Climate they belong: Therefore this method is to be followed for the more orderly and certain proceeding therein. First, a Circle nine foot over must be drawn, within which another Circle three inches from the outermost must be also made, in the Center whereof the name of the hour, the Angel of the hour, the Seal of the Angel, the Angel of the day predominant, wherein the work is undertaken.[315] Note, these attributes are to be inscribed betwixt the Circles round about with *Alpha* at the beginning, and *Omega* at the close.

When the Circle is composed, it must be sprinkled with holy Water, while the Magician saith. *Wash me O Lord, and I shall be whiter then Snow:*[316] And as for the Fumigations over them, this Benediction must be said; O *God of* Abraham, Isaac, *and* Jacob, *bless these thy subservient creatures, that they may multiply the force of their excellent odors, to hinder evil spirits and phantasms from entering the Circle, through our Lord. Amen.*

An Exorcism for the fire.

The Exorcist ought to have an earthen Censer, wherein to preserve the fire for magical uses, and the expiations and fumigations, whose consecration is on this manner.

By him that created Heaven and Earth, and is the God and Lord of all, I exorcize and sanctifie thee thou creature of Fire, that immediately thou banish every phantasin from thee, so that thou prove not hurtful in any kind: Which I beseech thee O Lord to confirm by sanctifying and making pure this creature of fire, that it may be blessed and consecrate to the honour of thy holy Name. Amen.

---

[315] The unknown author here seems to follow procedures derived from the Heptameron.

[316] The phrase comes from Psalm 51:7: "Purge me with hyssop, and I shall be clean: wash me, and I shall be whiter than snow" (*Asperges me, Domine, hyssopo et mundabor; Lavabis me, et super nivem dealbabor*). Its uses in texts of Magick is widespread, for instance its appearance in the *Heptameron* and the *Lemegeton.*

At the putting on the Garments,

Let the Magician say, *By the figurative mystery of this holy Stole or Vestment, I will cloath me with the armour of Salvation in the strength of the Highest.* **Ancor, Amacor, Amides, Theodonias, Anitor.** *That my desired end may be effected through thy strength* Adonai *to whom the praise and glory will for ever belong.*

Which Ceremonies being finished, the Exorcist shall proceed to the practical part of Invocation and Conjuration of all degrees of Spirits, having every utensil and appendix in readiness for the performance, and proceeding according to the method in these following Chapters.

Chap. VI.

How to raise and exorcize all sorts of Spirits belonging to the Airy Region.

The Garment which the Exorcist is cloathed withall at the performance of this action, ought according to the opinions of the chiefest Magicians, to be a Priestly Robe, which if it can no where be procured, may be a neat and cleanly linnen Vest, with the holy Pentacle fastned thereunto upon Parchment made of a Kids skin, over which an Invocation must be said, and then the Pentacle must be sprinkled with holy Water. At the putting on the Magical Garment, this Prayer must be repeated:

By the holy power **Adonai Sabaoth**, *And by the power and merit of thine Angels and Archangels, and by the vertue of holy Church, which thou hast sanctified, do I cloath me with this consecrated Garment, that what I am to practice may take effect through thy Name who art for ever and ever.*

Now as for the time of operation, and the manner thereof, The Instructions before set down, are sufficient to direct the Exorcist; only the Acter and his Scholar must be mindful in the way, as they go towards the place of Conjuration, to reiterate the sacred forms of Consecrations, Prayers, and Invocations, the one bearing an Earthen Vessel with consecrated fire, and the other the Magical Sword, the Book and Garments, till approaching nigh the place where the Circle is to be drawn, they must then proceed to compose it after the aforesaid manner. And at last Exorcize the Spirits on this following manner:

Seeing God hath given us the power to bruise the Serpents head, and command the Prince of Darkness, much more to bear rule over every airy Spirit: Therefore by his strong and mighty Name **Jehovah** *do I conjure you,* (naming the Spirits)*, and by his secret commands delivered to* Moses *on the* Mount*, and by his holy Name* **Tetragrammaton**, *and by all his wonderful Names and Attributes,* **Sadai, Ollon, Emillah, Athanatos, Paracletos**, &c. *That ye do here immediately appear before this Circle, in humane form, and not terrible or of monstrous shape, on pain of eternal misery that abides you, unless you speedily fulfil my commands,* **Bathar, Baltar, Archim, Anakin, Nakun**. *Amen.*

When the Exorcist hath finished this Conjuration, he and his companion shall continue constantly turning themselves to the East, West, North and South, saying, with their Caps in their hands, **Gerson, Anek, Nephaton, Basannah, Cabon**; and within a little space they will behold various apparitions upon the ground, and in the air, with various habits, shapes, and instruments; after that, he shall perceive a troop of armed men with threatning carriage appear before the Circle, who after they are conjured to leave off their phantasms, will at last present themselves before the Exorcist in humane form.

Then the Master must be mindful to take the consecrated Sword, and the cup of Wine into his hands; the Wine he shall pour into the fire, and the Sword he shall brandish in his right arm, being girded about with a Scarlet Ribbon; after this the Magician shall say, **Gahire, Gephna, Anepheraton**; then the Spirits will begin to bow unto the Exorcist, saying, *We are ready to fulfil thy pleasure.*

So that when the Magician hath brought the Spirits to this length, he may ask what ever he desireth, and they will answer him, provided the questions belong to that order whereof they are.

Now the properties wherein they excel, are these; They can give the gift of Invisibility, and the fore-knowledge of the change of weather; they can teach the Exorcist how to excite Storms and Tempests, and how to calm them again; they can bring news in an hours space of the success of any Battle, Seidge, or Navy, how farr off soever; they can also teach the language of Birds, and how to fly through the air invisibly.

'Twas through the assistance of these airy Spirits, that *Chanchiancungi*, the *Tartarian* Emperour did give the *Chinois* such a desperate rout near the year 1646. for it is reported, that he had constantly in his presence two Magicians, named *Ran* and *Sionam*, who perceived every motion of the *China*'s Army, and had intelligence by these Spirits of the Emperours private Counsels and Consultations.

And it is credibly reported by Magicians, that wonderful things may be with facility effected through the assistance of these aforesaid Spirits, so that the Exorcist must be very affable unto them, and gently dismiss them (when he is satisfied) in this following manner;

Seeing ye have willingly answered all our Interrogations and desires, we give you leave and licence. In the Name of the Father, Son, and Holy-Ghost, to depart unto your place, and be ever ready to attend our call; Depart, I say, in peace, and peace be confirmed betwixt us and you. Amen. ✠✠✠

After all these Ceremonies are finished, the Spirits will begin to depart, making obeysance as they go; and then the Master must demolish the Circle, and taking up all the Utensils repeat the *Pater Noster* as they are going away from the place of Conjuration.

Chap. VII.

How to obtain the familiarity of the Genius or Good Angel, and cause him to appear.

According to the former Instructions in conjuring Spirits, we must proceed to consult with the *Familiars* or *Genii*; first, after the manner prescribed by Magicians, the Exorcist must inform himself of the *name* of his good *Genius*, which he may find in the Rules of *Travius* and *Philermus*; as also, what *Character* and *Pentacle*, or *Lamin*, belongs to every *Genius*. After this is done, Let him compose an earnest Prayer unto the said Genius, which he must repeat thrice every morning for seven dayes before the Invocation.

The Magician must also perfectly be informed to what Hierarchy or Order the *Genius* belongs, and how he is dignified in respect of his Superiours and Inferiours; for this form of Conjuration belongs not to the Infernal or Astral Kingdom, but to the Celestial Hierarchy; and therefore great gravity and sanctity is herein required, besides the due observation of all the other injunctions, until the time approach wherein he puts the Conjuration in execution.

When the day is come wherein the Magician would invocate his proper *Genius*, he must enter into a private closet, having a little Table and Silk Carpet, and two Waxen Candles lighted; as also a Chrystal Stone shaped triangularly about the quantity of an Apple, which Stone must be fixed upon a frame in the center of the Table; And then proceeding with great devotion to Invocation, he must thrice repeat the former Prayer, concluding the same with *Pater Noster, &c.* and a *Missale de Spiritu Sancto.*

Then he must begin to Consecrate the Candles, Carpet, Table and Chrystal sprinkling the same with his own blood, and saying, *I do by the power of the holy Names* **Aglaon, Eloi, Eloi, Sabbathon, Anepheraton, Jah, Agian, Jah, Jehovah, Emmanuel, Archon Archonton, Sadai, Sadai, Jeovaschah,** &c. *sanctifie and consecrate these holy utensils to the performance of this holy work, In the Name of the Father, Son, and Holy Ghost, Amen.*

Which done, the Exorcist must say this following Prayer with his face towards the East, and kneeling with his back to the consecrated Table.

O thou blessed **Phanael** *my Angel Guardian, vouchsafe to descend with thy holy influence and presence into this spotless Chrystal, that I may behold thy glory and enjoy thy society O thou who art higher then the fourth Heaven, and knowest the secrets of* **Elanel**. *Thou that ridest upon the wings of the wind, and art mighty and potent in thy celestial and super-lunary motion, do thou descend and be present I pray thee, and desire thee, if ever I have merited thy society, or if my actions and intentions be pure and sanctified before thee, bring thy extertial presence hither, and converse with thy submissive Pupil, by the tears of Saints and Songs of Angels, In the Name of the Father, Son, and Holy Ghost, who are one God for ever and ever.*

This Prayer being first repeated towards the East, must be afterwards said towards all the four winds thrice. And next the 70. Psalm repeated out of a Bible that hath been consecrated in like manner as the rest of the utensils; which ceremonies being seriously performed; the Magician must arise from his knees, and sit before the Crystal bare-headed with the consecrated Bible in his hand, and the Waxen Candles newly lighted, waiting patiently and internally for the coming and appearance of the *Genius*.

Now about a quarter of an hour before the Spirit come. There will appear great variety of apparitions and sights within the glass; as first a beaten road or tract, and travelers, men and women marching silently along; next there will Rivers, Wells, Mountains and Seas appear: after that a Shepherd upon a pleasant hill feeding a goodly flock of Sheep, and the Sun shining brightly at his going down; and lastly, innumerable shews of Birds and Beasts, Monsters and strange appearances, noises, glances, and affrightments, which shews will all at last vanish at the appearance of the *Genius*.

And then the *Genius* will present it self amidst the Crystal, in the very same apparel and similitude that the person himself is in, giving instructions unto the Exorcist how to lead his life and rectifie his doings.

But especially (which is the proper work of every *Genius*) he will touch his heart and open his senses and understanding, so that by this means, he may attain to the knowledge of every Art and Science, which before the opening of his Intellect was lockt and kept secret from him.

After which, the *Genius* will be familiar in the Stone at the Prayer of the Magician.

Chap. VIII

A form of Conjuring **Luridan**
the Familiar, otherwise called **Belelah**

Luridan is a Familiar Domestick Spirit of the *North*, who is now become servant to **Balkin**, Lord and King of the *Northern* Mountains, he calls himself the *Astral Genius* of *Pomonia*, an Island amongst the *Orcades* beyond *Scotland*. But he is not particularly resident there; for in the dayes of *Solomon* and *David*, he was in *Jerusalem*, or *Salem*, being then under the name of **Belilah**; after that he came over with *Julius Cæsar*, and remained some hundred of years in *Cambria*, or *Wales*, instructing their Prophetical Poets in *British* Rhimes, being then surnamed *Urthin-Wadd Elgin*, from thence he betook himself unto this Island, *Anno* 1500. and continued there for 50 years, after which he resigned his Dominion to *Balkin*, and hath continued ever since an attendant unto this Prince.

He is a Spirit of the Air in the order of **Glauron**, and is said to procreate as mortals do; He is often sent by his Master upon errands to *Lapland*, *Finland*, and *Strik-finia*; as also to the most *Northern* parts of *Russia*, bordering on the *Northern* frozen Ocean: His office (being called by Magicians) is to demolish strong holds of Enemies, destroying every night what they build the day before; to extinguish fires, and make their Gunshot that it hath no power to be enkindled; for his nature is to be at enmity with fire; and under his Master with many Legions he wageth continual warrs with the fiery Spirits that inhabit the Mountain *Hecla* in *Ise-land*, where they endeavour to extinguish these fiery flames, and the inhabiting Spirits defend the flames from his Master and his Legions.

In this contest they do often totally extirpate and destroy one another, killing and crushing when they meet in mighty and violent Troops in the Air upon the Sea; and at such a time many of the fiery Spirits are destroyed, when the Enemy hath brought them off the Mountain to fight upon the water; on the contrary, when the battle is on the Mountain it self, the Spirits of the Air are often worsted, and then great mournings and doleful noises are heard both in *Iseland* and *Russia*, and *Norway* for many days after.

But to proceed to the form of conjuring this aforesaid Spirit, the Magician must draw a Circle in a Moonshine night in some solitary Valley; the Circle must be 18 foot over, and another Circle a foot distance within the same, being both drawn with chalk, and the Exorcist being girded about with two Snakes skins tyed together, and having many Snakes skins tyed to his cap, and hanging down before and behinde, must also with Chalk draw the form of a fiery Mountain at one side of the Circle on this manner:

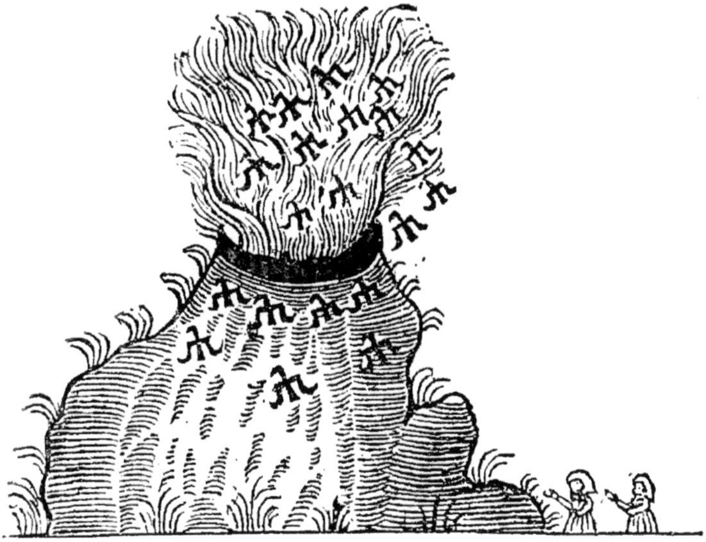

And round about the Mountain these following names must be wrote, **Glauron, Opotok, Balkin, Opotok, Urthin, Opotok, Swaknar, Nalah, Opotok**, ✠✠✠. After the Mountain is drawn, he must consecrate the same in these following words, **Ofron, Anepheraton, Baron Barathron, Nah halge tour hecla**, *In the Name of the Father, Son and Holy Ghost, Amen.* ✠✠✠. After the Magician hath consecrated the Mountain, he must write betwixt the circles these following words; **Urthin ✠ Malc hii ✠✠ Riddal Ratttron ✠ Agla ✠ Glaura ✠ Bashemo ✠ Phowah ✠ Elohim ✠ Emmanuel ✠ Amém.123** △ ✠ △ ✠ △ ✠.

Which done, he must begin to Invocate the Spirit on this following manner.

O ye Powers of the East, **Athanaton**; *of the West,* **Orgon**; *of the South,* **Boralim**; *of the North,* **Glauron**; *I charge and command you by the dreadful Names here mentioned, and the Consecration of this terrible Mountain, to present your selves one of every sort before this Circle by the power of* **Emmanuel**, *and his holy name.*

After this hath with fervency been thrice repeated, the Exorcist will hear great noises of Swords and fighting, Horses neighing, and Trumpets sounding, and at last there will appear four little Dwarfs or Pigmies naked before the Circle, their speech will be antient *Irish*; which afterwards being confined to a Triangle, they will interpret; the substance thereof will be from whence they came last, and what wonderful things they can do; Then the Magician must ask them, if they know one **Luridan**; a familiar; they will answer **Hamah ni trulloh Balkin**, he is Secretary or servant unto **Balkin**, and after the Exorcist hath charged them to bring the said **Luridan** unto him, they will immediately bring him like a little Dwarf with a crooked nose, and present him before the Magician in the triangle; then the Magician shall bind and tye him with the bond of obligation, and with his own blood, without any contract of conditions to be performed, that he will attend him constantly at his thrice repeating **Luridan, Luridan, Luridan**, And be ever ready to go whether he will, to the *Turks*, or to the uttermost parts of the Earth, which he can do in an hour, and destroy all their Magazines.

After the Magician hath so bound him, he shall receive from the Spirit a scrole written in this manner

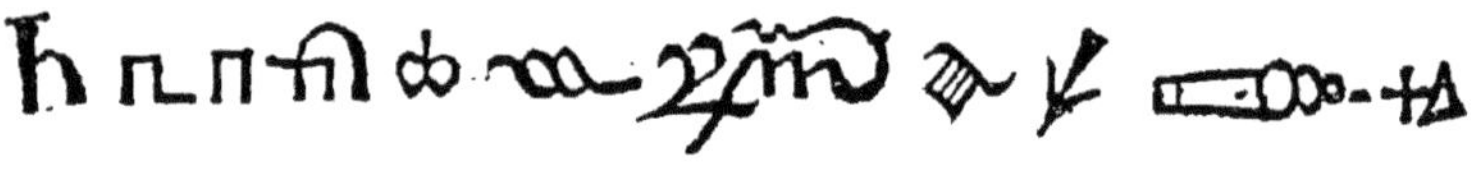

which is the Indenture to serve him for a year and a day; and then the Magician shall dismiss him for that time in the form of dismission.

Chap. IX.

How to Conjure the Spirit **Balkin**
the Master of **Luridan**

As in the former Chapter, the Exorcist is instructed to draw the form of the Mountain *Hecla* within the circle, so in this form of Conjuration he must do the same, adding these names to be written round the Mountain *Mathiel*; **Rahuniel, Seraphiel, Hyniel, Rayel, Fraciel.**[317] These are the names of

[317] Joseph H. Peterson identified these names as deriving from the angels of Mars

Olympick Angels, governing the *North*, and ruling over every airy Spirit that belongs unto the *Northern* Climate; so that the authority of these names must be used in the calling up of this Spirit, because he is a great Lord, and very lofty, neither will he appear without strong and powerful Invocations.

Therefore the Magician must make upon Virgin Parchment the two Seals of the Earth, and provide unto himself a Girdle made of Bears skin with a rough side next his body, and these names wrote round about in the outerside, **✠ Alpha ✠ Coronzon, Yah, Taniah, Adonay ✠ Soncas ✠ Damael ✠ Angeli fortes ✠ pur pur ✠ Elibra, Elohim ✠ Omega ✠ per flammam ignis ✠ per vitam Coronzon ✠** *Amen.* ✠. Also he must provide a black Priestly Robe to reach to his ankles, and a new Sword with **Agla** on the one side, and **On** upon the other; having likewise been very continent and chast for three days before the execution of his design: and when the appointed night approacheth, he must take with him an earthen pan with fire therein, and a little Viol with some of his own blood, as also some of the Gum or Rozin that comes from the Firr-tree.

And coming to the appointed place in some solitary Valley, the circle must be drawn with chalk, as the former, one circle within another, and these powerful names in the circumference, **Otheos on Panthon ✠ Breschit, Hashamaim, Waharetz Wahayah ✠ Tohu ✠ va Bohu ☆ ✠✠✠☆ magnus es tu ben Elohim qui super alas ventorum equitaris ✠.**[318]

This Circumscription is accounted amongst Magicians of all the most powerful and prevalent.

After this the Circle, Mountain, Fire, Turpentine, Girdle, Garments, Sword and Blood must be consecrated according to the foregoing forms of Consecration, adding also this to the end of the consecration.

Mighty art thou O **Adonay, Elohim, Ya, Ya, Aie, Aie, Aeimoy,** *who hast created the light of the day, and the darkness of the night, unto whom every knee bows in Heaven and on Earth, who hast created the* **Tohu** *and the* **Bohu,**[319] *that is stupor or*

---

atributed to North in the *Heptameron*: Rahumel, Hyniel, Rayel, Seraphiel, [Mathiel] Fraciel. (Esoteric Archives).

[318] Some of these words are identifiable from the Hebrew text of the first chapter of Genesis.

[319] "Tohu wa bohu (תֹהוּ וָבֹהוּ) is a Biblical Hebrew phrase found in the Book of Genesis 1:2 that describes the condition of the earth before God said, 'Let there be light' (Gen. 1:3). Precise translation of the phrase is difficult, since it is a Hebrew wordplay, like ve-ha-oniyyah hishevah le-hishaver in Jonah 1:4. Numerous interpretations of this phrase were made by various theological sources, though it is usually translated

numbness in a thing to be admired, and mighty are thy magnifcient Angels **Damael** *and* **Guael**, *whose influence can make the winds to bow, and every airy Spirit stoop; Let thy right hand sanctifie these consecrated utensils, exterminating every noxious thing from their bodies, and the circumference of this Circle. Amen.* **Calerna, Shalom, Shalom, Agla on Sassur, Tafrac, Angeli fortes.** *In Nomine Patris, Filii, & Spiritus Sancti. Amen, Amen, Amen.*

After that, he shall sweep the circle gently with a Foxes tayl, and sprinkle the same round with his blood, dipping also the Sword, or anointing it with the same, and brandishing the same in his right hand, he shall begin to conjure the Spirit on this following manner:

I Exorcize and Conjure thee thou great and powerful **Balkin**, *Lord of* **Glauron**, *Lord of* **Luridan**, *and of fifteen hundred Legions, Lord of the Northern Mountains, and of every Beast that dwells thereon by the holy and wonderful Names of the Almighty* **Jehovah, Athanato ✠ Aionos ✠ Dominus sempiternus ✠ Aletheios ✠ Saday ✠ Jehovah, Kedeth, El gabor ✠ Deus fortissimus ✠ Anapheraton, Amorule, Ameron ✠✠✠ Panthon ✠ Craton ✠ Muridon ✠ Jah, Jehovah, Elohim pentasseron ✠ ✠ trinus et unus ✠✠✠⛤** *I Exorcize and Conjure, I Invocate and Command thee thou aforesaid Spirit, by the powers of Angels and Archangels, Cherubim and Seraphim, by the mighty Prince* **Coronzon**, *by the blood of* Abel, *by the righteousness of* Seth, *and the Prayers of* Noah, *by the voyces of Thunder and dreadful day of Judgment; by all these powerful and royal words above said, that without delay or malitious intent, thou do come before me here at the circumference of this consecrated Circle, to answer my proposals and desires without any manner of terrible form either of thy self, or attendants; but only obediently, fairly, and with good intent, to present thy self before me, this Circle being my defence, through his power who is Almighty, and hath sanctified the same, In the Name of the Father, Son, and Holy Ghost. Amen.*

After the Magician hath thrice repeated this Conjuration, Let him immediately set the fire before him, and put the Rozin thereon to fumigate at the appearance of the conjured Spirits, and at the instant of their appearance he shall hold the Censer of fire in his left hand, and the Sword in his right, still turning round as the Spirits do.

For in a little space after the Invocation is repeated, he shall hear the noise of Thunders, and perceive before him in the Valley a mighty storm of Lightning and Rain; after a while the same will cease, and an innumerable company of Dwarfs or Pigmies will appear mounted upon Chamelions to march towards the Circle surrounding the same.

---

as 'waste and void', 'formless and empty', or 'chaos and desolation'." *Tohu wa-bohu.* Wikipedia.

Next comes **Balkin** with his Attendants; he will appear like the god *Bacchus* upon a little Goat, and the rest that follow will march after him afoot.

Assoon as they come near the Circle, they will breath out of their mouths a mist, or fog, which will even obscure the light of the Moon, and darken the Magician, that he cannot behold them nor himself; yet let him not be discomfited, or afraid, for that fog will be quickly over; and the Spirits will run round the Circle after **Balkin** their Lord, who rides upon a Goat; they will continue to surround the Circle, till the Magician begin the form of obligation or binding their Leader or King in this form, with the Sword in his right hand, the Fire and Rozin burning before him.

I conjure and bind thee **Balkin**, *who art appeared before me, by the Father, by the Son, and by the Holy Ghost, by all the holy Consecrations I have made, by the powerful Names of Heaven, and of Earth, and of Hell, that I have used and uttered in calling upon thee, by the Seals which thou here beholdest, and the Sword which I present unto thee, by this sanctified Girdle, and all the sanctified and potent things aforesaid, That here thou remain peaceably, and of thy present shape before the Northern quarter of this Circle, without injury to me in body, soul, or fortune; but on the contrary, to answer faithfully unto my demands, and not hence to remove, till I have licenced thee to depart, In the Name of the Father, Son, and holy Spirit. Amen.*

When he is thus obliged, he will alight from his Goat, and cause his Attendants to remove further into the Valley, then will he stand peaceably before the Circle to answer the Magician.

After this the Magician shall begin to demand into his own possession a Familiar to build or pull down any Castle or strong hold in a night; and that this Familiar bring with him the Girdle of Conquest, or Victory, that the Magician being girded with the same may overcome all enemies whatsoever.

And further, the Spirit is able to inform him of all questions concerning Thunder and Lightning, the Motions of the Heavens, the Comets and Apparitions in the air. Pestilence and Famine, noxious and malevolent blasts, as also of the Inhabitants of the *Northern* Pole, and the wonders undiscovered throughout the world.

Likewise if the Exorcist inquire concerning the habitations of starry Spirits, he will readily answer him, describing their orders, food, life, and pasttime truly and exactly.

After the Magician hath satisfied himself with inquiries, and curious questions unto the Spirit, there will come from amongst the company a little

Spirit of a span long, like a little *Ethiop*, which the great King Balkin will deliver unto the Exorcist to continue as a Familiar with him as long as his life shall last. This familiar the possessor may name as it pleaseth him.

The three last, who had this Spirit into possession, were three *Northern* Magicians, the first *Honduros* a *Norwegian*, who called it **Philenar**, and commanded it at his pleasure with a little Bell.

After him *Benno* his eldest Son injoy'd the same under the same name.

And *Swarkzar* a *Polonian* Priest was the last who enjoyed it under the Name of **Muncula**; all which names were imposed upon it, according to the pleasure of the Masters; and therefore the naming of this familiar is left to the discretion of the Exorcist.

Now when the Master hath taken this familiar into his custody and service, the Spirit **Balkin** will desire to depart, being wearied if the action continue longer then an hour. Therefore the Magician must be careful to dismiss him in this following form:

Because thou hast diligently answered my demands, and been ready to come at my first call, I do here licence thee to depart unto thy proper place, without injury or danger to man or Beast; depart, I say, and be ever ready at my call, being duly exorcised and conjured by sacred Rites of Magick; charge thee to withdraw with quiet and peace; and peace be continued betwixt me and thee, In the Name of the Father, Son, and Holy Ghost. Amen.

Then the Spirits company will begin to march about their Prince, and in a formal Troop will march along the Valley, whilest the Magician repeateth *Pater Noster*, &c. until the Spirits be quite out of sight and vanished.

This is a compleat form of conjuring the aforesaid Spirit, according to the Rules of Vaganostus the *Norwegian*.

Chap. X.[320]

An experiment of the dead.

FIRST fast and praie three daies, and absteine thee from all filthinesse; go to one that is new buried, such a one as killed himselfe or destroied himselfe wilfullie: or else get thee promise of one that shalbe hanged, and let him sweare an oth to thee, after his bodie is dead, that his spirit shall come to thee, and doo thee true service, at thy commandements, in all daies, houres, and minuts. And let no persons see thy doings, but thy fellow. And about eleven a clocke in the night, go to the place where he was buried, and saie with a bold faith & hartie desire, to have the spirit come that thou doost call for, thy fellow having a candle in his left hand, and in his right hand a christall stone, and saie these words following, the maister having a hazell wand in his right hand, and these names of God written thereupon, *Tetragrammaton* ✠ *Adonay* ✠ *Agla* ✠ *Craton* ✠ Then strike three strokes on the ground, and saie; Arise N. Arise N. Arise N. I conjure thee spirit N. by the resurrection of our Lord Jesu Christ, that thou doo obey to my words, and come unto me this night verelie and trulie, as thou beleevest to be saved at the daie of judgement. And I will sweare to thee an oth, by the perill of my soule, that if thou wilt come to me, and appeare to me this night, and shew me true visions in this christall stone, and fetch me the fairie *Sibylia*, that I may talke with hir visiblie, and she may come before me, as the conjuration leadeth: and in so dooing, I will give thee an almesse deed,[321] and praie for thee N. to my Lord God, wherby thou maiest be restored to thy salvation at the resurrection daie, to be received as one of the elect of God, to the everlasting glorie, Amen.[322]

[320] Here begins the material selected from Book XV from the first edition of Scot. In the first chapter of the original Book XV, Scot compares the erudite "conjurors" with the simple "witches." To exemplify how the conjurors act, the following chapters (2 to 4) repeat the text from the *Pseudomonarchia Daemonun*, and the fifth chapter presents a refutation of the ideas defended by these magicians. The sixth chapter presents only a few astrological tables, that here I put at the end of this section, being now Chapter XXIII; the original chapter VII has the "characters of the angels of thie seaven daies," that we reproduced on page 300 of this edition, and the Seals of the Earth, reproduced on page 316. The eighth chapter ("An experiment of the dead") of the original edition of Scot is here inserted as Chapter X. The following chapters (9 to 20) now follow the Roman numeration (XI to XXII).

[321] The meaning possibly being that charitable alms would be given on behalf of the deceased, so that he could enjoy merit.

[322] A note, probably by Scot, says: "*Ex inferno nulla redemptio, saith the scripture: Ergo you lie.*" The European magical eschatology often contradicted Christian orthodoxy, sometimes stating that human souls could enter and command legions of hell, or saying that the magician can invoke and even benefit from them. The Catholic Church came

The maister standing at the head of the grave, his fellow having in his hands the candle and the stone, must begin the conjuration as followeth, and the spirit will appeare to you in the christall stone, in a faire forme of a child of twelve yeares of age. And when he is in, feele the stone, and it will be hot; and feare nothing, for he or shee will shew manie delusions, to drive you from your worke. Feare God, but feare him not. This is to constraine him, as followeth.

I conjure thee spirit N. by the living God, the true God, and by the holie God, and by their vertues and powers which have created both thee and me, and all the world. I conjure thee N. by these holie names of God, *Tetragrammaton* ✠ *Adonay* ✠ *Algramay* ✠ *Saday* ✠ *Sabaoth* ✠ *Planaboth* ✠ *Panthon* ✠ *Craton* ✠ *Neupmaton* ✠ *Deus* ✠ *Homo* ✠ *Omnipotens* ✠ *Sempiturnus* ✠ *Ysus* ✠ *Terra* ✠ *Unigenitus* ✠ *Salvator* ✠ *Via* ✠ *Vita* ✠ *Manus* ✠ *Fons* ✠ *Origo* ✠ *Filius* ✠ And by their vertues and powers, and by all their names, by the which God gave power to man, both to speake or thinke; so by their vertues and powers I conjure thee spirit N., that now immediatlie thou doo appeare in this christall stone, visiblie to me and to my fellow, without anie tarrieng or deceipt. I conjure thee N. by the excellent name of Jesus Christ **A** and Ω the first and the last. For this holie name of Jesus is above all names: for in this name of Jesus everie knee dooth bow and obeie, both of heavenlie things, earthlie things, and infernall. And everie toong doth confesse, that our Lord Jesus Christ is in the glorie of the father: neither is there anie other name given to man, whereby he must be saved. Therefore in the name of Jesus of Nazareth, and by his nativitie, resurrection, and ascension, and by all that apperteineth unto his passion, and by their vertues and powers I conjure thee spirit N. that thou doo appeare visiblie in this christall stone to me, and to my fellow, without anie dissimulation. I conjure thee N. by the bloud of the innocent lambe Jesus Christ, which was shed for us upon the crosse: for all those that doo beleeve in the vertue of his bloud, shalbe saved. I conjure thee N. by the vertues and powers of all the riall names and words of the living God of me pronounced, that thou be obedient unto me and to my words rehearsed. If thou refuse his to doo, I by the holie trinitie, and their vertues and powers doo condemne thee thou spirit N. into the place where there is no hope of remedie or rest, but everlasting horror and paine there dwelling, and a place where is paine upon paine, dailie, horriblie, and lamentablie, thy paine to be there augmented as the starres in the heaven, and as the gravel or sand in the sea: except thou spirit N. doo appeare to me and to my fellow visiblie, immediatlie in this christall stone, and in a faire forme and shape of a child of twelve yeares of age, and that thou alter not thy shape, I charge thee upon paine of everlasting condemnation. I conjure thee spirit N. by the golden girdle, which girded the loines of our

---

close to this idea when it began to sell indulgences. Scot, as do several other Protestant theologians, often equates Catholic beliefs with magical practices.

Lord Jesus Christ: so thou spirit N. be thou bound into the perpetuall paines of hell fier, for thy disobedience and unreverent regard, that thou hast to the holie names and words, and his precepts. I conjure thee N. by the two edged sword, which *John* sawe proceed out of the mouth of the almightie; and so thou spirit N. be torne and cut in peeces with that sword, and to be condemned into everlasting paine, where the fier goeth not out, and where the worme dieth not. I conjure thee N. by the heavens, and by the celestiall citie of *Jerusalem*, and by the earth and the sea, and by all things conteined in them, and by their vertues & powers. I conjure thee spirit N. by the obedience that thou doost owe unto the principall prince. And except thou spirit N. doo come and appeare in this christall stone visiblie in my presence, here immediatlie as it is aforesaid. Let the great cursse of God, the anger of God, the shadowe and darknesse of death, and of eternall condemnation be upon thee spirit N. for ever and ever; bicause thou hast denied thy faith, thy health, & salvation. For thy great disobedience, thou art worthie to be condemned. Therefore let the divine trinitie, thrones, dominions, principats, potestats, virtutes, cherubim and seraphim, and all the soules of saints, both of men and women, condemne thee for ever, and be a witnesse against thee at the daie of judgement, bicause of thy disobedience. And let all creatures of our Lord Jesus Christ, saie thereunto; *Fiat, fiat, fiat*: Amen.

And when he is appeared in the christall stone, as is said before, bind him with this bond as followeth; to wit, I conjure thee spirit N. that art appeared to me in this christall stone, to me and to my fellow; I conjure thee by all the riall words aforesaid, the which did constraine thee to appeare therein, and their vertues; I charge thee spirit by them all, that thou shalt not depart out of this christall stone, untill my will being fulfilled, thou be licenced to depart. I conjure and bind thee spirit N. by that omnipotent God, which commanded the angell S. *Michael* to drive *Lucifer* out of the heavens with a sword of vengeance, and to fall from joy to paine; and for dread of such paine as he is in, I charge thee spirit N. that thou shalt not go out of the christall stone; nor yet to alter thy shape at this time except I command thee otherwise; but to come unto me at all places, and in all houres and minuts, when and wheresoever I shall call thee, by the vertue of our Lord Jesus Christ, or by anie conjuration of words that is written in this booke, and to shew me and my freends true visions in this christall stone, of anie thing or things that we would see, at anie time or times: and also to go and to fetch me the fairie *Sibylia*, that I may talke with hir in all kind of talke, as I shall call hir by anie conjuration of words conteined in this booke. I conjure thee spirit N. by the great wisedome and divinitie of his godhead, my will to fulfill, as is aforesaid: I charge thee upon paine of condemnation, both in this world, and in the world to come, *Fiat, fiat, fiat*: Amen.

This done, go to a place fast by, and in a faire parlor or chamber, make a circle with chalke, as hereafter followeth: and make another circle for the fairie *Sibylia* to appeare in, foure foote from the circle thou art in, & make no names therein, nor cast anie holie thing therein, but make a circle round with chalke; & let the maister and his fellowe sit downe in the first circle, the maister having the booke in his hand, his fellow having the christall stone in his right hand, looking in the stone when the fairie dooth appeare. The maister also must have upon his brest this figure here written in parchment, and beginne to worke in the new of the ☽ and in the houre of ♃ the ☉ and the ☽♋ to be in one of inhabiters signes, as ♋ ♐ ♓.

This bond as followeth, is to cause the spirit in the christall stone, to fetch unto thee the fairie *Sibylia*. All things fulfilled, beginne this bond as followeth, and be bold, for doubtles they will come before thee, before the conjuration be read seven times.

I conjure thee spirit *N.* in this christall stone, by God the father, by God the sonne Jesus Christ, and by God the Holie-ghost, three persons and one God, and by their vertues. I conjure thee spirit, that thou doo go in peace, and also to come againe to me quicklie, and to bring with thee into that circle appointed, *Sibylia* fairie, that I may talke with hir in those matters that shall be to hir honour and glorie; and so I charge thee declare unto hir. I conjure thee spirit *N.* by the bloud of the innocent lambe, the which redeemed all the world; by the vertue thereof I charge thee thou spirit in the christall stone, that thou doo declare unto hir this message. Also I conjure thee spirit *N.* by all angels and archangels, thrones, dominations, principals, potestates, virtutes, cherubim and seraphim, and by their vertues and powers. I conjure the *N.* that thou doo depart with speed, and also to come againe with speed, and to bring with thee the fairie *Sibylia*, to appeare in that circle, before I doo read the conjuration in this booke seven times. Thus I charge thee my will to be fulfilled, upon paine of everlasting condemnation: *Flat, fiat, fiat*; Amen.

Then the figure aforesaid pinned on thy brest, rehearse the words therein, and saie ✠ *Sorthie* ✠ *Sorthia* ✠ *Sorthios* ✠ I conjure thee *Sibylia*, gentle virgine of fairies, by the mercie of the Holie-ghost, and by the dreadfull daie of doome, and by their vertues and powers; I conjure thee *Sibylia*, O gentle virgine of fairies, and by all the angels of ♃ and their characters and vertues, and by all the spirits of ♃ and ♀ and their characters and vertues, and by all the characters that be in the firmament, and by the king and queene of fairies, and their vertues, and by the faith and obedience that thou bearest unto them. I conjure thee *Sibylia* by the bloud that ranne out of the side of our Lord Jesus Christ crucified, and by the opening of heaven, and by the renting of the temple, and by the darkenes of the sunne in the time of his death, and by the rising up of the dead in the time of his resurrection, and by the virgine Marie mother of our Lord Jesus Christ, and by the unspeakable name of God, *Tetragrammaton*. I conjure thee O *Sibylia*, O blessed and beautifull virgine, by all the riall words aforesaid; I conjure thee *Sibylia* by all their vertues to appeare in that circle before me visible, in the forme and shape of a beautifull woman in a bright and vesture white, adorned and garnished most faire, and to appeare to me quicklie without deceipt or tarrieng, and that thou faile not to fulfill my will & desire effectuallie. For I will choose thee to be my blessed virgine, & will have common copulation with thee. Therfore make hast & speed to come unto me, and to appeare as I said before: to whome be honour and glorie for ever and ever. Amen.

The which doone and ended, if shee come not, repeate the conjuration till they doo come: for doubtles they will come. And when she is appeared, take your censers, and incense hirwith frankincense, then bind hir with the bond as followeth.

I doo conjure thee *Sibylia*, by God the Father, God the sonne, and God the Holie-ghost, three persons and one God, and by the blessed virgine Marie mother of our Lord Jesus Christ, and by all the whole and holie companie of heaven, and by the dreadfull daie of doome, and by all angels and archangels, thrones, dominations, principates, potestates, virtutes, cherubim and seraphim, and their vertues and powers. I conjure thee, and bind thee *Sibylia*, that thou shall not depart out of the circle wherein thou art appeared, nor yet to alter thy shape, except I give thee licence to depart. I conjure thee *Sibylia* by the bloud that ranne out of the side of our Lord Jesus Christ crucified, and by the vertue hereof I conjure thee Sibylia to come to me, and to appeare to me at all times visiblie, as the conjuration of words leadeth, written in this booke. I conjure thee *Sibylia*, O blessed virgine of fairies, by the opening of heaven, and by the renting of the temple, and by the darknes of the sunne at the time of his death, and by the rising of the dead in the time of his glorious resurrection, and by the unspeakable name of God ✠ *Tetragrammaton* ✠ and by the king and queene of fairies, & by their vertues I conjure thee *Sibylia* to appeare, before the conjuration be read over foure times, and that visiblie to appeare, as the conjuration leadeth written in this booke, and to give me good counsell at all times, and to come by treasures hidden in the earth, and all other things that is to doo me pleasure, and to fulfill my will, without anie deceipt or tarrieng; nor yet that thou shalt have anie power of my bodie or soule, earthlie or ghostlie, nor yet to perish so much of my bodie as one haire of my head. I conjure thee *Sibylia* by all the riall words aforesaid, and by their vertues and powers, I charge and bind thee by the vertue thereof, to be obedient unto me, and to all the words aforesaid, and this bond to stand betweene thee and me, upon paine of everlasting condemnation, *Fiat, fiat, fiat*, Amen.

CHAP. XI.

A licence for Sibylia to go and come by at all times.

I conjure thee *Sibylia*, which art come hither before me, by the commandement of thy Lord and mine, that thou shalt have no powers, in thy going or comming unto me, imagining anie evill in anie maner of waies, in the earth or under the earth, of evill dooings, to anie person or persons. I conjure and command thee *Sibylia* by all the riall words and vertues that be written in this booke, that thou shalt not go to the place from whence thou camest, but shalt remaine peaceablie invisiblie, and looke thou be readie to come unto me, when thou art called by anie conjuration of words that be written in this booke, to come (I saie) at my commandement, and to answer unto me truelie and duelie of all things, my will quicklie to be fulfilled. *Vade in pace, in nomini patris, & filii, & spiritus sancti.* And the holie ✠ crosse ✠ be betweene thee and me, or betweene us and you, and the lion of *Juda*, the roote of *Jesse*, the kindred of *David*, be betweene thee & me ✠ Christ commeth ✠ Christ commandeth ✠ Christ giveth power ✠ Christ defend me ✠ and his innocent bloud ✠ from all perils of bodie and soule, sleeping or waking: *Fiat, fiat.* Amen.

CHAP. XII.

To know of treasure hidden in the earth.

Write in paper these characters following, on the saturdaie, in the houre of ☽, and laie it where thou thinkest practised if treasure to be: if there be anie, the paper will burne, else not. And these be the characters.

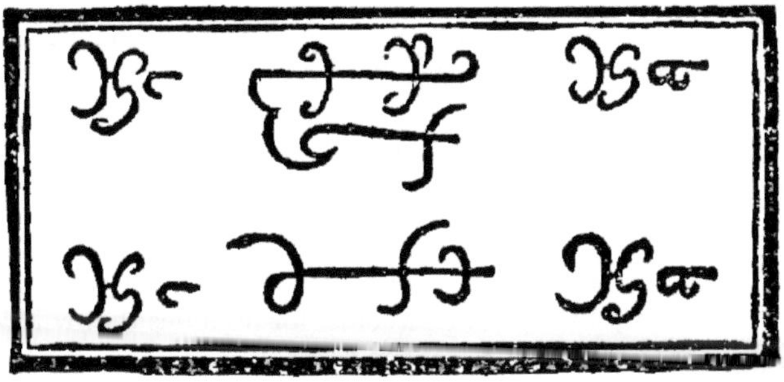

This is the waie to go invisible by these
three sisters of fairies.

IN the name of the Father, and of the Sonne, and of the Holie-ghost. First go to a faire parlor or chamber, & an even ground, and in no loft, and from people nine daies; for it is the better: and let all thy clothing be cleane and sweete. Then make a candle of virgine waxe, and light it, and make a faire fier of charcoles, in a faire place, in the middle of the parlor or chamber. Then take faire cleane water, that runneth against the east, and set it upon the fier: and ere thou washest thy selfe, saie these words, going about the fier, three times, holding the candle in the right hand ✠ *Panthon* ✠ *Craton* ✠ *Muriton* ✠ *Bisecognaton* ✠ *Siston* ✠ *Diaton* ✠ *Maton* ✠ *Tetragrammaton* ✠ *Agla* ✠ *Agarion* ✠ *Tegra* ✠ *Pentessaron* ✠ *Tendicata* ✠ Then reherse these names ✠ *Sorthie* ✠ *Sorthia* ✠ *Sorthios* ✠ *Milia* ✠ *Achilia* ✠ *Sibylia* ✠ *in nomine patris, & filii, & spiritus sancti,* Amen. I conjure you three sisters of fairies, *Milia, Achilia, Sibylia,* by the father, by the sonne, and by the Holie-ghost, and by their vertues and powers, and by the most mercifull and living God, that will command his angell to blowe the trumpe at the daie of judgement; and he shall saie, Come, come, come to judgement; and by all angels, archangels, thrones, dominations, principals, potestates, virtutes, cherubim and seraphim, and by their vertues and powers. I conjure you three sisters, by the vertue of all the riall words aforesaid: I charge you that you doo appeare before me visiblie, in forme and shape of faire women, in white vestures, and to bring with you to me, the ring of invisibilitie, by the which I may go invisible at mine owne will and pleasure, and that in all houres and minuts: *in nomine patris, & filii, & spiritus sancti,* Amen. ⌘ Being appeared, saie this bond following.

O blessed virgins ✠ *Milia* ✠ *Achilia* ✠ I conjure you in the name of the father, in the name of the sonne, and in the name of the Holie-ghost, and by their vertues I charge you to depart from me in peace, for a time. And *Sibylia,* I conjure thee, by the virtue of our Lord Jesus Christ, and by the vertue of his flesh and pretious bloud, that he tooke of our blessed ladie the virgine, and by all the holie companie in heaven: I charge thee *Sibylia*, by all the vertues aforesaid, that thou be obedient unto me, in the name of God; that when, and at what time and place I shall call thee by this foresaid conjuration written in this booke, looke thou be readie to come unto me, at all houres and minuts, and to bring unto me the ring of invisibilitie, whereby I may go invisible at my will and pleasure, and that at all houres and minuts; *Fiat, fiat*, Amen.

And if they come not the first night, then doo the same the second night, and so the third night, untill they doo come: for doubtles they will come, and lie thou in thy bed, in the same parlor or chamber. And laie thy right hand out of the bed, and looke thou have a faire silken kercher bound about thy head, and be not afraid, they will doo thee no harme. For there will come before thee three faire women, and all in white clothing; and one of them will put a ring upon thy finger, wherwith thou shalt go invisible. Then with speed bind them with the bond aforesaid. When thou hast this ring on thy finger, looke in a glasse, and thou shalt not see thy selfe. And when thou wilt go invisible, put it on thy finger, the same finger that they did put it on, and everie new ☽ renew it againe. For after the first time thou shalt ever have it, and ever beginne this worke in the new of the ☽ and in the houre of ♃ and the ☽ in ♋ ♐ ♓.

Chap. XIII.

An experiment following, of
Citrael, &c: angeli diei dominici
Saie first the praiers of the angels everie daie,
for the space of seaven daies.

Michael.	☉
Gabriel.	☽
Samael.	♂
Raphael.	☿
Sachiel.	♃
Anael.	♀
Cassiel.	♄

O Ye glorious angels written in this square, be you my coadjutors & helpers in all questions and demands, in all my busines, and other causes, by him which shall come to judge the quicke and the dead, and the world by fier. O *angeli gloriosi in hac quadra scripti, estote coadjutors & auxiliadores in omnibus quæstionibus & interrotionibus, in omnibus negotiis, cæterísque causis, per eum qui venturus est judicare vivos & mortuos, & mundum per ignem.*

Saie this praier fasting, called Regina linguæ

✠ *Lemaac* ✠ *solmaac* ✠ *elmay* ✠ *gezagra* ✠ *raamaasin* ✠ *ezierego* ✠ *mial* ✠ *egziephiaz* ✠ *Josamin* ✠ *sabach* ✠ *ha* ✠ *aem* ✠ *re* ✠ *b* ✠ *e* ✠ *sepha* ✠ *sephar* ✠ *ramar* ✠ *semoit* ✠ *lemaio* ✠ *pheralon* ✠ *amic* ✠ *phin* ✠ *gergoin* ✠ *letos* ✠ *Amin* ✠ *amin* ✠

In the name of the most pitifullest and mercifullest God of Israel and of paradise, of heaven and of earth, of the seas and of the infernalles, by thine omnipotent helpe may performe this worke, which livest and reignest ever one God world without end, Amen.

O most strongest and mightiest God, without beginning or ending, by thy clemencie and knowledge I desire, that my questions, worke, and labour may fullie and trulie accomplished, through thy worthines, good lord, which livest and reignest, ever one God, world without end. Amen.

Oh holie, patient, and mercifull great God, and to be worshipped, the Lord of all wisedome, cleare and just; I most hartilie desire thy holiness and clemencie, to fulfill, performe and accomplish this my whole worke, through thy worthiness, and blessed power: which livest and reignest, ever one God, *Per omnia sæcula sæculorum*, Amen.

Chap. XIV.

How to enclose a spirit in a christall stone.

THIS operation following, is to have a spirit inclosed into a christall stone or berill glasse, or into anie other like instrument, &c.

First thou in the new of the ☽ being clothed with all new, and fresh, & cleane araie, and shaven, and that day to fast with bread and water, and being cleane confessed,[323] saie the seven psalms,[324] and the letanie,[325] for the space of two daies, with this praier following.

---

[323] Having confessed to a priest; this passage betrays the religious affiliation of its author, although possibly the original text is before the Reformation in England.

[324] "The Penitential Psalms or Psalms of Confession, so named in Cassiodorus's commentary of the 6th century AD, are the Psalms 6, 32, 38, 51, 102, 130, and 143 (6, 31, 37, 50, 101, 129, and 142 in the Septuagint numbering). These psalms are expressive of sorrow for sin. Four were known as 'penitential psalms' by St. Augustine of Hippo in the early 5th century. The fifty-first Psalm (Miserere) was recited at the close of daily morning service in the primitive Church. Translations of the penitential psalms were undertaken by some of the greatest poets in Renaissance England, including Sir Thomas Wyatt, Henry Howard, Earl of Surrey, and Sir Philip Sidney. Before the suppression of the minor orders and tonsure in 1972 by Paul VI, the seven penitential psalms were assigned to new clerics after having been tonsured." *Penitential Psalms.* Wikipedia.

[325] "Litany, in Christian worship and some forms of Judaic worship, is a form of prayer used in services and processions, and consisting of a number of petitions. The word comes from the Latin litania from Ancient Greek: λιτανεία (litaneía), which in turn comes from Ancient Greek: λιτή (litê), meaning 'supplication'." *Litany.* Wikipedia.

I desire thee O Lord God, my mercifull and most loving God, the giver of all graces, the giver of all sciences, grant that I thy welbeloved *N.* (although unworthie) may knowe thy grace and power, against all the deceipts and craftines of divels. And grant to me thy power, good Lord, to constraine them by this art: for thou art the true, and livelie, and eternall GOD, which livest and reignest ever one GOD through all worlds. Amen.

Thou must doo this five daies, and the sixt daie have in a redines, five bright swords: and in some secret place make one circle, with one of the said swords. And then write this name, *Sitrael:*[326] which doone, standing in the circle, thrust in thy sword into that name. And write againe *Malanthon*, with another sword; and *Thamaor*, with another; and *Falaur*, with another; and *Sitrami*, with another: and doo as ye did with the first. All this done, turne thee to *Sitrael*, and kneeling saie thus, having the christall stone in thine hands.

O *Sitrael, Malantha, Thamaor, Falaur*, and *Sitrami,*[327] written in these circles, appointed to this worke, I doo conjure and I doo exorcise you, by the father, by the sonne, and by the Holy-ghost, by him which did cast you out of paradise, and by him which spake the word and it was done, and by him which shall come to judge the quicke and the dead, and the world by fier, that all you five infernall maisters and princes doo come unto me, to accomplish and to fulfill all my desire and request, which I shall command you. Also I conjure you divels, and command you, I bid you, and appoint you, by the Lord Jesus Christ, the sonne of the most highest God, and by the blessed and glorious virgine *Marie*, and by all the saints, both of men and women of God, and by all the angels, archangels, patriarches, and prophets, apostles, evangelists, martyrs, and confessors, virgins, and widowes, and all the elect of God. Also I conjure you, and everie of you, ye infernall kings, by heaven, by the starres, by the ☉ and by the ☽ by all the planets, by the earth, fier, aier, and water, and by the terrestriall paradise, and by all things in them conteined, and by your hell, and by all the divels in it, and dwelling about it, and by your vertue and power, and by all whatsoever, and with whatsoever it be, which maie constreine and bind you. Therefore by all these foresaid vertues and powers, I doo bind you and constreine you into my will and power; that you being thus bound, may come unto me in great humilitie, and to appeare in your circles before me visiblie, in faire forme and shape of mankind kings, and to obeie unto me in all things, whatsoever I shall desire, and that you may not depart from me without my licence. And if you doo against my precepts, I will promise unto

[326] These instructions follow Chapter XIII, with the name *Citrael* written *Sitrael*.

[327] A note (possibly) by Scot says: "A *weightie charge of conjuration upon the five K. of the north.*" "K." means *Kings*). Note the variation of the name "Malantha", previously written "Malanthon".

you that you shall descend into the profound deepenesse of the sea, except that you doo obeie unto me, in the part of the living sonne of God, which liveth and reigneth in the unitie of the Holie-ghost, by all world of worlds, Amen.

Saie this true conjuration five courses, and then shalt thou see come out of the northpart five kings, with a marvelous companie: which when they are come to the circle, they will allight downe off from their horses, and will kneele downe before thee, saieng: Maister, command us what thou wilt, and we will out of hand be obedient unto thee. Unto whome thou shall saie; See that ye depart not from me, without my licence; and that which I will command you to doo, let it be done trulie, surelie, faithfullie and essentiallie. And then they all will sweare unto thee to doo all thy will. And after they have sworne, saie the conjuration immediatlie following.

I conjure, charge, and command you, and everie of you, *Sirrael*, *Malanthan*,[328] *Thamaor*, *Falaur*, and *Sitrami*, you infernall kings, to put into this christall stone one spirit learned and expert in all arts and sciences, by the vertue of this name of God *Tetragrammaton*, and by the crosse of our Lord Jesu Christ, and by the bloud of the innocent lambe, which redeemed all the world, and by all their vertues & powers I charge you, ye noble kings, that the said spirit may teach, shew, and declare unto me, and to my freends, at all houres and minuts, both night and daie, the truth of all things, both bodilie and ghostlie, in this world, whatsoever I shall request or desire, declaring also to me my verie name.[329] And this I command in your part to doo, and to obeie thereunto, as unto your owne lord and maister. That done, they will call a certeine spirit, whom they will command to enter into the centre of the circled or round christall. Then put the christall betweene the two circles, and thou shalt see the christall made blacke.

Then command them to command the spirit in the christall, not to depart out of the stone, till thou give him licence, & to fulfill thy will for ever. That done, thou shalt see them go upon the christall, both to answer your requests, & to tarrie your licence. That, doone, the spirits will crave licence: and say; Go ye to your place appointed of almightie God, in the name of the father, &c. And then take up thy christall, and looke therein, asking what thou wilt, and it will shew it unto thee. Let all your circles be nine foote everie waie, & made as

[328] Third variation of the name; as well as Citrael, Sitrael and Sirrael it could be a result of typographical errors.

[329] Curious passage; the author expressed himself badly, and actually wants the name of the spirit (a classic notion of magic, which ensures the power of the magician over the spiritual creature); or, the word is a real name that man is unaware of, and that is the key to the understanding of its true essence.

followeth. Worke this worke in ♋ ♏ or ♓ in the houre of the ☽ or ♃. And when the spirit is inclosed, if thou feare him, bind him with some bond, in such sort as is elsewhere expressed alreadie in this our treatise.

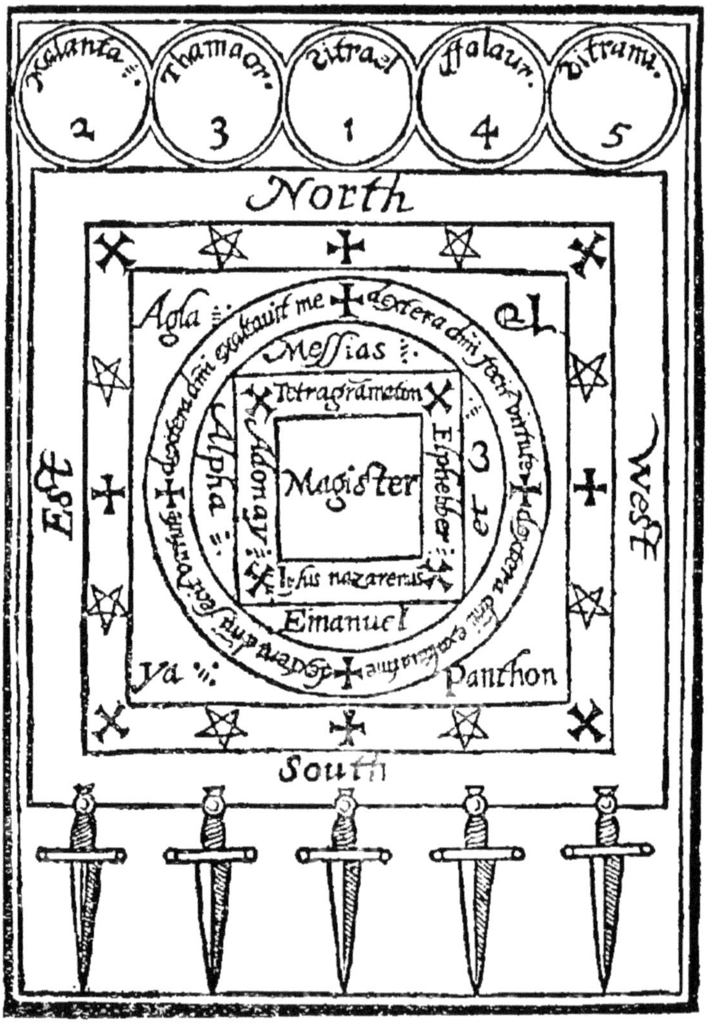

A figure or type proportionall, shewing what forme must be observed and kept, in making the figure whereby the former secret of inclosing a spirit in christall is to be accomplished, &c.

Chap. XV.

An experiment of Bealphares.

THIS is proved the noblest carrier that ever did serve anie man upon the earth, & here beginneth the inclosing of the said spirit, & how to have a true answer of him, without anie craft or harme; and he will appeare unto thee in the likenesse of a faire man, or faire woman, the which spirit will come to thee at all times. And if thou wilt command him to tell thee of hidden treasures that be in anie place, he will tell it thee: or if thou wilt command him to bring to thee gold or silver, he will bring it thee: or if thou wilt go from one countrie to another, he will beare thee without anie harme of bodie or soule. Therefore he that will doo this worke, shall absteine from lecherousnes and dronkennesse, and from false swearing, and doo all the abstinence that he may doo; and namelie three daies before he go to worke, and in the third daie, when the night is come, and when the stares doo shine, and the element faire and cleare, he shall bath himselfe and his fellowes (if he have anie) all together in a quicke welspring. Then he must be cloathed in cleane white cloathes, and he must have another privie place, and beare with him inke and pen, wherewith he shall write this holy name of God almightie in his right hand ✠ *Agla* ✠ & in his left hand this name ✠ 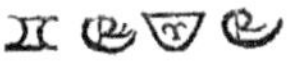 ✠ And he must have a drie thong of a lions or of a harts skin, and make thereof a girdle, and write the holie names of God all about, and in the end ✠ A and Ω ✠ And upon his brest he must have this present figure or marke written in virgine parchment, as it is here shewed. And it must be sowed upon a peece of new linnen, and so made fast upon thy brest. And if thou wilt have a fellow to worke with thee, he must be appointed in the same maner. You must have also a bright knife that was never occupied, and he must write on the one side of the blade of the knife ✠ *Agla* ✠ and on the other side of the knifes blade ✠ 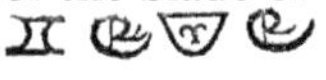 ✠ And with the same knife he must make a circle, as hereafter followeth: the which is called *Salomons* circle. When that he is made, go into the circle, and close againe the place, there where thou wentest in, with the same knife, and saie; *Per crucis hoc signum* ✠ *fugiat procul omne malignum; Et per idem signum* ✠ *salvetur quodque benignum,* and make suffumigations to thy selfe, and to thy fellowe or fellowes, with frankincense, mastike, *lignum aloes*: then put it in wine, and saie with good devotion, in the worship of the high God almightie, all together, that he may defend you from all evils. And when he that is maister will close the spirit, he shall saie towards the east, with meeke and devout devotion, these psalmes and praiers as followeth here in order.

The two and twentieth psalme.

O my God my God, looke upon me, whie hast thou forsaken me, and art so farre from my health, and from the words of my complaint?

And so foorth to the end of the same psalme, as it is to be founde in the booke.

This psalme also following, being the fiftie one psalme, must be said three times over, &c.

Have mercie upon me, O God, after thy great goodnes, according to the multitude of thy mercies, doo awaie mine offenses.

And so foorth to the end of the same psalme, concluding it with, Glorie to the Father and to the Sonne, and to the Holie-ghost, As it was in the beginning, is now, and ever shall be, world without end, Amen. Then saie this verse: O Lord leave not my soule with the wicked; nor my life with the bloudthirstie. Then saie a *Pater noster* an *Ave Maria,* and a *Credo, & ne nos inducas.* O Lord shew us thy mercie, and we shall be saved. Lord heare our praier, and let our crie come unto thee. Let us praie.

O Lord God almightie, as thou warnedst by thine angell, the three kings of *Cullen,*[330] *Jasper, Melchior, and Balthasar,* when they came with worshipfull presents towards *Bethleem: Jasper* brought myrrh; *Melchior,* incense; *Balthasar,* gold; worshipping the high king of all the world, Jesus Gods sonne of heaven, the second person in trinitie, being borne of the holie and cleane virgine S. *Marie,* queene of heaven, empresse of hell, and ladie of all the world: at that time the holie angell *Gabriel* warned and bad the foresaid three kings, that they should take another waie, for dread of perill, that *Herod* the king by his ordinance would have destroied these three noble kings, that meekelie sought out our Lord and saviour. As wittilie and truelie as these three kings turned for dread, and tooke another waie: so wiselie and so truelie, O Lord GOD, of thy mightifull mercie, blesse us now at this time, for thy blessed passion save us, and keepe us all together from all evill; and thy holie angell defend us. Let us praie.

Lord, king of all kings, which conteinest the throne of heavens, and beholdest all deepes, weighest the hilles, and shuttest up with thy hand the earth; heare us, most meekest GOD, and grant unto us (being unworthie) according to thy great mercie, to have the veritie and vertue of knowledge of hidden treasures by this spirit invocated, through thy helpe O Lord Jesus Christ,

---

[330] There is a town in Scotland called Cullen, famous for the three rocks in its beach, called "The Three Kings". A legend says that under every rock is buried a Scottish king, a Danish and a Norwegian. Another version attributes the association to the three wise men by the similarity between the name Cullen and "Culane" ("Cologne"). In the cathedral of Cologne (Cologne) in Germany there is a sanctuary with the supposed bones of the three Magi. There is also a Chapel of the Three Kings of Cologne in Bristol, England.

to whome be all honour and glorie, from worlds to worlds everlastinglie. Amen. Then saie these names ✠ *Helie* ✠ *helyon* ✠ *esseiere* ✠ *Deus æternus* ✠ *eloy* ✠ *clemens* ✠ *heloye* ✠ *Deus sanctus* ✠ *sabaoth* ✠ *Deus exercituum* ✠ *adonay* ✠ *Deus mirabilis* ✠ *iao* ✠ *verax* ✠ *anepheneton* ✠ *Deus ineffabilis* ✠ *so/doy* ✠ *dominator dominus* ✠ *ôn fortissimus* ✠ *Deus* ✠ *qui*, the which wouldest be praied unto of sinners: receive (we beseech thee) these sacrifices of praise, and our meeke praiers, which we unworthie doo offer unto thy divine majestic. Deliver us, and have mercie upon us, and prevent with thy holie spirit this worke, and with thy blessed helpe to followe after; that this our worke begunne of thee, may be ended by thy mightie power, Amen. Then saie this anon after ✠ *Homo* ✠ *sacarus* ✠ *muscolameas* ✠ *cherubozca* ✠ being the figure upon thy brest aforesaid, the girdle about thee, the circle made, blesse the circle with holie water, and sit downe in the middest, and read this conjuration as followeth, sitting backe to backe at the first time.

I exorcise and conjure Bealphares, the practiser and preceptor of this art, by the maker of heavens and of earth, and by his vertue, and by his unspeakable name *Tetragrammaton*, and by all the holie sacraments, and by the holie majestic and deitie of the living God. I conjure and exorcise thee *Bealphares* by the vertue of all angels, archangels, thrones, dominations, principats, potestats, virtutes, cherubim and seraphim, and by their vertues, and by the most truest and speciallest name of your maister, that you doo come unto us, in faire forme of man or womankind, here visiblie, before this circle, and not terrible by anie manner of waies. This circle being our tuition and protection, by the mercifull goodnes of our Lord and Saviour Jesus Christ, and that you doo make answer truelie, without craft or deceipt, unto all my demands and questions, by the virtue and power of our Lord Jesus Christ, Amen.

Chap. XVI.

To bind the spirit Bealphares,
and to lose him againe.

Now when he is appeared, bind him with these words which followe.

I conjure thee *Bealphares*, by God the father, by God the sonne, and by God the Holie-ghost, and by all the holie companie in heaven; and by their vertues and powers I charge thee *Bealphares*, that thou shalt not depart out of my sight, nor yet to alter thy bodilie shape, that thou art appeared in, nor anie power shalt thou have of our bodies or soules, earthlie or ghostlie, but to be obedient to me, and to the words of my conjuration, that be written in this booke. I conjure thee *Bealphares*, by all angels and archangels, thrones, dominations, principats, potestats, virtutes, cherubim and seraphim, and by their vertues and powers. I conjure and charge, bind and constreine thee *Bealphares*, by all the riall words aforesaid, and by their vertues, that thou be obedient unto me, and to come and appeare visiblie unto me, and that in all daies, houres, and minuts, whersoever I be, being called by the vertue of our Lord Jesu Christ, the which words are written in this booke. Looke readie thou be to appeare unto me, and to give me good counsell, how to come by treasures hidden in the earth, or in the water, and how to come to dignitie and knowledge of all things, that is to saie, of the magike art, and of grammar, dialectike, rhetorike, arythmetike, musike, geometrie, and of astronomic, and in all other things my will quicklie to be fulfilled: I charge thee upon paine of everlasting condemnation. *Fiat, fiat, fiat*, Amen.

When he is thus bound, aske him what thing thou wilt, and he will tell thee, and give thee all things that thou wilt request of him, without anie sacrifice dooing to him, and without forsaking thy God, that is, thy maker. And when the spirit hath fulfilled thy will and intent, give him licence to depart as followeth.

A licence for the spirit to depart

Go unto the place predestinated and appointed for thee, where thy Lord GOD hath appointed thee, untill I shall call thee againe. Be thou readie unto me and to my call, as often as I shall call thee, upon paine of everlasting damnation. And if thou wilt, thou maiest recite, two or three times, the last conjuration, untill thou doo come to this tearme, *In throno.* If he will not depart, and then *In throno*, that thou depart from this place, without hurt or damage of anie bodie, or of anie deed to be doone; that all creatures may knowe, that our Lord is of all power, most mightiest, and that there is none other God but he, which is three, and one, living for ever and ever. And the malediction of God the father omnipotent, the sonne and the holie ghost, descend upon thee, and dwell always with thee, except thou doo depart without damage of us, or of any creature, or anie other evill deed to be doone: & thou to go to the place predestinated. And by our Lord Jesus Christ I doo else send thee to the great pit of hell, except (I saie) that thou depart to the place, whereas thy Lord God hath appointed thee. And see thou be readie to me and to my call, at all times and places, at mine owne will and pleasure, daie or night, without damage or hurt of me, or of anie creature; upon paine of everlasting damnation *Fiat, fiat, fiat*; Amen, Amen.

The peace of Jesus Christ bee betweene us and you; in the name of the father, and of the sonne, and of the Holie-ghost: Amen. *Per crucis hoc signum*, &c. Saie *In principio erat verbum, & verbum erat apud Deum*; In the beginning was the word, and the word was with God, and God was the word: and so forward, as followeth in the first chapter of saint *Johns* Gospell, staieng at these words. Full of grace and truth: to whom be all honour and glorie world without end. Amen.

The fashion or forme of the conjuring knife,
with the names theron to bee graven or written.
A type or figure of the circle for the maister and his fellowes to sit in, shewing how and after what fashion it should be made.

This is the circle for the maister to sit in, and his fellowe or fellowes, at the first calling, sit backe to backe, when he calleth the spirit; and for the fairies make this circle with chalke on the ground, as is said before. This spirit Bealphares *being once called and found, shall never have power to hurt thee. Call him in the houre of ♃ or ♀ the ☽ increasing.*

Chap. XVII.

The making of the holie water

Exorciso *te creaturam salis, per Deum vivum ✠ per Deum ✠ verum ✠ per Deum sanctum per Deum qui te per Elizæum profetam in aquam mitti jussit, ut sanaretur sterilitas aquæ, ut efficiaris sal exorcisatus in salutem credentium; ut sis omnibus te sumentibus sanitas animæ & corporis, & effugiat atque discedat abe o loco, qui aspersus fuerit omnis fantasia & nequitia, vel versutia diabolicæ fraudis, omnisq; spiritus immundus, adjuratus per eum, qui venturus est judicare vivos & mortos, & sæculum per ignem, Amen. Oremus:*

Immensam clementian tuam, omnipotens ceterne Deus, humiliter imploramos, ut hanc creaturam salis, quam in usum generis humani tribuisti, bene ✠ dicere & sancti ✠ ficare tua pietate digneris, ut sit omnibus sumentibus salus mentis & corporis, ut quicquid ex eo tactum fuerit, vel respersum, careat omni immundicia, omniq; impugnatione spiritualis nequitiæ, per Dominum nostrum Jesum Christum filium tuum, qui tecum vivit & regnat in unitate spiritus sancti, Deus per omnia sæcula sæculorum, Amen.

To the water saie also as followeth[331].

Exorciso te creaturam aquæ in nomine ✠ patris ✠ & Jesu Christi filii ejus Domini nostri, & in virtute spiritus ✠ sancti ✠ ut fias aqua exorcisata, ad effugandam omnem potestatem inimici, & ipsum inimicum eradicare & explantare valeas, cum angelis suis apostatis, per virtutem ejusdem Domini nostri Jesu Christi, qui venturus est judicare vivos & mortos, & sæculum per ignem, Amem, Oremus:

Deus, qui ad salutem humani generis máxima quæque sacramenta in aquarum substantia condidisti, adesto propitius invocationibus nostris, & elemento huic multimodis purificationibus præparato, virtutem tuæ bene dictionis infunde, ut criatura tua mysteriis tuis serviens, ad abigendos dæmones, morbosq; pellendos, divinæ gratiæ sumat effectum, ut quicquid in domibus, vel in locis fidelium hæc unda resperserit , careat omni immundicia, liberetur à noxa, non illic resideat spiritus pestilens, non aura corrumpens, discedant omnes insidiæ latentis inimici, & si quid est, quod aut incolumitati habitantium invidet aut quieti, aspersione hujus aquæ effugiat, ut salubritas per invocationenm sancti tui nominis expetita ab omnibus sit impugnationibus defensa, per Dominum nostrum Jesum Christum filium tuum, qui tecum vivit & regnat, in unitate spiritus sancti Deus per omnia sæcula sæculorum, Amen.

---

[331] The first prayer *Exorciso te creaturam salis* etc. is to consecrate the salt, which is then placed in the water. These exorcisms are copied from practices used by the Church in the early centuries where even the "Oil creature" used in ointments was exorcised.

Then take the salt in thy hand, and saie putting it into the water, making in the maner of a crosse.

Commixtio salis & aquæ pariter fiat, in nomine patris, & filii, & spiritus sancti, Amen. Dominus vobiscum, Et cum spiritu tuo, Oremus:

Deus invictæ virtutis author, & insuperabilis imperii rex, ac sempermagnificus triumphator, qui adversa dominationis vires reprimis, qui inimici rugientis sævitiam superas, qui hostiles nequitias potens expugnas; te domine trementes & súplices deprecamur ac petimus, ut hanc creaturam salis & aquæ aspicias,benignus ilustres, pietatis tuæ rore sancti fices, ubicunq; fuerit aspersa, per invocationem sancti tui nominis, omnis infestatio immundi spiritus abjiciatur, terrórq; venenosi serpentis procul pellatur, & præsentia sancti spiritus nobis misericordiam tuam poscentibus ubiq; adesse dignetur, per dominum nostrum Jesum christum filium tuum, qui tecun vivit & regnat in unitate spiritus sancti Deus per omnia sæcula sæculorum, Amen.

Then sprinkle upon anie thing, and saie as followeth.

Asperges me Domine hyssopo, & mundabor, lavabis me, & supra nivem dealbabor. Miserere mei Deus, secundum magnam misericordiam tuam, & supra nivem dealbabor. Gloria patri, & filio, & spiritui santo: Sicut erat in principio, & nunc, & sempre, & in sæcula sæculorum, Amem. Et supra nivem dealbabor, asperges me, &c. Ostende nobis Domine sancte, pater omnipotens, æterne Deus, & mittere dignare sanctum angelum tuum de cælis, qui custodiat, foveat, visitet, & defendat omnes habitantes in hoc habitáculo, per Christum Dominum nostrum, Amem, Amen.

Chap. XVIII.

To make a spirit to appeare in a christall.

I do conjure thee N., by the father, and the sonne, and the Holie-ghost, the which is the beginning and the ending, the first and the last, and by the latter daie of judgement, that thou N. doo appeare, in this christall stone, or anie other instrument, at my pleasure, to mee and to my felow, gentlie and beautifullie, in faire forme of a boy of twelve yeares of age, without hurt or damage of anie of our bodies or soules; and certeinlie to informe and to shew me, without anie guile or craft, all that we doo desire or demand of thee to know, by the vertue of him, which shall come to judge the quicke and the dead, and the world by fier, Amen.

Also I conjure and exorcise thee N. by the sacrament of the altar, Marke how and by the substance therof, by the wisedome of Christ, by the sea, and by his vertue, by the earth, & by all things that are above the earth, and by their vertues, by the ☉ and the ☽ by ♄ ♃ ♂ and ♀ and by their vertues,[332] by the apostles, martyrs, confessors, and the virgins and widowes, and the chast, and by all saints of men or of women, and innocents, and by their vertues, by all the angels and archangels, thrones, dominations, principats, potestats, virtutes, cherubim, and seraphim, and by their vertues, & by the holie names of God, *Tetragrammaton*, *El*, *Ousion*, *Agla*, and by all the other holie names of God, and by their vertues, by the circumcision, passion, and resurrection of our Lord Jesus Christ, by the heaviness of our ladie the virgine, and by the joy which she had when she sawe hir sonne rise from death to life, that thou *N.* doo appeare in this christall stone, or in anie other instrument, at my pleasure, to me and to my felow, gentlie, and beautifullie, and visiblie, in faire forme of a child of twelve yeares of age, without hurt or damage of anie of our bodies or soules, and trulie to informe and shew unto me & to my felow, without fraud or guile, all things according to thine oth and promise to me, whatsoever I shall demand or desire of thee, without anie hinderance or tarrieng, and this conjuration be read of me three times, upon paine of eternall condemnation, to the last daie of judgement: *Fiat fiat*, *fiat*, Amen.

And when he is appeared, bind him with the bond of the dead above written:[333] then saie as followeth.

I charge thee *N.* by the father, to shew me true visions in this christall stone, if there be anie treasure hidden in such a place *N.*, & wherin it lieth, and how manie foot from this peece of earth, east, west, north, or south.

Chap. XIX.

An experiment of the dead.

FIRST go and get of some person that shalbe put to death, a promise, and sweare an oth unto him, that if he will come to thee, after his death, his spirit to be with thee, and to remaine with thee all the daies of thy life, and will doo thee true service, as it is conteined in the oth and promise following. Then laie thy hand on thy booke, and sweare this oth unto him. I *N.* doo sweare and promise to thee *N.* to give for thee an almesse everie moneth,[334] and also to praie for thee once in everie weeke, to saie the Lords praier for thee, and so to continue all the daies of my life, as God me helpe and holie doome, and by the contents of this booke. Amen.

---

[332] Note that ♀ is missing, possibly due to a printing error.

[333] It is uncertain to which of the previous conjures he is referring.

[334] Possibly meaning that alms would be given to some poor on behalf of the deceased, who would receive the corresponding spiritual benefit.

Then let him make his oth to thee as followeth, and let him saie after thee, laieng his hand upon the booke.

I *N.* doo sweare this oth to thee *N.* by God the father omnipotent, by God the son Jesus Christ, and by his pretious bloud which hath redeemed all the world, by the which bloud I doo trust to be saved at the generall daie of judgment, and by the vertues therof, I *N.* doo sweare this oth to thee *N.* that my spirit that is within my bodie now, shall not ascend, nor descend, nor go to anie place of rest, but shall come to thee *N.* and be verie well pleased to remaine with thee *N.* all the daies of thy life, and so to be bound to thee *N.* and to appeare to thee *N.* in anie christall stone, glasse, or other mirror, and so to take it for my resting place. And that, so soone as my spirit is departed out of my bodie, streightwaie to be at your commandements, and that in and at all daies, nights, houres, and minutes, to be obedient unto thee *N.* being called of thee by the vertue of our Lord Jesu Christ, & out of hand to have common talke with thee at all times, and in all houres & minuts, to open and declare to thee *N.* the truth of all things present, past, and to come, and how to worke the magike art, and all other noble sciences, under the throne of God. If I doo not performe this oth and promise to thee *N.* but doo flie from anie part thereof, then to be condemned for ever and ever. Amen.

Also I *N.* doo sweare to thee by God the Holie-ghost, and by the great wisedome that is in the divine Godhead, and by their vertues, and by all the holie angels, archangels, thrones, dominations, principats, potestats, virtutes, cherubim and seraphim, and by all their vertues doo I *N.* sweare, and promise thee to be obedient as is rehearsed. And heere, for a witnesse, doo I *N.* give thee *N.* my right hand, and doo plight thee my faith and troth, as God me helpe and holiedoome. And by the holie contents in this booke doo I *N.* sweare, that my spirit shall be thy true servant, all the daies of thy life, as is before rehearsed. And here for a witnesse, that my spirit shall be obedient to thee *N.* and to those bonds of words that be written in this *N.* before the bonds of words shall be rehearsed thrise; else to be damned for ever: and thereto saie all faithfull soules and spirits. Amen, Amen.

Then let him sweare this oth three times, and at everie time kisse the booke, and at everie time make marks to the bond. Then perceiving the time that he will depart, get awaie the people from you, and get or take your stone or glasse, or other thing in your hand, and saie the *Pater noster, Ave,* and *Credo,* and this praier as followeth. And in all the time of his departing, rehearse the bonds of words; and in the end of everie bond, saie oftentimes; Remember thine oth and promise. And bind him stronglie to thee, and to thy tone, and suffer him not to depart, reading thy bond 24 times. And everie daie when you doo call him by your other bond, bind him stronglie by the first bond: by the space of 24 daies applie it, & thou shalt be made a man for ever.

Now the Pater noster, Ave, and Credo must be said,
and then the praier immediatlie following.

O God of *Abraham*, God of *Isaac*, God of *Jacob*, God of *Tobias*; the which diddest deliver the three children from the hot burning oven, *Sidrac*, *Misac* and *Abdenago*, , and *Susanna* from the false crime, and *Daniel* from the lions power: even so O Lord omnipotent, I beseech thee, for thy great mercie sake, to helpe me in these my works, and to deliver me this spirit of *N.* that he may be a true subject to me *N.* all the daies of my life, and to remaine with me, and with this *N.* all the daies of my life. O glorious God, Father, Sonne, and Holie-ghost, I beseech thee to help me at this time, and to give me power by thine holie name, merits and vertues, wherby I may conjure & constreine this spirit of *N.* that he may be obedient unto me, and may fulfill his oth and promise, at all times, by the power of all thine holines. This grant O Lord God of hosts, as thou art righteous and holy, and as thou art the word, and the word God, the beginning and the end, sitting in the thrones of thine everlasting kingdoms, & in the divinitie of thine everlasting Godhead, to whom be all honour and glorie, now and for ever and ever, Amen, Amen.

Chapter XX.

A bond to bind him to thee,
and to thy N. as followeth.

I *N.* conjure and constreine the spirit of *N.* by the living God, by the true God, and by the holie god, and by their vertues and powers I conjure and constreine the spirit of thee *N.* that thou shalt not ascend nor descend out of thy bodie, to no place of rest, but onelie to take thy resting place with *N.* and with this *N.* all the daies of my life, according to thine oth and promise. I conjure and constreine thye spirit of *N.* by these holie names of God ✠ *Tetragammaton* ✠ *Adonay* ✠ *Agla* ✠ *Saday* ✠ *Sabaoth* ✠ *planabothe* ✠ *panthon* ✠ *craton* ✠ *neupmaton* ✠ *Deus* ✠ *homo* ✠ *omnipotens* ✠ *sempiternus* ✠ *ysus* ✠ *terra* ✠ *unigenitus* ✠ *salvator* ✠ *via* ✠ *vita* ✠ *manus* ✠ *fons* ✠ *origo* ✠ *filius* ✠ and by their vertues and powers I conjure and constreine the spirit of *N.* that thou shalt not rest nor remaine in the fier, nor in the water, in the aier, nor in anie privie place of the earth, but onelie with me *N.* and with this *N.* all the daies of my life. I charge the spirit of *N.* upon paine of everlasting condemnation, remember thine oth and promise. Also I conjure the spirit of *N.* and constreine thee by the excellent name of Jesus Christ, Α and Ω, the first and the last; for this holie name of Jesus is above all names, for unto it all knees do bow and obey, both of heavenlie things, earthlie things, and infernalles. Nor is there anie other name given to man, whereby we have anie salvation, but by the name of Jesus. Therefore by the name, and in the name of Jesus of *Nazareth*, and by his nativitie, resurrection and ascension, and by all that apperteineth to his passion, and by their vertues and powers, I do conjure and constreine the spirit of N. that thou shalt not take anie resting place in the ☉[335] nor in the ☽ nor in ♄ nor in ♃ nor in ♂ nor in ♀ nor in ☿ nor in anie of the twelve signes, nor in the concavitie of the clouds, nor in anie other privie place, to rest or staie in, but onelie with me N. or with this N. or with N. all the daies of my life. If thou be not obedient unto me, according to thine oth and promise, I N. do condemne the spirit of N. into the pit of hell for ever, Amen.

I conjure and constreine the spirit of N. by the bloud of the innocent lambe Jesus Christ, the which was shed upon the crosse, for all those that do obeie unto it, and beleeve in it, shall be saved and by vertue thereof, and by all the aforesaid riall names and words of the living God by me pronounced, I do conjure and constreine the spirit of N. that thou be obediente unto me, according to thine oth and promise. If thou doo refuse to doo as is aforesaid, I N. by the holie trinitie, and by his vertue and power doo comdemne the spirit of N. into the place whereas there is no hope of remedie, but everlasting condemnation, and horror, and paine upon paine, dailie, horriblie, & lamentablie the paines there to be augmented, so thicke as the stars in the firmament, and as the gravell sand in the sea: except thou spirit of N. obeie me N. as is afore rehearsed; else I N. doo condemne the spirit of N. into the pit of everlasting condemnation; *Fiat, fiat*, amen. Also I conjure thee, and constreine the spirit of N. by all angels, archangels, thrones, dominations, principats, potestats, virtutes, cherubim & seraphim, & by the foure evangelists, *Matthew, Marke, Luke*, and *John*, and by all things conteined in the old lawe and the new, and by their vertues, and by the twelve apostles, and by all patriarchs, prophets, martyrs, confessors, virgins, innocents, and by all the elect and chosen, is, and shall be, which followeth the lambe of God; and by their vertues and powers I conjure and constreine the spirit of N. stronglie, to have common talke with me, at all times, and in all daies, nights, houres, and minuts, and to talke in my mother toong plainelie, that I may heare it, and understand it, declaring the truth unto me of all things, according to thine oth and promise; else to be condemned for ever; *Fiat, fiat*, Amen.

Also I conjure and constreine the spirit of N. by the golden girdle, which girded the loines of our Lord Jesus Christ, so thou spirit of N. be thou bound, and cast into the pit of everlasting condemnation, for thy great disobedience and unreverent regard that thou hast to the holie names and words of God almightie, by me pronounced: *Fiat*, Amen.

---

335 In the original, the symbol ☉ was omitted, and an empty space left.

Also I conjure, constreine, command, and bind the spirit of *N.* by the two edged sword, which John saw proceed out of the mouth of God almightie except thou be obedient as is aforesaid, the sword cut thee in peeces, and condemne thee into the pit of everlasting paines, where the fier goeth not out, and where the worme dieth not; *Fiat,fiat,fiat*, Amen..

Also I conjure and constreine the spirit of *N.* by the throne of the Godhead, and by all the heavens under him, and by the celestiall citie new *Jerusalem*, and by the earth, by the sea, and by all things created and conteined therein, and by their vertues and powers, and by all the infernalles, and by their vertues and powers, and all things conteined therein, and by their vertues and powers, I conjure and constreine the spirit of *N.* that now immediatlie thou be obedient unto me, at all times hereafter, and to those words of me pronounced, according to thine oth and promise: else let the great cursse of God, the anger of God, the shadowe and darknesse of everlasting condemnation be upon thee thou spirit of *N.* for ever and ever, bicause thou hast denied thine health, thy faith, and salvation, for thy great disobedience thou are worthie to be condemned. Therefore let the divine trinitie, angels, and archangels, thrones, dominations, principats, potestates, virtutes, cherubim and seraphim, and all the soules of the saints, that shall stand on the right hand of our Lord Jesus Christ, at the generall daie of judgement, condemne the spirit of *N.* for ever and ever, and be a witnesse against thee, bicause of thy great disobedience, in and against thy promises. *Fiat, fiat,* Amen.

Being thus bound, he must needs be obedient unto thee, whether he will or no: proove this. And here followeth a bond to call him to your *N.* and to shew you true visions at all times, as in the houre of ♄ to bind or inchant anie thing, and in the houre of ♃ for peace and concord, in the houre of ♂ to marre, to destroie, and to make sicke, in the houre of the ☉ to bind toongs and other bonds of men, in the houre of ♀ to increase love, joy, and good will, in the houre of ☿ to put awaie enimitie or hatred, to know of theft, in the houre of the ☽ for love, goodwill and concord, ♄ lead ♃ tinne ♂ iron ☉ gold ♀ coppar ☿ quicksilver ☽ silver, &c.

Chapter XXI.

This bond as followeth, is to call him into your christall stone, or glasse, &c.

ALSO I doo conjure thee spirit *N.* by God the father, by God the Sonne, and by God the holie-ghost, **A** and **Ω**, the first and the last, and by the latter daie of judgement, of them which shall come to judge the quicke and the dead, and the world by fier, and by their vertues and powers I constreine thee spirit *N.* to come to him that holdeth the christall stone in his hand, & to appeare visiblie, as hereafter foloweth. Also I conjure thee spirit N. by these holie names of God ✠ *Tetragrammaton* ✠ *Adonay* ✠ *El* ✠ *Ousion* ✠ *Agla* ✠ *Jesus* ✠ *of Nazareth* ✠ and by the vertues thereof, and by his nativitie, death, buriall, resurrection, and ascension, and by all other things apperteining unto his passion, and by the blessed virgine Marie mother of our Lord Jesu Christ, and by all the joy which shee had when shee saw hir sonne rise from death to life, and by the vertues and powers therof I constreine thee spirit N. to come into the christall stone, & to appeare visiblie, as herafter shalbe declared. Also I conjure thee N. thou spirit, by all angels, archangels, thrones, dominations, principats, potestats, virtutes, cherubim and seraphim, and by the ☉ ☽ ♄ ♃ ♂ ♀ ☿, and by the twelve signes, and by their vertues and powers, and by all things created and confirmed in the firmament, and by their vertues & powers I constreine thee spirit N. to appeare visiblie in that christall stone, in faire forme and shape of a white angell, a greene angell, a blacke angell, a man, a woman, a boie, a maiden virgine, a white grehound, a divell with great hornes, without anie hurt or danger of our bodies or soules, and trulie to informe and shew unto us, true visions of all things in that christall stone, according to thine oth and promise, and that without anie hinderance or tarrieng, to appeare visiblie, by this bond of words read over by mee three times, upon paine of everlasting condemnation; *Fiat, fiat*, Amen.

Then being appeared, saie these words following

I Conjure thee spirit, by God the father, that thou shew true visions in that christall stone, where there be anie N. in such a place or no, upon paine of everlasting condemnation, *Fiat*, Amen. Also I conjure thee spirit N., by God the sonne Jesus Christ, that thou doo shew true visions unto us, whether it be gold or silver, or anie other metals, or whether there were anie or no, upon paine of condemnation. *Fiat*, Amen. Also I conjure thee spirit N. by God the Holie-ghost, the which dooth sanctifie all faithfull soules and spirits, and by their vertues and powers I constreine thee spirit N. to speake, open, and to declare, the true waie, how we may come by these treasures hidden in N. and how to have it in our custodie, & who are the keepers thereof, and how manie there be, and what be their names, and by whom it was laid there, and to shew me true visions of what sort and similitude they be, and how long they have kept it, and to knowe in what daies and houres we shall call such a spirit, N., to bring unto us these treasures, into such a place N. upon paine of everlasting condemnation ✠. Also I constreine thee spirit N. by all angels, archangels, thrones, dominations, principats, potestats, virtutes, cherubim & seraphim, that you doo shew a true vision in this christall stone, who did conveie or steale away such a N., and the spirit is where it is, & who hath it, and how farre off, and what is his or hir name, and how and when to come unto it, upon paine of eternall condemnation, *Fiat*, Amen. Also I conjure thee spirit N. by the ☉ ☽ ♄ ♃ ♂ ♀ ☿ and by all the characters in the firmament, that, thou doo shew unto me a true vision in this christall stone, where such N. and in what state he is, and how long he hath beene there, and what time he will be in such a place, what daie and houre: and this and all other things to declare plainelie, in paine of hell fier; *Fiat*, Amen.

A licence to depart.

Depart out of the sight of this christall stone in peace for a time, and readie to appeare therein againe at anie time or times I shall call thee, by the vertue of our Lord Jesus Christ, and by the bonds of words which are written in this booke, and to appeere visiblie, as the words be rehersed. I constreine thee spirit N. by the divinitie of the Godhead, to be obedient unto these words rehearsed, upon paine of everlasting condemnation, both in this world, and in the world to come; *Fiat, fiat, fiat*, Amen.

Chapter XXII.

When to talke with spirits, and to have true answers to find out a theefe.

THE daies and houres of ♄ ♂ ☿ and the ☽ is best to doo all crafts of necromancie, & for to speake with spirits, and for to find theft, and to have true answer thereof, or of anie other such like.

And in the daies and houres of ☉ ♃ ♀ is best to doo all experiments of love, and to purchase grace, and for to be invisible, and to doo anie operation, whatsoever it be, for anie thing, the ☽ being in a convenient signe.

As when thou laborest for theft, see the moone be in an earthie signe, as ♉ ♍ ♑ or of the aier, as ♊ ♎ ♒.

And if it be for love, favor or grace, let the ☽ be in a signe of the fier, as ♈ ♌ ♐, and for hatred, in a signe of the water, as ♋ ♏ ♓. For anie other experiment, let the ☽ be in ♈.

And if thou findest the ☉ & the ☽ in one signe that is called in even number, then thou maiest write, consecrate, conjure, and make readie all maner of things that thou wilt doo, &c.

To speake with spirits

Call these names, *Orimoth*, *Belimoth*, *Lymocke*, and say thus: I conjure you up by the names of the angels *Satur* and *Azimor*, that you intend to me in this houre, and send unto me a spirit called *Sagrigrit*, that hee doo fulfill my commandement and desire, and that also can understand my words for one or two yeares, or as long as I will, &c.

Chapter XXIII.

The names of the planets, their characters, together with the twelve signes of the zodiake, their dispositions, aspects, and government, with other observations

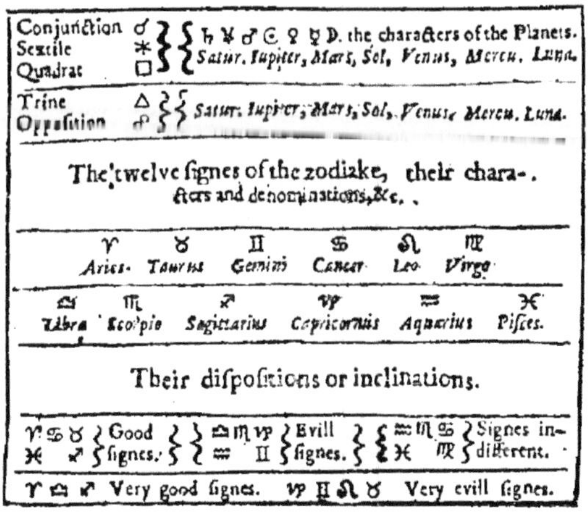

The disposition of the planets.

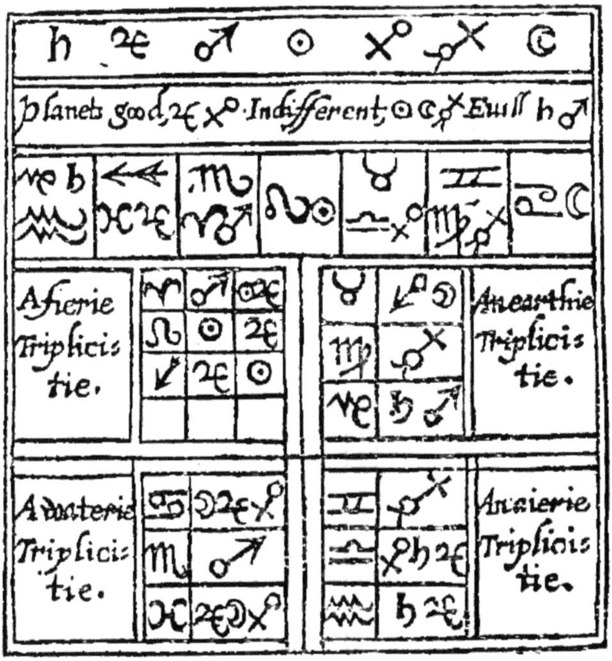

The aspects of the planets.

☌ Is the best aspect, with good planets, and woorst with evill.
✱ Is a meane aspect in goodnesse or badnesse.
△ Is verie good in aspect to good planets, & hurteth not in evill.
□ This aspect is of enimitie not full perfect.
☍ This aspect is of enimitie most perfect.

How the daie is divided or distinguished.

A daie naturall is the space of foure and twentie houres, accounting the night withall, and beginneth at one of the clocke after midnight.

An artificiall daie is that space of time, which is betwixt the rising and falling of the ☉ &c. All the rest is night, & beginneth at the ☉ rising.

Hereafter followeth a table, showing how the daie and the night is divided by houres, and reduced to the regiment of the planets.

The division of the daie, and the planetary regiment.

		1	2	3	4	5	6	7	8	9	10	11	12
day	lord	☉	♀	☿	☾	♄	♃	♂	☉	♀	☿	☾	♄
day	lord	☾	♄	♃	♂	☉	♀	☿	☾	♄	♃	♂	☉
day	lord	♂	☉	♀	☿	☾	♄	♃	♂	☉	☿	♀	☾
day	lord	☿	☾	♄	♃	♂	☉	♀	☿	☾	♄	♃	♂
day	lord	♃	♂	☉	♀	☿	☾	♄	♃	♂	☉	♀	☿
day	lord	☿	♀	☾	♄	♃	♂	☉	♀	☿	☾	♄	♃
day	lord	♄	♃	♂	☉	♀	☿	☾	♄	♃	♂	☉	♀

The division of the night, and the planetarie regiment.

		1	2	3	4	5	6	7	8	9	10	11	12
night	lord	♃	♂	☉	♀	☿	☾	♄	♃	♂	☉	♀	☿
night	lord	♀	☿	☾	♄	♃	♂	☉	♀	☿	☾	♄	♃
night	lord	♄	♃	♂	☉	♀	☿	☾	♄	♃	♂	☉	♀
night	lord	☉	♀	☿	☾	♄	♃	♂	☉	♀	☿	☾	♄
night	lord	☾	♄	♃	♂	☉	♀	☿	☾	♄	♃	♂	☉
night	lord	♂	☉	☿	☾	♄	♂	♃	☉	♀	☾	♀	☿
night	lord	☿	☾	♄	♃	♂	☉	♀	☿	☾	♄	♃	♂

Bibliography

A Hebrew-English Bible According to the Masoretic Text and the JPS 1917 Edition. Mechon Mamre, 2005. Web. <http://www.mechon-mamre.org/p/pt/pt0.htm>.

Agrippa, Henry Cornelius. *Fourth Book of Occult Philosophy.* London: Askin Publishers (Reprint), 1978.

Almond, Philip C. *England's First Demonologist: Reginald Scot & "The Discoverie of Witchcraft."* London: I. B. Tauris, 2011.

Athanassiadi, Polymnia (1999). The Chaldaean oracles: theology and theurgy. In Polymnia Athanassiadi & Michael Frede (eds.), *Pagan Monotheism in Late Antiquity.* OUP Oxford 149-183.

Augustine, S. "City of God and Christian Doctrine." Trans. Rev. Marcus Dods. Christian Classics Ethereal Library. Calvin College, 2005. Web. <http://www.ccel.org/ccel/schaff/npnf102.iv.html>.

—. *Obras Completas de San Agustín.* Trans. Santos Santamarta. Provided by the Federación Agustiniana Española. Madrid: Biblioteca de Autores Cristianos, 1990.

Becking, Bob, Karel van der Toorn, Pieter W. van der Horst, eds. *Dictionary of Deities and Demons in the Bible.* Grand Rapids, Michigan: Wm. B. Eerdmans Publishing Co.; Revised 2nd edition, 1999.

Betz, Hans Dieter Betz, ed. *The Greek Magical Papyri in Translation.* Chicago: The University of Chicago Press, 1986.

Bremmer, Jan N. and Jan R. Veenstra, eds. *The Metamorphosis of Magic from Late Antiquity to the Early Modern Period.* Leuven: Peeters, 2002.

Burnet, John. *Early Greek Philosophy.* London: A & C Black, Ltd, 1920.

Cassin, Barbara, ed. *Dictionary of Untranslatables: A Philosophical Lexicon: A Philosophical Lexicon.* Trans. and ed. Emily Apter, Jacques Lezra, and

Michael Wood. Princeton: Princeton University Press, 2013.
Catholic Encyclopedia. 1907-1912. *Catholic Encyclopedia.* Catholic Online. Web. <http://www.catholic.org/>.

Charles, R. H., Trans. *The Book of Enoch.* Oxford: Clarendon, 1893.

Crowley, Aleister. *Magick Without Tears.* Scottsdale, AZ: New Falcon Publications, 1991.

Drews, Robert. *The End of the Bronze Age: changes in warfare and the catastrophe ca. 1200 B.C.* Princeton: Princeton University Press, 1995.

Fuller, Hailey Marie, "From Daimon to Demon: The Evolution of the Demon from Antiquity to Early Christianity" (2013). UNLV Theses/Dissertations/Professional Papers/Capstones. Paper 1826.

Gager, John G., ed. *Curse Tablets and Binding Spells.* Oxford: Oxford University Press, 1999.

Heiser, Michael. "Deuteronomy 32:8 and the Sons of God." The Divine Council Com. <http://www.thedivinecouncil.com/DT32BibSac.pdf>

Hermann S. Schibli (1993). "Xenocrates' Daemons and the Irrational Soul." *The Classical Quarterly* (New Series), 43, pp 143-167.

Hesiod. *Hesiod, the Homeric Hymns, and Homerica.* Trans. Hugh G. Evelyn-White. Harvard: Harvard University Press/The Loeb Classical Library. Revised Edition. 1914.

Homer. *The Odyssey, rendered into English prose for the use of those who cannot read the original.* Trans. Samuel Butler. London: Longmans, Green, And Co. First Edition, 1900.

Iamblichus. *On The Mysteries of the Egyptians, Chaldeans, and Assyrians.* Trans. Thomas Taylor. London: Bertram Dobell (Second Edition), 1895.

—. *Theurgia or The Egyptian Mysteries.* Trans. Alexander Wilder. Whitefish, Montana: Kessinger Publishing, LLC; Reprint edition, 1942.

Jewish Encyclopedia. 1906. *Jewish Encyclopedia.* The Kopelman Foundation. Web. <http://www.jewishencyclopedia.com/>.

Justin (Martyr). "The Second Apology of Justin for the Christians Addressed to the Roman Senate." *Early Christian Writings*. N.p., n.d. Web. < http://www.earlychristianwritings.com/text/justinmartyr-secondapology.html/>

Kenny, Philip. "Socratic Knowledge and the Daimonion." *Aporia*. Vol. 13 .1. Spring 2003. Pp. 26-40.

Klaassen, Frank. *The Transformations of Magic: Illicit Learned Magic in the Later Middle Ages*. Pennsylvania: Pennsylvania State University Press, 2013.

Laurence, Richard, trans. *The Book of Enoch the Prophet*. London: Keegan Paul, Trench & Co., 1883.

Lehrich, Christopher. *The Language of Demons and Angels: Cornelius Agrippa's Occult Philosophy*. Leiden: Brill, 2003.

Martin, Dale Basil. "When Did Angels Become Demons?" *Journal of Biblical Literature*. Vol. 129, No. 4 (2010), pp. 657-677.

Mathers, Samuel Liddell MacGregor. *The Book of the Sacred Magic of Abramelin the Mage*. New York: Dover Publications, 1975.

McCracken, Andy. *The Book of Enoch: A Modern English Translation of the Ethiopian Book of Enoch*. Archive. N.p., n.d. Web. <http://archive.is/3hNvm>.

Meyer, Marvin and Paul Mirecki, eds. *Ancient Magic and Ritual Power*. Leiden: Brill, 2001.

Peterson, Joseph. *Heinrich Cornelius Agrippa: Of Occult Philosophy, Book III*. Esoteric Archives. N.p., 2000. Web. <http://www.esotericarchives.com/agrippa/agrippa3.htm>.

Reed, Annette Yoshiko. *Fallen Angels and the History of Judaism and Christianity: The Reception of Enochic Literature*. Cambridge: Cambridge University Press, 2005.

Ryland, J. E., trans. "Tatian's Address to the Greeks." *Early Christian Writings*. N.p., n.d. Web. < http://www.earlychristianwritings.com/text/tatian-address.html/>

Schodde, Rev. George H. *The Book of Enoch Translated from the Ethiopic*. Andover: W.F. Draper, 1882.

Scot, Reginald. *The Discoverie of Witchcraft.* London: Elliot Stock (Reprint), 1886.

Shaw, Gregory. *Theurgy and the Soul, the Neoplatonism of Iamblichus.* Pennsylvania: Pennsylvania State University Press, 1967.

Skinner, Stephen. *Techniques of Greaco-Egyptian Magic.* Minnesota: Llewellyn Publications, 2014.

Suchan, Vladimir. "*The Daemon of Socrates.*" All Academic Reserach. All Academic, Inc., n.d. Web. <http://citation.allacademic.com//meta/p_mla_apa_research_citation/2/7/6/3/3/pages276331/p276331-1.php>.

Tanaseanu-Döbler, Ilinca. *Theurgy in Late Antiquity: The Invention of a Ritual Tradition.* Göttingen, Germany: Vandenhoeck & Ruprecht, 2013.

Timotin, Andrei. *La Démonologie Platonicienne, Histoire de la notion de daimon de Platon aux derniers néoplatoniciens.* Leiden/Boston: Brill, 2012.

Viller, Marcel, F. Cavallera, J. de Guibert, dirs. *Dictionnaire de spiritualité ascétique et mystique. Doctrine et histoire.* Paris: Gabriel Beauchesne et ses Fils, 1932-1995. < http://www.dictionnairedespiritualite.com/>

Wikipedia contributors. *Wikipedia, The Free Encyclopedia.* The Wikimedia Foundation, Inc.

Wilder, Alexander, trans. *Theurgia or The Egyptian Mysteries By Iamblichus {Reply of Abammon, the Teacher to The Letter of Porphyry to Anebo & Solutions of the Questions Therein Contained}.* London: William Rider & Son Ltd., 1911.

Index

A

B

C

N

O

P

Q

R

S

T

Milton Keynes UK
Ingram Content Group UK Ltd.
UKHW020302060524
442231UK00009B/183

9 781907 881633